The Naked Christ

Distinguished Dissertations in Christian Theology

Series Foreword

We are living in a vibrant season for academic Christian theology. After a hiatus of some decades, a real flowering of excellent systematic and moral theology has emerged. This situation calls for a series that showcases the contributions of newcomers to this ongoing and lively conversation. The journal *Word & World: Theology for Christian Ministry* and the academic society Christian Theological Research Fellowship (CTRF) are happy to cosponsor this series together with our publisher Pickwick Publications (an imprint of Wipf and Stock Publishers). Both the CTRF and *Word & World* are interested in excellence in academics but also in scholarship oriented toward Christ and the Church. The volumes in this series are distinguished for their combination of academic excellence with sensitivity to the primary context of Christian learning. We are happy to present the work of these young scholars to the wider world and are grateful to Luther Seminary for the support that helped make it possible.

Alan G. Padgett
Professor of Systematic Theology
Luther Seminary

Beth Felker Jones
Assistant Professor of Theology
Wheaton College

www.ctrf.info
www.luthersem.edu/word&world

The Naked Christ
An Atonement Model for a Body-Obsessed Culture

DAN LÉ

☙PICKWICK *Publications* · Eugene, Oregon

THE NAKED CHRIST
An Atonement Model for a Body-Obsessed Culture

Distinguished Dissertations in Christian Theology #7

Copyright © 2012 Dan Lé. All rights reserved. Except for brief quotations in critical publications or reviews, no part of this book may be reproduced in any manner without prior written permission from the publisher. Write: Permissions, Wipf and Stock Publishers, 199 W. 8th Ave., Suite 3, Eugene, OR 97401.

Pickwick Publications
An Imprint of Wipf and Stock Publishers
199 W. 8th Ave., Suite 3
Eugene, OR 97401

www.wipfandstock.com

ISBN 13: 978-1-61097-788-3

Cataloging-in-Publication data:

Lé, Dan.

The naked Christ : an atonement model for a body-obsessed culture / Dan Lé, with a foreword by Graham McFarlane.

Distinguished Dissertations in Christian Theology #7

xii + 314 p. ; 23 cm. Includes bibliographical references and index.

ISBN 13: 978-1-61097-788-3

1. Jesus Christ—Crucifixion. 2. Atonement. 3. Human body—Religious aspects. I. McFarlane, Graham. II. Title. III. Series.

BT265.3 D300 2012

Manufactured in the U.S.A.

Content

Foreword by Graham McFarlane | vii
Acknowledgments | ix
Abbreviations | xi

Introduction | 1

Part 1: Nakedness and Clothing in a Body-Obsessed Culture

1 The Body-Obsessed Culture | 13
2 Nakedness and Clothing in a Body-Obsessed Culture | 34
3 Nakedness and Clothing in Metaphorical Language | 62

Part 2: Nakedness and Clothing in Biblical and Theological Contexts and Roman Crucifixion

4 The Antithesis of Nakedness and Clothing in the Bible | 89
5 The Antithesis of Nakedness and Clothing in Theology and Liturgy | 118
6 The Antithesis of Nakedness and Clothing in Crucifixion | 149

Part 3: Nakedness and Clothing in a Model of Atonement

7 The Making of the *Christus Nudus* Model | 173
8 The Legitimacy of the *Christus Nudus* Model | 211
9 The Effect of the *Christus Nudus* Model: A Conclusion | 237

Bibliography | 249
Index |

Foreword

WE INHABIT A WORLD in which everything is commodified—even the future. Everything, it would appear, has a price. This economic mindset is not new to the Western church. The genius of Dietrich Bonhoeffer was to critique his contemporaries' lack of appreciation of how much their salvation cost. He writes,

> Such grace is costly because it calls us to follow, and it is grace because it calls us to follow Jesus Christ. It is costly because it costs a man his life, and it is grace because it gives a man the only true life. It is costly because it condemns sin, and grace because it justifies the sinner. Above all, it is costly because it cost God the life of his Son: "ye were bought at a price," and what has cost God much cannot be cheap for us. Above all, it is grace because God did not reckon his Son too dear a price to pay for our life, but delivered him up for us. Costly grace is the Incarnation of God.
>
> Dietrich Bonhoeffer,
> *The Cost of Discipleship*. SCM, 1978, 37

In this book, the central topic of atonement is approached through the metaphor of "the naked Christ." It extends the cost—the sheer personal humiliation and suffering—exacted on Christ as he died on a Roman cross. It reminds us of the extent of love demonstrated by God in Christ. It goes beyond our traditions that protect Jesus' modesty on the cross and lays bare the kind of shame that a cross imposed on anyone unfortunate enough to die on one.

In his study of clothing and nakedness Dan Lé develops the metaphor of "nakedness" not only as a historical fact but also as a contemporary model of atonement. Through it he advocates an approach that deepens our understanding of the cross, not only in relation to the one who died there on our behalf, but also for his disciples today. There is much to be gained from this study, both historically and theologically. Yet—there is more to it than this. The contemporary Western church of the twenty-first century is a church addicted to cheap grace. God is too much perceived as our familiar friend and too little understood as our costly lover. Small wonder Bonhoeffer's words speak prophetically into our current lack of discipleship. Dan's proposal does two things. On the one hand, it empowers the reader to contemplate what God has done for us on the cross through a different model of atonement and perspective. This can only be a positive move. On the other hand, it provides an understanding of what it means to follow the naked Christ—of taking off our own life and being clothed with Christ. If there was ever a time when new stimuli were needed to help lead us into a deeper fellowship with Jesus Christ, then surely that time is now. This book may well help us on that task.

Graham McFarlane
London School of Theology

Acknowledgments

PRAISE GOD FOR HIS faithfulness through his blessings and provision; glory to his name! The journey from start to completion of this book has been long and arduous, but God has graciously provided me with great teachers and helpers. I would like to thank Dr Robin Parry and Pickwick Publications for their gracious help in the publication process of this book.

Second, I would like to express my deepest thanks to my PhD supervisor, Dr Graham McFarlane, whose expertise, encouragement, and friendship I can never repay. It would be hard to imagine the completion of this book without his challenging comments, sensitive guidance, and patience.

Third, I offer my gratitude to the Laing Scholarship for the financial support I have received throughout my PhD research. Immense heartfelt thanks also to OMF, Christchurch Westbourne, Mr and Mrs Tim and Zinnia Symonds and their friends who have faithfully supported me with love, prayers, and funding. To my Christian friends and fellow workers at the Vietnamese Chinese Christian Fellowship in Deptford, thank you! Your support and encouragement mean so much and your frequent prayers have been a tremendous blessing to me.

Fourth, I thank God for my friends at London School of Theology. Thank you my brothers and sisters who prayed, laughed, and cried with me. To members of Ramjets, the "tea family," all LST Frisbee fans and research fellows: thank you for sharing the journey with me! Thank you my friends: Philip Snelgrove, David Leeds, Virgil and Helena Tabry, who proofread my drafts. Thank you, St John's United Reform Church in Northwood for your love and support! God bless you! Great thanks also to Eastbury Church for welcoming, loving, and making me feel so much at home!

Last but not least, I would like to thank my dear scattered family—the Le Kieu clan! Despite the distance, I know I always have your prayers and support! Thank you mum and dad for teaching, trusting, and enduring with me all the way! Your sacrificial love truly moves me toward the exemplary self-emptying love of the *Christus nudus*!

Abbreviations

AH	*Adversus Haeresies*. Irenaeus. In *Ante-Nicene Christian Library 5: AH* I.1–IV.30, and *Ante-Nicene Christian Library 9: AH* IV.31–V.36
ANF	*Ante-Nicene Fathers*. Edited by Alexander Roberts and James Donaldson. Peabody, MA: Hendrickson, 2004
ANCL	*Ante-Nicene Christian Library*. Edited by Alexander Roberts and James Donaldson. Edinburgh: T. & T. Clark, 1869
BAR	*Biblical Archaeological Review*
BST	Bible Speak Today
CBQ	*Catholic Biblical Quarterly*
CC	*Calvin's Commentaries*. John Calvin. 1847. Reprint. Grand Rapids: Eerdmans, 1948–50.
CD	*Church Dogmatics*. Karl Barth. Translated by G. T. Thomson et al. Edited by Geoffrey William Bromiley, Thomas F. Torrance, and G. T. Thomson. Edinburgh: T. & T. Clark, 1936–77
CDH	*Cur Deus Homo*. Saint Anselm. In *St. Anselm: Basic Writings*, translated by S. N. Deane. La Salle: Open Court, 1962
CTJ	*Calvin Theological Journal*
EQ	*The Evangelical Quarterly*
ERT	*Evangelical Review of Theology*
ExpT	*Expository Times*
FOC	*Fathers of the Church*. Washington, DC: The Catholic University of America Press, 1961
GOTR	*Greek Orthodox Theological Review*

HTR	*Harvard Theological Review*
IJST	*International Journal of Systematic Theology*
Institutes	*Institutes of the Christian Religion.* John Calvin. In *The Library of Christian Classics*, translated by Ford Lewis Battles, edited by John T. McNeill. Vol. 1: bk. 1.1–3.19; Vol. 2: bk. 3.20–4.20. Philadelphia: Westminster, 1960
JAP	*Journal of Applied Psychology*
JBL	*Journal of Biblical Literature*
JETS	*Journal of the Evangelical Theological Society*
JRH	*Journal of Religious History*
JSNT	*Journal for the Study of the New Testament*
JSOT	*Journal of the Study of the Old Testament*
JSOTSup	*Journal of the Study of the Old Testament Supplement*
JTS	*Journal of Theological Studies*
LW	*Luther's Work.* Edited by Jaroslav Pelikan and Helmut T. Lehmann. St. Louis, MO: Concordia, 1958
NIBC	New International Biblical Commentary
NICNT	New International Commentary on the New Testament
NIGTC	New International Greek Testament Commentary
NIVAC	The NIV Application Commentary
NPNF	*Nicene and Post-Nicene Fathers.* Edited by Philip Schaff. Grand Rapids: Eerdmans, 1979.
NTS	*New Testament Studies*
SJT	*Scottish Journal of Theology*
SVTQ	*St. Vladimir's Theological Quarterly*
TPC	The Preacher's Commentary
VT	*Vetus Testamentum*
WA	*Weimarer Ausgabe*
WBC	Word Biblical Commentary
WTJ	*Wesleyan Theological Journal*

Introduction

> Salvation is found in no one else, for there is no other name under heaven given to men by which we must be saved.
>
> —Peter the Apostle[1]

AT 9:09 ON THE 26 October, 2009,[2] in a ceremony in Soc Son (Ha Noi), the Vietnam Buddhist Shangha and the Ha Noi municipal authorities began the casting of an eighty-five-tonne copper statue of Thánh Gióng (Saint Gióng)—the legendary hero of the Phu Linh commune. Not only is this statue one of the major projects set up to commemorate the millennial founding anniversary of Thang Long—Ha Noi in 2010,[3] it is also a legendary folklore icon of "salvation" for the Vietnamese people. Legend has it that, after a miraculous birth, the three-year-old Gióng suddenly grew into a giant, and promptly chased the invaders out of the country with an iron sword and groves of bamboos while riding on an iron horse.[4] After reaching the top of Soc Mountain and removing his armor, the hero and his horse flew into the sky from the mountain. In order to show deep gratitude to the valiant man, the king conferred on him the title: "Heavenly King of Phu Dong"[5] and set up a temple in his memory.

1. Acts 4:12. All biblical references are taken from the New International Version.

2. I.e., 9:09 on 9 September, 2009 Lunar Calendar, according to Nhandan.com.vn, Dantri.com.vn and Vnexpress.net, see Nhandan, "Hanoi starts casting of Thanh Giong statue"; Đô, "Khởi đúc tượng Thánh Gióng"; Nguyễn, "Đúc tượng Thánh Gióng 85 tấn vào ngày 'trùng cửu'."

3. The statue will be placed at the Soc Temple on Soc Mountain, and requires a total investment of approximately US$2.8 million, half of which will be spent on the cast.

4. Nhandan, "Giong"; Overland Club Vietnamese Culture Class, "Vietnamese folk literature."

5. My translation of *"Phù Đổng Thiên Vương,"* compared to the Overland Club Vietnamese Culture Class's translation "General of God who came to help and protect people."

Perhaps an icon such as this has been built upon many layers of cultural belief concerning more perfected concepts of salvation that it represents. In particular, the elements that are necessary for this icon to be considered salvific are: heroism, miracles, supernatural manifestation, and big-scale impact. Yet, over time, such an icon can become no more than a statue of historical and cultural heritage. For the younger Vietnamese generations today, this icon is only a reminder of a mythical legend.

The same question mark is placed over the atonement debate today: how do Christians start talking about the cross and its salvific narrative to a culture that is so accustomed to consumption, entertainment, and hedonism while being so desensitized to violence? Surely, cultural changes have effectively pushed the gospel's atonement narrative into a list of several alternative stories. Once an entertainment culture has reduced the naked body of Christ into artistic interpretations and various fictional narratives, the crucifix remains no more than an interesting narrative that appears over and over again in the media, either intensified with sanguinary physical torments or encrypted with esoteric codes.[6] It is clear then, the naked body of Christ has lost its scandal, tension, and theological vitality of cosmological disclosure to the flow of deconstructionism in a pluralistic culture. Consumerism now substitutes emotional solutions, entertainment and academic achievement substitute wisdom, and emotional promiscuity and supernatural activities substitute a spiritual relationship with God.[7] In a body-obsessed culture that emphasizes body appearance, fashion, and nudity, the cross has become irrelevant. A naked Christ has become misunderstood, shunned, re-shaped, re-imaged, and domesticated into an artistic expression,[8] or at best another meaningless, barbaric, and gruesome death of the ancient Roman world.

---

6. E.g., Kazantzakis, *The Last Temptation of Christ*; Fina and Scorsese, *The Last Temptation of Christ*; Brown, *The Da Vinci Code*; Gibson, *The Passion of the Christ*; Grazer and Howard, *Da Vinci Code*.

7. Bauman, *Postmodern Ethics*, 23; Bauman, *Liquid Modernity*, 69; Kellner, "Popular Culture and the Construction of Postmodern Identities," 153. New Age activities and psychic spies (such as Derren Brown) are becoming more popular, especially in an entertainment culture.

8. A bronze sculpture of a naked Christ by Yuri Orekhov, on display in the Modern Art Museum, Moscow, Russia, (on September 10, 2009, patroned by Zurab Tseretely, President of Russian Academy of Fine Arts), has been criticized by some Russian believers for profaning the image of the Savior and should therefore be removed from the museum (Zumapress, "Sculpture of Naked Christ Caused Scandal in Moscow").

Soteriologically, this problem has been identified, but the naked body of Christ on the cross has not received enough attention, let alone its theological contribution to the picture of atonement drawn out. Indeed, the nakedness of Christ has been considered irrelevant or unimportant, and has even been accused of overemphasizing the suffering of the cross as a scandalous ordeal.[9] Therefore, it is imperative to keep recovering the scandal of that mangled body because, on the one hand, the cross is restricted by social propriety that domesticates it, and, on the other, it is distorted by postmodern body-obsessed depictions. The tension of God's wisdom in the folly of the cross appears to have been compromised by both social propriety and fictional fantasies. Time has never been riper for a fresh model that revitalizes the distinctiveness of the gospel's atonement narrative while at the same time employs a symbol that attracts the attention of a body-obsessed, entertainment culture. Such a model of atonement must move beyond the "what" of a barbaric 2,000-year-old execution into the "how" of humanity's at-one-ment with God.

Why Construct Another Model?

The reason for this book is twofold. On the one hand, a body-obsessed culture is increasingly driven by an urge of self-centrism and body-centrism, especially the nude and clothed forms of the body.[10] Underlying this body-obsession is a thirst for an alternative human ontology, which this book identifies as a self-seeking notion of atonement. Subsequently, this notion of atonement stimulates a quest for another human ontology that is "free" of flaws, starting with cosmetic surgery, strict diets, fitness, and body appearance. However, this body-obsessed notion of atonement is problematic because it perpetuates shame and promotes a concept of salvation without any concept of grace. As this book will point out later, a body-obsessed culture seeks for a means of rescuing itself by pursuing body perfection and body modification. This is a stage where a

---

9. Even amongst those within academic circles, Edersheim, Thoby and Lagrange and lately Viladesau deny the tradition of a naked Christ by the theory of "decency" or a "concession of decency" (Edersheim, *The Life and Times of Jesus the Messiah*, 584; *Sanhedrin* 6.3–4, in Danby, *Mishnah*; Lagrange, *The Gospel according to Saint Mark*, 168; Tinsley, "Coming of a Dead and Naked Christ," 32; Viladesau, *The Beauty of the Cross*, 22).

10. The effect is an inevitable change in our understanding of nakedness, i.e., "our obsession with the body-perfect, and the connectedness of nakedness, bodiliness, sexuality and sin" (Wilson, "Nakedness, Bodiliness and the New Creation," 44).

body-obsessed culture has confused the *body* and the *self*, and falls prey to a consumer notion of atonement, hoping that "salvation" to the *body* can be extendable enough to be equated to the atonement of the *self*. Body modification, including the mutation of genetic protocols, can be interpreted as "salvation seeking."[11] As a result, for a body-obsessed culture the naked body and its clothing are among the first platforms where the human-ontological changes happen.[12] However, such a notion of "salvific modification" with a hope for body-perfect and a better-evolved humanity (or humanities) is only a symptom of a hazardous pathway to an endless "salvation hunt" that might subsequently be followed by almost insurmountable sociological implications.

On the other hand, while a body-obsessed culture seeks to perfect its own notion of atonement, the salvific narrative of the gospel is seriously downplayed in an individualized and secularized society.[13] Models of atonement and their metaphors such as battle, sacrifice, legal court, and ancient ritual rites might come across as anachronistic and primitive to a postmodern society, while models with an endeavor to intellectually rationalize the mystery of atonement have become theologically heavy and off-putting.[14] There is, then, a clear need to hold a balance between safeguarding traditional theological content and at the same time communicating the scandal of the cross to a body-obsessed culture in a fresh and attractive language that stimulates engagement and dialogue. In recent years, several attempts have proposed to revitalize this engagement,[15] yet the naked crucifix has not received adequate attention.[16]

---

11. Ertelt, "Scientist says British Human Cloning Bill Would Allow Human-Chimp Mating."

12. Bauman, *Liquid Life*, 89–92.

13. Bauman, *The Individualized Society*, 157; Bauman, *Postmodernity and Its Discontents*, 181; Brown, *The Death of Christian Britain*, chapters 2–3.

14. Grenz, *A Primer on Postmodernism*, 161.

15. Green and Baker, *Recovering the Scandal of the Cross*; cf. Boersma, *Violence, Hospitality, and the Cross*; Schmiechen, *Saving Power*; McKnight, *A Community Called Atonement*; Terry, *The Justifying Judgement of God*.

16. Closest to the originality of this book are the works of Frank ("Naked but Unashamed," 122–34) and Jordan ("God's Body," 284); however, these works lack a wider cultural and anthropological analysis as well as biblical and theological criteria to propose an adequate model of atonement.

What Is New?

This book will draw attention to the naked body of Christ through the contribution and consolidation of archeological, historical, and cultural evidence.[17] However, this is not an end in itself. Rather, the language of nakedness and clothing is employed to construct a model of atonement called *Christus nudus* in order to dialogue with a body-obsessed culture on the significance of the cross. While the language of "being clothed with Christ" and "putting on Christ"[18] has been prevalently discussed, the language of nakedness has been of a lesser concern. In fact, nakedness has only been referred to in theological discussion and commentaries where a cultural interaction is required.[19] Therefore, if an atonement model employs the theological meanings of nakedness and clothing it also opens an exciting opportunity for the scandal and tension in the narrative of the cross to once again touch base with a body-obsessed culture.

A Justifiable Methodology

There are several methodological questions that this book endeavors to answer, such as "what does *Christus nudus* comprise of?" or "what makes it tick?"; yet more importantly, this book endeavors to point out why a body-obsessed culture needs *Christus nudus*.

How can such a test be possible? Clothing and nakedness are extensive cultural and anthropological fields, but they do not cover as much of

---

17. Klausner, *Jesus of Nazareth*; Blinzler, *The Trial of Jesus*; Hengel, *Crucifixion*; Tzaferis, "Crucifixion—The Archaeological Evidence"; Fitzmyer, "Crucifixion in Ancient Palestine, Qumran Literature, and the New Testament"; Neyrey, "Despising the Shame of the Cross: Honor and Shame in the Johannine Passion Narrative"; Neyrey, *Honor and Shame in the Gospel of Matthew*; Keener, *A Commentary on the Gospel of Matthew*; Kenner, *Matthew*; Kenner, *The Gospel of John*.

18. Gal 3:27; Col 3:9–12.

19. This does not necessarily imply that the content of these discussions are insignificant. In fact, some major works by Aune, Neyrey, Harris, and Kim have touched on various themes connected to nakedness (Aune, *WBC—Revelation 6–16*; Neyrey, "Cross"; Neyrey, *Honor*; Harris, *The Second Epistle to the Corinthians*; Kim, *The Significance of Clothing Imagery in the Pauline Corpus*.) Nevertheless, none of these studies have mentioned an atonement model. Nakedness and clothing are no longer new topics, in fact they have been extensively engaged with during the time of the early Church Fathers. Most probably, starting with the interpretation of Adam and Eve's nakedness and the controversial naked baptism and public bath in the Greco-Roman culture and the association of the nakedness of Christ with his humanity. Augustine's *The City of God* is also an obvious example.

an extensive area in theology.[20] Most obvious are shame and mutilation in Lemos,[21] or the shame and honor of crucifixion in Neyrey.[22] However, the idea of using metaphors of nakedness and clothing for a model of atonement remains original for this book.[23] It might first appear problematic that the metaphors of nakedness and clothing have not been found in any specific biblical texts on atonement.[24] A "naked Christ" is not recorded in any of the Synoptic Gospels. However, it is still possible and legitimate to construct a model of atonement using the metaphors of nakedness and clothing (1) from a linguistic approach with an anthropological and biblical understanding of the metaphors, and (2) from the traditional theological and liturgical interpretations of nakedness and clothing. Thus, methodologically speaking, using fresh metaphors does not necessarily imply a total change of the content of theology according to the social context.

This book will present evidence from anthropological and sociological perspectives, linguistic compatibility of the biblical witness, and most importantly a comparative study of three classical models in relation to the new model. While this book may appear to be a research of a multidisciplinary nature, all these aspects are ultimately essential for the construction of an evangelical response to a body-obsessed notion

20. For female nakedness and its religious meanings see Miles, *Carnal Knowing*, 21–53, 81–169. For nude baptism: meanings of nakedness and embodiment, its implications in relation to resurrection and renewal of creation, the challenge of human brokenness and the anticipation of God's restoration, see Wilson, "Nakedness," 46–49. Other works that have relevant touches on the topic of nakedness are various but mainly thematic. See Smith, "The Garments of Shame," chapter 1, 1–23 [originally in *History of Religions* 5 (1966) 217–38]; Goodson, *Therapy, Nudity, and Joy*; Gorham and Leal, "Naturism and Christianity," 13. More evidence on the metaphorical use of Christ's nakedness in Calvin's writings and the homilies on penitential nakedness in early English sermons, with reference to an atonement model, will be presented later.

21. Lemos, "Shame and Mutilation."

22. Neyrey, "Cross"; Neyrey, *Honor*.

23. Works by Smith ("Garments" and *Map*), Gorham and Leal ("Naturism") have given an essential foundation for Christian understanding of nakedness, yet with no specific reference to a fresh model of atonement. Hengel (*Crucifixion*), Green and Baker (*Recovering*) recover the scandal of the cross, but not with the particular intention of viewing the cross through the scope of nakedness and clothing. Calvin's interpretation of Christ's nakedness and justification as clothing of righteousness unfortunately has not provided adequate elaboration as to what "nakedness" means in the light of atonement (Calvin, *CC—John*, 230).

24. Johnson has done some significant general work on the topic of nakedness in the Bible (Johnson, "Clothing and Nakedness in the Bible").

of atonement. Therefore, methodologically, since the *Christus nudus* model is designed to build a contemporary soteriological dialogue, the ultimate question it must answer is systematic in nature. McIntyre points out that new models have the tendency to be "replacement-oriented,"[25] but this is not the intention of the *Christus nudus* model. As will be pointed out later in chapter 8, within a kaleidoscopic fashion, introducing a fresh model does not necessarily imply a dismissal of contributions made by existing models; rather, the *Christus nudus* model compiles and compares itself with the classical models in order to establish its own contribution. Moreover, employing a kaleidoscopic perspective does not necessarily mean that this book holds a relativistic view of atonement, or denies any "norm." In fact, by following a kaleidoscopic perspective, on the one hand, history and tradition can be safeguarded from oversimplification and, on the other, the biblical diversity and a multifaceted nature of atonement can be promoted. Like McIntyre's critique of "liberation," *Christus nudus* considers the figure of the naked Christ as an axis connecting the many models.[26]

Therefore, the *Christus nudus* model will be tested by its ability to meet three objectives: (1) recovering the scandal of a domesticated cross, (2) producing an up-to-date response to a myopic body-obsessed notion of atonement, and (3) representing the cross in a kaleidoscopic fashion that umbrellas three classical models. Through the construction and testing of this model, metaphors of nakedness and clothing are employed to elaborate the problematic cultural shift away from traditional values, which in turn causes the traditional teachings of atonement to become downplayed. Yet at the same time, the *Christus nudus* model aims not to lose the core theological content contributed by the classical models.

Mapping Out the Journey

This book is divided into three parts. Part One explores the legitimacy of nakedness and clothing in an anthropological context of a body-obsessed culture. Chapter 1 clarifies the making of a body-obsessed culture. From the link between identity and the body, it is argued that the body and its expression through clothes are a vital part of human communication. So much so that the body has become both a "laboratory" and an ultimate "public courtroom" that has the verdict as to whether an individual is

25. McIntyre, *The Shape of Soteriology*, 28.
26. McIntyre, *Shape*, 51, 63.

rejected or accepted, condemned or atoned. Chapter 2 draws from the origins of clothing and an anthropological review of cultural concepts of nakedness and clothing to provide a wider perspective of shame, modesty, and human relation. The naked and clothed body, although varied in forms and structures, is still foundational for bodily communication and relational concepts in most cultures. Chapter 3 presents a linguistic approach to a rhetorical and epistemological understanding of nakedness and clothing. The "conceal-reveal" and "object-containment" models reflect how shame and modesty work within the capacity of metaphors. Nakedness and clothing are legitimate cognitive metaphors that have the natural sociological and psychological development of a body-obsessed culture. Through this metaphorical linguistic approach, this book will establish a connection that makes sense of a naked Christ in an atonement dialogue with a body-obsessed culture.

In Part Two, this book moves away from an anthropological ground into the specific grounds of the Bible and Christian theology, not only to claim the legitimacy of the metaphors of nakedness and clothing, but also to examine the theological topics that employ them. Chapter 4 investigates how the Bible employs the contrast between nakedness and clothing. In particular, the Mosaic theory has proposed that the sense of shame in nakedness at the fall was the cause for the origin of clothes. Yet an investigation into the biblical notion of nakedness points to a wider lens for human relations. Chapter 5 focuses on the use of nakedness and clothing in the theologies of sin, shame, covenant, eschatology, and the interchange between old and new in baptism. At the end of this part, chapter 6 extends the shame and honor motif of the Roman crucifixion into the suffering and glory of a naked Christ. The significance of the antithesis between nakedness and clothing in the context of the naked crucifix uncovers the omitted symbol of a naked Christ, while at the same time points out the need to construct and validate an atonement model called *Christus nudus*.

Part Three holds the nakedness of Christ and the clothing language of atonement at the center of the *Christus nudus* model. Chapter 7 is the main construction of the model. Within the *kenosis-theosis* framework, the *Christus nudus* model retells the narrative of the ultimate clothing that God initially intended for humanity—an intimate relationship with him. Moving from nakedness (sin, shame, and suffering) to clothing (righteousness, justification, forgiveness, and honor), the model finally points to the *telos* of glorification (union with God through being clothed with Christ). Subsequently, chapter 8 will test out the legitimacy and compatibility of the *Christus nudus* model in constructive negotiation and kaleidoscopic correlation between its contribution and three classical models. Through this test, limitations of the model will also be indicated. Finally, this part will end with a conclusion on the theological implications and impact of the *Christus nudus* model on a body-obsessed culture in anthropological, soteriological, and methodological terms. In response to a body-obsessed view of atonement, which was built upon a consumer acceptance of a standardized body through body-modification, the *Christus nudus* model offers an interpersonal dimension of atonement, wherein nakedness that is beyond the genitals can be covered by Christ—the type of clothing that can never perish. Thus, the emphatic *telos* in the actualization of "putting on Christ" is the unique hope for true atonement and humanity through the cosmological *Christus nudus*.

PART 1

Nakedness and Clothing in
a Body-Obsessed Culture

I

The Body-Obsessed Culture

ADMITTEDLY, THE HUMAN BODY has been a human obsession probably from the time humans first walked on the earth. The more humans live, the more they understand the body and the stronger the obsession they have for it, no matter how far from assured they are about its referent.[1] Therefore, the historical discourse on the body has been examined according to a variety of perspectives: the body is a subject in the terminologies and data of biochemical-medical science,[2] of a plethora of philosophical dialogues,[3] and an obsession of religions,[4] as well as sociology.[5]

It has been widely recognized that the Western world is increasingly driven by the force of brand consumerism, under the dictatorship of an image-dominating media culture.[6] What has not been fully recognized is the fact that consumerism and image dictatorship also encourages the emergent body-obsessed culture to interpret nakedness and clothing in a new light. Accordingly, a model of atonement that employs metaphors

---

1. Coakley, "Introduction: Religion and the Body," 2–3.

2. Cregan, *Sociology of the Body*, 13–14.

3. From Aquinas, Aristotle, Descartes to Kant and Freud, to modern social philosophy of Foucault, French social theory of Sartre, and structuralist Marxism, see Turner, "The Body in Western Society," 15–17; Brown, *The Body and Society*, 26–29, 34–35, 47–48, 108–9, 163–66, 425–26.

4. *Religion* 19 (1989) 197–273. Coakley has compiled this discourse into a wide range of academic perspectives from ancient philosophy to various contemporary religious and secular modern thoughts (Coakley, *Religion*).

5. Moltmann-Wendel, *I Am My Body*, 4–9; Cregan, *Sociology*, 13–14.

6. Lasch, *The Culture of Narcissism*, 47–48; Klein, *No Logo*, 7–12, 15–26, 28–30, 45–46.

of nakedness and clothing must take into account how a body-obsessed culture defines nakedness and clothing, and the subsequent adjustments created by those definitions.

The notion of a *body-obsessed culture* begins with the notion of a *body-obsessed being* since human beings are fundamentally bodily creatures.[7] This chapter explores the relationship between a body-obsessed *culture* and body-obsessed *beings* and the mutual influence between the two. Particularly, on the one hand, the psycho-economical spectrum evidences the shift from a being as an *embodied* being to a body-*obsessed* being; on the other, the socio-economical spectrum suggests that the body-obsessed *culture* is in fact the result and the expansion of that body-obsessed *being* under the encouragement of its very own social development. Hence, in essence, the focus of this chapter will be devoted to three areas: (1) The internal body: "I am my body"; (2) The external body: "Body is our measurement," and (3) The body-obsessed culture and consumer clothing.

The Psycho-Economical Spectrum: The Internal Body

"We sometimes speak as if we have bodies, rather than are bodies."[8] "If the body begins to stop functioning, we make those around us insecure. And in such crises we have another experience, namely that we *are* bodies."[9] Human embodiment—the physical and mental experience of existence—is the condition that makes human-human and human-world relations possible.[10] However, the step from being *embodied* to being body-*obsessed* must not be surmised. The definition of a body-obsessed being, at the grass-root level, begins with the crucial question: *what constitutes a human being?*[11]

---

7. From religious and scientific perspectives, this is accepted as fact. Wright claimed that all creatures need a body to live in this metaphysical world, for the devils and angels do not exist in a bodily way (Wright, *Man in the Process of Time*, 36–37); Carruthers, *Introducing Persons*, 194.

8. Kenny, *The Metaphysics of Mind*, 17; Turner, "Western," 18–19.

9. Moltmann-Wendel, *Body*, 1.

10. Cregan, *Sociology*, 3.

11. In other words, what is it that composes the *true self* in human being? For further research and discussion, see Moreland and Rae, *Body & Soul*, 179–81, 201–2.

Body and Self: Body-Identity and Self-Identity

René Descartes' statement "*Cogito, ergo sum*" ("I think, therefore I am")[12] is a foundational statement of Western philosophy, for it verifies the existence of humanity.[13] The sense of self-awareness and existence in "*cogito, ergo sum*" points to the existence of an entity called *self*. That *self*, according to many schools of psychology, is the cognitive representation of one's identity.[14] In philosophy, the self is broadly defined as the essential qualities that make a person distinct from all others.[15] Most philosophical definitions of self are expressed in the first person.[16]

For Socrates and Plato, the soul is the essence of the self.[17] Aristotle, also following Plato, defined the soul as the core essence of a being, but argued against it having a separate existence.[18] For Avicenna and Descartes, the self is independent of the senses. Avicenna's "Floating Man" states that the soul is a substance.[19] He concludes that the idea of the self is not logically dependent on any physical thing, and that the soul should

---

12. René Descartes' original statement was "Je pense donc je suis," from his *A Discourse on Method*, 27; Descartes, *The Meditations and Selections from the Principles*, 132: it was intended to replace Aristotle's philosophy and traditional Scholastic Philosophy then used in Universities; Baird and Kaufmann, *Philosophic Classics*, 374–75.

13. Descartes was not the first to mention it; Plato spoke about the "knowledge of knowledge" (Greek *noésis noéseós*) and Aristotle explains the idea at length in *Nicomachean Ethics*, 1170a25ff in Aristotle, *The Nicomachean Ethics*, 240–41. Alternatively, Augustine writes in *The City of God* 11.26, 335: "Si [. . .] fallor, sum" ("If I err, I am.") Additionally, another predecessor to Descartes is Avicenna's "Floating Man," which is a thought experiment on human self-awareness and self-consciousness, see Nasr and Leaman, *History of Islamic Philosophy*, 315.

14. James, *The Principles of Psychology*, Vol. 1: 216–21, 291–305; Sedikides and Spencer, *The Self*, 4–14, 52–64.

15. Locke's theory of consciousness as the basis of personal identity in Locke, *An Essay Concerning Human Understanding*, 309.

16. Descartes, *Discourse*, 27; Locke, *Understanding*, 475; Baird and Kaufmann, *Philosophic*, 375–76, 386–92; and James, *Psychology*, Vol. 1: 291–93.

17. Plato's *Crito* (Sorabji, *Self*, 167, 177–78); Copleston, *Aquinas*, 156–61; Flew, *Body, Mind, and Death*, 43–45.

18. *De Anima* (On the Soul,) 408b1f., in *The Complete Words of Aristotle: The Revised Oxford Translation*, Vol. 1: 651.

19. Dales, *The Problem of the Rational Soul in the Thirteenth Century*, 7–8: In Avicenna's *Liber sextus naturalium*, or *De anima*, Avicenna argues that the soul and body are separate substances. The human personality resides in the soul. The soul is not mixed with the body, nor is it dependent on it. Its relation to the body is accidental rather than substantial, for if it were substantial, then the soul would perish with the body.

not be seen in relative terms, but as a primary given, a substance.[20] This argument was later refined and simplified by René Descartes in epistemic terms when he stated: "I can abstract from the supposition of all external things, but not from the supposition of my own consciousness."[21]

The relationship between the self and the body is thus divided into two views: (1) a materialist (or secularist) view holds that all a human being is and has is the body,[22] while (2) the dualist view holds that there is a body-soul combination within a person,[23] wherein the will controls the body.[24] Whatever the perspective, the self is a complex subject that defines many forms of spirituality.[25] However, in a body-obsessed culture, this discourse on the relationship between the self and the body must take into account the fact that, to a large extent, the body affects a person's identity and perception of the world and subsequently the self.[26] In fact, the biological body has developed its own perception even before

---

20. Sorabji, *Self*, 134–35, 222, 314.

21. Nasr and Leaman, *Islamic*, 315; Adamson and Taylor, *The Cambridge Companion to Arabic Philosophy*, 103. Descartes' proposition, which holds that the soul is separate from the body, however, is based on the fact that the body is independent of the mind and what it thinks. He does not appear to distinguish between mind, spirit and soul as faculties for rational thinking (Rozemond, *Descartes' Dualism*, 1998).

22. Midgley, "The Soul's Successor: Philosophy and the 'Body,'" 53. This view might find support in Dennett's deflationary theory of the self, which argues that the selves are not physically detectable. In this sense, they are convenient fiction, like the centre of gravity of a hoop is a point in thin air. People constantly tell themselves stories to make sense of their world, and they feature in the stories as a character, and that convenient but fictional character is the self [Dennett, "The Self as a Center of Narrative Gravity," 103–12; Dennett, "Why Everyone is a Novelist," 1016, 1028–29.]

23. More on dualism, see Carruthers, *Introducing*, 87–194.

24. Barth, *CD* III.4, 358–60; Moltmann-Wendel, *Body*, xii, 42; Lloyd, *Introduction to Psychology*, and Lloyd, *The Man of Reason*.

25. For instance, see Hall's bipolar self: (1) the ego (the learned)—a superficial self of mind and body, and (2) an egoic creation (the self which is sometimes called the True Self, the I or I AM, the Atman in Hinduism, the Observing Self, or the Witness, see Hall, *Self Unfoldment by Disciplines of Realization*, 38–46; Kohut, *The Analysis of the Self*, 25: Grandiose and idealized selves.

26. LaFollette, *Personal Relationships, Love, Identity, and Morality*, 58–59; Churchland, *Scientific Realism and Plasticity of Mind*, 89–116. A materialistic view of the body might even argue that physical behaviour, which exhibits life or consciousness, can ultimately be explained without bringing in non-physical principles. In other words, the only ultimate and fundamental laws of the universe are physical (Braine, *The Human Person*, 1).

the mind becomes aware of its cognition.[27] Alternatively, intellectual and volitional activities such as silent thought and spiritual longings depend on the activity of the brain,[28] which holds the central control of the body. Therefore, it can be further argued that the self and its identity are dependent on the body.

The body is the *only* channel through which we live and experience the physical world. When we see people, we see their bodies;[29] we relate as and through our embodied beings.[30] As a result, in a surveillance culture such as Western society, for example, bodily evidence is demanded as proof of human identity,[31] due to the close connection between mental and physical events.[32] Indeed, Glover demonstrates that this connection is internally unique to each body, different from that external perception.

> My body is also something I am aware of. I do not perceive it in the same way others do, and this contributes to my sense that its frontiers are mine. . . . The body is not controlled from outside: its control system, the brain is inside it. . . . To see someone is to see a body. And bodies tell us a lot about people. We learn about their age, their sex, and perhaps their race, something about their strength, their state of health and their weight. We learn about their attractiveness, and we can see something of how they think of themselves and how they want to be seen. From their posture and from their style of bodily movement we may get an impression of their mood or even their job.[33]

---

27. Popper and Eccles point out that a newborn baby is a developing body, but not yet a person with a unity of body and mind (Popper and Eccles, *The Self and Its Brain*, 115).

28. It is even argued that when a person dies, the body ceases to exist and that person also ceases to exist (Kenny, *Metaphysics*, 31); Young, *Philosophy and the Brain*, 86, 102: our senses in the skin and the nervous cortical centres make us believe that our selves are our bodies. This is an anthropological and medical fact.

29. Glover, *The Philosophy and Psychology of Personal Identity*, 69–70.

30. Cregan, *Sociology*, 5–6.

31. Lyon, *Surveillance Society*, 70. It is also called "forensic identity" with a political nature (Gabriel and Lang, *The Unmanageable Consumer*, 82–83).

32. LaFollette, *Personal*, 58; Kenny, *Metaphysics*, 97. Self-identity is no doubt closely related to body, which changes greatly and constantly (Popper and Eccles, *Self*, 101; particularly the physical basis, 115).

33. Glover, *Identity*, 69–70.

The body provides a compelling and convenient definition of identity.[34] From childhood, human beings learn about the function and the meaning of having a body, its capacity and limitations.[35] As such, the body is vital for any sense of self in a biological world: through it we discover the existence of that which is beyond what we can see or feel.[36] Therefore, because embodiment is empirical, it is almost anyone's first thought that the body is identified as "self," body-identity is personal identity.[37]

Certainly the self depends on the body,[38] especially for a perception of the physical world, but there is a limit to this dependence. For instance, observation shows that if the body survives an operation, which cuts away parts of the body or the brain, the integrity of the self still exists.[39] Moreover, there is more to the self than how the body determines it. Cognitive or religious experiences, which occur beyond the verification of the body, are also capable of shaping the self.[40] Therefore, a definition of the self that maintains the body as central to the self-identity above all other aspects is an obvious body-obsessed definition. The self, in this instance, is called a "body-obsessed being."

Body-Dependence and Body-Obsession

The *nude* body certainly has an important place in human identity development.[41] The naked body is one of the first and foremost sources of

---

34. Donath, "Identity and Deception in the Virtual Community," 29.

35. LaFollette, *Personal*, 70; Giddens, *Modernity and Self-Identity*, 56.

36. For instance, Kenny suggests that knowledge can be felt without philosophical reflection or empirical enquiry (Kenny, *Metaphysics*, 98).

37. Noonan, *Personal Identity*, 2–3.

38. The Greek notion of the ghost in the machine is thus important. In this view, the body can feel as if being "trapped" (Bultmann, *The Second Letter to the Corinthians*, 136, following Lietzmann and Windisch); Glasson, "2 Corinthians v. 1–10 *versus* Platonism," 146–47.

39. Popper and Eccles, *Self*, 115; Swinburne, *The Evolution of the Soul*, 147: by this test of "brain cutting" we conclude that the brain is the core of the body, which determines whose body it is; however, parts of the brain can be lost without interference with our personality.

40. James, *Psychology*, Vol. 1: 291–400; Locke, *Human*, 310–21.

41. Physical, motor, and cognitive development (Dworetzky, *Human Development*, 147–49). Interestingly, Irenaeus also established this connection in his interpretation of Adam and Eve (Steenberg, "Children in Paradise: Adam and Eve as 'Infants' in Irenaeus of Lyons," 1–22).

data, from which a child develops its gender and identity.[42] Subsequently, not only does body change (e.g., during puberty, pregnancy, disability) affect the development of self-image and body image;[43] bodily discoveries also affect one's gender identity, attraction, and sexuality,[44] before one settles with so-called a "sexual preference" or "sexual orientation."[45] Alternatively, one's identity is shaped by cultural upbringing and immediate social propriety[46] that dictates how one should feel when a nude body is exposed, or to consider it a "breaking of social norms."[47] Therefore, not only does the naked body influence the way one relates to oneself (gender identity, body-image, and self-worth), it also affects the way one relates to others in a wider context.

When body-identity is conceived as self-identity there is an obvious dependence of the self on the body that eventually builds up an obsession for the body. This body-obsessed self arguably originates from an act of merging the body and the self: first, the self depends on the body's natural survival defense instinct to exist and secondly, the self builds up a cognitive understanding where its identity slowly becomes established in the body.[48] However one might ask a significant question, what makes the self believe that it can define itself through the body? Surely, body-dependence develops into body-obsession through an intensifying process of psychological and sociological effects imposed by the environment.[49] Bordo suggests that the obsessive body practices of contemporary culture

---

42. Dworetzky, *Development*, 164–69: gender role acquisition; Freud's theory of *penis envy* (ibid., 166) is relevant to the idea suggested above, although Freud's theory has not been widely accepted. However, this does not mean to neglect or overemphasize the role of anatomical genitalia over that of many other factors in forming gender identity (Pattison, "Gender Identity," 487–89).

43. Abi-Hashem, "Self-Esteem," 1085.

44. Bolt, "Interpersonal Attraction," 642.

45. Herek, "Homosexuality," 149–50; Rosenak and Looy, "Homosexuality," 571. Alternatively, one might argue that there is no solid ground for a concept of "orientation" (Anderson, *On Being Human*, 125–28).

46. Carey, *I Believe in Man*, 109–10.

47. Farley, *Good & Evil*, 54–59.

48. The merging of the body and the self has been noted (Eagleton, *The Illusion of Postmodernism*, 71).

49. The contribution of the adaptable nature is the shift from survival to self-actualization, ideally becoming everything that one is capable of becoming. Maslow's pyramid of needs is an excellent example for this (Maslow, *Motivation and Personality*, 15–22, chapters 11–13).

are not to be portrayed as bizarre or anomalous but as logical manifestations of anxieties and fantasies fostered by our culture.[50]

While the body-dependent self exists at the natural, economic level, the body-obsessed self is the result of an environmental intensification and modification imposed by society's concept of body on the self.[51] With the rise of popular culture, the influence of "celebrity," image categorization,[52] and media dictatorship,[53] the body-obsessed self is pressurized to be a body that can meet the demands of the postmodern self. Consequently, the body-obsessed self must appear in a fit, attractive, and productive body that is updated with the dictation of the image-controlling media and popular culture.[54] The self's dependence on the body has now made the individual more sensitive to sensuality and pleasure and thus prompting a personal desire for bodily modification and enhancement.[55] In this sense, the body becomes a visible carrier of the desires of the self, including sexual orientations and practices.[56] Furthermore, the body even becomes a "tool" to redefine identity. For example, body fitness becomes the channel through which women define themselves, expressing a sense of liberation, and projecting a successful, independent, enterprising, and fulfilled image.[57] The self is no longer content with a healthy body. It demands a fit body, one that is more capable of work and narcissistic hedonism. From a sexual theoretical standpoint, the more attractive the body or the more genetically superior it appears, the better chances of mating and procreation.[58] Therefore, the more attractive the

---

50. Bordo, *Unbearable Weight*, 15.

51. James, *Affluenza*, 28–30, 73–74, 123–29, 132–39, 143; James, *The Selfish Capitalist*, 62–65, 71–84; de Graaf, *Affluenza*, 123–24, 198–205.

52. Gabriel and Lang, *Unmanageable*, 84–85; Kellner, "Popular," 145–48.

53. Fiske shows how media demonstrates the way representational codes and techniques both shape and "decode" our perception (Fiske, *Television Culture*, 45–47, 314–19).

54. Certain looks are dictated by media as more desiring (Nixon, "Exhibiting Masculinity," 304; Bordo, *Unbearable*, 320–21: footnote 12). Therefore, there is a need to see through the illusions and mystifications of the image dominated culture (Bordo, *Twilight Zones*, 22).

55. Bordo, *The Male Body*, 69–83.

56. Lyon, *Postmodernity*, 83; Giddens, *The Transformation of Intimacy*, 28–34.

57. Willis, *Specifying*, 7–25; Miles, *Consumerism*, 102–3.

58. Darwinian natural selection is especially relevant to physical attraction and modern civilized societies (Cash, "Sexism and 'Beautyism' in Personnel Consultant Decision Making," 301–10; Clark and Mills, "Interpersonal Attraction in Exchange

person, the more attention, the more social opportunities, popularity, and even fame may follow.⁵⁹

In the shift from economic sufficiency to competitive consumerism, the postmodern body is exhausted by the demands of the self in achieving social position, material power and narcissist attractiveness.⁶⁰ Therefore, to the postmodern self, any body-perception that goes against the flow of this logic is often seen as dull and sluggish if not abnormal, problematic, and rejectable.

The Socio-Economical Spectrum: The External Body

Unlike the internal body, the external body is concerned with changes that happen to the body to a large scale.⁶¹ Particularly, the dualistic notion of body and soul, such as the Augustinian body, where body is subjected to the self, flesh is to be dominated by spirit, and the ancient Greek and Hebraic views, which separate the soul from the body,⁶² are now replaced by the cementing of soul and body.⁶³ Religious views of the body, which see the body as the "flesh" and, therefore, a threat that should be subjected to control,⁶⁴ are now replaced by the consumer external presentation of freedom and pleasure.⁶⁵ This is a shift of cognition wherein intellectual and spiritual knowledge is slowly outdated and replaced by experiential knowledge of the body. In fact, certain feminist

---

and Communal Relationships," 12–24; De Santis and Kayson, "Defendants Characteristics of Attractiveness, Race, & Sex and Sentencing Decisions," 679–83).

59. Cash, "Sexism," 301–10; Clark and Mills, "Interpersonal," 12–24; Lorenz, "Do pretty people earn more?"

60. Bauman, *Life*, 91.

61. For further detail see Cregan, *Sociology*, 2–15.

62. Bordo, *Unbearable*, 3; Dales, *Problem*, 4–5: prior to the third quarter of the twelfth century, Latin Christian thought on the soul had been most heavily influenced by Augustine and the pseudo-Augustinian works. This tradition held that the soul was an immortal spiritual substance, created by God and infused into the body of each individual. The soul was thought to rule the body in this life, to be capable of an independent existence and would be eternally punished or blessed as its actions in this world merited. In short, it was in the soul that the human personality resides, for which Augustine had defined man as a soul using a body (*De immortalitate animae* 9 [16], 10 [17], "The Immortality of the Soul," 34–37; *De quantitate animae* 13 [22], "The Magnitude of the Soul," 83).

63. Lash, *Sociology of Postmodernism*, 56.

64. Turner, "Western," 20–23.

65. Ibid., 32, 36.

views discard the notion that the body is inherently corrupted, arguing, rather, that discourse on the body must start from creation.[66] Similarly, Dyer suggests: "[A]n intellectual or spiritual knowledge about the body is different from experiential knowledge of the body—both are socially constructed, but the latter is always in a dynamic material and physical relationship with the body, is always knowledge in and of the body. Intellectual or spiritual knowledge on the other hand divorces social construction from that which it constructs, divorces knowledge about the body from knowing with the body."[67]

With the discovery of the scientific body, the human body becomes more materialized and secularized.[68] Scientific human anatomy redirects the body to the experiential knowledge, subjecting the body under experiments and experiences, and at the same time, putting religious and intellectual values into question.[69] The brain is now the centrality of the anatomy and is responsible for the "body-image." "*Modernity* witnessed the advent of the clinic, the disappearance of the signifier, as doctors came to know the body and its organ as 'in-themselves.' Corporeal penetration through physiology meant that experimentation replaced deduction and that bodies were to be regulated, their interior movements made calculable."[70]

On the one hand, scientific anthropology cements the self (identified as the brain) and body, arguing that as soon as the brain is dead, the identity and sense of self will cease to exist. This puts pressure on the body as the ultimate and decisive factor of existence. On the other hand, a scientific pathway has given license to the body to make the most of its existence.[71] Accordingly, the consumer body replaces the bounded and dominated body.

---

66. Moltmann-Wendel, *Body*, 35–36.

67. Dyer, *Only Entertainment*, 122–23.

68. Turner, "Western," 29; Donzelot, *The Policing of Families*, 12–25.

69. For specific reference to the body and sexuality, see Giddens, *Transformation*, 175–77, 180–81.

70. Lash, *Sociology*, 57; Turner, "Western," 35–36; however, this does not mean it is free from a bodily crisis, such as AIDS, 37.

71. Green, *Body, Soul, and Human Life*, 21–23, 38–46.

The Shift from the Regulated Body to the Consumer Body

As the body has become a subject for science and an object for alteration it is the target for a perpetuating circle of bodily experiential desires and pleasures. While the regulated body is restricted from indulging in pleasure beyond the fulfilment of bodily needs, the consumer body is liberated and pursues desires, facilitated by commercial advertizing, which cannot in principle be quenched.[72] The body shifts from having needs that demand satisfaction into having needs that demand the perpetual arousal for further satisfaction. In short, the desire for satisfaction, not satisfaction *per se*, is the goal of the consumer body. Consequently, in a consumer society, virtues in a producer's body are seen as counterproductive and therefore deplorable because the consumer body is autotelic.[73]

This notion of a consumer body comes as a result of social change.[74] In a productivist society, a person is defined by what he/she *does*; in a consumer society however, a person is defined by what he/she *buys*.[75] The development of consumerism, accordingly, opens up endless opportunity for experimentation with innovative and deviant lifestyles.[76] Consequently, the body is not only expected to be capable of receiving and broadcasting information, but also flexible enough to be a "molded" product of the inner self, and to be tested beyond the limits of existing spiritual and intellectual knowledge.[77] The body, which was seen as threatening and dangerous if not adequately controlled and regulated by cultural process,[78] is now rejected for being a profound denial of human emotionality.[79] As a result, re-definition of the body exposes the body to the experimentation and the goal of consumer satisfaction.

With the cultural shifts into postmodern consumerism, the obsession for the body also mistakes the appearance of the body for self-identity. There appears to be no distinction between identity and self-image,

---

72. Bauman, *Life*, 92.

73. Ibid., 91.

74. Kellner, "Popular," 153.

75. Smith, *Zygmunt Bauman*, 156–57. In exchange for Descartes' "I think therefore I am" is "I consume therefore I am" (Latimer, "All-Consuming Passions," 161).

76. Turner, "Western," 32.

77. Rose points out the false sense of self that has been invented as the result of psychological-based technology (Rose, *Inventing Our Selves*, 101–15).

78. Turner, "Western," 20; Bynum, *Fragmentation and Redemption*, 146.

79. Adorno and Horkheimer, *Dialectic of Enlightenment*, 231.

self-image and mere image.[80] It has been pointed out that the consumer body is associated with the display of logos, labels, and trademarks.[81] If products and logos represent lifestyle and identity,[82] then the more choices and logos available[83] the wider the range of identities from which to select.[84] Consequently, identity can be customized and personalized, grouped and materially labelled.[85]

Image-Dominance and the Bipolar Consumer Body

There is a certain truth in the statement that at the heart of the consumer identity crisis is the fundamental craving for respect and self-love:[86] people are caught in an endless cycle of lacking ego-ideal, and are unsuccessful in long-term relationships.[87] This craving for respect and connection is worsened by the myth that the attractiveness of ready-made patterns can bring fulfilment and satisfaction to the torments of self-construction and thirst for approval,[88] or even sustain personal identity. However, in order to associate the craving for acceptance and approval with the consumer logo identity, it is essential to note the dictatorial character of image-dominance by various media, which grants physical attractiveness a very high value.[89] This has a significant effect on human relations, especially on how people are judged, whether for employment, social

---

80. Gabriel and Lang, *Unmanageable*, 92.

81. Cross, *Time and Money*, 163. The presentation of self through fashion is argued to be the basic form of discretionary and open-ended consumption (Flugel, *The Psychology of Clothes*, 229–30).

82. Kellner, "Popular," 163–67.

83. Ransome, *Work, Consumption & Culture*, 144; Klein, *Logo*, 28.

84. Bauman, *Modernity and Ambivalence*, 206; Clammer, "Aesthetics of the Self: Shopping and Social Being in Contemporary Urban Japan," 195: "Shopping is not merely the acquisition of things: it is the buying of identity"; Kellner, "Popular," 158.

85. Construction of group identity and group belonging, see Ransome, *Consumption*, 144–145; Simmel in Frisby and Featherstone, *Simmel on Culture*, 196. For further sociological commentary on social group identity formation, see Giddens, *Sociology*, 274–78; Boudon and Bourricaud, *A Critical Dictionary of Sociology*, 185–86.

86. Gabriel and Lang, *Unmanageable*, 96.

87. Ibid., 95; James, *Selfish*, 65–69.

88. Bauman, *Modernity*, 206.

89. Particularly from a male perspective for choosing partners, respectively; see Buss, *The Evolution of Desire*, 57–58, 60–63. It is argued that judging by appearances is natural because sexual attraction, imagination, art, and other major sectors are unthinkable without it (Tietje and Cresap, "Is Lookism Unjust?," 37).

opportunities, friendship, sexual behavior, or marriage.[90] On that account, the body must strive to achieve the set models to receive approval; on the contrary, failure to do so results in self-dissatisfaction with overall appearance.[91] As a result, in a consumer society, the image of the body is heavily shaped and dictated by the media in the popular culture, like a common rule and standard set by certain chosen models presented by the media.[92] "Women and, to a lesser degree, men are not only affected by images in the media, they also want to see themselves represented differently. They are clamoring for change and willing to put their money on their predilections."[93]

The effect of image-dominance begins with an idealized body presented in the media,[94] with a standard that has been chosen and projected in a way that its audience can identify and emulate.[95] Yet, in order to indoctrinate its concept of "body-perfect," the media must target most strongly those who are dissatisfied with their shape,[96] or have a neurotic body. Consequently, in a consumer culture that is plagued with an identity crisis the body appears to be bipolar: on the one hand, the hedonistic body encourages consumers to be narcissistic while, on the other hand, the neurotic body alerts of bodily flaws and defects against the ideal hedonistic body.

First, certain assumptions hold that indulgence in bodily desires and hedonistic sensuality are rooted in a view that considers the body to be

---

90. Lorenz, "Pretty." It has even been said that attractive people tend to be extrovert, popular, happy and attractive and as a result receive more attention that helps them develop the necessary social skills (Cash, "Sexism," 301–10; Clark and Mills, "Interpersonal," 12–24; Santis and Kayson, "Defendants," 679–83).

91. This dissatisfaction of bodily appearance exists in both genders (Bordo, *Male*, 1999, 186–93; Monteath and McCabe, *The Influence of Societal Factors on Female Body Image*, 708–27; Garner, "Survey Says: Body Image Poll Results."

92. Garner, "Survey": "The media play an important role as a cultural gatekeeper, framing standards of beauty for all of us by the models they choose." Cf. James, *Selfish*, 71–84; Bordo, *Unbearable*, xix, xxxi, 42–47.

93. Garner, "Survey."

94. Kellner, "Popular," 153.

95. Garner, "Survey." Bordo observes that the rules of femininity have come to be culturally transmitted more and more through the deployment of standardized visual images (Bordo, "The Body and the Reproduction of Femininity," 17; Kellner, "Popular," 150).

96. Garner, "Survey."

the totality of a person.[97] However, this is unnecessarily so in a consumer society where the body is constantly seduced to be desirably hedonistic and playful with mass leisure, nudism, and mass holidays.[98] Featherstone rightly points out: "Within a consumer culture the body is proclaimed as a vehicle of pleasure. . . . Consumer culture permits the unashamed display of the human body."[99]

The hedonistic body is most prominent in a society's sexual mores: enhancement products for male genitals and cosmetic surgery abound and legally invade the consumer market;[100] sex toys and similar products are more prevalent and accessible.[101] The sexual body, highly valued in the advertizing industry,[102] *must* appear sexually alluring and is meant to be both desirable and desired.

What is problematic about this hedonistic body, as Bauman points out, is that as the enhancement of bodily sensations becomes the focus of life politics, as the ultimate purpose the consumer body tends to be a prolific source of perpetual anxiety.[103] Consequently, the hedonistic body is subjected to a perpetual process of body experimentation and alteration in order to maintain itself.[104] The body becomes the location of style, subjected to alternation, mutation, and enhancement, and has to be plastic and malleable enough to be moulded into any desired appearance.[105] Therefore, Lasch makes an important observation: the culture of mass consumption encourages narcissism, a new kind of self-consciousness or vanity through which people have learned to judge themselves not merely against others but through others' eyes.[106] As a result, the hedonistic and narcissistic body, which must be achieved, earned, or purchased,[107] becomes the foundation for an economy that results in the emergence of a neurotic body.

97. Wright, *Process*, 37.
98. Turner, "Western," 36.
99. Featherstone, "The Body in Consumer Culture," 21–22.
100. Not only in the form of drugs such as Viagra, but also mechanic forms such as Andro-Medical (www.maxhim.co.uk).
101. E.g., www.passion8.co.uk.
102. Taylor, "Fashion—Dress Up the Soul," 235.
103. Bauman, *Life*, 91.
104. For instance, well-being is defined by "fitness" (Bauman, *Life*, 93).
105. Lyon, *Postmodernity*, 81; Bauman, *Intimations of Postmodernism*, 194.
106. Lasch, *Narcissism*, 56–59, 84–86; Bauman, *Intimations*, 194.
107. James, *Selfish*, 156–65; James, *Affluenza*, 302–11.

The neurotic body is one that looks and criticizes incompleteness or defection and slowly turns its victims into the myth that modification is needed to be "good" (or "better"). The problem, however, is that although cosmetic surgery, obsessive dieting, and physical training are necessary to preserve the cultural standardized images,[108] the image projected by media creates an anxiety that potentially pressurizes the body into neurosis and disorder. This external pressure subsequently exacerbates low self-esteem and body dysmorphic disorder, which are closely linked with one's perceived appearance,[109] causing chronic social anxiety equally in men and women,[110] and even to the extreme of suicide.[111] For instance, one of the major concerns of the postmodern body is to lose weight and keep fit, in order to protect the body image.[112] For men, being muscular has become very significant to masculinity.[113] Although research shows that the relationship between masculinity and muscle is often beyond the actual limits of human physiology,[114] the male body that has muscle dissatisfaction also suffers from a low self-esteem.[115]

Consequently, it is noted that increasing numbers of people spend increasing amounts of time looking in the mirror on a quest for perfection

---

108. Bordo, *Unbearable*, 24–25.

109. Phillips, *The Broken Mirror*, 95–130.

110. American Psychiatric Association, *Diagnostic and Statistical Manual of Mental Disorders*, 429–84, 589; Bordo, *Unbearable*, 35: anorexia nervosa and bulimia in the female body.

111. Phillips and Menard, "Suicidality in Body Dysmorphic Disorder," 1280; Phillips, "Suicidality in Body Dysmorphic Disorder," 58–66.

112. Kashubeck-West, "Separating the Effects of Gender and Weight-loss Desire on Body Satisfaction and Disordered Eating Behavior." Website such as http://www.herbalvitality.info/ gives a broad perspective of what products consumers are searching for.

113. Pope, *The Adonis Complex*, 1–61; McCreary, "The Drive for Muscularity and Masculinity," 83–94; Mahalik, "Development of the Conformity to Masculine Norms Inventory," 3–25.

114. Pope, "Evolving Ideals of Male Body Image As Seen Through Action Toys," 65–72.

115. Olivardia, "Biceps and Body Image," 112–20. Even worse, not only does muscle dissatisfaction create personality disorder, it also exposes men to other disorders such as the "Adonis Complex," "Bigorexia," "Reverse Anorexia," etc., or urges them to find a solution in muscle-building supplements and anabolic steroids (Davis, "Personality Correlates of a Drive for Muscularity in Young Men," 349–59; Kimmel and Mahalik, "Body Image Concerns of Gay Men," 1185–90; Ridgeway and Tylka, "College Men's Perceptions of Ideal Body Composition and Shape," 209–20).

and willingly consume anti-ageing cosmetics and surgery.[116] This implies that not only does the image projected by possessions, physical attractiveness, clothes, and appearance replace personality, experience, and skills, but also that it serves as gauges of personal identity, health, and happiness.[117] Accordingly, the enhancement of the body to increase pleasure expresses the bi-polar manner of hedonism and the neurosis-therapeutic mentality of the consumer body-obsessed culture. Therefore, the neurotic body enslaves the body within a framework that is dictated by society's acceptance, which is a different "socially regulated" norm.[118]

The Body-Obsessed Culture and Consumer Clothing

In many ways, the self depends on the senses of the body and the bodies of others for information and communication.[119] In fact, the form and appearance of the body is the highest priority after the biological well-being of that individual. Particularly in communication, the body speaks about the person before the person speaks.[120] This explains why in most societies the appearance of a person's body, through clothes or bare skin, signifies his or her identity and relation to community. Therefore, nakedness and clothing are especially relevant to the body's appearance, if not the most decisive factor.

The expression of thoughts and ideas through dressing and clothing in modern fashion, said to have begun around the fourteenth century,[121] has been the most intimately and widely experienced area of socio-cultural life.[122] How we dress speaks of who we are, where we are going, and how we feel inside. It plays a part in the development of our ethics

---

116. Gabriel and Lang, *Unmanageable*, 95; Garner, "Survey."

117. Garner, "Survey"; Lasch, *Narcissism*, 92–93.

118. Bauman, *Life*, 100.

119. E.g., facial expression (Darwin, *The Expression of the Emotions in Man and Animals*, 32); Douglas, *Purity and Danger*, 22.

120. Identity in our culture often starts with appearance, or how we adorn ourselves (Taylor, "Fashion," 226). This chapter only takes into account a fraction of bodily communication, focusing on the contrasting images of nakedness and clothing with limited reference to the expression of self-identity through clothing as body-communication. Chapter 2 of this book will explore anthropological nakedness and clothing in greater detail.

121. Paulve and Boye, *In Fashion*, 1–25; Benedict, "Dress," 32.

122. Connor, *Postmodernist Culture*, 190.

and morality.[123] More importantly, it shapes what happens in our contemporary society in terms of identity, meaning, and shapes.[124] In other words, clothing is an unspoken language that can signify and define.[125] As a result, the communicative body is clothed with the linguistic codes of fashion—a competitive display between skin and clothes. The inner skin and the outer skin are both richly loaded with symbolic language. Although this phenomenon might be culturally varied, the parallel expression of skin and clothes displays the status and statement of the body identity, through which the self exhibits in a society.[126]

From the examination of the internal and external bodies it can be argued that in a body-obsessed culture the body is the centre of desires, pleasures, consumption, logo identity, enhancement, and modification. Since the hedonistic body carries such heavy sexual overtones, nakedness and clothing, which are most intimate to the body, are affected in significant ways.[127] In particular, fashion has increasingly facilitated the consumer self to express its hedonistic body. What underlies fashion speaks volumes about the self's obsession for its body. The body becomes conflated into the commodity values of clothing and nakedness and vice versa: the naked (or clothed) body must obtain commodity values for entertainment and hedonism that, on the one hand, are compatible with the dictation of the media culture while, on the other, feed the growth of a neurotic body so that the two contrasting notions perpetuate consumerism. In fact, for McDowell, the crucial body communication now is more concerned with money than with beauty.[128] Clothing has become the arena within which the wares of consumerism are most visibly expressed.[129] Fashion and advertizing become blurred.[130] The body (of different shapes,

---

123. Taylor, "Fashion," 225.

124. Ibid., 222–23.

125. Hall, "The Work of Representation," 37; Drane, *Celebrity Culture*, 54–55. Tattooing and body piercing are also included in adornment and fashion (Taylor, "Fashion," 223). Consumers use the effect of labels and logos for economic status (Barnard, *Fashion as Communication*, 110).

126. Beaudoin, *Virtual Faith*, 43; Leach, *Culture and Communication*, 55–56, 61. This is only one side of the coin since society also influences and shapes the way clothing communicates (Craik, *The Face of Fashion*, 225; Miles, *Consumerism*, 102).

127. Baudrillard, *Symbolic Exchange and Death*, 105.

128. McDowell, *The Designer Scam*, 57.

129. Miles, *Consumerism*, 90.

130. Grenz, *Postmodernism*, 37.

colors, appearances) is now adorned with different "glamorous" clothing with specific trends of thoughts and ideas, while shoppers are exploited because they are locked into the necessity of appearing with and revealing certain identities.[131] Consumers' shopping habits have been altered to believe that luxuries are in fact necessities.[132]

In such a consumer society where clothing is a "transitional object" that bridges the internal and the external worlds,[133] the relationship between self-image and clothing is essential. Moreover, as significant as clothing and fashion are to the body and the self, McDowell suggests that the scams of fashion have abused and misled people into believing that high fashion is a birthright, a proof of worth, an adjunct of character, even an indication of social desirability.[134] As Bordo points out, these identity crises, which give clothing and fashion the ability to provide self-gratification, stability and belonging in the modern consumer capitalism,[135] must be the manifestation of anxiety and fantasies.[136] Television programmes, such as *How to Look Good Naked*,[137] might appear to discourage anxiety and fear and encourage acceptance of the body but still they cannot escape the pressure and demand of a style-controlling and image-dominant culture.[138]

The implications of the phenomenon of consumer fashion are enormous. First, consumption of fashion and music is the leading activity of the post-war youth culture,[139] but along with this consumer fashion is the "freedom" to play with one's identity according to the whims of fashion and indoctrinations of popular culture.[140] Therefore, people are less used to making choices; rather, they become passive in decision making, expecting the popular culture to tell them what they need to do and choose

---

131. Langman, "Neon Cages," 66.
132. McDowell, *Designer*, 138; Miles, *Consumerism*, 97.
133. Gabriel and Lang, *Unmanageable*, 88–89.
134. McDowell, *Designer*, 225.
135. Miles, *Consumerism*, 104.
136. Bordo, *Unbearable*, 15.
137. Wan and Porter, "How to Look Good Naked?"; Wan, *How to Look Good Naked*.
138. Miller, "Therapy of Fashion," 269–70: dress therapy.
139. Furlong and Cartmel, *Young People and Social Change*, 60–61; Steward, "The Adolescent as Consumer," 203–26.
140. Kellner, "Popular," 174.

from the "ready-made" selves.[141] Secondly, while choice-making ability has been paralyzed, image dominance and the bipolar consumer body exploits the notion of a neurotic body to give birth to a false and myopic concept of atonement: shop to save. The point regarding atonement/salvation through the body cannot receive enough emphasis, especially within its connection with the bipolar hedonistic-neurotic body.

Summary and Conclusion

The body in a contemporary consumerist culture has shifted away from traditional values. The shift from spiritual and intellectual knowledge into experiential and experimental knowledge releases the postmodern body from being bounded into a medical-scientific one that is modifiable and malleable. Central to the body-obsessed culture is a bipolar-hedonistic-neurotic body, one that is subjected to bodily desires, pleasures, consumption, consumer identity, body enhancement, and modification.

In a body-obsessed culture, the body is idolized into a standardized measurement of acceptance and rejection. Therefore, the rejection of a person's body is immediately and automatically equated with the rejection of the whole *being*. Accordingly, when the concept of acceptance and rejection is interpreted as the focal balance of "salvation" or "atonement," a person's body becomes the starting point for the quest for atonement. Generally, atonement has been defined as having the propensity to become a problem from within, now it is also undermined by a problem from without. Subsequently, there is no longer a role model or absolute view of the body. Instead, the body is prey to consumer values: identity of the body becomes subjected to personal choice; the body itself becomes plastic, changeable, and modifiable, depending on the selection, a "pic-n-mix" of features appointed by the self. However, this self-designed body, as a result of self-made identity, becomes distorted and faces its own problematic symptoms: obsessive diet, obesity and eating disorders, body dysmorphia, plastic surgery, and a sexual body of excessiveness and abuse. The specific implication for nakedness and clothing in such a body-obsessed culture is that they must be compatible with a hedonistic-neurotic body. In this sense, nakedness and clothing exhibit a sense of

---

141. Smith, *Bauman*, 180. It is even said that there is no fashion; there is only fashions, no rule, only choices (Ewen and Ewen, *Channels of Desire*, 249–51; Turner, "Western," 33; Gabriel and Lang, *Unmanageable*, 96).

obsession for the body and carry many, if not all, of the problematic symptoms of the body.

As a result, atonement theories are facing an extremely self-focused culture where not only does the self identify itself with the body; it also identifies the body as the exhibition of atonement. The self mistakenly identifies approval of appearance as "atonement" and "salvation," and subsequently wishes to rightfully earn atonement. And since atonement is "earnable," a saviour is no longer needed and no one can claim someone else's atonement. Yet, a notion of atonement such as this is only a phantom. On the one hand, if atonement is "earnable" and everyone is a separate entity that is responsible for its own atonement, then the concept of sin is grossly distorted. The greatest sin is that which was committed against the self for failing to be a complete and autonomously self-saving entity. And atonement ultimately becomes dependent on self-forgiveness through the acquiring of the correct clothes or the development of the correct "look" or body. On the other, a self with this notion of salvation is caught up in a predicament: its atonement appears to be autonomous since it depends on self-forgiveness; yet at the same time, this self-earned atonement is determined as an achievement or a failure depending on others' judgement, a process which the self autonomously allows to take place.

Alan Mann rightly suggests that a "sinless" society is plagued by self-shame and "self-deficiency,"[142] and consequently longs for ontological coherence. Yet, this is only a superficial symptom. A closer inspection reveals a body-obsessed self in confusion between being autonomous and being dependent on others in its quest for another human ontology. Such a self is convinced that its commodified body can offer life-changing experiences through superficial changes and sustaining bodily experience, yet at the same time it is caught in the dilemma of a hedonist-*but*-aging body. However, sooner or later the body will fail to keep up with the self's expectation. Such a need for atonement appears to be identified with an innate crisis of the self, which is the self's failure at being in itself an autonomous and complete self, but needs and depends on the others for completeness. Gradually it becomes a norm that such a notion of atonement is almost impossible and always a struggle for the self. Yet, the self continues to focus its efforts on addressing its innate matter before the problem it has with the others. It identifies atonement with the act

---

142. Mann, *Atonement for a "Sinless" Society*, 5.

of *self-saving* the body rather than depending on other bodies and *being saved* by another body.

Such a body-obsessed culture offers a space within which a Christian atonement model may be constructed that recommends the *telos* of a resurrection body. In the *Christus nudus* model, true atonement comes from an exemplary cruciform body of Christ, a body that connects with body-renouncement, and not body-enhancement. Before addressing this matter, the next chapter will look particularly at the wider anthropological notion of nakedness and clothing with an intention to understand the wider relational context of the body.

2

Nakedness and Clothing in a Body-Obsessed Culture

EVER SINCE HUMAN BEINGS walked on planet Earth, food and clothes have been basic needs.[1] Admittedly, excepting the most extreme environments, humans can survive without clothes but never without food. Natural historians and anthropologists tend to explain the origin of clothes in terms of physical need and social-cultural development.[2] The concepts of nakedness, they explain, may have been developed within the growth and flowering of culture and society, manifesting through clothes and ornaments.[3] As cultures develop, wherever clothes are mentioned,

---

1. Anthropologists and historians usually refer to Charles Darwin (*The Descent of Man and Selection in Relation to Sex*) to explain humanity's existence and the biological needs for food and clothes. Humankind is one of many biological species (Hewes, "The History of Man's Culture," 137–38); Attenborough, *Life on Earth: A Natural History* by David Attenborough, DVD.

2. Attenborough, *Life*, 2:12:05–2:14:20: It is argued that about one million years ago, the *Homosapiens* (lit., "wise Man") in Europe faced colder weather and had to adopt a cave for protection and sewn clothes of animal skins; Hatt, *Clothes of the Ancient World*, 4.

3. Hatt, *Clothes*, 4–5: clothes were never used for practical purposes alone; in fact, modesty became an important reason for clothing after the rise of Christianity and Islam; Barney, *Clothes and the Man*, 25: clothing is not only used for medical protection, but also for adornment and modesty.

in sociology,[4] in psychology,[5] in philosophy and spirituality,[6] nakedness is also mentioned. Nakedness even becomes more colorful in the Arts,[7] anatomical science,[8] fashion, improvized traditions, and religions.[9] If clothing has an origin and a development then arguably the concepts of covering and uncovering the naked body must have originated and developed in parallel.

Clothing is perceived differently in each culture. To some cultures, clothing is as intimate as one's skin,[10] giving anthropological, social, and religious identity;[11] to others, it is only one of many ways to obtain a "good look." Consequently, nakedness and the body are also perceived differently, yet they mutually complement one another in the structure of most cultural norms and social propriety.

The intention of this chapter, therefore, is to answer two important questions: (1) What can we learn about the concepts of nakedness in

---

4. Brown, *Body*, 315–17, 437–38.

5. For an analysis of the psychological perception of the body and bodily nakedness (i.e., why does one feel naked and what to do with the body?) see Wright, *What is Man?*, 26–40. If a person is his/her body, then the outward look and the state of the clothed/unclothed body does affect one's self-identify and self-awareness (Glover, *Identity*, 85). The psychological perception of a person's naked body also has to do with the feeling of guilt and shame (Timpe, "Shame," 1074–75). Bodily perception, sexual anatomy, size of genitals, and sexual shame are all associated with nakedness (Hastings, *Treating Sexual Shame*, 91–94).

6. In the Bible, nakedness is interpreted as a spiritual state in 2 Cor 5:1, Rev 16:15 (Knutson, "Naked," 480) or the Greek philosophical and metaphorical concept of the naked soul *psuchè gumnè tou sòmatos* (Perniola, "Between Clothing and Nudity," 239).

7. Lewinski, *The Naked and the Nude*; Nochlin, *Bathers, Bodies, Beauty*, 13. For Chrétien, (*Hand to Hand*, 85), nudity is not only about a body without clothes, but also about the absence of clothes, the unclothed or denuded being of the body, and the act where the body exposes itself. Moreover, imagery and poetic nudity are also included art (Ostriker, *The Nakedness of the Fathers*).

8. Kuriyama, *The Expressiveness of the Body and the Divergence of Greek and Chinese Medicine*, 129–30; Smith, *The Victorian Nude*, 22; Schiebinger, "Skeletons in the Closet," 42–82.

9. Most clearly in Coakley, *Religion*, 100, 248–50; Cargal, "Nakedness," 994: In the Bible the term "nakedness" is understood in a wide range from complete nudity to inadequately clothed; Miles, *Carnal*, xii–xiv.

10. Clothes form the conscious and subconscious sense of self, an identity, and connect not only with memory, history, ritual, sexuality, and sensuality but also social and cultural relations (Dunseath, *A Second Skin*, vii–viii).

11. Perniola, "Between," 237.

relation to the origin of clothes? (2) How differently could nakedness be understood among cultures?

Concept of Nakedness and the Origin of Clothing

What do we think when we put on our clothes each morning? Has it to do with the color or the feel of the clothes? Is it about the people we meet and the places we attend? Possibly there are no overt reasons, and thus little if any reflection is given to why human beings wear clothes, or when they actually started wearing clothes. While it is suggested that the development of dress started about 5,000 years ago "in the ancient civilizations of Egypt and Mesopotamia,"[12] ultimately we cannot know for certain when human beings started wearing the *primary* form of clothing, although we can guess why human beings started wearing clothes.

Information collated from cultural and historical researches allow anthropologists and historians to propose a number of theories regarding the origin of clothes. The following theories, taken from Hiler's *From Nudity to Raiment*, are the most discussed.[13] Admittedly, no single theory will answer thoroughly the question of the origin of clothing by its own argument.[14] Moreover, there are always overlaps between the seven theories. However, through them, not only does a clearer explanation of why people wear clothes emerge, but also an understanding of how nakedness might have come to be understood. We turn, then, to Hiler's schema.

Chinese Mythology (Economic Theory)

The Economic Theory is based on the myths of ancient China and Greece. Chinese myths say that Pan-Kou or Hon-Tun created the world 129,600 years ago. Then, humankind appeared and while struggling to survive, discovered clothes.[15] Meanwhile, the early Greek commentators also held to the ancient theory that humans adopted clothes as a protection against the elements.[16] These myths suggest that humans, at an early

---

12. Horn and Gurel, *The Second Skin*, 17.

13. Hiler, *From Nudity to Raiment*, 1.

14. Since no one knows exactly why or when people began wearing clothes, each of these theories offers important answers but is unable to independently provide all answers (Hatt, *Clothes*, 4; Hiler, *Raiment*, 1).

15. Hiler, *Raiment*, 2.

16. Ibid., 2.

stage, learned to survive low temperatures by adopting and creating for themselves protective clothes of different materials from leaves to animal skins. The myths provide ideal support for an economic theory, which is based mainly on the *protective function* of clothes. In addition, Horn and Gurel claim that there is archaeological and pre-historical evidence from as early as 500,000 to 300,000 years ago that prove the adoption of animal fur for protection.[17] However, did humans start wearing clothes only because they needed protection from the cold weather? Some scholar believes so,[18] but there may have been many other easier ways to find warmth including caves and houses, fire or emigrating to warmer climates. Perhaps the "movable warmth" of clothing was considered a better option for convenience, but humans also needed protection from thorns, rocky and rough surfaces, insects, and heat. Moreover, it is with uncertainty that clothing appeared because of low temperatures alone, as protection might not have been an issue for those who lived in the areas with hotter climate.[19] That said, the protective function of clothes might not be the only reason humans adopted clothes.[20] They might have decorated themselves with different styles of adornment. Hoebel points out: "If he wears not so much as a G-string, he certainly sports a nose, ear, or lip plug, or bears his tattoos or scarifications, or paints his face, or curls his hair, or cuts it off, or blackens his teeth, or knocks them out, or perhaps merely files them to a point."[21] Consequently, since low temperatures are not the only explanation of Economic Theory, let alone being the only factor that generated a concept of nakedness, it is possible to find answers from the other theories.

Mosaic Theory (Shame Theory)

The second theory, based on shame, appears to have survived the passing of time and is widely accepted.[22] This theory emphasizes that there

---

17. Horn and Gurel, *Skin*, 11–12.
18. Knight Dunlap, in Benedict, "Dress," 31–32.
19. Ratzel, *The History of Mankind*, Vol. 1: 93; Goodson, *Therapy*, 156.
20. Horn and Gurel, *Skin*, 24.
21. Hoebel, *Anthropology: The Study of Man*, 326.
22. Hiler, *Raiment*, 4; Horn and Gurel, *Skin*, 19. Ellis (*Psychology of Sex*, Vol. 1, 58) argues that modesty is independent of clothing and may have been developed long before the discovery of either ornament or garments. Ellis, however, is inconsistent in his view (Hiler, *Raiment*, 4).

is an innate instinct of modesty or decency that leads humans to adopt a bodily covering.[23] Saint Augustine of Hippo attributes this theory of modesty and shame to the genital organs.[24] However, this theory also has its critics. First, it has been considered that the story of the Garden of Eden in Genesis 2–3 is a Jewish mythical explanation of the origin of clothing.[25] Secondly, since shame associated with nakedness does not exist in every culture, people think that shame and modesty are parts of *cultural* propriety, not human biological instincts,[26] and thus do not originate clothing.[27] Horn and Gurel point out:

> Most people in the world do use dress to conceal parts of the body but the parts it conceals vary from culture to culture. Modesty, or a sense of shame associated with an unconcealed body part, is not universal. What is covered or left uncovered varies among societies. Even within one particular culture, variations occur depending on age, sex, subcultural groupings, locations, and situational factors. And even if we accept the theory that feelings of natural shame are common, a number of illustrations can be cited to disprove the assumption that such shame is necessarily associated with a lack of clothes.[28]

One can argue that the sense of shame associated with clothes or bodily adornments, or the lack of them, exists in most cultures. But primitive tribes, whose members wear no clothes, prove that modesty in covering nakedness could be a learned rather than built-in ability from birth.[29] The concept of nakedness in this theory, therefore, faces the question of the origin of human morality and modesty, i.e., from where do human beings get the ability to examine what is or is not modest? Moreover, the unclear relation between bodily shame and the act of disobedience (eating from the tree of knowledge)[30] makes the story of the Garden of

---

23. Hiler, *Raiment*, 4.

24. Augustine, *City*, 14:17.

25. Wallace, *The Eden Narrative*, 145.

26. Hoebel, *Anthropology*, 252–53.

27. Welby, *"Naked and Unashamed": Nudism from Six Points of View*, 22–23; Westermarck, *The History of Human Marriage*, 208.

28. Horn and Gurel, *Skin*, 19.

29. Goodson, *Therapy*, 155; for an extensive collection of evidences see Ellis, *Psychology*, 8–35; Bloch, *Anthropological Studies on the Strange Sexual Practices of All Races and All Ages*, 140.

30. Most Biblical scholars suggest that Gen 3:7 involves disobedience and shame

Eden stand out as a *miraculous* and *one-off* event that happened only to Adam and Eve. So, it might be argued that only the first man and woman held this concept of nakedness. How their shame of nakedness was (or was not) passed on to the whole mankind is left unexplained.

Theory of Possession

Ratzel believes that clothing is connected with the idea of possession in marriage, arguing that "[a] man would force his woman to cover herself to diminish her sexual attraction to other men."[31] The woman, thus, clothes herself to indicate that she belongs to *a* husband. But this theory actually seems to associate much more with sexual attraction than possession and, therefore, creates two different views of nakedness. "Nakedness" means "sexually attractive" but also means "available-for-dating-purposes," while the covered body means "not sexually attractive" but also means "preoccupied."[32]

A different perspective derived from this theory might make more sense with the "property possession" aspect of the Economic Theory. Horn and Gurel explain that "the earliest garments may have developed from the need for protection from intense cold. The protection theory is still obviously important in explaining dress today. However, as soon as physical needs are provided for, any further creation or accumulation of items can serve only to gain greater prestige for the owner."[33] Here, the theory involves the function of clothes as exhibitions of property, rewards and approval.[34] Therefore, since clothing serves to show ownership or to gain prestige, nakedness can be associated with poverty. This provides a better explanation for materialism and the desire for more properties. However, this theory leaves out the shame of nakedness—an element that is shared by both the rich and the poor.

(Adar, *The Book of Genesis*, 22; Cargal, "Nakedness," 944; Morris, *The Genesis Record*, 115; Blocher, *In the Beginning*, 135–37). Nakedness becomes shameful and abnormal because of disobedience (Knutson, "Naked," 480).

31. Hiler, *Raiment*, 6.

32. Ibid., 6: a married woman covered herself "as a means of diminishing her sex attraction."

33. Horn and Gurel, *Skin*, 40.

34. Ibid., 28–30.

Theory of Sexual Attraction

According to Hiler, the Sexual Attraction Theory of Westermarck is the most reasonable theory, which is also "the least open to fatal objections."[35] The theory proposes that the origin of clothing springs from the need to enhance one's sexual beauty.[36] "[I]t seems to be beyond doubt that men and women began to ornament, mutilate, paint, and tattoo themselves chiefly in order to make themselves attractive to the opposite sex,—that they might court successfully, or be courted."[37]

Here, the thinking is contradictory to that of Ratzel, which holds that clothes are to conceal attraction,[38] not to be "a sexual lure."[39] Certainly, "[f]eathers and beads of different colours, flowers, rings, anklets, and bracelets are common embellishment"[40] that could prove the predilection for ornaments and the desire for decoration. However, in what ways do clothes enhance sexual attraction? Does "more clothes" mean "more attractive," "fewer clothes" mean "less attractive," and "more colorful clothes" mean "higher level of sexual excitement"? Or does the act of taking clothes off increase the sexual attraction? In this view, the undecorated naked body, where sex really happens, is deemed "boring" and clothes become fetishistic objects. Moreover, because of its focus on sexuality, there is a weakness to this theory. Horn and Gurel point out, "[i]t is very unlikely that primitive peoples, who had been naked, would realize that parts of the body would be more alluring if covered and would for that reason alone start to cover parts of the body."[41]

---

35. Hiler, *Raiment*, 8; for physical attractiveness sexual attractiveness and sexual arousal see Dion, "Physical Attractiveness, Sex Roles and Heterosexual Attraction," 12–13; Tesser and Reardon, "Perceptual and Cognitive Mechanisms in Human Sexual Attraction," 124; Bloch, *Anthropological*, 142.

36. For psychological perspectives of attractiveness see Jones, *Physical Attractiveness and the Theory of Sexual Selection*, 19: Jones applies Darwin's theory of sexual selection to argues for the outward cues associated with mate-values (ibid., 24) in the psychological analysis of sexual selection and physical attractiveness (ibid., 42); Smith and Sparks, *The Naked Child: Growing Up Without Shame*, 91–92.

37. Westermarck, *Marriage*, 172. For Ellis, in some cultures clothes serve the purpose of drawing attention to the sexual organs (Ellis, *Psychology*, 60).

38. Hiler, *Raiment*, 6.

39. Horn and Gurel, *Skin*, 22.

40. Westermarck, *Marriage*, 165.

41. Horn and Gurel, *Skin*, 24.

Nakedness and Clothing in a Body-Obsessed Culture 41

In other words, even if it were true that clothes serve the purpose of enhancing sexual attraction, to say that such an association *initiates* clothing is to omit other aspects such as protection, modesty, adornment and decoration, to show skills, and to highlight identity.[42]

Totemistic Theory

This theory proposes that clothes were originated by spiritual beliefs or religions of some sort. Clothes are worn because people hold certain beliefs that have to do with ornaments or garments. Hiler says: "Totemism and Trophyism both have the elements of ornamentations and clothing. One might have to do with the origin of religious garments, the other might have to do with the caste in its relation to clothing."[43]

What are the beliefs that actually originate the idea of clothes? People might cover themselves because of the significance of sexual organs,[44] or because of fear of spiritual attack, or to avoid irreverence toward the gods or spirits; such beliefs may possibly create a concept of nakedness where to be naked means to feel shame, fear and vulnerability while being clothed suggests holiness, protection and reverence.[45]

However, clothing and religions have a much more complicated association than what at first appears. While wearing clothes is an expression of some people's beliefs, stripping off is an expression of the beliefs of others.[46] Later we shall look at some aged religions,[47] which express renunciation through the unadorned body.[48]

Therefore, religious nakedness, as described in the Totemistic Theory, could either be discouraged due to a fear, not of harsh weather, but of spiritual forces. Or, in contrast, it could be encouraged for its spiritualized expression of renunciation.[49] However, it is unlikely that humans

---

42. Ibid., 28–30.

43. Hiler, *Raiment*, 9.

44. Welby, *View*, 22–23.

45. Hiler, *Raiment*, 8–9; Horn and Gurel, *Skin*, 30.

46. Fox (Script writer) and Schiber (Executive Producer), *Shocking Asia*, DVD, chapter 7:43:30.

47. Jain Cultural Reseach Society, *Jainism, the Oldest Living Religion*.

48. The concept of *prosadhopavàsa* prohibits bodily adornment with garlands, perfumes or ornaments (Sinha, *The Philosophy of Jainism*, 109; Jain Darshan Vidya Varidhi Divakar, *The Nudity of Jain Saints*, 4–5).

49. Physical austerity is common [Mehta, "Jaina Yoga," 21; Kulkarni, *Sudies in Jain*

need protection from spiritual forces more or before they need protection from the harsh weather. Both religious concepts of putting on and stripping off must have been improvized from the most essential forms of protection: physical and economic.

Theory of Amulets

According to this theory, clothes were worn as "life giving substances" in the form of magical properties.[50] And since humankind were not formerly used to clothes, ornaments associated with charms are the very first forms of adornment. This theory overlaps with the previous Totemistic Theory in that it originates from the practices of spiritual and religious beliefs. Yet, it is also distinctive in that it highlights how people carry on wearing clothes, which are the "further improvisation"[51] of ornaments, without the attachment of beliefs. However, if that is true, wearing clothes is only a habit, yet it is uncertain how such a habit, which is rooted in fear of evil forces,[52] triggers shame. This theory is incomplete.

Aesthetic Theory

This theory holds that aesthetics is an instinct: as animals show their preference for colors, human beings also have a preference for beauty.[53] There is an overlap with the Theory of Sexual Attraction mentioned above. The Darwinian notion of mate selection appears to fit quite well: the purpose of being beautiful is to choose a better life partner.[54] However, the difference found in the Aesthetic Theory is its concern solely with beauty in general without the sexual connotations. In other words, human beings can be creative merely for the sake of beauty and pleasing appearance alone. Interestingly, this theory does not have space for the cultural shame of nakedness. If this theory were correct, nakedness and

---

Literature, 519; Divakar, *Saints*, 4–5].

50. Hiller, *Raiment*, 9.

51. Ibid., 9.

52. Benedict, "Dress," 31.

53. Ibid., 10–11; Hall, *From Hoopskirts to Nudity*, 134–35, 143: Aesthetic desire results in the wearing of clothes to express personality, taste, mental attitudes, character, and individuality.

54. Hiler, *Raiment*, 2; Jones, *Attractiveness*, 11: attractive women are more likely to get married; Benedict, "Dress," 30; Darwin, *Descent*, 253–65; Ridley, *The Red Queen*, 129–30, 263–65.

undressing would only imply an abruption of beauty enhancement rather than an abruption of cultural norms, unless that culture deliberately chooses its concept of aestheticism to be social propriety.

Summary

The two latter theories are quite short compared to the former ones, partly because they overlap the previous theories,[55] but overall, these seven theories provide a relevant background to put the atonement model *Christus nudus* to the test.

Bar the Modesty Theory, the use of clothing has acquired a great many evolutionary values. In these theories, environments are important factors that make human beings adopt and improvize ornaments and materials for better living conditions. This suggests that no common original concept of nakedness can be assumed; rather, various concepts of nakedness appear to have gradually developed, possibly after the discovery of clothing. Hence, according to this process, the concept of nakedness is better perceived as a product of the human psyche seeking to satisfy some anthropocentric needs, be they physical protection, sexual attraction, social acceptance, or social status.

These theories of the origin of clothing raise questions regarding the origin and the nature of our cultural concepts of nakedness and the development of clothing in relation to modesty and social propriety. In the following section we will explore how these concepts of nakedness are expressed in human cultures.

Cultural Concepts of Nakedness

What is nakedness? Is it defined by the absence of what we habitually wear or is it a product of cognitive reasoning and habitual thinking? Or both? Even if Perniola is correct in his assertion that human beings are distinct from animals because of clothes,[56] it is possible that some people cannot understand the word *nakedness*. That is to say, we may know for certain that the word has a specific meaning in a specific context, depending on who is looking and who is naked.[57] Satlow's approach to the notion

---

55. For a more extensive discussion see Johnson et al., *Fashion Foundations*, part 1; Steele, "Clothing."

56. Perniola, "Between," 237.

57. Bastian, "The Naked and the Nude," 35.

of nakedness possesses a careful consideration of possible contexts and cultures. "Nakedness is not merely being without clothing (although it can be); it can also carry sociocultural and theological meaning. Again, *who* is naked and in what context he or she is naked convey different meanings: Is he or she naked in a locker room, at a strip-show, or at an academic conference? Nakedness can also convey ritual meaning. In the same manner that societies make assumptions that allow clothing to transmit meaning, so too do they make assumptions about nakedness."[58]

Scholars have rightly understood that nudity, social propriety, and modesty are "produced and reproduced in historically specific contexts."[59] While it may be obvious to those who use the word "naked," to understand that it means "to uncover," for those who have never been covered, nakedness may not even be a concept that exists in their understanding. Ableman explains: "Now true nakedness is rare. By true nakedness is meant, in this context, the nakedness of people whose body surface is both unadorned (with clothing or ornamentation) and unmodified (by tattooing, painting or scarification). But for the present, 'nakedness' can be taken as meaning unconcealed. Thus a naked tribe is one in which, although ornaments or even clothing may be worn, no systematic attempt is made to hide the body or its functions."[60] Therefore, to understand the function of clothes in a culture is to understand its view of nakedness. In this chapter we will examine how differently the concept of nakedness can be understood in a number of cultures and worldviews.

In many modern and civilized societies, such as twenty-first-century Britain and America, nudity has been adopted as entertainment in many forms,[61] although this adoption has been found in some ancient cultures.[62] Yet in these societies nudity does not carry neutral connotations

---

58. Satlow, "Jewish Constructions of Nakedness in Late Antiquity," 431.

59. Masquelier, "An Introduction," 2–3.

60. Ableman, *Anatomy of Nakedness*, 9.

61. The amount of nudity in adult entertainment more than doubled between 1997 and 2002 both in the number of scenes and duration (Broadcasting Standards Commission and Independent Television Commission, *Briefing Update*, 2–7); Reyes and Matussière, *Female Nudes*, 116–18: nude photography and artistic expression of sexuality; Bernard, *Total Exposure*, x–xiv: nudity, romance, sex and fascination that feed the curiosity about celebrity bodies.

62. The idea of art and the beauty of the body have been modified and re-modified in the Greek culture of the Eastern Empire, in the second century, and again in the Christian Empire (Goldhill, "Viewing and the Viewer: Empire and the Culture of Spectacle," 42–45).

and people often complain about nudity on television and in films.[63] Media products are censored to restrict unsuitable viewers, with warnings of nudity, sex, bad language, and violence. It is often emphasized that there is *always* a social and intellectual way to consider the artistic and aesthetic beauty of the body,[64] but, of course, in reality that pure artistic view is not the only view existing in society. There is always a lurking erotic gaze that has to do with sexual lust and fornication.[65] As a result, moral debates and movements become heated.[66] Nudism, for instance, is a clear example.

Nudist View of Nakedness

Modern nudism, Welby claims, may well have originated in Germany.[67] In 1903 Richard Ungewitter advocated a hygienic and moralistic practice of nudity called nudism, to which some people named a "rebellion against Victorian clothing,"[68] a "cult of frankness,"[69] or even an example of "pseudo-salvation."[70] What is nudism? Welby answers this question by focusing on what is *not* nudism. He states that, "[n]udism is not an excuse for sexual orgies or licensed promiscuity. It is not a channel for exhibitionism or pruriency. Nor are all Nudists vegetarian fanatics and believers in Nature-cures."[71] Nudists who practice nudism believe that it is not a sexual phenomenon and enjoy recreation without clothes.[72]

In *Love's Clarity: A Fruit of Experience, Insight, and Action*, Zimmermann writes about the nudist view of shameless nakedness: "Whoever walks in such a garment of light, conscious and wholly unembarrassed, is, as if by a spell, more protected from sexual desire than is the finishing-school girl with her thousand secrets, or the monk behind thick walls, or

---

63. Whitehouse, *Cleaning-Up TV*, 23.

64. Goldhill, "Viewing," 70.

65. For Greek erotica and early Christianity see Gaca, *The Making of Fornication*.

66. Smith, *Victorian*, 217–20; Nelson, *Nudity and Sexual Activity in the Media*, 6–8: the harm caused to children and society by nudity and sexual actvities in the media.

67. Welby, *The Naked Truth about Nudism*, 26; Ross, *Naked Germany: Health, Race and the Nation*.

68. Goodson, *Therapy*, 179.

69. Kidner, *Genesis*, 69.

70. Blocher, *Beginning*, 175.

71. Welby, *Truth*, 23–24.

72. Hartman and Fithian, "Nudism."

the pious sister in her massive white blinkers."[73] By stating this, Zimmermann implies that nudists are not only shameless about their nakedness but are also unperturbed by the nudity of others, because the nudity of others is not associated with sexual shame, sexual arousal, sexual connotation, or voyeurism of any sort. Even so, many people are not convinced and are still suspicious enough to relate nudists to some second century fanatic religious groups who adopted nudity.[74] Wilkinson argues that the two types of nudism: deed (exposing bodily) and word (euphemistically) "often have a common motivation, exhibitionism and a desire to shock."[75] In other words, for Wilkinson, nudism is a form of "libertarian propaganda and shocking for shocking's sake,"[76] that overcomes the feeling of shame primarily attached to a *civilized* person. But such a statement neglects the practical contribution of nudism to human health. Welby claims that nudism is based on sane and healthy principles with logic and commonsense,[77] and with a strong medical argument: the skin needs air like lungs, and sunlight to produce vitamin D.[78]

However, does nudism have a future merely because of the medical contribution it makes? This remains a debatable issue even today. Probably both sides of the controversy have gone too far into two opposite extremes. Nudist activists would agree with Zimmermann, who condemns voyeurism for being small-minded and hypocritical, arguing that nudity should not be naturally covered with shame unless there are lustful desires and pride. Zimmermann makes an interesting point by comparing human genitals to flowers—the sexual organs of plants;[79] but his explanation of shame being a result of lustful fantasies, low self-esteem, and enviousness[80] neglects the reality and the historical formation of social propriety. On the contrary, moralists fear that the doctrinaire teaching of nudism affects the moral conduct of the members of the society similarly to what happened in the Hellenistic Age.[81] Again, such thinking will only color nudity with a sexual connotation, and consequently, relegate

73. Zimmermann quoted by Szeemann, "Here I Am Human Here I Am Free," 3.
74. Welby, *Truth*, 25–26.
75. Wilkinson, *Classical Attitudes to Modern Issues*, 81–82.
76. Wilkinson, *Attitudes*, 108.
77. Welby, *Truth*, 26.
78. Ibid., 42–44.
79. Zimmermann, "Free," 3–4.
80. Ibid., 3–4.
81. Wilkinson, *Attitudes*, 96.

the topic to other unhealthy taboos. Having briefly looked at the nudist view of nakedness, we understand that nudity could be accepted and celebrated in daily social life.[82] There is a similar acceptance for nudity but at a different level. We now turn to the religious perspective, which respected and celebrated nakedness as a virtue.

Religious Nakedness as a Virtue

As previously mentioned, the renunciation connotation of nakedness may be found in both ancient and more contemporary religions. This religious virtue is found in Hinduism, Jainism, Buddhism, among the ancient Arabs religions and Greek saints, and even in the Hebrew Bible (1 Sam 19:24 and Isa 20:2).[83]

In Jainism, nakedness is a symbol for the "highest pitch of Renunciation and Divinity of man."[84] Although not every kind of nudity would be seen as a virtue,[85] Divakar argues that this view of nakedness should be respected and its practice allowed because it has a spiritual significance and has been respected for thousands of years.[86] Digamber (also called Digambar or Digambara) Jain Saints are naked saints who follow twenty-eight root duties,[87] including the twelve vows (*Vratas*) within the process of six stages of development (*Sarva-virati-gnasthàna*).[88] The chief goal of these rites, rituals and vows is to liberate the *Atma* (soul) from the body and make it free,[89] because the mundane body, including its sexual passions, is seen as a source of contamination, and therefore, it should be left unadorned, undecorated and unattractive.[90]

---

82. For a substantial development of German nudism, see Ross, *Germany*, 2005.

83. Divakar, *Saints*, 5–13; Ramaswamy, *Walking Naked*, 74, 81, 167, 170–75.

84. Divakar, *Saints*, 2; for a wider concept of renunciation see Laidlaw, *Riches and Renunciation*, 216–29.

85. Fohr, "Restriction and Protection—Female Jain Renouncers," 169–70: It is true that nudity is necessary for those who want to reach the state of *moksa*, but a male *muni* can be completely naked whereas a nun *àryikà* cannot because clothing is necessary for her morality. When a nun renounces her clothing she encounters great difficulties because of the traditional Indian culture and the moral restriction *maryàdà*.

86. Divakar, *Saints*, 16–17.

87. Prasadji, *A Comparative Study of Jainism and Buddhism*, 276–80.

88. Gandhi, *Religion and Philosophy of the Jainas*, 186, 222.

89. Kasliwal, "Concept of Soul in Jaina Philosophy and Its Scientific Interpretation," 4–5.

90. Gandhi, *Religion*, 129, 204–5, 220.

Buddhism, on the one hand, is said to have adopted the duty of *achelaka* of Jainism,[91] and on the other, exerted vital influences on Jainism.[92] Yet both Jainism and Buddhism are said to have emerged from the same Bràhmanical asceticism, or it could be considered that little distinction is made between them and Hinduism.[93] The virtues of abstention and self-discipline of these two religions effectively explain why nakedness could be seen differently.

Greek Beauty of Nakedness

Along with the religious practice of nakedness, the ancient Greeks also found nudity significant in terms of beauty and philosophy.[94] In contrast to the Jewish view, they thought that "the human body was the highest form of beauty, and although they draped themselves artistically in vestments of exquisite texture and coloring, they did not forget the body beneath."[95] It is not that the Greeks were barbarians. In fact, their developments in intellectual thinking, art, law, and science contributed immensely to our world today. That is to say, there are both appropriate and inappropriate forms of nakedness in their culture. For instance, it was considered unseemly to walk about naked in public, and yet nakedness manifested through their sculpture and games was deemed pure and beautiful.[96] "[T]hese highly-cultured people encouraged their girls and boys, young men and young women to practise games and exercises together in a state of nudity—partly to ensure freedom of movement unencumbered with irksome garments; partly, we may assume, that the sight of the beautiful physique of some would impel the admiration and emulation of others less well favoured."[97]

---

91. Prasadji, *Comparative*, 280; Bhagchandra, "Contribution of Jainism to the Development of Buddhism," 162.

92. Verma and Bakshi, *Hinduism, Buddhism and Jainism in Ancient India*, 192; Uno, "Some Relationships between Buddhism and Jainism," 46.

93. Dwivedi, *Essentials of Hinduism, Jainism & Buddhism*, 2–4, 76; Prasadji, *Comparative*, 304.

94. Stewart, *Art, Desire, and the Body in Ancient Greek*, 3; Marinatos, *The Goddess and the Warrior*, 1–31.

95. Welby, *View*, 23–25; Stewart, *Art*, 34; Goodson, *Therapy*, 158–61.

96. Welby, *View*, 23–25; Stewart, *Art*, 24.

97. Welby, *View*, 23–25; Goodson, *Therapy*, 160.

Perniola suggests: "Here, the ideal human figure was presented as essential nude. In their celebration of nudity, the Greeks distinguished themselves from all other peoples. For them, nudity was not a matter of shame, ridicule, or dishonor. Rather, nudity assumed a paradigmatic significance that involved clarity of vision (an aspect of Greek religious experience) with an athletic perspective (aristocratic in origin) that viewed victory as its glorious celebration as an end to be most energetically pursued."[98] This, then, explains why nakedness was imported into Greek art, and not into Sumerian, Assyrian, Babylonian, or Egyptian art.[99] And yet, if the body was such a glorious form of beauty why did the Greeks wear clothes? Clothes were seen only as ornaments to exalt beauty and richness, not to cover indecency. "Even when civilisation reached a state of luxury and grandeur, however, the sight of the naked body was by no means regarded as something indecent."[100]

Was nakedness always seen to be perfectly good in Greek culture? Not always. Alternative views about the body, such as degradation and shame,[101] might appear contradictory to the common view of nakedness. "This idea of degradation occurs also in Homer. Odysseus threatens to teach Thersites his place by stripping from him the garments that cover his 'shame' (*aidos*); and the body of Hector that Achilles drags behind his chariot round the walls of Troy is naked. Of course, the nakedness of captives might be simply the result of despoliation; but the idea that nakedness could be cause for mockery persists, being attributed, for instance, to barbarians by Plato."[102]

Moreover, Platonic thinking taught that the body was the tomb of the soul.[103] Nakedness, then, became a philosophical aspect of the relationship between the soul, the mind and the body. Indeed, the metaphor "naked truth" is derived from "a conflation of the concept of truth as visual precision and the idea that eternal forms are the ultimate objects of intellectual vision."[104] Perniola continues: "From this foundation, the

98. Perniola, "Between," 238.
99. Wilkinson, *Attitudes*, 82–83.
100. Welby, *View*, 23.
101. Aune, *Revelation 6–16*, 898.
102. Wilkinson, *Attitudes*, 83.
103. Reale, *A History of Ancient Philosophy*, 157; Lane, *The Lion Concise Book of Christian Thought*, 12.
104. Both Greeks and Indians agree that nudity is a state of purity and honesty (Goodson, *Therapy*, 162).

entire process of knowledge becomes an unveiling of the object, a laying it entirely bare and an illumination of all its parts. The body itself then came to be considered an obstacle, a tomb of the soul. Only when the soul is naked—*psuchè gumnè tou sòmatos,* the soul stripped of the body (*Cratylus* 403b)—does it acquire complete freedom."[105]

Later, the Gnostic hope in nakedness concerned deliverance from the earthly *soma,* and hope for a heavenly garment.[106] This is possibly derived from the previous Platonic view that deems the body as a tomb and a "prison-house" from where the soul of the dead appears naked before the judge.[107] Here, human beings seek to escape bodily life with all of its misleading bodily senses because only after death has the soul the freedom of a disembodied state.[108] Therefore, this teaching makes the Greek view of nakedness quite confusing for, on one hand, the body possesses a beauty that is worth celebrating; on the other, the soul is encouraged to be delivered from that same body because it is a "prison-house" of misleading senses.

Nevertheless, on the whole, nakedness was common in Greek culture and considered to be something of special significance,[109] not only in social life but also in ritual and religious practices.

The Orientals and Nakedness

Comparing the Greek view of nakedness with that of the Orientals, Welby says: "One was concerned almost entirely with form, as in the case of the Greeks, and the other with richness of embellishment, favoured by the Orientals. . . . The Orientals, perhaps, scorned the nude form as being insignificant; as being unable to give pleasure to the eye without rich and colourful trappings. In their case, to a great extent, clothes made the man."[110]

Rightly so, a traditional Vietnamese proverb says: "Silk makes beauty, manure makes rice."[111] It is clear that clothes were important to

---

105. Perniola, "Between," 239.
106. Bultmann, *Corinthians,* 137.
107. Bultmann, *Corinthians,* 136; Glasson, "Corinthians," 146–47.
108. Glasson, "Corinthians," 146–47.
109. Wilkinson, *Attitudes,* 83.
110. Welby, *View,* 23.
111. My translation of "*Người đẹp vì lụa, lúa tốt vì phân*"; cp. "Silk makes a pretty man, measure makes rice crops more fertile" in Vo, *Vietnamese Proverbs, Folk Poems*

the ancient Orientals, but does this imply that they viewed nakedness as indecent? Not necessarily! For instance, nudity in public bathhouses was considered natural in Japanese daily socialisation,[112] so much so that people did not appear to adopt the modern Western concept of nakedness.[113] Alternatively in some Asian cultures, a woman was not allowed to show her fingertips; a Chinese woman was not permitted to show her feet;[114] upper class Chinese women were not to appear unclothed even in the presence of her doctor,[115] and the Han Chinese women would force her three-year-old daughter to bind her feet and keep them painfully small in order to be considered marriageable.[116]

Besides, Oriental minds tended to eradicate intangible conflicts in order to live in peace and harmony with the self. Confucianism, for example, stressed the importance of ethical shame over conventional shame, even to the extreme of minimizing the significance of conventional shame.[117] Therefore, shame and nudity may well have been overlooked by the mind that was so strongly orientated to community, traditions, respect, discipline, and obedience. Garrett asserts that this mentality was manifested very clearly in the clothing tradition.

> Throughout most of China's long history there has been a common style of dress within each social stratum of the Han people, unlike other countries where traditional dress often varied greatly from region to region. The reasons for this uniformity stem from the approach to life evolved by the Chinese. To the Han Chinese man, his place within the clan, the extended family descending from one male ancestor, was and remains of vital importance. He was keenly aware of his responsibilities, not only to future generations and the importance of producing male heirs to continue the linage, but also of his great obligation to those who went before, his ancestors. Filial piety and success in terms of bringing wealth and honour to the clan were his duty. In doing this he was required to act in a way worthy of his ancestor. His clothes, especially, were a "uniform," donned to show

---

and Folk Songs, 90.

112. Goodson, Therapy, 165.

113. Kawano, "Japanese Bodies and Western Ways of Seeing in the Late Nineteenth Century," 151–53.

114. Westermarck, Marriage, 206–8.

115. Goodson, Therapy, 165.

116. Garrett, Chinese Clothing, 91–92.

117. Norden, "The Virtue of Righteousness in Mencius," 168–70.

his place in the hierarchy. Everyone—man and woman—had a designated place in society, in part due to a complex system of dress regulations which was imposed, in one form or another, over the centuries.[118]

Nudity, then, was not only considered less significant than clothing and tradition, but was almost ignored in the light of how one should live with the self. This is in clear contradiction with the West, where such views of nakedness, either exalting nudity or neglecting its blatant existence, are foreign and difficult to grasp, due to the fact that the Western view of nakedness has formed and developed differently from that of Asian and Oriental cultures.

The Development of the Notion of Nakedness in the Christian West

Onians argues that the basis of modern European thought is Greek philosophy and science.[119] On one hand, it is argued that the human body in Greek culture comes to dominate the Western representational tradition[120] with all its notions of art and erotica.[121] On the other, the Western view of nakedness is rooted in the Jewish Bible and further modified throughout the history of Christianity. The Torah, especially Genesis 2–3 and Exodus 20:26,[122] has introduced a robust Jewish view of nakedness that influenced the Christian view in a very distinctive way. Miles points out that "the story of Adam and Eve provided the Christian West with a palimpsest on which attitudes toward bodies, sexuality, and women were inscribed."[123] Wilson adds that: "The Eden myths run deep in our culture, telling us that sin is about sex is about nakedness is about shame. Conversely, innocence is also about nakedness, is about childlikeness, is about sexlessness."[124]

Indeed, within the context of Christian mission, argues Masquelier, nakedness implies "darkness, disorder, and pollution" of the body which

---

118. Garrett, *Chinese*, xiii.
119. Onians, *The Origins of European Thought*, 1.
120. Stewart, *Art*, 3.
121. Ibid., 24, 34, 156.
122. Exod 20:26.
123. Miles, *Carnal*, 85.
124. Wilson, "Nakedness," 43.

is corruptible by nature. As a result, the visible erotic qualities, weakness and ugliness of the body, are demonstrable of the failure of humankind before the dark power of sin and the Devil.[125] And yet, in secular Western views of nakedness, there is also an element of beauty, where nakedness appears in figurative arts as eroticism and exhibitionism.[126] Therefore, there is a bipolar perception of nakedness that is a consequence of many influences, especially from the Jewish and Greco-Roman cultures.

Jewish Abhorrence of Nakedness

While the Greeks perceived nudity as somewhat significant and positive, their Near Eastern counterparts, including the Hebrews, found nudity degrading and profane.[127] Epstein points out that the attitude of the ancient Jew to bodily nakedness is reflected in the early chapters of Genesis.[128] Yet the early chapters of Genesis include two notions of nakedness: one is without shame before the fall (2:25), the other demonstrates shame after the fall (3.7). If nakedness is seen as degrading and shameful throughout the Bible,[129] then, in what way should we interpret nakedness in Genesis 2:25? Unfortunately, the rabbis of late antiquity (70 C.E.–500 C.E.) did not address the exegetical, cultural, and theological questions regarding the meaning of "nakedness" in Genesis 2:25.[130] Whether or not this ambiguity has something to do with the Jewish *imagination* of Adam's extraordinary physical qualities before the fall,[131] nakedness is negatively viewed in the Jewish mentality.

It has been held that Jewish nakedness is concerned with religious holiness, superiority, gender, and personal modesty,[132] depending on the tradition in which it is rooted, rabbinic or non-rabbinic. Both male and female nakedness are never perceived as good, not even neutral, but

---

125. Masquelier, "Introduction," 2.
126. Perniola, "Between," 237.
127. Ibid., 237; nakedness is generally seen as bad (Satlow, "Constructions," 430).
128. Epstein, *Sex Laws and Customs in Judaism*, 25.
129. Ibid., 26.
130. Satlow, "Constructions," 430.
131. Physical qualities like lofty stature, radiant skin, etc., see Moore, *Judaism*, Vol. 1, 479.
132. Satlow, "Constructions," 431–32.

loathsome. In Epstein's words, it would be superficial to say that this revulsion was synonymous with sexual modesty.[133]

Male nakedness is the exposure of the penis.[134] It is said, "the word shame (*aschemosune*) is a euphemism for the genitals in Jewish contexts."[135] The prohibition in Exodus 20:26 is usually interpreted with the implication that exposure of the penis is a great offense to God. There are alternative interpretations for this prohibition. Perniola thinks that the prohibition seeks to emphasize the importance of the priestly robe, which reflects Yahweh's glory (*chabod*).[136] Fretheim suggests that the prohibition establishes Israel as distinctive from idolatrous neighbors.[137] That said, neither interpretation provides good enough evidence to claim that God abhors nakedness.

Nevertheless, in Jewish culture bodily exposure is abhorrent and profane; and there were restrictions that clearly approve this view. Jewish males would urinate with their backs to the Temple. They did not recite God's word, read the Torah or do anything holy in the presence of nakedness, not even greet one another with "shalom" in the bathhouse.[138] In other words, nakedness is barred from holy spaces.[139] The ultimate aim is to avoid the offense against the *sancta* where God is present.

Outside the context of sancta, nakedness in normal social life is unremarkable, although it is still neither a "proper" behavior nor advisable. In practice, male nakedness has much to do with power and social hierarchy: superiors should not appear naked to inferiors. Naked people are, therefore, looked upon with disgust, but there was no further comment on how nakedness should be displayed. A man can bathe with anyone but his father, brother-in-law, his master or teacher, because respect and fear might decrease if the nakedness of a superior is revealed.[140]

Besides, the Jewish view of nakedness has a strong sexual connotation. Exercising holiness can also mean one should not have sex naked,[141]

---

133. Epstein, *Customs*, 26.
134. Satlow, "Constructions," 431.
135. Witherington III, *Revelation*, 210.
136. Perniola, "Between," 237–38.
137. Fretheim, *Interpretation Exodus*, 243.
138. Satlow, "Constructions," 432–33.
139. Epstein, *Customs*, 27–28.
140. Ibid., 33; Satlow, "Constructions," 437–40.
141. Satlow, *Tasting the Dish: Rabbinic Rhetoric of Sexuality*, 308.

not have sex in the day,[142] and not gaze upon a naked body. "The rabbis connect the word 'holiness' itself to male modesty. According to an oft-cited tradition, Rabbi Judah the Patriarch is called 'our holy rabbi' (שודקה וניבר) because he never looked at his own penis (*b. Sabb.* 118b)."[143]

Yet modesty is also a virtue that is associated with chastity.[144] There is a strong sexual connotation in the concept of gazing upon the naked body. If a woman bathes with men (equal to letting them gaze upon her nakedness), she is to be divorced by her husband since no Jewish woman should appear naked to the gaze of a man.[145] This has great implications for the concept of female nakedness.

Female nakedness is not seen as an offense against God or his holiness. It does not relate to social hierarchy, but is conceived mainly with regard to female modesty and propriety in subjection to men.[146] On that account, female nakedness has much to do with a woman's marital status, her reputation and head covering.[147] "The rabbis view female nakedness, unlike male nakedness, predominantly as a marker of moral character; it rarely has significance vis-à-vis the sacred. Respectable Jewish women should not go out in public naked; and conversely, if a naked woman is seen in public, she must not be a respectable Jewish woman. 'In public,' of course means in front of men."[148]

To some rabbinic traditions female nakedness is seen as sexual temptation.[149] "The primary rabbinic understanding of female nakedness is that it arouses sexual passion in men. The rabbis frequently exhort (rather than prohibit outright with a legal ruling) men not to look at women in any state of dress or undress for fear that they will be led

142. Satlow, "Constructions," 434–35.

143. Ibid., 433.

144. Moore, *Judaism*, Vol. 2, 272; Epstein, *Customs*, 29; Job 24:15 and Prov 7:9.

145. Epstein, *Customs*, 30–31; Satlow, "Constructions," 442.

146. Satlow, "Constructions," 440.

147. Epstein, *Customs*, 32; Satlow, "Constructions," 442. However, this view of nakedness has now clearly changed, for a general response from Jewish feminist perspective (Marx, "Gender in Israeli Liberal Liturgy," 207: gender unequality; Lerner, "Pacing Change," 181–82; Brettschneider, "Jewish Feminism, Sexuality, and a Sexual Justice Agenda," 243, 249: liberation of sexuality; Litman, "If the Shoe Doesn't Fit, Examine the Soul," 250–51, 257: gender and sexuality; for a diversity of voices see Schreiber, *Hide and Seek*, 150–95).

148. Satlow, "Constructions," 444.

149. Ibid., 442; Satlow, *Tasting*, 155; *Talmud*, "Derek 'Erez Rabbah," 536, 540. Avoiding such temptation is a virtue ("Kallah," 407–8).

into sexual misconduct."[150] Within Jewish culture, then, the image of female nakedness contains so strong a sexual connotation that there are so many extreme restrictions. For example, men should not look at women,[151] especially those wearing colorful clothes or when they do laundry. Men should not look at women's heels for it is equal to looking at their vaginas:[152] looking at a woman's vagina being a euphemism for intercourse with her. While hard to believe, born-blind children are even said to have looked at their mothers' vaginas.[153]

Jewish views of nakedness in late antiquity reflect very clearly both theocentrism and androcentrism: nakedness is seen as bad, profane, and sexual. It is important, therefore, to note that this is also the view that affected the attitude of the early Christian church towards nakedness. However, Jewish attitudes toward nakedness were not the only influence. In fact, the Roman Empire was the political setting within which the church expanded. And therefore, it was inevitable for Greco-Roman views to influence the formation of subsequent Christian views of nakedness.

Greco-Roman Society and Nakedness

While the Roman Empire adopted certain elements of the Greek attitude toward nakedness,[154] it also modified its concept of nakedness, as Aune points out: "The Romans, in contrast, tended to disapprove of Greek forms of public nudity (Cicero *Tusc. Disp.* 4.70). In comparing Greek and Roman statuary, Pliny observes that Greek statues of prominent males are characteristically nude, while Roman statues are clothed (*Hist. nat.* 34.18)."[155]

---

150. Satlow, "Constructions," 440–41.

151. *Talmud*, "Kallah," 403.

152. "Heel" refers to the female genitalia (Satlow, *Tasting*, 308). For a discussion on Jeremiah 13 see Eslinger, "The Infinite in a Finite Organical Perception (Isaiah vi 1–5)," 152.

153. Satlow, *Tasting*, 306; Satlow, "Constructions," 441. However, according to the *Talmud*, it is the parents' fault, not the child's. Deformity of children such as being lame, blind, dumb or deaf are caused by, correspondingly, looking at the heel, looking at genitals, kissing genitals, and talking while having sex (*Talmud*, "Kallah," 403–4).

154. Young Roman youths stripped off at the baths and during exercises (Balsdon, *Romans and Aliens*, 33).

155. Aune, *Revelation 6–16*, 898.

Besides, while the Romans had a probable alternative preference for revealing nakedness, they retained the Greek public bath.[156] As a result, the Romans did not actually impose a completely different view of nakedness; rather, they formed a mixed view of nakedness. How did this mixed view work? The Greek appreciation for beauty appears to be limited only to public baths.[157] An element of sexual shame still exists but this did not stop people from being naked.[158] On the contrary, being naked without shame was a way of exhibiting social superiority.[159] Wilson explains that, "to the Graeco-Roman mind, nakedness was an indication of nobility and intellectual superiority. Nakedness also indicated spiritual refinement. It was a *theological* statement. . . . Social status was the issue. A Roman woman expressed wealth, social ease and spiritual maturity as she stripped to her jewellery before society. That she could do so without shame, without signs of sexual exhibitionism on her part, was a measure of her birth."[160]

Accordingly, in such a social setting, the feeling of sexual shame did exist. Rather, the significant social status that public nakedness brought about was irresistible. Therefore, in Roman culture bodily shame does not always damage one's status; on the contrary, it could be a means to a convenient life.

Early Christianity and Nakedness

Under the influence of the Greco-Roman culture, the concept of nakedness in early Christianity went through a significant period of development. Platonism was influential in Athens and Corinth and was even studied with great thoroughness by Philo at Alexandria,[161] a Hellenized Jew who sought to combine Judaism and Greek philosophy.[162] As we have seen above, Judaism and Greek philosophy had contrasting views of nakedness and the body: Judaism teaches that the body is created by God,

---

156. Welby, *View*, 23–25. The Roman Bathhouse in Bath, United Kingdom, is an obvious example of this.
157. Wilkinson, *Attitudes*, 101.
158. Wilson, "Nakedness," 44.
159. Brown, *Body*, 315.
160. Wilson, "Nakedness," 44.
161. Glasson, "Corinthians," 146.
162. Hillar, "Philo of Alexandria (c.20 BCE–40 CE)."

whereas Platonism views the body as a tomb and a "prison-house."[163] Philo asserted that the body was evil by nature and a "dwelling place of endless calamities," which plots against the soul.[164] Philo also interpreted the Old Testament from a Greek perspective to emphasize his point. "The High Priest shall not enter the Holy of Holies in his robe, but laying aside the garment of opinions and impressions of the soul, and leaving it behind for those that love outward things and value semblance, shall enter naked with no colored borders or sound of bells . . . "[165]

Although the early Christian church was heir to both Greek and Near Eastern concepts,[166] nakedness was still a controversial issue: for some, social nakedness was unproblematic, while for others, it was unacceptable.[167] To the Christian saints, nudity was interpreted along the line of original sin: a "reminder" of the loss of innocence,[168] a consequent "state of deceit and concealment," a mark of the loss of a "privileged condition," and Eve's subjection to Adam.[169] In addition, early Christians destroyed representations of nude deities of the ancient world,[170] because they saw nakedness as a demonic power.[171] Besides, the prevalent social practice of nude bathing was condemned by some Christian writers and church fathers,[172] and was even forbidden by the emperors[173] on the grounds that it encouraged adultery,[174] or on the basis of extreme attitudes toward sex (such as, the idea that having sex is to "thwart the purpose of God").[175] Therefore, it is no surprise that Christian naturists of the time were referred to as "Gnostic heretics."[176]

163. Glasson, "Corinthians," 146–47.
164. Ibid., 147.
165. Philo of Alexandria, *Legum allegoria* 2:56, 259; Perniola, "Between," 239.
166. Brock, "The Robe of Glory: A Biblical Image in the Syriac Tradition," 247.
167. Wilson, "Nakedness," 45.
168. Walters, *The Nude Male*, 66.
169. Miles, *Carnal*, 93–96. The nude female body is seen as wicked and decadent, and a failure to protect not only female sexuality but also male sexuality (Polinska, "Dangerous bodies: women's nakedness and theology," 49–51).
170. Wilkinson, *Attitudes*, 99.
171. Walters, *Male*, 82.
172. Epstein, *Customs*, 29.
173. Wilkinson, *Attitudes*, 100.
174. Wilson, "Nakedness," 44.
175. Ibid., 45.
176. Goodson, *Therapy*, 171. Later attitudes toward nakedness reflected

However, in contrast, baptismal nakedness was a "cherished symbol."[177] For example, the association between the "naked Christ"[178] and the "naked new converts" was expressed not only in nude baptism,[179] but also in a motto for the Christian lifestyle of that time. Jerome's famous adage *"nudus nudum Jesum sequi"* or *"nudus sequi nudum Christum"* (naked to follow a naked Christ),[180] signified "innocence and purity" or the "willing self-deprivation"[181] for the prudish horror of Christ's death.[182] This interpretation is similar to that of Saint Bernard of Clairvaux and Saint Francis.[183] Living out the human essence in nakedness before the fellows, to the delight of God, is to confess the brokenness of the body and witness to God's "salvific participation."[184] Indeed, nudity went beyond the limit of baptism and formed a metaphor for a lifestyle of renunciation. Nakedness meant freedom—"To see is not to lust, not is to be seen either to lust, to invite lust or to be threatened."[185]

Renaissance and After

According to Gorham and Leal, Medieval moral theology distinguished four symbolic meanings: *nuditas naturalis* (natural state), *nuditas temporalis* (poverty), *nuditas virtualis* (innocent), *and nuditas criminalis* (lust).[186] On the one hand, nudity was common in the public baths of

---

Greco-Roman society, such as the medieval Adamite sects, the Brothers and Sisters of the Free Spirit (Perniola, "Between," 239), Carpocrations, Adamianis, Encratites and Marcosians (Goodson, *Therapy*, 170; Gorham and Leal, "Naturism," 13), all of whom held different combinations of beliefs, philosophies, and practices of nakedness.

177. Wilson, "Nakedness," 45.

178. Walters, *Male*, 82–83. Part two of this book will explore more fully the notion of the Naked Christ (Melito of Sardis, *Homily on the Passion* 16:96–97, 179). Arguably, the risen Christ was also naked (John 20:6) (Knights, "Nudity, Clothing, and the Kingdom of God," 178).

179. Miles, *Carnal*, chapter 1.

180. Ibid., 63.

181. Walters, *Male*, 82–83.

182. Ibid., 66, 82; Hengel, *Crucifixion*, 21.

183. Gorham and Leal, "Naturism," 13; Miles, *Carnal*, xii; Walters, *Male*, 74–75; Constable, "Nudus Nudum Christum Sequi and Parallel Formulas in the Twelfth Century," 84n.8.

184. Wilson, "Nakedness," 49.

185. Ibid., 48.

186. Gorham and Leal, "Naturism," 13; Bottomley, *Attitudes to the Body in Western*

medieval and renaissance societies.[187] Female nudity, from the fourteenth to mid seventeenth centuries, was also prevalent.[188] Aristocrats were allowed to bathe naked in the late thirteenth century under Edward IV.[189] On the other hand, nudity was condemned.[190]

Clearly the tension between shameless nakedness and shameful nakedness remains. The same tension is found in today's "innocent" nude art,[191] and the ethics of pornographic materials.[192] More recently, the social movement of nudism, as we have discussed above, is also one of the significant issues of modern social politics and ethics. In modern Christianity, the growing phenomenon of Christian nudism,[193] leaves a rather tentative conclusion. It is concluded by Gorham and Leal that there is no essential conflict between Christianity and naturism,[194] but putting this into practice requires a sensible consideration of the modern culture heritage, wherein the nakedness of the secularized body has always been viewed as mundane.[195]

Summary and Some Conclusions

Throughout this chapter, the undressed body has been the subject of our cultural exploration of nakedness and clothing. We have visited some

---

Christendom, 180.

187. Wright, *Clean and Decent: The Fascinating History of the Bathroom and Water Closet*, 23.

188. Gorham and Leal, "Naturism," 14: building upon Ribeiro, *Dress and Morality*, 52, 175n.26.

189. Fisher, *The Complete Poetry of Geoffrey Chaucer*, 364: line 422.

190. For example, in the seventeenth century, Jacques Boileau said: "God hates nakedness, because he is purity itself; the Devil loves it, because he is impure: God hates nakedness, because it is a sign of our defeat and overthrow; and the Devil loves it, because it is a mark of his Trumph . . ." (quoted in Ableman, *Anatomy*, 36); Cooke, *A Just and Seasonable Reprehension of Naked Breasts and Shoulders*, 49–50.

191. Lewinski, *Naked*; Nochlin, *Bathers*, 13; Chrétien, *Hand*, 85.

192. Gorham and Leal, "Naturism," 14; Thielicke, *Theological Ethics I: Foundations*, 552.

193. Boyd, "Christian Naturism"; Natura Fellowship, "Naturist Christians."

194. Gorham and Leal, "Naturism," 24.

195. This section is notably brief due to lack of space and, therefore, does not cover, for example, Victorian nudity (Smith, *Victorian*) or attitudes and changes caused by political, economical, and religious factors. However, there is an apparent tension between attitudes toward the naked body and clothing that this section deems necessary to take into account.

major social and anthropological settings with drastically different views on nakedness and clothing. The influence of the two contrasting views (Jewish and Greco-Roman) and the long dominance of Christianity have left the notion of the naked body in a state of tension: on the one hand, it is seen as sexual and a taboo; on the other, artistic, narcissistic, and hedonistic.

Regarding theories concerning the origin of clothing, the economic theory appears to fit better with the cultural shifts that produce a postmodern consumer body-obsessed culture, as mentioned in chapter 1. With the emergence of a modern productivist society, especially the secularization of the body and its clinical disposition, nakedness carries not only economic and ethical values but is also commodified in a materialistic, hedonistic, and speedily globalizing consumer body-obsessed culture. Consequently, modesty and the ethical values of clothing become subjected to change and become prey to the perceptions of postmodern relativism.

The cultural understanding of nakedness and clothing, in this chapter, establishes sufficient anthropological ground for an investigation into the biblical imageries of nakedness and clothing. Subsequently, an understanding of aspects of linguistic and theological imageries is needed, especially in a body-obsessed culture, where the theological meaning of a naked Christ has been reduced to a hollow product of entertainment and artistic expression.

3

Nakedness and Clothing in Metaphorical Language

THIS CHAPTER WILL EXPLORE the activities of the emotional and imaginative forms of symbolism,[1] as well as observe evidence offered by metaphor-theories for a consistent model, where nakedness and clothing can operate as *emotive* metaphors.[2] It is hoped this will show how the "mark of genius"[3] is articulated,[4] not only through the particular use of

1. Langer's *presentational* (*Philosophy in a New Key*, 141); Foss' sensationalism and rationalism (*Symbol and Metaphor in Human Experience*, 47–69); Dillistone, *Christianity and Symbolism*, 26; Cox, "Psychology and Symbolism," 56–59; Verspoor, "What are the Characteristics of Emotional Metaphors?" 5.

2. There is insufficient space to present fully the discussion of linguistic science and the poetic analysis of literary texts; however, it is important to be aware of some important works in this field. Croft and Cruse, *Cognitive Linguistics*, chapters 3, 8; Stockwell, *Cognitive Poetics: An Introduction*, 105–20; Evans and Green, *Cognitive Linguistics: An Introduction*, part II: chapters 5–13; Evans, *A Glossary of Cognitive Linguistics*; Geeraerts and Cuyckens, *The Oxford Handbook of Cognitive Linguistics*; Rohrer, "Embodiment and Experientialism," 25–47.

3. "To have command of metaphor is the mark of genius." (Aristotle, *Poetics*, 1459a, in Barnes, *The Complete Works of Aristotle*, Vol. 2, 2334–35).

4. For an analysis that is necessary to cover the academic requirements and resonates with recent scholarship, see extensive surveys on metaphorical language and symbolism in Dillistone (*Christianity*, 1955); Verspoor, "Emotional"; Need, *Human Language and Knowledge in the Light of Chalcedon*, part II; and Stordalen, *Echoes of Eden*, 48–78. See also biblical metaphors analysis in Walker, "Grounding Biblical Metaphor in Reality," 214; Perdue, *Wisdom in Revolt*, chapters 1–3: 22–72; Macky, *The Centrality of Metaphors to Biblical Thought*, 8–25; Korpel, *A Rift in the Clouds: Ugaritic and Hebrew Description of the Divine*, chapters 1–2: 1–87; Stienstra, *YHWH is the Husband of His People: Analysis of a Biblical Metaphor with special reference to Translation*,

bodily metaphors of nakedness and clothing but in the wider context of the language of shame and sin.

In the previous two chapters we have examined a body-obsessed culture wherein the body and its appearance holds an important communicative power that influences society's activities, thinking patterns, and even social dilemmas. Such a reality is foundational for an anthropological understanding of nakedness and clothing. In this chapter we will examine the cognitive aspect of nakedness and clothing with specific reference to metaphorical language and symbolism. This seeks to understand the coherence between psychology and language in the employment of metaphors such as nakedness and clothing. This chapter will seek to explore: (1) the relationship between cognition and symbolism, (2) the heuristic experience of nakedness and clothing that affects cognition, and (3) the natural legitimacy of metaphors of nakedness and clothing.

Cognition, Symbolic Language, and Metaphorical Language

It is important to note that while metaphorical language is only a small part in linguistic epistemology, it is one of the dominant foundations for cognitive theories because thought itself is fundamentally metaphorical.[5] From a utilitarian perspective, the human need to communicate has turned words into effective communicative tools through a process of observing similarities and connections.[6] Every new experience or new idea evokes some metaphorical expression or the borrowing of at least some other facts or experiences that are already familiar.[7] This phenomenon happens automatically and unconsciously.[8] For Lakoff and Johnson, this ability is also known as *cross-domain mappings*,[9] which is the ability to form more complex conceptual structures based on pre-conceptual

---

chapters 1–2, 4–6.

5. Built upon Lakoff and Johnson, (*Metaphors We Live By*). Cf. Evans, "Cognitive Linguistics," 7; Evans, et al., "The Cognitive Linguistics Enterprise: An Overview," 16.

6. Dillistone, *Christianity*, 137–38; Stancliffe, "Symbolism and Preaching," 100.

7. Langer, *Key*, 141; Langer, *Feeling and Form*, 35–36, 189, 238–39; Stancliffe, "Preaching," 99; Lakoff and Johnson, *Live*, 29.

8. Lakoff and Johnson, *Live*, 55; Lakoff, "A Figure of Thought," 215–25. It is even proposed that metaphor is stored in memory (Carroll, *Psychology of Language*, 47–48, 197–99, 354–56).

9. Evans, et al., "Enterprise," 16; Rull, "The Emotional Control Metaphors," 180; Lakoff and Turner, *More Than Cool Reason*, 38–39, 131–35.

or embodied experiences. This phenomenon of recognising and relating to similarities is specifically distinctive in humans.[10] However, there are divisions and sub-divisions in that ability which the philosophy of language defines as sign, symbol, analogy, allegory, simile, metonymy, or other figures of speech.[11] This phenomenon is also subjected to a division of intellectual and emotional sides (for example, signs are logical whereas symbols are sensory),[12] or to a division of its changeability (for example, surviving the coming and going of trends and fashions, or being controlled by poetic mastery).[13]

Origin of Metaphor

Richards suggests that humans cannot convey three sentences of ordinary fluid discourse without using metaphors.[14] The discovery of the phenomenon of metaphor is not new,[15] but the question of its origin can appear unimportant compared to the question of how it operates. The heuristic approach of metaphor argues that symbols and metaphors come to exist through experiences.[16] For Coleridge, the dichotomy of the body and mind implies that the body can prompt thoughts or can be the instrument of the mind; therefore, touch and feelings lay at the root of the senses and the growth of the mind—the cradle of metaphors.[17] Lakoff and Johnson assert and also affirm to have discovered that the only similarities relevant to metaphors are *experiential*, not *objective*.[18]

---

10. Dillistone, *Christianity*, 13, 23–24; Langer, *Key*, 29.

11. For a variety of this linguistic phenomenon, see Need, *Chalcedon*, part II and Stordalen, *Echoes*, 48–78; Black, *Models and Metaphors*, 27–28, 35, 237; Way, *Knowledge Representation and Metaphor*, 22–23, 122–49; Evans, et al., "Cognitive." 17.

12. Roberts, *Critique of Poetry* (in Dillistone, *Christianity*, 20–21).

13. Lewis, *The Poetic Image* (in Dillistone, *Christianity*, 22).

14. Richards, *The Philosophy of Rhetoric*, 92.

15. The first occurrence of the word "metaphor" is in Isocrates, *Evagoras* (Stanford, *Greek Metaphor*, 3).

16. Most clearly in the works of Johnson and Coleridge following Kant (Miall, "The Body in Literature: Mark Johnson, Metaphor, and Feeling," 191–210; Johnson, *The Body in the Mind*, 34).

17. Coleridge, II.897, II.2495 (in Miall, "Johnson," 15); Coleridge, *Collected Letters of Samuel Taylor Coleridge*, 897; Coleridge, *The Notebooks of Samuel Taylor Coleridge*, I.1575, II.2495.

18. An experientialist perspective (Lakoff and Johnson, *Live*, 235; Lakoff, *Women, Fire, and Dangerous Things*, 446–53: conventional metaphors are derived from

It should be stressed further that metaphors are not only dependent on but also create "experiential similarities."[19] These experiential similarities can be perceptual and sensory imageries that are based on the correlation between sense data and the non-linguistic world.[20] The body, therefore, becomes an important ground for bodily experience and metaphorical expressions.[21] Recent feminist philosophers[22] also hold that the incorporating of the body into discourse is both essential and urgent. Surely, cognitive linguistics benefits from the findings of cognitive neuroscience on image schemas, to argue for the existence of conceptual metaphors and cross-domain mappings.[23] Therefore, the generation of images in the mind integrating the bodily experiences into words happens intrinsically when there is a need of interpreting new experiences. When we say something is *just* a metaphor, the statement suggests that metaphors are somehow less accurate and less truthful than literal description,[24] but in fact metaphors are the most appropriate means of expressing truth.[25] McFague presses the point that we think metaphorically.[26] Therefore, a metaphor only comes to be used if it has some cognitive value that could be commonly experienced and expressed.[27]

---

experience, rather than objective characteristics of the concepts involved). Also see Rohrer, "Embodiment," 12.

19. Indurkhya, *Metaphor and Cognition*, 79.

20. Brown in Paivio and Begg, *Psychology of Language*, 263–87; Verspoor, "Emotional," 16.

21. Goschler, "Embodiment and Body Metaphors," 36; Goschler examines the various aspects of body metaphors in different contexts. More significant is the *linguistic action*, which uses body parts as the source domain (Pauwels and Simon-Vandenbergen, "Body Parts in Linguistic Action: Underlying Schemata and Value Judgements," 36–40).

22. Jaggard and Bordo, *Gender, Body, Knowledge*.

23. Rohrer, "Embodiment," 3; Miall, "Johnson," 1–2.

24. Boersma, *Violence*, 104.

25. Ibid., 105; Gunton, *The Actuality of the Atonement*, 37–38; Wright, *The New Testament and the People of God*, 63.

26. McFague, *Metaphorical Theology*, 16, 35; Brümmer, *The Model of Love*, 8; Need, *Chalcedon*, 7, 87. Following McFague (*Metaphorical*, 42), Boersma (*Violence*, 105) goes so far as to claim all human language is metaphorical.

27. Aquinas in Need, *Chalcedon*, 77–78. Cultural values are crucial for the existence of metaphors (Lakoff and Johnson, *Live*, 22–23); MacCormac, *A Cognitive Theory of Metaphor*, 181–206.

Defining Metaphor

A metaphor is best defined in its original Greek form, meaning "carry across."[28] However, that sense of carrying across needs clarification. Aristotle puts it: "Metaphor is the application of an alien name by transference."[29] This transference has to maintain a tension, so-called "is and is not."[30] "There must always be some element of unlikeness, even incongruity, in the employment of a word or a group of words in a metaphorical way. This does not mean that no elements of likeness remain; if such were the case the metaphor would lose its power. It does mean that when a metaphor is first presented, we recognize at once that language is being employed in an unusual way."[31]

Alternatively, McFague contends that a metaphor is seeing one thing as something else, or imagining "this" in terms of "that" because of the inability to describe exactly what "this" is.[32] Macky insists that metaphors are not words but rather speech acts, wherein words are employed in metaphorical ways.[33] That said, most people would agree that the heart of metaphor is speaking about one thing in terms of another.[34] Dillistone, however, classifies metaphors more specifically as another type of symbol where there exists a sense of "distance" and "togetherness," "contrast" and "similarity," "tension," and "communion."[35] While some argue that no generally acceptable definition of this phenomenon is given,[36] most biblical scholars tend to accept some variant of the interactionist view proposed by Richards and Black.[37]

---

28. Need, *Chalcedon*, 89; Boersma, *Violence*, 100.

29. Aristotle (*Poetics*, 1457b, 7–8); Walker, "Grounding," 214.

30. McFague, *Metaphorical*, 13; McFague, *Models of God*, 33; Brümmer, *Model*, 8; Need, *Chalcedon*, 8.

31. Dillistone, *Christianity*, 160.

32. McFague, *Metaphorical*, 15; McFague, *Models*, 33.

33. Macky, *Centrality*, 8–25; Kittay and Lehrer, "Semantic Fields and the Structure of Metaphor," 31–63.

34. Need, *Chalcedon*, 7, 90; McCloskey, "Metaphor," 215; Lakoff and Johnson, *Live*, 112.

35. Dillistone, *Christianity*, 34–35; Boersma, *Violence*, 101.

36. Stordalen, *Echoes*, 51–52; Noppen, et al., *Metaphor: A Bibliography of Post-1970 Publications*; Noppen and Hols, *Metaphor II: A Classified Bibliography of Publications 1985 to 1990*.

37. Stordalen, *Echoes*, 52; Black, *Models*, 22–47, built upon Richards, *Rhetoric*, 89–112; Doyle, "Howling Like Dogs—Metaphorical Language In Psalm LIX," 70;

One way of defining metaphor is to show how it works. According to Richards[38] and Black,[39] metaphor consists of two parts: tenor and vehicle. Richards distinguishes "tenor" as the literal aspect of metaphor, and "vehicle" as offering the figurative sense. These two parts (tenor and vehicle) are "target" and "source" in Lakoff and Johnson's definition.[40] "Target" is the unfamiliar or abstract aspect, whereas "source" is more often familiar and concrete.[41] When metaphor occurs, we have the application of one system of meaning (the one that is familiar and concrete) applied to another (the one that is still abstract); that is to produce new meanings or clarify the abstract concept.[42]

Another way to define metaphor is to distinguish its characteristics. A figure of speech is a device that manifests itself in many forms that overlap metaphor in their characteristics, such as metonymy, synecdoche,[43] simile,[44] allegory, and parable.[45] For example, a *simile* is a comparison: A is *like* B. A *metaphor* is an act of putting an object into a different framework or giving it a different framework it did not have before: A (taken out of its framework) *is* B (A at B's framework). An *allegory* is a picture with symbolic meaning; a *parable* is story-like; *emblem* functions like an image or sign; an *analogy* creates similarities, resemblance, or parallel,[46]

Grohmann, "Ambivalent Images of Birth in Psalm VII 15," 445.

38. Richards, *Rhetoric*, 93, 97: vehicle is the image, and tenor is the underlying idea.

39. Black, "Metaphor," 24–27; Black, "More About Metaphor," 19–43.

40. Lakoff and Johnson, *Live*, 147–84; Lakoff, *Women*, 276–78; 386–88; Lakoff and Turner, *Reason*, 63, 162–65, 196–203; End and Danks, *Comprehension of Metaphors: Priming the Ground*, 11–13.

41. Rull, "Control," 180; Stordalen, *Echoes*, 52 (built upon Lakoff and Turner, *Reason*, 20); Richards, *Rhetoric*, 93; Macky, *Centrality*, 47, 49–50.

42. Need, *Chalcedon*, 103 (built upon Black, *Models*, 38); Soskice, *Metaphor and Religious Language*, 46.

43. For example, "the ham sandwich" (Evans et al., "Cognitive," 17).

44. Black (*Models*, 25–47) argues that metaphor has the formation A is B, whereas in a simile, A is *like* B; similes as a specific type of metaphor is a view from Aristotle (Diebler, "A Philosophical Semantic Intentionality Theory of Metaphor," in Verspoor, "Emotional," 8).

45. Unlike metaphors, allegory has been explained as a structural principle in literature, a rhetorical strategy and a process of signification (Frye, *Anatomy of Criticism: Four Essays*, 89–91; Rosenberg, *King and Kin: Political Allegory in the Hebrew Bible*, 12). Allegory normally has the form of a story (Stordalen, *Echoes*, 56).

46. For the distinction between negative and positive analogy see Stebbing, *A Modern Introduction to Logic*, 250; McIntyre, "Analogy," 17.

while *imagery* is a figure of speech of metonymy, a substitution for a thing that is meant. Indeed, as Need points out, the family features of these figures of speech makes a close definition of metaphor especially difficult.[47]

Function, Recognition, and Meaning of Metaphor

Dillistone suggests that the basic function of a metaphor is to provide transference from the expected to the unexpected, from the usual to the surprising.[48] In this way, metaphor provides a similarity between things that might not be previously noticed, and characterizes the abstract in terms of the concrete.[49] In other words, metaphor not only changes the perspective of the reader or listener,[50] but can also function as a means to understand the domain of one experience in terms of the conceptual structure of another.[51] A certain view might consider metaphorical language an abuse of language,[52] but Boersma concretely establishes that metaphor actually has four functions:[53] a quick description, an "extra" that enriches creativity,[54] a means of shaping and transforming one's environment, a divine means to avoid idolatrous claims to knowledge.[55]

Recognition of metaphors, Verspoor suggests, happens when there is a violation of the interpretative norm.[56] However, recognizing metaphor depends heavily on the interpretation of meanings or the comprehensibility of a sentence. Therefore, the most important aspect of metaphor is its meaning. Some propose that the key to understanding metaphor is to recognize the common features between the topic and the vehicle (the

---

47. Need, *Chalcedon*, 90.
48. Dillistone, *Christianity*, 160.
49. Lakoff and Johnson, *Live*, 112; Rohrer, "Embodiment," 12–13.
50. Verspoor, "Emotional," 5 (built on Kittay's "perspectival theory"); Indurkhya, *Metaphor*, 246–52.
51. Lakoff, "The Metaphorical Logic of Rape," 73–79.
52. E.g., Hobbes (in Gunton, *Actuality*, 29).
53. Boersma, *Violence*, 102–4.
54. Franklin, "Art, Imagination, and Theology," 5. Sole focus on this function can result in a tendency to see metaphor as decorative (Need, *Chalcedon*, 90) or a happy trick of words (Richards, *Rhetoric*, 90).
55. Theorists argue that metaphors also perform cognitive functions (Black, *Models*, 30–34; Soskice, *Religious*, chapters 6–8; Stordalen, *Echoes*, 52; Needs, *Chalcedon*, 98).
56. Verspoor, "Emotional," 6; MacCormac, *Cognitive*, 3–4.

metaphor and that which it stands for).⁵⁷ This is done by mapping aspects of both domains, at the same time,⁵⁸ or imposing one domain on the other.⁵⁹ The way this imposition takes place depends on the cultural experience.⁶⁰ The question of whether metaphor has a meaning, or how to understand that meaning is no longer a recent debate.⁶¹ Kittay proposes that a metaphorical transference of meaning is not a simple displacement of an atomistic meaning but a move from one system to another; metaphorical meaning is a second-order meaning.⁶² However, as Black argues, metaphors need not permanently change their meanings; in fact, there is a fluid concept of words and meanings,⁶³ which constitute their "tantalizingly elusive" nature.⁶⁴ Interpretation of metaphors, therefore, depends on a set of conventional beliefs,⁶⁵ while a negotiation between the domains takes place.⁶⁶

Metaphors, in turn, can be classified into types. *Dead metaphors* are those that take on a former metaphorical sense as part of a regular lexical sense, or have turned into idioms or a cliché.⁶⁷ *Retired metaphor* tends to be regarded as a word, not a statement or to be confused with conventional metaphor, which contains the conventional *metaphorical* sense.⁶⁸ Brettler suggests that *retired metaphor* does not produce affiliated metaphors like those that are more traditional.⁶⁹

57. End and Danks, *Comprehension*, 11–13.
58. Gibbs, "Comprehending Figurative Referential Descriptions," 56–66.
59. Katz, "On Choosing the Vehicles of Metaphors," 486–99.
60. Sapir, "The Anatomy of Metaphor," chapters 1–2: 3–66; Holland and Quinn, *Cultural Models in Language and Thought*; cf. Lakoff and Johnson, *Live*, 22.
61. Lycan, "An Irenic Idea about Metaphor."
62. Kittay, *Metaphor*, 138, 141.
63. Black, "How Metaphors Work: A Reply to Donald Davidson," 188.
64. Ibid., 192.
65. Built on Black's "interaction theory" (Indurkhya, *Metaphor*, 286–301).
66. Miall, *Metaphor: Problems and Perspective*, 17–18, 29–33, 107–13.
67. Starting with Lakoff and Johnson (1980), in Rohrer, "Embodiment," 12; Macky, *Centrality*, 135–55; Stordalen, *Echoes*, 53; Verspoor, "Emotional," 5–6; Lycan, "Irenic."
68. Stordalen, *Echoes*, 53. Stordalen does not give any example here, but one can think of examples from the English language such as: a computer mouse, kidney beans, head teacher, forerunner, to lose face, to lend a hand or to catch someone's name.
69. Brettler, *God is King: Understanding an Israelite Metaphor*, 21; Soskice, *Religious*, 73; Kurz's three types of metaphors (1) novel-creative, (2) traditional, and (3) lexicalized or "retired" (Kurz, *Metapher, Allegorie, Symbol*, 19).

Nakedness and Clothing as Heuristic Metaphors of Shame and Modesty

Heuristic experience and cultural phenomenon can be a resource for metaphorical language.[70] This is especially significant to cultures where nakedness and clothing are associated with shame and modesty.[71] This entails a twofold process: (1) the heuristic experience of physical vulnerability relates itself to the emotive vulnerability of shame, thanks to the "spatial" dimension of metaphors;[72] and (2) theories on shame suggest that what is deep-rooted and underlies the feeling of shame is the notion of "concealing" and "revealing,"[73] which is foundational to the physical perception of nakedness and clothing. Such correlation is possible because metaphorical language provides a means for dialogue and interaction between conscious and unconscious sectors of the psyche.[74] It is equally possible to borrow sensory data to express thoughts, as it is to express feelings.[75]

It follows that if nakedness is associated with shame, then shame can be referred to in the symbol of nakedness. Consequently, shame that occurs in other cultural contexts and social settings, which are not associated with bodily nakedness, can borrow the notion of shame in nakedness to depict certain emotional states like guilt or embarrassment. Alternatively, the effect can also be applied to clothing, which represents honor and modesty. Hence, shame and modesty can be expressed through the "conceal-reveal" model of nakedness and clothing within the logic of emotive metaphors.

Shame and the Metaphorical Model of Conceal-Reveal

Emotions are generally understood in terms of orientational metaphors (e.g., happy is up, sad is down)—a result of systematic correlation between emotions and sensory-motor experiences.[76] Similarly, feelings of

---

70. Lakoff and Johnson, *Live*, 117–19; Rohrer, "Embodiment," 13.
71. See chapter 2.
72. Johnson, *Mind*, 34.
73. Timpe, "Shame," 1074–75.
74. Cox, "Psychology," 56–59.
75. Verspoor, "Emotional," 5.
76. Ibid., 12; Rull, "Control," 186. Rull is more precise in his description of emotion as being an object that could be "contained," (ibid., 184). This "object-containment"

shame and embarrassment occur through a desire to be concealed or hidden from public view or opinion.[77] In this sense, the logic of shame is expressed congruously through an agreement on what is concealed or revealed between people of the same culture.[78] In this way, an "object-containment" model has depicted shame as an object to be concealed or revealed.

In the "conceal-reveal" model and the "object-containment" model the observer is crucial. A highly systematic explanation of shame proposes that there are two types of exposure that trigger embarrassment: one is of physical functions of elimination and sexuality,[79] the other is of sentiment related to self-respect.[80] Although much distinction should be made between shame and embarrassment,[81] it is important to emphasize that both shame and embarrassment share the discomfort and awkwardness of being exposed to the observer.[82] Therefore, the "object-containment" model and the "conceal-reveal" model would not work without an observer.[83]

Moreover, the "conceal-reveal" model underlying shame remains congruous with the "object-containment" and "observer" models, despite

---

model provides a facility of "conceal-reveal" for the emotional feelings of guilt and shame.

77. Miller, *Embarrassment: Poise and Peril in Everyday Life*, 1; Timpe, "Shame," 1074–75.

78. Lakoff and Johnson, *Live*, 117–19; Johnson, *Mind*, xii–xiii; Rohrer, "Embodiment," 13.

79. Freud, *The Interpretation of Dreams*, 242–48; Wilcox, "Naked in Old English: The Embarrassed and the Shamed," 279–81; Paster, *The Body Embarrassment: Drama and the Disciplines of Shame in Early Modern England*, 144–47.

80. Timpe, "Shame," 1074–75; McFarland and Baker-Baumann, *Shame and the Body Image*, 3.

81. Embarrassment can trigger shame but embarrassment itself is triggered by less fundamental transgressions whereas shame is attached to more serious moral values (Wilcox, "English," 278).

82. Wilcox, "English," 278; Miller, *Embarrassment*, 6; Edelmann, *The Psychology of Embarrassment*, 56.

83. Timpe, "Shame," 1074–75. Alternatively, would contemporary therapeutic models concur? Could this not be a dysfunction of a damaged sense of *self* without any other objective party? Evidence suggests that relationship within the self is possible (Mann, "Sinless," 81: narrative therapy; Watts, "Shame, Sin and Guilt," 64: distinction between *self* and *others*). Therefore, it is arguable that self alienation can be understood as a divided self wherein a part of it becomes an *objective observer*—a form of self-judgment, as much individualistic and autonomous as self-design and self-termination.

what triggers the feelings of embarrassment and shame. This conclusion can be drawn from an anthropological study of shame and modesty relating to nakedness and clothing. In cultures where nakedness and clothing are associated with moral-ethical values and social propriety, the conceal-reveal model of shame is significantly relevant to the concealment of the body.[84] Alternatively, in cultures where modesty is not solely expressed through the concealment of genitals, the conceal-reveal model of shame is expressed through the concealment of other body parts, or through the existence of certain body paintings or tattoos.[85]

However, the coherence between shame and the "conceal-reveal" model is challenged, especially when concealment does not mean modesty,[86] or even imposes shame.[87] This implies nothing more than the need to distinguish the "conceal-reveal" model of shame and that of the heuristic metaphors of nakedness and clothing.[88]

Modesty and the Concealment of a Sexual Body

At times, modesty has been understood as an instinctive and biological factor that has caused humans to wear clothes for most of recorded history,[89] but the instinctiveness of this "modesty" appears to have been mistaken with the sexual instinct of the human body. For example, a more Freudian viewpoint holds that modesty has to do with whether or not the physical elimination functions and sex are covered.[90] Here, shame is identified with the exposure of the sexual body: as long as the sexual body is covered, shame is also "hidden" away. Therefore, bodily modesty is equal to the concealment of the shame of the sexual body. In reality, however, concepts of modesty and shame underlying the sexual body are mercurial and heavily dependent on cultural viewpoints. Modesty can-

---

84. However, there is little evidence that the shame of nakedness initiated the formation of social modesty as indicated in chapter 2; Smith and Sparks, *Child*, 91.

85. Ableman, *Anatomy*, 9, 40; Westermarck, *Marriage*, 206–8.

86. Hoebel, *Anthropology*, 252–53.

87. Ableman, *Anatomy*, 15.

88. This "conceal-reveal" model will be mentioned further in later chapters.

89. Flugel, *Clothes*, 53–67. This is also the opinion of many psychologists on the origins of clothes (Adams, *Naked We Came: A More or Less Lighthearted Look at the Past, Present, and Future of Clothes*, 20).

90. Wilcox, "English," 285; Smith and Sparks, *Child*, 108; Freud, *Dreams*, 242–48; Langner, *The Importance of Wearing Clothes*, 72.

not be interpreted as an instinctive fear that requires concealment solely on grounds that are connected to sex,[91] because such an interpretation appears inconsistent among different customary habits,[92] and religious practices,[93] not to mention the various economic views.[94]

The idea of sexual modesty remains relative and conventional among cultures. In some, modesty exists without the shame underlying the sexual body. For example, genital concealment in the Mundirucú culture expresses modesty through the sitting in a modest manner (for a naked woman) and the careful putting on and taking off of the sheaths covering a man's private parts.[95] In this sense, sexual modesty is associated with how the genitals are concealed, and not as a contrast with the shame of exposure. This confirms that sexual modesty is "a habit, not an instinct."[96] This cultural example of customary modesty explains why the concealment of the sexual body might be irrelevant in some cases where the concept of obscenity appears meaningless,[97] or in some cases where concealment might impose shame.[98] In addition, because modesty is customary, there is a possibility for change and adaptation between cultures.[99] The evidence for this is the process of civilisation and differing rates of culture adaptation,[100] reactions of shame and resistance.[101] This adaptation appears to follow a single-direction; once the body is no longer seen as morally neutral, it probably will never be seen as such again.[102]

What does this inconsistency mean and where does it leave us? The inconsistency regarding sexual modesty and concealment of the

91. E.g., Ellis, *Psychology*, 1.

92. Crawley, "The Sexual Background of Dress," 72–76; Smith and Sparks, *Child*, 108–14.

93. Rudofsky, *The Unfashionable Human Body*, chapters 1–2; Cooke, *Reprehension*, 4, 47–50; Smith and Sparks, *Child*, 97–98.

94. Adams, *Naked*, 19–20, 24; Langer suggests inferiority and superiority complexes are the thriving force for adornment (Langer, *Wearing*, 12).

95. Murphy and Murphy, *Women of the Forest*, 54.

96. Hoebel, *Anthropology*, 252–53. Ellis also acknowledges the force of tradition in modesty that cannot be reasoned, yet appears incongruous when he presumes that modesty is instinctive (Ellis, *Psychology*, 70).

97. Wilkinson, *Attitudes*, 81.

98. Ableman, *Anatomy*, 15.

99. Hoebel, *Anthropology*, 328.

100. Kawano, "Japanese," 151.

101. Ableman, *Anatomy*, 15.

102. Ibid., 36.

body among cultures implies that sexual modesty must not be seen as identical to the sense of modesty in the "conceal-reveal" model. In cultures where modesty is associated with the concealment of a sexual body it also functions as a contrast entity to shame, which is associated with the exposure of the body. Alternatively, in cultures where sexual modesty is *not* identified as a contrast entity to shame, no assumption can be made that the "conceal-reveal" model is nullified. Therefore, an appropriate view of modesty should acknowledge an overlap between sexual modesty and modesty in the "conceal-reveal" model of shame, yet concealment of a sexual body is not the determining factor of a "conceal-reveal" model of shame.

The Relational Aspect of Shame and Metaphorical Language of Guilt and Sin

Bodily shame is subjected to an observer, most probably another human being who is capable of feeling ashamed and is able to see the exposure.[103] The driving force of shame appears to be the fear of disapproval for breaking conventional or traditional codes,[104] either deliberately or accidentally, because generally people do not want to be condemned, ill-thought of, blamed, or mocked.[105] This means that there is a *relational* aspect of shame that disjoints the individual from the observer or the "power of custom."[106]

There are many similarities and differences between shame and guilt.[107] However, the relational aspect of shame (between the observer and the victim of shame) is negotiable to the concepts of guilt and sin. In this way, while shame and embarrassment are the results of a disruption of conventional agreement, wherein the victim of shame suffers from the predicament, guilt and sin are the result of a disruption of a relational

---

103. Lemos, "Shame," 228; Gilmore, "Honor, Honesty, Shame: Male Status in Contemporary Andalusia," 101.

104. Ellis, *Psychology*, 70.

105. Westermarck, *Marriage*, 208–9; McFarland and Baker-Baumann, *Image*, 3.

106. Westermarck, *Marriage*, 209.

107. Piers and Singer, *Shame and Guilt*, 15–22; Tangney, "Shame," 266–69; Barrett, et al., "Avoiders versus amenders: Implications for the investigation of shame and guilt during toddlerhood?" 481–505; Freud, "Three Essays on the Theory of Sexuality," 153–243; Kitayama, et al., "Culture, Self, and Emotion," 439–64; Tangney et al., "Are Shame, Guilt and Embarrassment Distinct Emotions?" 1256–69.

agreement that might damage both parties. Additionally, the language of sin and guilt can also be depicted through an "object-containment" model,[108] especially when sin and guilt are seen as the "dirt and abject" of a relational entity,[109] that can be "hidden," "taken" away, "washed," "cleansed," and "wiped."[110]

The relational aspect of sin and shame can be expressed in various ways. First, sin and shame are both unseen but can be felt between the parties involved. Secondly, both sin and shame can be seen as relational objects or "opponents," e.g., "struggle" with sin/shame; "being released" from sin/shame; "being captivated" by sin/shame, or Christ "overcame" sin, or Christ "bore" our shame, etc. Thirdly, although the difference is clear: shame is an emotional phenomenon whereas sin can be a forensic problem, the relational aspect of both shame and sin makes it possible for the two notions to be complementary parts of each other. For example, when a husband stripped his wife in public, as a sign of a divorce, he not only stripped her status and exposed her shame, but also condemned her infidelity. Shame in this sense exists alongside sin in the judgment of the gazing public. Finally, self-shame and self-sin can be defined through a chronic failure to relate to the self, its body image, and bodily shame. Body image, which is the mental representation or internal picture of the outer physical body,[111] needs to compete to be attractive and to feel secured by acceptance.[112] However, when the body image is disparaged by aging,[113] accidents and clinical disfigurement,[114] abuse,[115] or bodily dysmorphia,[116] bodily shame is inevitable. Bodily shame occurs as a result of a violation of one's body image, which obstructs a normal relationship with the self. This point is an alternative interpretation of shame to an *objective observer* mentioned above.

---

108. Johnson, *Mind*, 29; Rohrer, "Embodiment," 17–18.
109. Gunton, *Actuality*, 119.
110. Lakoff and Johnson, *Philosophy in the Flesh*, 37–38.
111. McFarland and Baker-Baumann, *Image*, 77.
112. Gilbert, "Body Shame," 6–14.
113. McGee and Gott, "Shame and the Ageing Body," 75–81.
114. Coughlan and Clarke, "Shame and burns," 155; Carr, "Body Shame," 98; Kent and Thompson, "The Development and Maintenance of Shame in Disfigurement," 103; Kellett, "Shame-Fused Acne," 135–36.
115. Andrews, "Body Shame and Abuse in Childhood," 256.
116. Veale, "Shame in Body Dysmorphic Disorder," 267.

After all, what does the relational aspect of shame, guilt and sin mean to our metaphorical use of nakedness and clothing? As we have examined above, a metaphor occurs when there is a shift or a carrying over of a word from its normal use to a new one. In an emotive metaphor the shift occurs through the similarity between the feelings the new situation and the normal situation arouse.[117] This allows us to conclude that nakedness and clothing can be used metaphorically to express conventional feelings and unfold the relational aspect of shame, guilt and sin in a relationship thanks to the cognitive "object-containment" and "conceal-reveal" models.

Nakedness and Clothing as Emotive Metaphors in Religious Language

Religious language has been perceived,[118] at times, to be a language that can be "picked up" along the way like the rules of a game.[119] In other words, the nature of religious language reflects the nature of a metaphor—religious language uses human concepts to explain mystery.[120] The "fluid" nature of metaphor[121] provides the possibility for variants of metaphor to express complicated theological discourse, especially in preferable ways.[122] The function of metaphors and analogies in theology is to illuminate by picturing something partially unknown.[123] Nevertheless they aid in the apprehension of truth, not fact; in other words, there is a further

---

117. Cox further asserts that the third term, which will bring the two sides (conscious and unconscious) of the psyche together, is filled with symbols (Cox, "Psychology," 56); Richards, *Practical Criticism*, 221.

118. Fawcett, *The Symbolic Language of Religion*, 29, 86–93; McIntyre, *Faith, Theology and Imagination*, chapters 6–7; Porter, *The Nature of Religious Language*, 201–11, 284–306; Palmer, *Analogy*, chapters 4–6: 81–164; Ramsey, *Models For Divine Activity*, 40–55; Ramsey, *Religious Language*, chapters 3–4; Sherry, *Religion, Truth & Language Games*, chapters 2: 7–9.

119. Donovan, *Religious Language*, 88; the influence of Wittgenstein's theory of language-games is acknowledged, 91.

120. Russsell, *The Prince of Darkness*, 123: "Any affirmation about God can be no more than a metaphor."

121. Black, "Davidson," 192.

122. TeSelle, *Speaking in Parables*, 138.

123. Lyall, "Of Metaphors and Analogies: Legal Language and Covenant Theology," 2n.1.

reality to which a metaphor points.[124] The significance of a symbol is not unlimited due to the limit created by the relationship between symbol and that which is symbolized, i.e., the symbol can only reveal what is present within it.[125] Therefore, the error of failing to distinguish between metaphor and its significance, or any attempt to synthesize different but related metaphors will result in making them into one self-consistent whole and pressing a single metaphor or analogy too far.[126]

The defining differences between typology, analogy, and intertextuality in religious language lie with the different functions and significance that metaphors retain among these phenomena. At times, the decorative nature of metaphor is emphasized,[127] probably because of the fact that metaphor can appear to be a complex system of resemblances or a form of sub-language that can be esoteric or unintelligible. Such features can also be found in the employment of the metaphors of nakedness and clothing, especially when they are "stretched" to create a theological point. Therefore, there are styles and fashions where the metaphors of nakedness and clothing are employed. Nakedness and clothing can function separately or become *relational emotive metaphors* and together function as a model that depicts a broken relationship.

Model, Analogy, and Metaphors

"Model" has a wider use in contemporary philosophical discussion; it carries natural logical overtones, takes us at once into a logical context,[128] and relates to the "world of experience" and "secular" situations,[129] yet it is incapable of escaping solecism and inadequacy.[130] There are a wide range of models, which serve different purposes, symbolically or descriptively, with different restrictions and limitations,[131] but the ultimate aim of using a model is to form a discourse that is most reliable, licensed by, and consistent with the widest possible range of models.[132] The more a model

124. Ibid., 2.
125. Fawcett, *Symbolic*, 29.
126. Lyall, "Metaphors," 3–4.
127. Or a happy trick of words (Richards, *Rhetoric*, 90; Need, *Chalcedon*, 90–94).
128. Ramsey, "Talking about God: Models, Ancient and Modern," 76.
129. Ibid., 79; Fawcett, *Symbolic*, 69.
130. Ramsey, "Talking," 84, 96; Fawcett, *Symbolic*, 71, 87.
131. Fawcett, *Symbolic*, 70–76.
132. Ramsey, "Talking," 84, 89, 94; therefore, the supply of models can never be

can exist successfully in competition with other models, the more justifiably it provides discourse about what the cosmic disclosure discloses.[133]

The religious model, however, is distinct from the scientific one,[134] due to its affective evocativeness and the mixture of theological intuition and philosophical assumption regarding its potential in describing God.[135] The popular position holds that models in theology are fluid and expressive while the language of the sciences is rigorous and "objectively" true; models in theology are a necessary part of human expression in religion while science is concerned with permanent truth.[136] This is the precise point where theological language linguistically differs from its scientific counterpart. Theological models are more intimate to metaphors, both in nature and in operation. In fact, it can be said that models are related to metaphors and are to some degree an extension of metaphors,[137] and therefore indispensable in the way human language and knowledge work.

A religious model can be formed by an "extra-system" of metaphors or as a collection of *root metaphors*, which comprise of some very fertile metaphors.[138] In this fashion, the metaphorical language of clothing is an extra-system that is attached to an existing model. For example, the bride of Christ borrows the cultural concept of clothing to depict a glorious spiritual condition of the church and the relationship with Christ.[139] Surely, the process of preparing the bride[140] becomes an extra-system that is added to the existing metaphor/model in order to extend its theologi-

---

exhausted, ibid., 85.

133. Ibid., 90.

134. Fawcett, *Symbolic*, 91.

135. Soskice, *Religious*, 108–9, 116–17.

136. Need, *Chalcedon*, 116. Need points out that in the light of Chalcedon, models pervade theological discourse at its most fundamental level; theology is saturated with usages of metaphors and models, 117.

137. Ibid., 116; McFague contends that a model is in essence a sustained and systematic metaphor (*Metaphorical*, 67); Barbour (*Myths, Models and Paradigms*, 43), following Black, treats models as "systematically developed metaphors"; Soskice (*Religious*, 101) keeps them separate but "metaphor arise when we speak on the basis of models." This book holds that metaphors and models are two separate things but can overlap and interchange, albeit not to the extent of alternation but can be utilized together in the same setting in order to achieve a better-desired explanation.

138. McFague, *Metaphorical*, 26–27; McIntyre, *Imagination*, 129; for an extensive study on root metaphors see Goatly, *The Language of Metaphors*, chapter 2: 41–81.

139. Fung, "Some Pauline Pictures of the Church," 97–100; Muirhead, "The Bride of Christ," 178.

140. Batey, "Paul's Bride Image: a Symbol of Realistic Eschatology," 179.

cal capacity. An alternative effect can be found in the negotiation with the Adam-Christ typology, i.e., the bride corresponds with the Second Eve.[141] The "extra-system" attached to any existing model has to be compatible with the dichotomy of the existing model. In the Adam-Christ typology, nakedness and clothing must carry the contrast and division of functions that are both suitable and complementary to the contrasts that already exist in the typology in question.[142]

Like model, analogy and symbolism are common means to account for the meaning of religious language.[143] McIntyre, building upon Stebbling, suggests that the strength of analogy depends upon at least two considerations: (1) initial resemblance and the comprehensiveness of the properties, which ought to be connected,[144] and (2) a principle, which asserts that the more comprehensive the inferred properties are, the less likely the conclusion is to be true. Accordingly, analogy opens up new vistas of possibility and plays a penultimate role in theological thought. We are prone to allow analogical description to be a substitute for a more rigorously disciplined investigation of the subject.[145] McIntyre warns of the error of seeking to impose upon analogy too rigid a structure, which forces it to become univocal.[146]

Religious Models of Nakedness and Clothing[147]

"[T]he history of clothes, with their symbolic meanings, is a fascinating one. Dress has been intimately associated with national identity, with class

141. Muirhead, "Bride," 179.

142. Part Two of this book will explore how this dichotomy of nakedness and clothing varies in different contexts, and part three will explore how these metaphors may be employed in a model of atonement.

143. Hook, *Religious Experience and Truth*; Campbell, *The Language of Religion*, 92; Aquinas, *Summa Theologiae*, I: 13; Aquinas, *Summa Contra Gentiles*, I: 34; Anderson, *The Bond of Being*; Phelan, *St. Thomas and Analogy*; McInerny, *The Logic of Analogy*; Mascall, *Existence and Analogy*; Farrer, *Finite and Infinite*; Hawkins, *The Essentials of Theism*.

144. McIntyre, "Analogy," 18; Stebbing, *Modern*, 253.

145. McIntyre, "Analogy," 18.

146. Ibid., 20. Besides, McIntyre believes that analogies must be carefully scrutinized for positive and negative content and be graded accordingly.

147. The word "model" here implies a "setting" wherein both metaphors of nakedness and clothing work as a team. The "naked-clothed" model is a name for such a setting in light of similar cognitive models such as "object-containment" and "conceal-reveal."

structure, with professional qualifications, with conventions of a particular period, with stages of growth and aging, with artistic performances and celebrations. In no department of life, however, has distinctiveness of clothing been more obviously symbolic than in the sphere of religion."[148]

As we shall explore the concepts of nakedness and clothing in the Bible and theology in later chapters, only a brief discussion will be presented here with a few examples pointing out the analogical characteristic of a "naked-clothed" model. We argue that the "naked-clothed" model is preserved by the power of a drama between the two metaphors, i.e., there is a certain degree of negotiation in constructing a model that is compatible to the target domain. Moreover, the compatibility between metaphors and correspondent meanings in the target domain must be established by a rhetoric discipline.

(1) The first example is a philosophical consideration of clothing and nakedness in the sense of transparency.[149] In this case, the idea of uncovering, baring and exposing an object is both rhetorical and poetic; thus, nakedness is borrowed to express a metaphorical and philosophical exposure. To say, "death is naked before God" is to say that God sees and knows death clearly; or in other words, there is no cover or barrier that keeps God from the full knowledge of death.[150] Accordingly, in the "conceal-reveal" model, to strip a person naked is an act of exposing the bareness of the body, from which many cultural implications can be made, with a richer relational aspect.

(2) Similarly, in the example of nude baptism, the putting off of clothes does not hold a philosophical sense of transparency but expresses the rejection of the old nature and the putting on of the new nature. Nudity is a metaphor for the emptiness of the self, reflecting the transition in the Adam-Christ typology between old and new: nudity does *not* signify the old, but the act of stripping signifies self-emptying and re-clothing with new clothes signifies the imitation of Christ.[151] Surely this sign of admittance into Christian fellowship,[152] to an extent, is an oft-repeated symbolism.[153]

---

148. Dillistone, *The Power of Symbols*, 50.
149. E.g., Job 26:6; further explanation will be offered in chapters 4 and 5.
150. McKenna, *TPC—Job*, 177; Janzen, *Interpretation—Job*, 177.
151. Mazza, *Mystagogy: A Theology of Liturgy in the Patristic Age*, 155–64.
152. George, "The Number of the Sacraments," 166.
153. Dillistone, *Symbols*, 53; Dillistone, *Christianity*, 169, 182–99.

Being associated with circumcision,[154] baptism signifies a break and renunciation of the flesh to engage in a new life of righteousness.[155] This self-exposure is about being vulnerable, not to condemnation, but by faith in grace, to a divine provision. "This image was central to Jesus' own teaching. No patching of new cloth on old garments! It became central for those converting to the Christian faith in the Mediterranean world. Putting off and putting on. Divesting oneself of the old life, old habits, old weakness. Clothing oneself with new habits, new strengths and above all with Christ Himself."[156]

(3) Alternatively, in the example of penitential nakedness, an emotive-relational model of shame is established in the comparison between the shame of confession on earth and the eschatological shame on the Day of Judgment.[157] The special point of this homiletic framework is that it also allocates nakedness in the philosophical sense of transparency,[158] with a possible intention to express the confession of sins as a practice of religious transparency.[159]

(4) Similar to the penitential model, the punitive model of nakedness and clothing also carries a comparison, but a comparison between an adulterous naked wife who is associated with a broken spiritual vow or spiritual infidelity and a spiritual relationship between humanity and God. The analogy of a naked adulterous wife being stripped by her husband in public is clearly a symbolic announcement of the divorce,[160] and

---

154. Cp. Colossians 3 in Dillistone, *Christianity*, 199–202. Circumcision is a mark of covenant with God (Lods, *Israel From Its Beginnings to the Middle of the Eighth Century*, 200) that gives a cultural and religious identity (Wagner, "Piety, Jewish," 800; Hall, "Circumcision," 1025; a mnemonic sign of covenant with God, 1027).

155. Thornton, *The Common Life in the Body of Christ*, 227–29, 414–16.

156. Dillistone, *Symbols*, 53–54.

157. Pope, *Homilies of Ælfric: A Supplementary Collection*, II: 770–81 (Emphasis and translation from Wilcox, "English," 282n.18); Napier 46 (quoted by Wilcox, "English," 297n.24); Scragg, *The Vercelli Homilies and Related Texts*, 366–80; Ericksen, "Penitential Nakedness and the Junius 11 *Genesis*," 270–71n.23–26; Godden, "An Old English Penitential Motif," 222; the embarrassment in the Doomsday, in the sermon on Sunday after Pentecost (*Catholic Homilies* II. 36), Pope, *Ælfric*, homily 27 (II: 770–81).

158. The homily *Vercelli* 22 (Pope, *Ælfric*, II: 770–81); Godden, "Motif," 222; Ericksen, "Penitential," 271n.26.

159. Again, this *penitential nakedness* calls for penitence using the main interpretation of Genesis 2–3 and Matt 22:1–14 (Wilcox, "English," 298n.47).

160. Ruiz, *Ezekiel in the Apocalypse*, 372; Wolff, *Hosea*, 32–34.

thus can be classified to the group of symbolic actions.[161] This symbolic action is employed as a metaphor for the breaking of relationship between Israel and Yahweh, and therefore, it becomes a sign of punishment in a judgmental prophecy. This punitive metaphor of nakedness is unique in its distinctive intertextual meaning of condemnation, unlike the encouraging connotation in the penitential model.

(5) The philanthropic model of nakedness and clothing holds fast to the tradition of almsgiving, particularly the religious language of renunciation and social welfare in the story of Boniface,[162] and Francis of Assisi's motto "Naked to follow the naked Christ."[163] The employment of the metaphors of nakedness and clothing reinforces many theological points: (1) renunciation of material life, (2) care for the poor and needy in society, (3) imitation of Christ, and (4) even soteriology.[164] In this framework, the punitive and transparent meanings of nakedness are completely irrelevant, and therefore, creating an irregularity in the use of nakedness and clothing.

(6) In the spiritual-condition model, nakedness and the degree of clothing become a metaphorical scale measuring the spiritual state of the soul before God.[165] In this framework, nakedness implies a state of being rejected and subject to judgment, whereas clothing is a state of being justified in righteousness and accepted before God. This particular model is very significant to the soteriological model that this book is testing.[166]

A Possible Soteriological Model Using Nakedness and Clothing

Christian thought at times borrows the symbols of nakedness and clothing to enrich the demonstration of theological ideas. However, in that process there are some important points to note. First, the various uses of nakedness and clothing share a *universal rhetoric phenomenon*—the

---

161. Dillistone, *Christianity*, 169, 174.

162. Gregory I, *Dialogues*, 40; Ericksen, "Penitential," 258: footnote 3: he would sometimes leave the house and later return without his coat or even without his shirt, for, as soon as he saw anyone in need of clothes, he would give up his own.

163. Trexler, *Naked Before the Father: The Renunciation of Francis of Assisi*, 4.

164. Chapter 7 will explore the connection between giving clothes to the naked and Christian salvation (Cyprian, Jerome and Augustine).

165. Hodge, *Second Epistle to the Corinthians*, 116.

166. Calvin, *CC—John*, 230.

"conceal-reveal" model.[167] Clearly from the examples above, nakedness and clothing can maintain a *contrast* and *complementary* relationship. That relationship is crucial to maintain the internal coherence of a model, and therefore play-roles of nakedness and clothing cannot afford to be overlapped.

Secondly, while employing nakedness and clothing language, theological language cannot escape the necessity of *cross-domain mappings* that metaphor theories point out. Nakedness and clothing are flexible enough to provide *consistency* and *compatibility* between metaphors and concepts in many target domains. The example models show that the metaphors of nakedness and clothing are flexible enough for certain irregularities; not only depending on the cultural views,[168] but also the literal creativity (for instance, both the metaphors of nakedness and of clothing can independently symbolize shame).[169] This is not to say these irregularities are limitless. Any model can easily appear cryptic and incoherent when stretched too far by a juxtaposition of meanings that do not belong to the target domain.[170]

Lastly, there is an ongoing *constructability* in the understanding of nakedness and clothing within the conventional values of a culture. It is a mistake to claim that a metaphor of nakedness and clothing can retain its indigenous meaning without adopting more meanings over the course of time. In most cultures, generally, these metaphors can express shame and modesty, reward and punishment, but these meanings may not necessarily remain unaltered or appear foreign in some other frameworks. Therefore, with these points in mind, a model that employs nakedness and clothing is *not* descriptive, but analogical.[171]

---

167. The clearest example is Johnson, *Mind*, 34; Timpe, "Shame," 1074–75; Wilcox, "English," 278; Miller, *Embarrassment*, 6; Edelmann, *Embarrassment*, 56.

168. Especially with regards to shame (Lemos, "Shame," 228; Gilmore, "Honor," 101).

169. Nakedness is shameful, (e.g., the concept of porno-prophet in Guest), but at times nakedness is glorious (the Greek eschatological concept of naked soul, or the shameless naked baptisand in the early centuries of Christianity, or the philanthropic notion of imitation of the Naked Christ); clothing of shame in poetic literature (Job 8:22; Pss 34:5; 35:26; 44:15; 69:7; 83:16; 109:29; 132:18), or the shame of inappropriate dressing at the wedding feast of Matt 22:1–14 (Wilcox, "English," 298n.47).

170. The recent debate on soteriological models, which will be explored in later chapters of this book, has shown that analogical models have certain limits.

171. Fawcett, *Symbolic*, 86.

In order for the metaphors of nakedness and clothing to be employed in an atonement model, they must possess a compatibility with the doctrine. There must be enough flexibility for the chronic problem of sin, confession of sins, and the ongoing reception of forgiveness, in accordance with the contemporary concept of atonement, which focuses on shame and sin in the body. The later chapters of this book will gradually lead the argument into a reflection of these metaphors within an association with sin in the framework of Genesis 2–3, with covenantal theology, with the interpretation of the cross, and the robe of righteousness and salvation (Ps 132:16).[172] What this chapter points out is that a model, which employs the emotive-relational metaphors of nakedness and clothing, might increase the liveliness of its ontology because of a combined impact between emotion and epistemology.

Summary and Conclusion

The heuristic experience of the body is an abundant source for metaphorical language because it has more experiential and shared values for communication. The cultural consistency between metaphorical language and social conventions, proposed by metaphorical language theories,[173] can only verify that nakedness and clothing become emotive metaphors where cultural conventions consider them as appropriate. However, due to the ability of adaptation, it is probable that these metaphors might be transferred from culture to culture.

With regard to shame, the "conceal-reveal" and "object-containment" models provide possibility for negotiation with the cognition and epistemology of nakedness and clothing. Moreover, the "observer" in the "conceal-reveal" model gives shame, nakedness and clothing a relational aspect, which allows the facility made of nakedness and clothing to speak of shame and guilt in the narrative of a relationship.

---

172. Leupold, *Exposition of the Psalms*, 914–15: increasing of quality between priest garb, garment of righteousness, garment of salvation; Kraus, *Psalms 60–150*, 481: "bearers of salvation," to them the "oracle of salvation" is entrusted; Anderson, *The Book of Psalms*, Vol. 2: Psalms 73–150, 882–83: linking to Isa 11:5; 61:10; Briggs and Briggs, *A Critical and Exegetical Commentary on the Book of Psalms*, Vol. 2: 471: attributes are often represented as clothing put on, priests were bearers of his righteousness and salvation; Kidner, *Psalms 73–150: A Commentary on Books III–V of the Psalms*, 450: Isa 61:10.

173. Lakoff and Johnson, *Live*, 22–23.

As we look to argue that metaphors of nakedness and clothing can be employed to communicate the message of the cross, an assessment of the adequacy of these metaphors is needed. This chapter only presents the boundaries within which metaphors can be used and how they place before us opportunities for communication and dialogues. So far we have confirmed that metaphors of nakedness and clothing are capable of constructing a compatible model for the theological discourse of sin based on the relational aspect of shame and guilt. In the following chapters, an investigation will be carried out on biblical texts; and the religious and theological notions of nakedness and clothing will be examined in greater depth.

PART 2

Nakedness and Clothing in Biblical
and Theological Contexts
and Roman Crucifixion

4

The Antithesis of Nakedness and Clothing in the Bible

HISTORICALLY, CHRISTIANS BELIEVE THAT the biblical writers were inspired by the Holy Spirit while being influenced and limited by the cultures in which they lived and to which they wrote.[1] Therefore, in order to examine how the antithesis of nakedness and clothing is recorded, portrayed, and conveyed by the writers, one has to face the challenge of interpreting and analyzing the text with a considerable awareness of its linguistic and cultural concepts.[2] Despite various references of the term "naked/nakedness,"[3] a rich collection of concepts of nakedness is preserved from different perspectives of social and historical settings.[4] Therefore, the aim of this chapter is to unpack the particular develop-

---

1. Fee and Stuart, *How To Read The Bible For All Its Worth*, 20: "In speaking through real persons, in a variety of circumstances, over a 1500-year period, God's Word was expressed in the vocabulary and thought patterns of those persons and conditioned by the culture of those times and circumstances." Gorman, *Elements of Biblical Exegesis*, 69–74; Barton, "Historical-Critical Approaches," 9–11; Dockery, et al., *Foundation for Biblical Interpretation*; White, "Inspiration and Authority of Scripture," 19–23; Walton, "Cultural Background of the Old Testament," 256–57; Seifrid, "Cultural Background of the New Testament," 489–90; Carroll, "Introduction: Issues of 'Context' within Social Science Approaches to Biblical Studies," 14–16; Plantinga, "Two (or More) Kinds of Scripture Scholarship," 20–23.

2. Historical contexts, including time and culture, and literary contexts are crucial areas for consideration when doing exegesis (Fee and Stuart, *Worth*, 23–24).

3. The word "naked/nakedness" appears 104 times (eighty-seven verses) in the KJV and forty-nine times (forty-seven verses) in the NIV (Robinson, "Nudity, As Mentioned in the Bible").

4. For a brief summary see Utriainen, "Naked and Dressed," 132–49.

89

ment of the concepts of nakedness in the light of commentators' interpretations. The central question concerns not only how *differently* the concept of nakedness has been understood, but also to what extent it has been *addressed* in the Bible.

Garden Of Eden—
The Birthplace of Nakedness and Symbolism

In chapter 2 we have mentioned briefly one of the oldest theories of the origin of clothes—the Mosaic theory.[5] This theory originates from an interpretation of Genesis 3:7, which refers to the discovery of nakedness of "the first man."[6] The "discovery" is founded on the text's implications of two conditions of nakedness: a prelapsarian condition *without* shame, which only Adam and Eve possessed, and a postlapsarian condition *with* shame.[7] The notion of nakedness in Genesis 2:25 is crucial to the "birthplace" or "discovery" idea. However, it is a problematic passage due to its particular similarities to certain ancient myths,[8] and thus prompts further examination. The intention of this chapter is to look for an appropriate interpretation of this "birthplace of nakedness."

A Primitive Condition and Mythical Symbolism

Numerous theorists have proposed that Genesis 2:25 is foundational to the interpretation of Genesis 3:7; but their claims vary widely. Some hold to the interpretation of childlike and innocent nakedness;[9] others hold to

---

5. Genesis 3:7–11, respectively; Hiler, *Raiment*, 4; Horn and Gurel, *Skin*, 19.

6. Augustine, *City*, 14:16–17, 24; Adar, *Genesis*, 23; Kass, *The Beginning of Wisdom*, 106; "first man" also in the symbolic sense of "parents of the whole human race" (Wenham, "Original Sin in Genesis 1–11," 321).

7. Gen 3:7 is contrast to Gen 2:25, Davidson, *Genesis 1–11*, 41; Cassuto, *Commentary on the Book of Genesis*, 148.

8. For example, the idea that the text might have been influenced by Babylonian folklore (Robinson, "Nudity"); Adapa myth and Enkidu episode in Gilgamesh Epic (Westermann, *Genesis 1–11*, 245–48); Wallace, *Narrative*, 104, 114, 129; Veenker, "Forbidden Fruit," 71–73; *Pesiqta de-Rabbi Eliezer* 20:46a–50b.7 and *Genesis Rabbah* 97, as quoted in Nissan Rubin and Admiel Kosman, "The Clothing of the Primordial Adam as a Symbol of Apocalyptic Time in the Midrashic Sources," 170–71.

9. For more on children theory, see Irenaeus, *AH* IV.38.3 (Steenberg, "Children," 1–22); Gunkel, as quoted by Westermann, *Genesis*, 1984, 235.

the theory of sexual innocence.[10] It is also held that nakedness in Genesis 2:25 is not a state but a literary preparation for 3:7, i.e., there was no historical or chronological fall,[11] or that 2:25 is simply a non-biblical and mythical idea of a blessed original state.[12] Following this line of thought, certain feminist perspectives press on even further to reject the "sin and fall" motif, arguing that Genesis 2:25 should be seen as immaturity, as opposed to maturity inferred in Genesis 3:7.[13] However, such a rejection of the "sin and fall" motif risks the danger of dismissing and clashing with the prominent theological model of "sin and salvation" in the "Adam-Christ" typology of Pauline theology.[14] It also shows ignorance of this motif in post-Biblical Hebrew and Aramaic literature before the Mishnah.[15] Could any plausible interpretation of Genesis 2:25 be made that would meet the requirements of a critical evaluation of the primordial state and, at the same time, be consistent with the "sin and fall" model?[16]

One of the earliest Christian interpretations considers the innocent couple, Adam and Eve, as the "infants of paradise."[17] Irenaeus refers to Adam and Eve as literal children, not childlike,[18] whereby with such a

10. Augustine, *City*, 14:24, 54–55; O. Procksch, as quoted by Westermann, *Genesis*, 1984, 235; Skinner, *A Critical and Exegetical Commentary on Genesis*, 71; Shuster, *The Fall And Sin*, 62–63.

11. Genesis 2:25, then, hold in suspense of the "not yet" element to be resolved in Genesis 3:7 (Westermann, *Genesis*, 1984, 234–35); Wenham, "Original," 312: paradigm of sin and consequences.

12. Rad, *Genesis: A Commentary*, 75.

13. Bechtel, "Rethinking the Interpretation of Genesis 2:4B–3:24," 84; Wolde, *A Semiotic Analysis of Genesis 2–3*, 160–73; Wolde, *Stories of the Beginning*, 72–73: Wolde criticizes the "sin and fall" motif of taking a human-centered view and a naïve preference of sinfulness and guilt to inexplicability; Jobling, "The Myth Semantics of Gen. 2:4b–3:24," 41–49; Clines, "The Tree of Knowledge and the Law of Yahweh," 9.

14. Powell, *The Fall of Man*, 21–23. Wenham suggests that the author of Genesis would have been generally sympathetic with Paul's and Augustine's interpretation (Wenham, "Original," 326). The Adam-Christ typology, therefore, is a result of this "sin and fall" motif.

15. Jesus ben Sira 25:24; 4 Ezra 3:20; Pseudo-Ezra 7:118; 2 Baruch 23:4, 17:2–3, quoted by Vermes, "Genesis 1–3 in Post-Biblical Hebrew and Aramaic Literature before the Mishnah," 223–24.

16. Blocher uses the terms *astray* and *stumble* rather than "fall" (Blocher, *Beginning*, 135).

17. Irenaeus, *AH* IV.38.3; Steenberg, "Children," 1–22.

18. Irenaeus, *AH* III.22.4; Steenberg, "Children," 4; Smith, "Chiliasm and Recapitulation in the Theology of Ireneus," 313, 318, 331: Eve was actually considered prepubescent; Balthasar, *The Scandal of the Incarnation*, 60–61: *AH* III.22.4.

child-like mentality they were ignorant of their nakedness.[19] Gunkel takes a similar view that they were children, but as Westermann points out, if the couple were children in Genesis 2:25 and adults in 3:7, the change between the two passages would cause a problem for intelligibility.[20] The infant theory can be combined with the route of the mandate of procreation in Genesis 1:28 only if, as Irenaeus appears to suggest, Genesis 2:25 refers to the time when Adam and Eve were still children and not able to understand procreation. Consequently, there must be a period of time in which they would have grown up and developed this understanding,[21] but this "period" is ambivalent.

The next theory, however, holds that before the fall nakedness was not unknown to the adult couple,[22] yet they remained sexually innocent.[23] When they gained the knowledge of good and evil, sexual knowledge was included and they had the capacity to procreate.[24] Wolde explains:

> The tree of knowledge stands for the capacity for discernment, with sexual awareness as one of its exponents. By contrast, the tree of life represents eternal life; it stands for life without death. To eat of both trees at the same time would mean that the human being would have the capacity both to have children and to go on living for ever. That would be a bit too much of a good thing, and the earth would get over-populated. So the moment that the human being eats from the tree of knowledge, the tree of eternal life is prohibited.[25]

However, it is important to note that the text does not point to a prohibition either from the tree of life or sex because, far from it, God blessed sex![26] The view that holds that there was no sex in the Garden

19. Irenaeus, *AH* III.22.4.

20. Westermann, *Genesis*, 1984, 235.

21. Irenaeus, *AH* III.22.4.

22. Augustine, *NPNF1-2*, 276.

23. They had never experienced sexual arousal nor did they know sex could be evil, thus they looked upon their sexual organs in the same way as upon their mouths, faces or hands (Cassuto, *Genesis*, 137).

24. Wolde, *Stories*, 47–48, 50. Taken from the time of Saint Ambrose and Jerome, this view holds that Adam and Eve engaged in sexual relations only after the fall (Hunter, "On the Sin of Adam and Eve," 291–92); Bonhoeffer, *Creation and Fall*, 78; Brichto, *The Names of God*, 83–84. Shuster argues that the sexual overtones can hardly be denied (Shuster, *Fall*, 62–63).

25. Wolde, *Stories*, 48.

26. Wallace, *Narrative*, 103.

of Eden creates an internal contradiction with the narrative regarding the command to multiply in Genesis 1:28. It is also interesting to note that certain variation of this interpretation can press as far as seeing the "eating" of the "fruit" as a metaphor for sexual intercourse, and falls into the pitfall of inconsistency. In particular, if the "forbidden fruit" is Adam's penis,[27] then what is the fruit of the tree of life, or how did Eve know the "fruit" was good for food and gaining knowledge, and how did Eve "give" the fruit to her husband, who was standing nearby? Obviously, since the commandment to multiply is separate from that of the eating from the tree, by no means can sex be the "forbidden fruit."

Alternatively, Augustine's theory of sexual innocence holds that before the fall humans exercised control over their sexual organs by their own will, but after the fall they were no longer able to do so,[28] i.e., the genitals became insubordinate.[29] According to some scholars, this idea of sexual overtone is undeniable when it is analyzed within the context of shame after the fall, because our physical shame is concentrated upon the sexual organs.[30] However, this overtone of sexuality appears to reflect a cultural element and certain illicit sexual references in the Bible, since nakedness is associated not only with sexuality but also with judgment.[31] In this case, it is quite clear that there is no evidence supporting a relationship between the sense of shame of nakedness in Genesis 3 and sexual relations.[32] Therefore, the knowledge of good and evil cannot be solely connected with the awareness of sex, if interpretation is to be faithful to the narrative.[33]

In the story of the fall, as Shuster points out, the sudden discovery of nakedness should not be limited only to the matter of sexuality.[34]

---

27. Veenker, "Forbidden," 57–73.

28. Augustine, *City*, 14:24; Miles, *Carnal*, 116.

29. I.e., male erection (Kass, *Wisdom*, 107). Besides, both Adam *and* Eve were aware of their new sexuality (Carmichael, "The Paradise Myth," 49).

30. Shuster, *Fall*, 62–64; Miles, *Carnal*, 114; White, *Narration and Discourse in the Book of Genesis*, 137. Westermann points out that Procksch's theory has no support for sexual elements in shame, yet acknowledges that it is largely responsible for the sexual interpretation of Gen 2–3 in the Christian era (Westermann, *Genesis*, 1984, 235).

31. Ezek 16:36 and Hab 2:15; Brownlee, *Ezekiel 1–19*, 235–36.

32. Ryken, et al., *Dictionary of Biblical Imagery*, 582.

33. Adar, *Genesis*, 26; Brueggemann, *Genesis*, 42.

34. Shuster, *Fall*, 65.

Nakedness was also about vulnerability and defenselessness[35] and poverty.[36] As a result, the next interpretation proposes that Adam and Eve could have had some forms of clothes before the eating of the fruit. The fact that Adam and Eve made clothes infers a possible previous state of being covered. In other words, the realization may have been a psychological reaction of memory, to which the Semitic approach refers the loss of the "robe of glory."[37] There are a number of exegetical reasons for this: (1) the wordplay *'or* (skin) and *'or* (light),[38] (2) the Syriac understanding of the tense of the verb *clothe* in Genesis 3:21, which implies God *had clothed* them before the fall, and (3) Syriac interpretation of Psalm 8:6: in honor and glory did you *clothe* him.[39] This view, however, cannot justify the statement "they were *naked* yet without shame."[40] There is a semantic problem here: either, the notion of *prelapsarian clothing* is a product of imagination[41] or it points to an inadequate description of prelapsarian nakedness from a postlapsarian viewpoint of nakedness.[42] It is logically impossible for one notion (the initial condition) to be expressed in two opposite terms (*naked* yet *clothed*), unless both or one of these two terms are to be understood metaphorically!

This possibility of symbolism leads us to the next view, which holds that the state of shameless nakedness in Genesis 2:25 is a metaphor.[43] Yet,

---

35. Magonet, "The Themes of Genesis 2–3," 43.

36. Wambacq (*Mélanges B. Rigaux*, 547–56) and Haag (*Mensch am Anfang*, 50) quoted in Wenham, *WBC—Genesis 1–15*, Vol. 1, 71; However, building upon Coppens ("La nudité des protoplastes," 380–83), Wenham holds that because Gen 3:7 should be aligned with Gen 9:20–27 (and Exod 20:26; 28:42–43), Gen 2:25 must function as reiterating the contentment of the couple and Gen 3 explains how clothing comes to exist according to the norm of a Sumerian custom for modesty (ibid., 72).

37. Brock, "Robe," 247. This argument is based on the book of 1 Enoch 62:15–16, and Daniel 10:5, 12:7; *Book of Jubilees* 3:23–31 (100–150 CE) and *Apocalypse of Moses* 15–30, 20:4, 21:1–6, (20 BCE—70 CE) in Lambden, "From Fig Leaves to Fingernails," 82–84; *Pesiqta de-Rabbi Eliezer* 20:46a—50b.7 and *Genesis Rabbah* 97, as quoted in Rubin and Kosman, "Clothing," 170–71.

38. Aune, *Revelation 6–16*, 897.

39. Brock, "Robe," 248–49; Aaron, "Shedding Light on God's Body in Rabbinic Midrashim," 303–9.

40. Augustine, *On Marriage and Concupiscence* 6, as quoted by Shuster, *Fall*, 65.

41. Moore, *Judaism*, Vol. 1, 479.

42. As Milne rightly points out, our everyday language is shaped by fallen experience (Milne, *Know the Truth*, 129).

43. Bechtel argues that the symbolic mode of communication has not been adequately considered (Bechtel, "Rethinking," 80).

there are variants, within this view, with specific reference to the "sin and fall" motif:

(1) The story is only a collection of metaphors, which points neither to the theology of the fall nor a historical fall. Westermann holds that the element of "before and after" should only be seen as stylistic and literary. In other words, the intention of the narrator is merely to present an event that caused the current human reality and not to make reference to a historical fall.[44] The shameless condition in Genesis 2:25 simply implies nothing more than the absence of shame in the garden.[45]

(2) The occurrence of nakedness and clothing between Genesis 2:25 and 3:7 should not be interpreted within the "sin and fall" motif; rather, a new motif should be in place. For example, Bechtel holds that there was no fall. Rather, Genesis 2:25 and 3:7 are metaphors for immaturity and maturity.[46] Alternatively, Baker intends to replace the "sin and fall" motif with "choice and consequences."[47]

(3) The metaphors of nakedness and clothing remain as metaphors operating within a myth, which has been heavily influenced by intertextuality. This allows an academic reader to argue for an interpretation as long as it achieves its scholarly aims, depending on the relevance and quality of the interest behind the interpretation.[48] This includes a possible argument for the theory of original sin and/or the "sin and fall" motif.

In this book, in order to be consistent with the "sin and fall" motif,[49] Genesis 3:7 must be associated with "sin," and 2:25 must be understood as a sinless condition,[50] just as the allusion to the Garden of Eden is found in the New Testament writings. However, within that "sin and fall" motif, a symbolic view of nakedness in Genesis 2:25 demands an adequate

44. Westermann, *Genesis*, 1984, 235.

45. Ibid., 236; Westermann is either inconsistent in this matter (his previously claim that there was no separation between the primordial state and the fallen state [235–39] is incoherent with his concepts of "loss" and "transgression" [250–51]), or he has not given a name to the different conditions in comparison to the eating of the fruit.

46. Bechtel, "Rethinking," 80; maturation of sexual differences (ibid., 84); sexual maturation (ibid., 88).

47. Baker, "The Myth of Man's 'Fall,'" 237.

48. Stordalen, *Echoes*, 75 (influenced particularly by Hans-Georg Gadamer and Paul Ricoeur).

49. Rad, *Genesis*, 101–2; Brueggemann, *Genesis*, 49.

50. Building upon the interpretation of Paul and Augustine (Wenham, "Original," 326).

argument for its function in the narrative. As the complex notion of shame is evident in the narrative, we argue that shameful nakedness is most plausible operating as an emotive metaphor,[51] for a cognitive concept of "sin."[52] In consistency with the cognitive metaphor theories,[53] it is probable that shame can be used as a metaphor for sin.[54] Nakedness, which represents shame, can take on the metaphorical function of shame, and at the same time function as an awkward consequence of a relational agreement. In this way, nakedness and clothing become valid metaphors for different spiritual states while explaining the origin of clothing and civilization.[55] Therefore, this symbolic interpretation can satisfy the historical elements within a symbolic view,[56] as well as the textual consideration of civilization and cultures,[57] and most importantly the traditional motif of "sin and fall."[58]

When the Eyes Were Opened: Nakedness and the "Sin and Fall" Motif

A number of scholars have attacked the "sin and fall" motif. Baker, for instance, argues that the "sin and fall" interpretation is dangerously composed of a careless analysis of the narrative, and therefore must be replaced by the "choice and consequences" motif.[59] However, the "choice

---

51. Emotive metaphors in this sense can be understood as an "inside view," providing the assumption of a shared experience or understanding (Boomershine, "The Structure of Narrative Rhetoric in Genesis 2–3," 118).

52. If in this context sin is understood as "brokenness," "awkwardness" or a "desire to heal/conceal" then such brokenness and innate division can be borrowed from shame. See also the discussion of shame and embarrassment (Wilcox) in chapter 3.

53. Or there is some form of association between these two concepts where nakedness finds favor as an emotive metaphor employed to describe an obscure notion that is unconscious (Cox, Evans, Coleridge and Mark Johnson, following Kant's *Imagination*.)

54. As indicated in chapter 3, although the Hebrew word for "shame" does not carry the meaning of "guilt" like our English word for shame (Wenham, *Genesis*, 71), it could function as a metaphor for sin, nonetheless, due to its ambivalent and ambiguous nature. We shall come back to this later in chapter 5.

55. Westermann, *Genesis*, 1984, 251–52.

56. Bechtel, "Rethinking," 80; Wenham, "Original," 317.

57. Westermann, *Genesis*, 1984, 235, 251–52; Wenham, *Genesis*, 72; Wallace, *Narrative*, 145.

58. Wenham, "Original," 321, 326.

59. Baker, "Myth," 237. Even if this rejection coheres with the wider biblical motif

and consequence" motif cannot explain why God also gave the Serpent a curse: the Serpent is punished for making no clear choice, and God appears to be arbitrary.[60] Alternatively, Williams suggests that the "sin and fall" motif is about the human instinct of blaming and judging.[61] He argues that Jews knew the reality of sin and guilt, but avoided abstracting formulas that considered all humans sinners because of Adam's disobedience, and thus, for Judaism through centuries the story is not of much use.[62] Williams might find support in Beattie who holds that the "sin and fall" motif is a specimen of *derash* in Rabbinic terminology which serves a homiletic purpose rather than exegesis.[63] However, this view only points to the fact that, if the "sin and fall" motif is dismissed, a perfect God can appear to have created humans evil and punished them for his own sport.[64]

Interestingly, Wolde criticizes the "sin and fall" motif for being human-centered and because through it people feel safer being guilty than remaining in uncertainty.[65] Although Wolde's point of human-centeredness might seem reasonable, it is only so in relation to the cultural scope and values of propriety in human relationships,[66] or the changing between prelapsarian and postlapsarian states.[67] Wolde's objection especially falls short when the "sin and fall" motif places emphasis, not on

---

"the righteous live by faith," it is unnecessary to discard the "sin and fall" motif.

60. A single-dimensional view might even show sympathy toward the Serpent for making no obvious choice (Beattie, "What is Genesis 2–3 About?," 9), but if a "choice and consequence" motif dismissed the "sin and fall" motif, it would fail to give an adequate explanation for the curses on the Serpent. Thus there is a need for alternative readings: a "literal" reading might interpret the story as offering a contrast "before and after" (Westermann, *Genesis*, 1984, 235), or "immaturity and maturity" (Bechtel, "Rethinking," 80–84, 88); whereas a "mythical" reading might take the story to mean an explanation for clothing (Wallace, *Narrative*, 145).

61. Williams, "Genesis 3," 278.

62. Ibid., 279.

63. Beattie, "Genesis," 8.

64. Ibid., 10.

65. Wolde, *Stories*, 73.

66. Chapter 2 of this book mentions Jewish nakedness in relation to God's presence, and nakedness between superiors and inferiors.

67. For an interpretation that focuses on the chance of immortality that Adam and Eve could have taken, see Barr, *The Garden of Eden and the Hope of Immortality*, 57.

human *conditions*, but on *relationships*, the latter being a reflection on a different condition.[68]

Surely, "sin and fall" is not only about the state of human morality, but also about the relationship between humans and God.[69] Therefore, this book argues that the metaphors of nakedness and clothing represent the conditions of the relationships: the narrative presentation of Adam and Eve reflects the more general relation between humans and God.[70] Put simply, shameful nakedness represents a broken relationship whereas clothing represents a restored relationship.[71] The inexplicability of a broken relationship can be conveyed through the predicament, awkwardness, fear and shame of the metaphor of nakedness and thus reinforce the revelatory nature of metaphors.[72] Rooted in the Israelite mores,[73] such metaphors of nakedness and clothing are both suitable and effective in the interpretation of the story. Other cultures, wherein nakedness and clothing do not have these symbolic values,[74] will certainly struggle to understand the point of the narrative.

The crucial question of our hypothesis is: how exactly does nakedness operate as a metaphor or a sign for corruption in the "sin and fall" motif? In order to answer this question, it is important to note that the narrator moves from an ambiguous and mysterious notion of primeval nakedness to a concept, which clearly has an anthropological dimension. This is important because, as we have discovered in chapter 2, anthropological shame and modesty is a process of culturally learned

68. The story tells us about the couple's human shortcoming in making choices and obedience. However, at a deeper level, the shortcomings that the couple finally committed originates from a lack of trust in their relationship with their Creator (Shelton, *Cross and Covenant*, 23–26).

69. Eve's inclination to the words of the Serpent—a created animal—rather than to the words of the Creator indicates that her choice has disqualified trust in her relationship with God (Augustine, *City*, 14:3, 14:11–13; Luther, *LW*, Vol. 1, 141, 167; Roberts, *Creation and Covenant*, 125).

70. If these metaphors are replaced by concepts of wholeness and brokenness, the point of the story will remain adequate without the cultural elements of shame and the origin of clothing.

71. This symbolic phenomenon only operates with an appropriate cultural antithesis.

72. Walker, "Grounding," 218.

73. Vawter, *On Genesis*, 76; a means of social control than act of shaming (Bechtel, "Rethinking," 84).

74. This happens if a culture does not hold nakedness as immodesty, or whose theory of origin of clothes disagrees with Genesis' concept of shame.

experience. The narrator's strategy of refocusing from the "mysterious" shameless nakedness to its anthropological nature creates an ambiguous relationship between the cultural shame of nakedness and the theological "knowledge of good and evil." That lack of clarity, we propose, makes it possible to intentionally foster a "sin and fall" motif with the concepts of guilt, shame and fear.

Surely, the text does not say the couple *saw*, but they *knew* or became aware of their nakedness,[75] as in realizing something they previously had not known. As we see, the eyes are opened but the ability to see is lost in the text; rather, it is replaced by the knowledge of good and evil.[76] The pairing of the epistemological "knowledge of good and evil" and the awareness of bodily nakedness,[77] poses questions to the distinctive mythical nature of the narrative: Are "the knowledge of good and evil" and "bodily awareness" separate or are they one and the same thing?[78] Does the knowledge of good and evil prompt the ability to have bodily awareness, and therefore bring about a sense of disappointment?[79] Or is it the "awareness of nakedness" that prompts the realization of good and evil?[80] The answer is rather complicated.

Starting with the tree of knowledge Beattie claims that it is problematic that God's *advice* becomes a solemn *prohibition*[81] from which the sense of "commandment" originates. However, this bold assumption is unfaithful to the text. Certainly, if it were the case that God only gave *advice*, it would be impossible to justify the notion of "death" as the consequence of a *neutral* choice. It is unlikely that any *advice* could be delivered in the solemn seriousness of death; rather, a *caution* or *commandment* would be more appropriate. Indeed, the divine warning (rather than advice) comes where the story reaches its turning point, for which the dis-

75. Wolde, *Stories*, 47. Metaphorically, it is the enlightening of the eyes (Clines, "Tree," 11).

76. It is important to note that the couple had been told about the concept of "knowledge of good and evil" without experiencing it (Gen 3:4).

77. Kass, *Wisdom*, 106.

78. Wallace refers to universal knowledge wherein cultural development, sex and civilization are included and applied (Wallace, *Narrative*, 128–29).

79. Adam and Eve realize how vulnerable they truly are (Towner, *Genesis*, 45); more dependent on God (Magonet, "Themes," 44); embarrassment replaced enjoyment (McCurley, *Genesis, Exodus, Leviticus, Numbers*, 23).

80. In Adar's view, having a moral awareness or knowing what is pleasant and what is unpleasant (Adar, *Genesis*, 25).

81. Beattie, "Genesis," 10.

ease of shame subsequently takes place as a testified consequence. This dis-ease makes it possible to interpret guilt and sin but most important of all the brokenness of the human-God relationship. This dis-ease requires the facilitation of a corresponding complex metaphor; therefore, the narrator inserts the emotive metaphor of nakedness, by creating a semantic pairing between the notion of shame and the other sense of metaphorical transparency hinting at guilt.[82]

While the notion of shame is a dominant issue in the narrative,[83] it is fear-based[84] and appears to be shared between a cultural-anthropological level and that of a spiritual level. There appear to be two layers of shame: the former arguably comes from a cultural and learned experience;[85] the latter is prompted by the knowledge of "good and evil," from which readers sense a profound inner division that is understood as guilt.[86]

On the one hand, as Wenham points out, the reactions of the couple suggests urgency and desperation because the innocent serenity is shattered.[87] Something so dark and negative has happened to their perception of nakedness that many scholars mistakenly identify it with the mystery of sex.[88] However, there is little evidence in the act of hiding that could support this cultural-anthropological notion of sexual shame.[89] At its best, this sense of shame carries an etiological sense of clothing and culture[90] or, as White suggests, the objective limits of gender differences.[91]

82. Chapter 5 will examine further this aspect of guilt and shame.

83. Davidson, *Genesis*, 41; McCurley mixes shame, guilt and nakedness together (*Proclamation*, 23); Schaeffer only focuses on fear and guilt, not shame (*Genesis in Space and Time*, 91).

84. Adam was afraid (not ashamed) of his nakedness Gen 3:10; Barr, *Immortality*, 63; cf. Gowan, *From Eden to Babel*, 56.

85. This is consistent with the understanding of the Israelite mores or an anthropological explanation of clothes and civilization, while operates as a metaphor in the mystery of the fall (Vawter, *Genesis*, 76; Westermann, *Genesis*, 1984, 235, 251–52; Wenham, *Genesis*, 72).

86. Rad, *Genesis*, 75; Brueggemann, *Genesis*, 1982, 49–50; Davidson, *Genesis*, 41.

87. Wenham, *Genesis*, 76.

88. Building upon Ehrlich (Ehrlich, *Randglossen zur hebräischen Bibel*, Vol. 1, 1908, Genesis, 1–256), and McKenzie (*Theological Studies*, Vol. 15, 1954, 562–63), see Speiser, *The Anchor Bible—Genesis: Introduction, Translation, and Notes*, 26.

89. Cassuto, *Genesis*, 137; Wallace, *Narrative*, 103.

90. Francis Landy, "The Song of Songs and the Garden of Eden," 524; language of genitals (ibid., 526); Wallace, *Narrative* (ibid., 145); Westermann, *Genesis*, 1984, 235, 251–52; Wenham, *Genesis*, 72.

91. White, *Narration*, 133.

On the other hand, the act of hiding includes a sense of shame that extends beyond the embarrassment of bodily nakedness. Adam and Eve hide among the trees although they are already wearing their aprons made of fig leaves.[92] The couple's subsequent blaming of each other also indicates: (1) a separation in their initial unity in addition to their disharmony with God and (2) guilt, or at least the fear of being responsible. Shuster helpfully points out that there is more to the act of hiding, because Adam and Eve must have known that their clothes were not enough to hide themselves from God[93] (i.e., bodily nakedness does not appear to be the only factor that causes shame). Furthermore, White proposes that the exact objects, which the couple try to cover up, are their foliages from the fig trees because those coverings represent a change in their consciousness.[94] However, it could be further argued that the new human condition—the state of knowing "good and evil"—is *not* what is being hidden. Rather, the brokenness of the relationship with God is that which Adam and Eve attempt to hide. Accordingly, Blocher emphasizes that the inner division, which makes the couple realize the limitation of being a creature, produces disappointment and shame.[95] Hence, an *inner* division adds to the *external* distance that has occurred between them and God.

In addition to the overlapping of shame and hiding, the semantic pairing is constructed with the help of an additional metaphorical phenomenon. On the one hand, shame causes a desire to be hidden and concealed. On the other hand, nakedness represents "transparency" and reality. The overlapping of the two can operate as a metaphor for the exposure of some shameful and indecent act previously committed.[96] This is coherent with the fact that the realization of nakedness was the immediate result of the act of transgression.[97] Consequently, the narrative employs a cultural concept of nakedness in order to convey a dual-indication of both *symptom*[98] and *effect*[99] concerning the new human

---

92. Morris, *Genesis*, 115.
93. Shuster, *Fall*, 62.
94. White, *Narration*, 139.
95. Blocher, *Beginning*, 174.
96. Rad, *Genesis*, 1972, 91.
97. Adar, *Genesis*, 22.
98. Ryken et al., *Imagery*, 780.
99. Barr, *Immortatlity*, 64–65.

condition. Therefore, by employing nakedness as a metaphor, the author seeks to interweave the anthropological-cultural values and the mystery of the "sin and fall" motif. The couple hide because they feel the dis-ease when thinking of facing God, for they know they have to give account for disobeying the command the moment they meet God again. It is reasonable to consider that nakedness hints at the dis-ease caused by the broken state of the couple's relationship with God. In other words, the "sin and fall" motif employs the dis-ease involved in the shame of nakedness in order to indicate a broken spiritual relationship via an act of disobedience.

In a nutshell, the pairing of *the awareness of bodily nakedness* and *the knowledge of good and evil* should be interpreted within the intention of the narrator's figure of speech. The mysterious nature of the realization of nakedness[100] in the narrative gives power and enables it to become a metaphor pointing to the mystery of the fall, particularly the dis-ease of brokenness. To human perception, especially within the boundary of the "sin and fall" motif, the taint of failure and defeat is irremovable and therefore the concept of nakedness is often considered a symbol of shame, vulnerability and sexuality. It cannot be overemphasized that this motif is crucial, especially for those interpretations that propose the state of being naked/or clothed before God,[101] or in a soteriological model.[102]

Vulnerability

While it remains in dispute that the notion of nakedness in Genesis marks the failure of Adam and Eve, most commentators agree that the curses following their actions result in severe consequences on the land and a life of suffering and hard labor.[103] In other words, the land on which human welfare depends[104] now produces thorns and thistles (Gen 3:17–18).[105]

---

100. For White, the narrator posits an inner "mechanism," "operating" independently to the human will (White, *Narration*, 137).

101. Kidner, *Genesis*, 69; Kessler and Deurloo, *Commentary on Genesis*, 56–57.

102. Purchas, "Sermon III. Nakedness. Gen. iii. 11: 'Who told thee that thou wast naked?'" 31–32; cf. Morris, *Genesis*, 115.

103. This is a "sentence" (Brueggemann, *Genesis*, 50). This curse on the fertility of the land is similar to that of Deut 33:13–15 (Cassuto, *Genesis*, 168); McCurley, *Proclamation*, 24; Blocher, *Beginning*, 183; Kidner, *Genesis*, 71–73.

104. Gowan, *Eden*, 59.

105. Thorns and thistles are eloquent signs of nature marking man's self-defeat and God's judgment (Kidner, *Genesis*, 72).

Consequently, human vulnerability increases[106] not only because of the shortage food supply but also because of the weariness of hard labor to sustain their existence.[107] Besides, the provision of garments of skin is commonly understood as an act of God's love and care in terms of their moral, physical,[108] or even relational needs.[109] The vulnerability of humanity at this point is consistent with both the anthropological approach and the Mosaic origin of clothes.[110] Therefore, the primary significance of the word "nakedness" is best reflected in the concepts of defenselessness and poverty,[111] which in turn lead to suffering and insecurity.

Basic Needs

Biblically, the naked body usually depicts a physical state of vulnerability and weakness or simply the imperfection, limitation, and the vulnerability of humans in general, departing life as they enter it—naked and helpless.[112] This is succinctly stated in Ecclesiastes 5:15[113] and Job 1:21,[114] both the rich and the poor will depart life empty-handed and naked. Accordingly, Aquinas rightly points out, "Man is mortal like the other animals."[115] There is as much universality with regard to human needs for food and clothes as there is for suffering in the harshness of temperatures and natural calamities.[116]

For this reason, nakedness and clothing are expressed very clearly through the theme of curses and blessings,[117] first to Adam and Eve, then

---

106. Kass, *Wisdom*, 106.

107. Skinner, *Genesis*, 83; McCurley, *Proclamation*, 24; Davidson, *Genesis*, 45; Kidner, *Genesis*, 73; with hard labor and pain (Adar, *Genesis*, 22).

108. Kidner, *Genesis*, 72; McCurley, *Proclamation*, 25.

109. Kessler and Deurloo, *Genesis*, 56–57.

110. See chapter 2.

111. Magonet, "Themes," 43.

112. Longman III, *The Book of Ecclesiastes*, 167; Hammond, *In Understanding Be Men*, 75–76.

113. Provan, *The NIV Application Commentary Ecclesiastes/Song of Songs*, 128; Longman III, *Ecclesiastes*, 167; Whybray, *Ecclesiastes*, 101; Crenshaw, *Ecclesiastes*, 123–24; Brown, *Ecclesiastes*, 61; Andersen, *Job*, 88; Janzen, *Job*, 44.

114. Job 1:21 (Atkinson, *The Message of Job*, 24).

115. Aquinas, *Summa Theologica*, Ia. lxxvi. 3, *ad* 2, in Gilby, *Aquinas Philosophical*, 211; cf. Farley, *Good*, 43, 72, 122; Augustine, *City*, 12:21, 366.

116. Farley, *Good*, 43, 72.

117. The similarity to ancient Near Eastern treaties has been pointed out by several

to the people of Israel. Deuteronomy 28:45–48 is a good example where, as scholars suggest,[118] ancient Israel understood its relationship to the Lord in this particular political model of treaty, i.e., nakedness in this context is found in a list of curses and punishments,[119] including hunger, thirst, dire poverty, and enslavement as a price for disobedience to God.[120] Brown explains that the covenant has two directions: (1) God's promised blessings (28:1–4), and (2) self-determined curse (28:15–58).[121] Mayes suggests that this list of curses was proclaimed for the acts of disobedience that were already committed.[122]

More importantly, as Weinfeld believes, the theme of "curses," which resonates through the imagery of nakedness, is associated with the dramatized version of nakedness depicted in Isaiah 20.[123] Besides the physical exposure to harm and pain, health risk and lack of sanitation, nakedness also involves the mental sense of disgust or shame in slavery, exploitation and suffering, as trophies of wars were normally treated.[124] The imagery of nakedness in Isaiah 20:3, according to many scholars, is a metaphorical warning for the vulnerability of defeat and captivity as a result of trusting in Egypt.[125] In this case, nakedness refers to exile,

---

scholars: McCarthy, *Treaty and Covenant*, 122–23; Hillers, *Treaty Curses and the O.T. Prophets*; Hillers, *Covenant*, 131–32; Hillers, *Lamentations*, 92–93; Weinfeld, *Deuteronomy and the Deuteronomic School*, 116–17, 129–30.

118. For typical Deuteronomic theology of curses and blessings, see Maxwell, *Deuteronomy*, 283. This list of curses draws on common ancient Near Eastern materials (Millar, "Living at the Place of Decision," 76).

119. Rad, *Deuteronomy*, 175; Mann, *Deuteronomy*, 148. This typical Near Eastern treaties tradition is seconded by Miller (*Deuteronomy*, 197).

120. Maxwell, *Deuteronomy*, 283, 287; Wright, *Deuteronomy*, 281. It is clear that this is "a relationship in which choices and acts determine outcomes and consequences" (Miller, *Deuteronomy*, 198).

121. Brown, *The Message of Deuteronomy*, 267; Jordan, *The Law of the Covenant*, 66–67; McCarthy, *Old Testament Covenant*, 13–30.

122. Mayes, *Deuteronomy*, 356.

123. Weinfeld, *Deuteronomy*, 136–37.

124. Buchanan, *A Critical and Exegetical Commentary on the Book of Isaiah: I-XXXIX*, 346; Oswalt, *The Book of Isaiah 1–39*, 384; Brueggemann, *Isaiah 1–39*, 167; Lemos, "Shame," 225–41; Goulder, *Isaiah as Liturgy*, 66.

125. It is probable that this is a totally naked state, probably not because of the same word *arôm* but the lack of a clear indication (Webb, *The Message of Isaiah*, 97–98); Herbert, *The Book of the Prophet Isaiah: Chapters 1–39*, 128; Clements, *Isaiah 1–39*, 175. The prophecy is not only about Israel but also about Egypt and Cush (Miscall, *Isaiah*, 59; Childs, *Isaiah*, 145).

Suffering and Grief

The vulnerability of humanity means they are subjected to suffering.[127] The metaphor of nakedness conveys the idea of suffering, and this is particularly linked to Christian suffering.[128] Basic needs such as lack of clothing,[129] shame and suffering are familiar to the Christian life.[130] Romans 8:35[131] and 2 Corinthians 11:27[132] express the same idea: Christians may be exposed to poverty and vulnerability, to suffering and disgrace and to very humble and lowly positions and circumstances.[133] The same term for "nakedness" is used in both of these passages,[134] and is translated from the Greek γυμνοτης, meaning lack of clothing or human deprivation.[135] Nakedness caused by poverty adds to the Christian life vulnerability and suffering.

Additionally, grief, pain and sorrow are expressions of suffering and vulnerability. At times "disrobing" is adopted to express all these

---

126. Brueggemann, *Isaiah 1-39*, 167; Blenkinsopp, *Isaiah 1-39*, 323; Delitzsch, *Prophecies of Isaiah*, 373-74; Conrad, *Reading Isaiah*, 119-20.

127. Kitwood, *What is Human?* 117-23. This is understood not only in terms of physical vulnerability but also psychological shame (Sherlock, *The Doctrine of Humanity*, 159-60).

128. Surely this is characterized in Paul's life (Cranfield, *Romans: A Short Commentary*, 211; Osborne, *Romans*, 228). Suffering might be considered separating Christians from the love of Christ (Murray, *The Epistle to the Romans*, 330).

129. Such needs pose questions to God's providence (cp. Matt 6:25-26) (Stott, *The Message of Romans*, 257).

130. Fitzmyer, *Romans*, 534.

131. Lack of clothing affects health and normal relationships (Dunn, *Romans 1-8*, 505).

132. Nakedness represents the lack of the ordinary necessities of life, see Harris, *Corinthians*, 810; Wilson, *2 Corinthians*, 149; Best, *Second Corinthians*, 112; Belleville, *2 Corinthians*, 293; Kruse, *The Second Epistle of Paul to the Corinthians*, 197; Fisher, *Commentary on 1 & 2 Corinthians*, 421.

133. Jewett, *Romans: A Commentary*, 547; Moo, *Romans 1-8*, 586; Stuhlmacher, *Paul's Letter to the Romans*, 140; Barnett, *The Second Epistle to the Corinthians*, 547; McCant, *2 Corinthians*, 138; Furnish, *II Corinthians*, 519.

134. Bultmann, *Corinthians*, 217.

135. Dunn, *Romans*, 505; Balz, "γυμνος, γυμνοτης," 265.

aspects.[136] Micah 1:8–10 expresses sorrow, grief, and pain through the act of walking about barefoot and naked,[137] even including mourning and rolling in the dust. These are the expressions not of ordinary grief and pain, but of that which seems to be so unbearable that there is no other way to show and express it other than through nakedness. At this emotional breakdown even basic needs are neglected. Therefore, nakedness becomes a tool for expressing mental and emotional needs, which are even greater or more urgent than the physical.

Social Justice

As nakedness signifies a lack of basic necessities, the metaphorical use of this concept conveys not only sufferings in general but also ethical and social injustice. For instance, in the book of Job nakedness was employed as a metaphor of violation of social justice (Job 24:7–10). In fact, Job was accused of stripping people naked and leaving them in desperation for clothes and essential daily needs (22:6).[138] In this case, nakedness is a metaphor for the vulnerability caused by exploitation and social injustice. If food and clothes are the basic rights of a human being, exploiting someone to the extreme of exposing their nakedness is a crime against justice: taking away the rights to protect one's life. "Man is nothing without clothes, not only because the poor will be deprived of their dearest possessions, but also in a general sense, because nudity leaves a person 'void, empty.'"[139]

Similarly, the theme of social justice is also expressed very clearly in the prophetic writings. Isaiah 58:7 speaks about the true form of fasting and worship that has to be as applicative as sharing food and clothing to the hungry and naked.[140] Furthermore, Ezekiel 18:7–16 highlights this theme on a level that is much more personal to an individual's righteousness and responsibility.[141] This is the very theme that Jesus emphasized. The parable of the sheep and goats in Matthew 25:36–43 uses the word

---

136. Disrobing was included in the customary mourning rites (2 Sam 3:31) (Anderson, *2 Samuel*, 62–63).

137. Kaiser, *Micah-Malachi*, 34; Knutson, "Naked," 480.

138. McKenna, *Job*, 158.

139. Vogelzang and Bekkum, "Meaning and Symbolism of Clothing in Ancient Near Eastern Texts," 273.

140. Watts, *Isaiah 34–66*, 275; Brueggemann, *Isaiah 40–66*, 189.

141. Duguid, *The NIV Application Commentary: Ezekiel*, 239.

γυμνοτης, translated from the Hebrew "*arôm*" in Genesis 3:7,[142] meaning nakedness.[143] Jesus expects the poor, the vulnerable, and the naked to be taken care of and to be clothed as a fulfilment of "justice and mercy" in the Old Testament (Isa 58:7; Mic 6:8).[144]

This particular theme of social justice has clearly and repeatedly been emphasized by the church fathers.[145] On the one hand, the effect of that salvation urges an outward expression of the fruits of righteousness and repentance[146] reflecting a representative model of atonement: as Christ clothes us when we are naked, we clothe the needy.[147] Not doing so results in leaving Christ lying "at the door naked and dying."[148] On the other hand, another expression of Christian philanthropy proposes that social justice is not the result but the cause of salvation. For example, Cyprian of Carthage instructs: "Let us give clothes to Christ on earth so that we may receive the clothing of heaven."[149] "Let us give to Christ earthly garments, that we may receive heavenly raiment; let us give food and drink of this world, that we may come with Abraham, and Isaac, and Jacob to the heavenly banquet."[150]

Cyprian's philanthropy and theology appear to have brought the act of "clothing the naked" to the level of redemption,[151] or the subsequent

142. Oepke, "γυμνος, γυμνοτης, γυμναζω, γυμνασια," 773–76; for an extended study on the word *arôm* and *gymnos* see Rockel, "The Bible, Society and Nudity." Unfortunately, at the time this research completed, Rockel's study had been partly removed.

143. The NIV changes the meaning into "needed clothes." Nakedness here is listed among other needs (Hagner, *Matthew 14–28*, 743–44; Keener, *Matthew*, 1997, 361–62).

144. Although as Green points out, there is a danger to limit the gospel to "social action" (Green, *Matthew*, 262), it is necessary to bring on board the echo of Old Testament social justice (France, *The Gospel according to Matthew*, 357; Harman, *Isaiah*, 386; Childs, *Isaiah*, 478; Brueggemann, *Isaiah 40–66*, 189; Kaiser, *Micah–Malachi*, 72–73; Achtemeier, *Minor Prophets I*, 353).

145. Francis of Asisi sets an excellent example for this lifestyle of alms giving (Trexler, *Father*, 4, 42–43). Augustine instructed that Christians should clothe the naked to be clothed by Christ with the "wedding garments" (*NPNF1-6*, 408).

146. Wesley, *Sermons on Several Occasions*, Sermon 33, 51–56; Sermon 43, 219–23.

147. Augustine puts it the other way round (*NPNF1-6*, 408).

148. Jerome, in *NPNF2-6*, 36: Letter XXII.

149. Cyprian of Carthage, in Davies, *Born to New Life*, 97.

150. Cyprian, *ANCL8-2*, 19.

151. Cyprian, *De Lapsis and De Ecclesiae Catholicae Unitate*, 51–53, 99: to show penance is to follow the naked Christ, to shine light in good works.

cleansing of sins.[152] In short, the metaphors of nakedness and clothing are highly important for an ethic of social justice, for they express strongly the contrast between the desperation of poverty and social welfare.

Defeat

Since nakedness is understood as vulnerability, it is used to portray the defenseless position of defeat. However, while carrying almost a similar expression of vulnerability in grief, or the "basic physical needs" in poverty, the notion of nakedness in defeat expresses a greater need—the urgent need for safety and dignity. While the context of Amos 2:16 is about the defeat of Israel's army, the case of defeat in 1 Samuel 19:20–24[153] portrays a rather embarrassing captivation. Here, Saul's nakedness was a sign of his defeat before God's sovereignty, and this is different from the religious extreme of self-abasement or self-renunciation.[154] It is clear that the Spirit of God prevented Saul's attack and had him captured and deposed[155] although some say he was subordinate to the prophet and to God.[156]

Additionally, an interesting incident of defeat is found in Acts 19:16, where some Jewish magicians were attacked, humiliated, beaten, and stripped naked by the very spirits they tried to exorcize.[157] The word "naked" in this passage conveys the immediate humiliation, which is the result of a careless approach to exorcism. It indicates a desperation and urgency for safety rather than dignity and decency.[158] It also implies a sense of shame for having done something improperly.

The story of the disciple "fleeing-naked" stands out in this theme of defeat. Mark 14:50–52 is the only account of the story in the Bible where a young disciple of Jesus ran off naked, leaving his clothes behind as Jesus' enemies came to seize him. Commentators give much space and

---

152. Cyprian, *ANCL13-2*, 2: The treatise VIII—On work and alms; Prov 16:6.

153. Evans, *1 & 2 Samuel*, 90–91.

154. See chapter 2.

155. Chafin, *1 & 2 Samuel*, 148–49; Brueggemann, *First and Second Samuel*, 145–46.

156. Robinson, *1 & 2 Samuel*, 109; Johnson, "Nakedness as a form of Symbolic Expression in the Old Testament."

157. Walaskay, *Acts*, 180.

158. The phrase employed by Taylor is "desperation in the extreme" (Taylor, *The Gospel according to St. Mark*, 561).

attention to the identity of this young disciple as well as the purpose and relevance of this story.[159] However, as we examine the use of nudity in this passage we can agree that the young man's identity is no more important than the fact that he ran off naked.

Brooks suggests that Mark might have wanted to associate the shame in nakedness with anyone who abandoned Jesus.[160] This argument makes a lot of sense given the context of the arrest of Jesus. Yet, is there more to it? Edwards emphasizes the abandonment of the disciples by making a connection with Amos 2:16, which we have mentioned above.[161] We can understand Edwards' intention, but perhaps the only common link between these two contexts is the idea of running for one's life. Wright, on the other hand, links this detail to the story of Adam and Eve.[162] But again, perhaps the story in Mark can only relate, to some extent, to the fear and desperation mentioned in the Garden of Eden.

In the case of the disciples, Jesus asked for them not to be arrested (John 18:8–9). The fear that overwhelmed the disciples was not because they had done something wrong but for the pain of persecution. Mark's gospel records that they could not, and were not allowed to defend Jesus (John 18:10–11), and had to follow from a distance (John 18:15). The incident was full of confusion, fear, and hesitation and therefore certain commentator suggests that it is unnecessary to spiritualize the question of nudity here.[163] Yet, there are good reasons for the occurrence of such an unusual detail.[164] Schweizer redirects us to the main point of the story: the arrest of Jesus. "The isolation of the Son of Man is absolute. Even the brief incident concerning the young man simply intensified the atmosphere, which seems to say, 'save yourself if you can.'"[165]

Having looked at various viewpoints it is probable that nudity in this incident plays a part in the story of Jesus' arrest, especially in

---

159. See detailed discussions in Haren, "The Naked Young Man," 525–31; Hatton, "Mark's Naked Disciple," 35–48; Jackson, "Why the Youth Shed His Cloak and Fled Naked," 273–89.

160. Brooks, *Mark*, 239.

161. Edwards, *The Gospel according to Mark*, 441.

162. Wright, *Mark for Everyone*, 200.

163. Cole, *Mark*, 302.

164. At least two reasons can be given: (1) Jews considered public nakedness unpleasant, and (2) the contrast of *naked to follow the Naked Christ* and *naked running away from Christ*.

165. Schweizer, *The Good News according to Mark*, 319.

consideration of the vulnerability and helplessness of the disciple who runs away naked. This state of defeat reflects exactly what Jesus meant by "scattered sheep without a shepherd" in Matthew 26:31.[166] Fleddermann makes a strong point when, by looking at the verb *skandalizein*, he characterizes the flight of the disciple as unbelief, in contrast to Jesus' acceptance of God's will.[167]

Sexual Metaphors and Euphemism

Sexual connotations are most obviously attached to the concept of nakedness.[168] In particular, they are often associated with the dialogue between nakedness and clothing, namely semi-nakedness.[169] Boman points out the difference between the Hebrew and the Greek candor: while the Hebrews tend to talk about nakedness, but do not show it, the Greeks tend to show nakedness but do not talk about it.[170] As highlighted in chapter 2, the tradition of the Christian West understands nakedness as sexual and lustful and therefore the concept of nakedness could be pushed to the extreme of evil lust and wickedness. For example, the female nude body, especially the vagina, is interpreted as lust and readiness for collaboration with the devil.[171] However, such extremities of hostility against nakedness are rooted in the simplest employment of nakedness as a euphemism for sexual immoralities. In the nature of the semantics and semiotics of the biblical texts, hostile attitudes toward nakedness, rather than what nakedness stands for, are simply the products of presumptuous misjudgment.

Sexual Law in Leviticus

In Leviticus 18:6–23, Moses told the Israelites not to uncover the nakedness of a close relative or member of the same family, a euphemism for incestuous relations.[172] Far from interpreting this euphemism of nakedness

---

166. Fleddermann, "The Flight of a Naked Young Man," 416.

167. Ibid., 416, building upon Schenke (*Studien zur Passionsgeschichte des Markus: Tradition und Redaktion in Markus 14, 1–42, 401–4*).

168. The word "naked" in Leviticus is used purely with sexual connotation (Seevers, "עָרָה," 527–28).

169. Watson, *Agape, Eros, Gender*, chapter 2; Gorham and Leal, "Naturism," 7.

170. Boman, *Hebrew Thought Compared with Greek*, 77–84.

171. Polinska, "Dangerous," 51: Prov 30:15–16.

172. Sherwood, *Studies in Hebrew narrative & Poetry*, 73; Tidball, *Leviticus*,

in the light of the honor/shame motif and a cultural educative process,[173] Bonar points out that these moral obligations are not ceremonial precepts, but an amplification of the seventh commandment.[174] The phrase "uncovering nakedness" is understood as sexual intercourse.[175] The term ערוה means nakedness and is a technical term for the genitals.[176] However, it is noteworthy that there is a great variety of interpretations for this euphemism depending on whose nakedness,[177] family kinship,[178] or other cultural variations.[179]

People who committed these sexual transgressions would be cut off from the community, or put to death (Lev 18:25–29; 20:23–24).[180] Therefore, if sexual abominations always provoke horrific punishments there is little need to explain why euphemisms, such as nakedness, cannot escape condemnation and hostility.

Sexual Symbolism in Prophecies[181]

As nakedness is employed as a euphemism for sex, it also occurs in prophetic words that use the metaphor of adultery or sexual debauchery.

220–21; Milgrom, *Leviticus 17–22*, 1536–37; Hartley, *Leviticus*, 294; Rushdoony, *The Institutes of Biblical Law*, 368–69; Johnson, "The Law of Moses, Nakedness, Worship and Close Relatives."

173. Gerstenberger, *Leviticus: A Commentary*, 250.

174. Bonar, *Commentary on Leviticus*, 330.

175. Gerstenberger, *Leviticus*, 247–48; Demarest, *Leviticus*, 195–97; Wenham, *Book of Leviticus*, 253–54; uncovering nakedness is a euphemism for sexual intercourse, (chapter 19) (Balentine, *Interpretation Leviticus*, 155–56); as "copulate" in Milgrom, *Leviticus 17–22*, 1534.

176. Hartley, *Leviticus*, 282n.6.d. Since there is no biblical term for genitals, the word 'erwâ applies to both sexes, Milgrom, *Leviticus*, 2000, 1534.

177. Most clearly in Leviticus 18 (Milgrom, *Leviticus*, 2000, 1536–45; Ellens, *Women in the Sex Texts of Leviticus and Deuteronomy*, 81–84).

178. Nakedness also means "flesh and blood" or "one flesh" (Wenham, *Leviticus*, 255); Snaith, *Leviticus and Numbers*, 123.

179. For example, in the Talmudic tradition nakedness can refer to forbidden marriages, "Masseketh Soferim," 253–54, chapter 9: rule 8.

180. Noth, *Leviticus*, 134; Balentine, *Leviticus*, 156; *Mishnah Sanhedrin*, 7:4 (Neusner, *The Mishnah*, 596–97).

181. Chapter 5 will explore more fully the notion of "porno-prophet." Weems, *Battered Love*, 60; Brownlee, *Ezekiel*, 236; Ogilvie, *Hosea, Joel, Amos, Obadiah, Jonah*, 46; and Renkema, *Lamentations*, 134.

Habakkuk 2:15 is an excellent example of this.[182] Roberts further emphasizes that Habakkuk's metaphor exposes the brutality of imperialistic conquest that strips away the dignity of the conquered for the conqueror's selfish and insatiable gratification.[183] It is clear in the text that this vulgar form of entertainment at the expense of others' nakedness is associated with sexual impurity and the degradation of the body as a result of drunkenness.[184] However, while it is suggested that nakedness is associated with drunkenness and sexual impurity,[185] Roberts emphasizes further that the metaphor might have been rooted in the actual practice of leading naked war prisoners, as depicted in Isaiah 20:4 and 2 Chronicles 28:15, due to the subsequent judgmental degradation.[186]

Shame Versus Dignity

In the Bible, the concept of nakedness is associated with shame while clothing is associated with dignity and respect.[187] This reflects the culture of ancient Near East where nakedness can be taken as a loss of identity: man is nothing without clothes.[188] The development of this convention between the shame of nakedness and the dignity of clothing has progressed from the fall of Adam to the degradation and humiliation of Noah, to the Old Testament prophetic depiction of Israel as a harlot.[189] We now explore the development between the shame of nakedness and the degradation of stripping clothes.

---

182. Kaiser, *Micah–Malachi*, 175.

183. Roberts, *Nahum, Habakkuk, and Zephaniah*, 124.

184. Robertson, *The Books of Nahum, Habakkuk, and Zephaniah*, 201. Robertson suggested here a homosexual act based on Ham's story in Gen 9:21 and Lev 20:17–19 (ibid., 201–2).

185. Ward, "A Critical and Exegetical Commentary on Hababkkuk," 17; Smith, *Micah–Malachi*, 111; and Haak, *Habakkuk*, 70.

186. Roberts, *Habakkuk*, 124; Keil and Delitzsch, *Commentary on the Old Testament, Vol.7 Isaiah (1866)*, 546; McKenna, *Isaiah 40–66*, 193; Johnson, "Nakedness as Judgement."

187. However, covering and taking away shame are not the same thing (Gorham and Leal, "Naturism," 9).

188. Vogelzang and Bekkum, "Symbolism," 273; shame in death (Pattison, *Shame*, 311–12).

189. Singgih, "Let Me Not be Put to Shame," 80–81.

Humiliation

Scholars suggest that mutilating the enemies' bodies was a common wartime practice in the ancient Near East,[190] with a specific intention of bringing dishonor.[191] For instance, the story in 2 Samuel 10:4 records that Hanun, an Ammonite king, brought shame and indignity to David's messengers by exposing their buttocks and shaving half of their beards. It is important to note that the shame in this story is not only about semi-nakedness but also about the beard, the garment, and the act of sending away. Being inflicted as such is equal to being forced into a lower status.[192] Chapman even suggests that this was an act of feminization.[193] Consequently, from the perspective of politics and warfare, nakedness is a form of humiliation and affliction.

However, this political affliction through nakedness is not consistent with the Hebrew culture, first due to the association between nakedness and superiority, and secondly in light of the Law of Moses. For instance, in the story of 1 Samuel 24:4, David respected the superiority of king Saul, the anointed; and as a result, although Saul was David's political enemy, he was saved from David because of his "righteous body."[194] Similarly, the story of the battle between Israel and Judah in 2 Chronicles 28 also points to an inconsistency of this inflicting nakedness. Clearly, Israel won the battle but the prophet Oded convicted the people of Israel to change their attitude toward their countrymen from Judah. Those "prisoners" and "trophies of war," previously humiliated by nakedness,[195] were then clothed, taken care of, nursed and fed. The political infliction of nakedness is not to be practiced among the people of God. Surely, war, slavery and insult were never meant to exist among the people whom God had set free and to whom God gave human dignity.[196]

---

190. Lemos, "Shame," 225–41; Olyan, "Honor, Shame, and Covenant Relations in Ancient Israel and Its Environment," 201–18; Hobbs, "Reflections on Honor, Shame, and Covenant Relations," 501–20.

191. Olyan, "Covenant," 213n.37. Clearly, this mutilation and degradation does not exclusively belong to one culture. We will explore later how the Roman crucifixion inflicted its victims with shame (McIlroy, "Honour and Shame," 3).

192. Lemos, "Shame," 233.

193. Chapman, *The Gendered Language of Warfare in the Israel-Assyrian Encounter*, 220. Also see the theme of social and gender hierarchy in chapter 1 of this book.

194. Satlow, "Constructions," 439–40.

195. Johnstone, *1 & 2 Chronicles*, 181.

196. Durham, *Exodus*, 196–98; Fretheim, *Exodus*, 142–46.

Disrespect

The concept of human dignity is present not only in the story of Adam and Eve but also in Noah's ambiguous story.[197] Genesis 9:20–23 records that Noah planted a vineyard, got drunk, and exposed his nudity in his own tent. His son Ham saw his nakedness but the result was that Ham's children, Canaan, were cursed. Noah's other sons Shem and Japheth, who respectfully covered his nakedness, were blessed for doing so. However, there are questions that need answers: What did Ham really do?[198] Why did his actions result in such a terrible curse? Why were Ham's children cursed and not Ham himself?[199] And, why was the story included in the Bible at all?[200]

To some Rabbis, the interpretation of this passage is linked to Leviticus 18:7–8: Ham must have done something of a sexual nature (penetrated or emasculated) rather than just seeing Noah's nakedness.[201] Some interpret Ham's sin as "castration, sodomy, or incest (intercourse with Noah's wife)."[202] However, while the story appears to carry such ambiguous sexual connotations, there is no clarity with regards to the evidence for Ham's sin. Bible commentators and interpreters can only provide various additional comments without relying on explicit evidence.[203]

Obviously there is no evidence in this text indicating that Ham "delighted" or "reproached laughing" or "took pleasure" in Noah's nakedness. In fact, the text does not mention any explicit sexual or moral

---

197. For a detailed discussions, see Bergsma and Hahn, "Noah's Nakedness and the Curse on Canaan (Genesis 9:20–27)," 25–40; Robertson, "Current Critical Questions Concerning the 'Curses of Ham' (Gen 9:20–27)," 177–88; Steinmetz, "Vineyard, Farm, and Garden," 193–207.

198. Especially in Bergsma and Hahn, "Nakedness," 25–40.

199. Robertson, "Current," 180. Bassett ("Noah's Nakedness and the Curse of Canaan a Case of Incest?" 235) suggests that "to see a man's nakedness" is to have sexual relations with his wife, and thus Canaan is the result of the incest between Ham and Noah's wife.

200. For a comparative study on the motifs of sin in the stories of the Garden of Eden, Cain and Abel and Noah, see Steinmetz, "Vineyard," 197–99.

201. Satlow, "Constructions," 437–38; Ross, *Holiness to the Lord*, 343–44.

202. Gowen, *Genesis 1–11*, 109; Bassett, "Incest," 234–35. It is difficult to accept the view of incest, because Ham does not need to wait for Noah to get drunk and it would not make sense when the other two brothers cover their father's nakedness (ibid., 237).

203. For example, Calvin suggests Ham must have had a perverse attitude toward his father's nakedness, Calvin, *CC—Genesis*, Vol. 1, 302; Briscoe, *Genesis*, 103. However, such oral tradition is not traceable (Bassett, "Incest," 232–37).

dimensions. Interestingly, Speiser argues that the term *pudenda* relates to exposure and does not necessarily imply sexual offenses.[204]

Therefore, is there an alternative interpretation of this text? Perhaps, in terms of cultural propriety, especially within the Hebrew system of respect, we can agree with Gowen that seeing someone naked could be one of the most extreme ways to dishonor that person.[205] However, in order to give this text a fair interpretation we need to draw attention to other details. For example, the narrative records that Ham saw his father's nakedness, but remains silent regarding why Ham turned up at his father's tent; neither does it provide any hint as to whether this was merely an accident.[206] Gowen suggests that Noah probably deserves part of the blame because of his uncontrollable behavior;[207] but although he deserves being blamed for abusing wine, he should not be blamed for being naked in his own tent—his private space. Assuming that Ham accidentally turned up at his father's tent[208] the question should not only be "What wrong did he do?" but also "What did he fail to do?" Kass suggests that without disturbing Noah, Ham engages in an act of patricide and incest just by viewing and telling.[209] However, this interpretation can be established further within a cultural understanding of a son's duty in helping his drunken father.[210]

Accordingly, the appropriate explanation for this incident should be founded within the context of family relation. The narrative should be seen as an example of moral code pointing toward a pattern of living with boundaries and definitions for family, respect, and appropriateness in social conduct.[211] Ham saw his father's nakedness but did nothing to relieve the shameful condition he was in due to his drunkenness.

204. Speiser, *Genesis*, 61.

205. Gowen, *Genesis 1–11*, 108.

206. Kass, *Wisdom*, 206.

207. Gowen, *Genesis 1–11*, 108.

208. Eilberg-Schwartz stresses that a son's trespassing upon the spot where the nakedness of his father has been exposed is equal to uncovering his nakedness (Eilberg-Schwartz, *The Savage in Judaism*, 171). However, if Ham's actions were intentional, there is no need for his brother's to intrude into the tent again, even simply to cover Noah's nakedness.

209. Kass, *Wisdom*, 204–5.

210. Westermann, *Genesis*, 69; Pritchard, *Ancient Near Eastern Texts*, 150; Rogerson, *Genesis 1–11*, 72.

211. See also how ethnic hatred could be generated in some interpretations of the curse on Ham (Gowen, *Genesis 1–11*, 110).

The clear contrast between his actions and his brothers' should be interpreted as carrying an educative nature, purposefully aiming at depicting a better family, as Westermann sums up most adequately: "The curse of Canaan makes sense if we remember what is at stake: a continuity between generations that was vital for the world. This continuity demanded an unbroken chain of tradition from one generation to the next. The chain could remain unbroken only if those departing were respected by those arriving. Respect for elders was an imperative for group self-preservation. Here Noah represents the group. This is why he curses his son for disrespect."[212]

Noah's story can be understood as a cultural statement of family relation or how shame and honor operate with kinship. Along with other themes such as infliction, war, humiliation, incest, and sexual sins, nakedness is a symbol that is relevant to human dignity, the system of shame and respect within cultural propriety and the family-kinship relation. Surely, the word "naked/nakedness" might appear in different places and narratives but human relation is an important underlying motif.

Summary and Conclusion

The biblical concept of nakedness is most appropriately categorized into three themes despite its complex and random development. Theme (1) *shame* is fundamental and foundational. It is first expressed at the beginning of the postlapsarian notion of nakedness in Genesis, alongside fear and an understated notion of guilt. Theme one is the foundation for theme (2) *vulnerability*. In contrast to prelapsarian nakedness, which is described as innocent and good, postlapsarian nakedness is seen as the fruit of disobedience, failure, sinfulness, and evil. The vulnerability of the first human couple can be understood in the total exposure of sin and failure before the gaze of God. The couple's shame, which urged them to hide behind the covering of fig leaves, expresses vulnerability. Alternatively, when a secret is laid bare, it becomes naked to the awareness of the audience. Furthermore, as a result of the expulsion out of Eden, nakedness not only marks the shame of the first couple's self-defeat but also exposes true human vulnerability to the harsh reality of the environment. More importantly, the notion of shame in nakedness that hints toward sin also connotes a *spiritual* vulnerability—the distortion of sin. Consequently, under the effect of sin, sexuality and nakedness also bear

---

212. Westermann, *Genesis*, 1988, 69.

an ineradicable remark of lust and immorality,[213] thus forming theme (3) *sexuality*. Nakedness, body, and sexuality are interlinked; therefore, to speak about the naked anatomy is to speak about the procreative function of the body.[214] Sexual carnal pleasure and lust have also been prevalent interpretations of the fall.[215] Subsequently, the condemnation of sexual lust becomes more and more vigorous especially in prophetic interpretation. The imagery of an adulterous woman is used to portray the unfaithfulness of Israel,[216] and to speak of the kind of punishment and shame that God reserves for those who indulge in sin.[217] Furthermore, the interweaving of the three themes *shame, vulnerability*, and *sexuality* gives power to the message that employs the metaphor of nakedness. The power of abnormal imageries draws the attention of the audience, while at the same time, the cultural abhorrence for nakedness creates a "tension" that the message intends to achieve.

However, the employment of the metaphor of nakedness does not stop here. It appears that a turn of culture and social philosophy can contribute enormously to the use of this concept. Crossing the physical and mental boundaries, nakedness and its connotation of vulnerability were adopted to figuratively address the spiritual state after death,[218] or to construct an understanding of what will happen at the *parousia*.[219] Chapter 5 will give a better exposition of these theological topics.

---

213. Augustine, *City*, 47–55.

214. Wilkinson, "The Body in the Old Testament," 209.

215. Starting with Augustine, *City*, 54–55; Lane, "Lust," 21–35.

216. Setel, "Prophets and Pornography," 92; Motyer, *Isaiah*, 355; Ogilvie, *Hosea*, 134.

217. Guest, "Hiding behind the Naked Women in Lamentations," 413–45; Renkema, *Lamentations*, 134; Dijk-Hemmes, "The Metaphorization of Woman in Prophetic Speech," 162–70; Eslinger, "Perception," 145–69.

218. 2 Cor 5:3–4; Cassidy, "Paul's Attitude to Death in 2 Corinthians 5:1–10," 215–17; Craig, "Paul's Dilemma in 2 Corinthians 5:1–10," 145–47; Hettlinger, "2 Corinthians 5:1–10," 180; Osei-Bonsu, "Does 2 Cor. 5:1–10 Teach the Reception of the Resurrection Body at the Moment of Death?" 89–90.

219. Revelation 16:15; Aune, *Revelation 17–22*, 897–99; Hemer, *The Letters to the Seven Churches of Asia*, 191, 201; Thomas, *Revelation 1–7*, 312–15; Wall, *Revelation*, 209.

5

The Antithesis of Nakedness and Clothing in Theology and Liturgy

THIS CHAPTER SEEKS TO analyze and assess the value and significance of the antithesis of nakedness and clothing, particularly in theological discourses.[1] We will start with the "sin and fall" motif, wherein the concept of nakedness prompts new hermeneutical and theological questions concerning original sin, with particular regard to the metaphorical role of nakedness in relation to the "brokenness" or "lack of wholeness" in the concepts of sin and shame. Subsequently, the contrast between nakedness and clothing (emptiness, vulnerability and shame versus protection and wealth) suggests a possible dialogue that could facilitate a prophetic and covenantal theology using relational metaphors. We shall examine the theological significance of nakedness and clothing in a covenantal relationship with specific reference to the concepts of curses and blessing. Additionally, the antithesis of nakedness and clothing also functions metaphorically in eschatology and the notion of the intermediate state. Therefore, we will also explore the particular relationship between philosophy and biblical interpretation and how that elucidates Paul's intention of using the concept of nakedness to depict his theological point. Finally, we shall examine the ritual symbols of nakedness and clothing in the early centuries Christian baptism and how the metaphors of na-

---

1. This chapter will pay special attention to the metaphorical value of nakedness and clothing. See Stordalen, *Echoes*, 52; Macky, *Centrality*, 87–114; Caird, *The Language and Imagery of the Bible*, 224; Black, *Models*, 237, who builds upon Richards, *Rhetoric*, 89–138.

kedness and clothing became theologically interwoven in this aspect of liturgy.

Nakedness, Shame, and the Original Sin

Following from the previous semantic discussion in chapter 3 and the biblical discussion in chapter 4, this section focuses on the relationship between the realization of nakedness and shame, and the concept of "original sin" proposed by the "sin and fall" motif of creation theology.[2] The central question is: how far can the metaphors of nakedness and clothing support the "sin and fall" motif, with particular reference to hamartological implications?

In the fall narrative, the immediate result of disobedience is not the state of nakedness but the realization of it, and the induced feelings of shame, which is clearly indicated by the desperation and fear of the couple: nakedness is unpleasant and there is a need for a defense.[3] At this point in the narrative there is a tension: on the one hand, the major theological focus is on the relationship between the couple and God, thus "guilt and shame," which appear to be associated with nakedness, are arguably a demonstration of sin. On the other hand, nakedness is one of the keys to the mythos of the Eden story;[4] without which the story cannot point to a relationship between humanity and God. Therefore, there must be an appropriate interpretation of the interplay between nakedness and clothing in the light of sin and shame, which can make sense in this "relational" story.

The Link between Nakedness, Sin, and Shame

The three elements: nakedness, shame, and sin are closely connected in a clear circle: the eating (actualization of the lack of trust in God's command) is equal to sin, which causes the awareness of nakedness and the subsequent unpleasant sense of "shame," which points to what had

---

2. Blocher, *Original Sin*, 16–17; Rad, *Genesis*, 75; and to some extent chronological time and proto-history (Wenham, "Original," 312, 318–21). This is to be distinguished from the view which holds that we cannot speak of a historical fall because there was never a time when humankind had fellowship with God (Westermann, *Genesis*, 1984, 53).

3. Wenham, *Genesis*, 76; Gowan, *Eden*, 50, 56; clothing therefore become the first defense.

4. Brichto, *Names*, 83.

previously been good,[5] and hence, the resulting "guilt" of sin.[6] Therefore, the element of shame in nakedness must have been the result of sin, because sin (the act of eating the fruit) brings about the change in the human mind.[7] If sin had not been carried out through the act of eating, the couple would have remained ignorant of their nakedness and would not have hidden away for fear of breaking God's command. In fact, as Kierkegaard points out, this act of eating is an actualization of a lust to violate the command,[8] and this lust could be interpreted as a failure of trust in the couple's relationship with God. The question is then, what actually brought about the broken condition of the human-God relationship: was it sin or was it just a lack of trust?

Much has been said on this notion of trust, but is mainly associated with the question why God withheld the knowledge of good and evil from the couple.[9] After all, what was so bad about the knowledge of good and evil? Barr suggests that this knowledge of good and evil helps Adam and Eve perceive their nakedness,[10] and therefore brings about

---

5. Gregory of Nyssa thought that humankind is made of a hybrid mixture of earthly and divine, so that they could enjoy the earthly sensuality yet at the same time being created in God's likeness and having the knowledge of the Giver. Different from the animals, which do not have the ability to apprehend the higher and therefore only seek for sensual goods, humans are not determined by their bodily appetites. Smith, "The Body of Paradise and the Body of the Resurrection," 209–11; Alternatively, Augustine suggests that Adam was free from physical ills (Wenham, "Original," 309).

6. Wenham, *Genesis*, 76.

7. Wolde, *Stories*, 47.

8. Kierkegaard, *The Concept of Anxiety*, 40–41.

9. At this point in this book, the "knowledge of good and evil" refers to the postlapsarian knowledge after the eating of the fruit, which causes Adam and Eve to experience their nakedness in a different and uneasy state. Epistemologically, this "knowledge of good and evil" is realized through the dis-ease of shame in nakedness and is to be distinguished from that of Gen 3:4. This "knowledge of good and evil" is achieved through a conscious choice to be "autonomous," which the self, out of independence and freewill, discards God's command with a view to acquire the knowledge through eating the fruit (hence playing God's role in choosing its own destiny despite the warning of fatal consequence). At the realization of shame in nakedness, the distinction between good and evil, on the one hand, reveals the evil consequence of the choice for autonomy and, on the other hand, reveals the Ultimate Good (God), and that the prohibition was the boundary that protected the created humanity in his perfect and good intention. In this way, postlapsarian "knowledge of good and evil" is a gateway to the realization of sin and evilness in all things that are other than God and autonomous entities that refuse to be dependent on God.

10. Barr, *Immortality*, 11; Shuster, *Fall*, 68.

propriety,[11] but God wanted to keep the knowledge and eternal life for himself.[12] Similarly, Wolde suggests that God's prevention makes sense because it is too much of a good thing for humans to keep multiplying and at the same time living forever.[13] However, these interpretations appear to give the precarious impression that the couple was only benefiting from the thinking function of their minds,[14] and the freedom they were given, without necessarily sinning against God with an intention. In this view, God is put in a bad light: it was the Creator who had not trust humans with the knowledge of good and evil in the first place. There is a dangerous assumption here that there is equality between the parties in the human-God relationship. Is this lack of trust then the root of sin?

Surely the notion of trust reveals a conscious human choice, which is enacted in the breaching of the given command. Therefore, the "sin and fall" motif makes sense of the narrative when sin is understood as the completion of doubt and lack of trust in God. Lack of trust does not directly lead to a broken relationship, the choice to linger and prolong that distrust does. In the light of this understanding, the story makes sense relationally: the couple did not want to face God because they should have had a better comprehension of the trustworthiness of their previous human-God relationship.

Vawter suggests that the shame Adam and Eve felt has nothing to do with sin because shame is not in itself necessarily a mark or consequence of personal sin.[15] Similarly, Barr suggests that Adam's act of hiding is associated, not with guilt, but with the embarrassment of his nakedness.[16] However, God completely ignored Adam's fear and shame of nakedness but pressed him to confess his guilt.[17] Moreover, the couple not only hid but also blamed each other.[18] The blaming indicates the fear that is beyond the fear of nakedness, namely, the responsibility for the act of eating. Therefore, the sense of shame in nakedness is accompanied by the sense of guilt. Finally, the shameful state of nakedness results in

11. Barr, *Immortality*, 11, 63–65.

12. Ibid., 11–12.

13. Wolde, *Stories*, 47–48.

14. For example, Augustine believes that God created Man with the mind to think so that Man would rule over the animals (Augustine, *City*, 12.21–22).

15. Vawter, *Genesis*, 76.

16. Barr, *Immortality*, 11, 63.

17. Wenham, *Genesis*, 77; Wilcox, "English," 287.

18. Wenham, *Genesis*, 78; Schaeffer, *Genesis*, 92.

curses and expulsion.[19] The severe consequence of eating the fruit makes the story carry more than a simple "choice and consequence" motif, but points to a serious motif of "sin and consequence."

Sin, Shame, and "Brokenness"[20]

Shame caused by nakedness after the fall is a sign of internal brokenness. The specific awkwardness that makes the couple fear and their need for covering indicate an internal "brokenness" as a result of sin, in contrast to their previous state of innocence and ignorance.[21] This sense of shame subsequently points to an ethical sense of shame,[22] which makes the narrative not only meaningful in the context of modesty, but also of evilness.[23] There appear to be two notions of shame here, which Wilcox distinguishes from each other: one is embarrassment, which is triggered by less fundamental transgressions; the other is shame, which is more serious and carries moral value.[24]

Westermann opposes this ethical interpretation of shame by arguing that it is ambivalent; because, while shame can be a reaction to a mistake,[25] it diverts the doer away from the same mistake; and therefore concludes that shame should not be restricted to a reaction to sin or sensuality.[26] Another reason to reject the sense of guilt in this story is the fact that the Hebrew term for shame does *not* carry the overtones of personal guilt that the English sense of "shame" includes.[27] However, while the absence of a clear sense of guilt might be acknowledged linguistically, the *dis-ease* in the story is undeniable. This *dis-ease* is self-evident first and foremost as an "internal brokenness." Surely, the lack of guilt in

---

19. Wenham, *Genesis*, 78; Westermann rejects the view that these curses imply punishment, however, he does not offer a reason why the snake was also cursed (*Genesis*, 1988, 23; *Commentary*, 253).

20. The terms "brokenness" and "moral taint" (Oshana, "Moral Taint," 363–64) imply a *negative* sense of shame. For an alternative view on positive/negative shame, see Watts, "Shame," 54–55.

21. Ryken et al., *Imagery*, 780.

22. Thus, Ericksen construes that Adam and Eve were stripped both materially and spiritually (Ericksen, "Penitential," 266).

23. Blocher, *Beginning*, 176.

24. Wilcox, "English," 278.

25. Westermann, *Creation*, 94–95.

26. Westermann, *Commentary*, 236.

27. Wenham, *Genesis*, 71.

shame does not mean that shame is any less awkward. Yet, this "internal brokenness" happens within a relational context and thus brings about an "external brokenness." Even if guilt is not inferred in the first instant of shame, the second context of shame definitely induces guilt. Therefore, the foundation for an interpretation of sin in the fall narrative is established by the fact that shame illuminates sin by a sense of "brokenness," which both Adam and Eve share.

SHAME AS BROKENNESS

The *first* "brokenness" that must be emphasized is an innate broken relationship with the self—a state of inner conflict in the self-relation.[28] Augustine's sexual theory, for example, suggests that the shame of nakedness and the loss of genital control are the immediate punishment.[29] Augustine's theory of nakedness is built upon sexual arousal as the brokenness of nakedness and sinful lust. For Augustine, nudity is understood as erotically alluring and tempting,[30] due to the lust with which humans are affected because of disordered desires.[31] After the lure comes the lust:[32] since nakedness strongly connotes sexuality, it admittedly becomes the object of human lust.[33] The crucial point to be taken from Augustine is the *inability* to control (or precisely the loss of control), which points to a "broken" state of fallen humanity wherein a person's sin is perpetuated because sin has twisted natural desires into inordinate and disordered ones.[34]

---

28. White, *Narration*, 128, 137–38: the inner concealment spontaneously gives rise to outer concealment; Kass, *Wisdom*, 106–8: a lack of wholeness and control, without and within, and the deep connection between sexual self-conscious and shame is universal; Riezler, "Comment on the Social Psychology of Shame," 457–65; Rad, *Genesis*, 85: a loss of inner unity; Blocher (*Beginning*, 176) also accords to Augustine's theory of sexuality and control.

29. Augustine, *City*, 13.13, 14:24. Korsmeyer puts it that the "natural action of human hormones is a divine punishment" (Korsmeyer, *Evolution & Eden*, 35–36).

30. This is understood with the exception of visual disability or asexuality (cf. Augustine, *City*, 19.3).

31. Augustine, *City*, 14.16–19; Lane, "Lust," 25–27; Court, "Pornography," 854–55: pornography is one form of sexual lure that abuses nudity.

32. Fairlie, *The Seven Deadly Sins Today*, 175–90; Lane, "Lust," 31–33.

33. Lane points out that sexual lust, for Augustine, is the most blatant instance of concupiscence, not the essence of it (Lane, "Lust," 33). However, this needs to be developed further, namely, that it was the *first* to appear.

34. Lane, "Lust," 33.

Sin as Relational Brokenness

The *second* "brokenness" must refer to a relational aspect. Blocher demonstrates how the notion of shame in fallen humanity plagues them in their dysfunctional relationship with God.[35] In the fall narrative, the eating of the fruit is interpreted as the sin of "disobedience," "pride," and "lust and coveting."[36] In the "sin and fall" motif, nakedness is marked with shame, yet shame reflects a broken and dysfunctional relationship: both vertically (humans-God) and horizontally (human-human).[37] The relational brokenness is expressed through the act of hiding, despite the fact that God is omniscient.[38] The fear of the couple, which is the horror of being naked and unmasked before God,[39] becomes a barrier that separates them from God.[40] The act of blaming divides Adam and Eve when they pass their guilt from one to the other.[41] Therefore, the realization of nakedness leads to the realization of a relational brokenness in their relationship with God and with each other.

Sin, Shame, and a Metaphor of Brokenness

Following Pascal, Blocher argues that the doctrine of original sin in the fall narrative alone is able to illuminate the problems of evil:[42] Adam's role in the biblical doctrine sheds remarkable light on the "empirical" fact of human universality.[43] There are firm foundations for this establishment. McKenzie suggests that the authors and audience of a primeval tale would have thought they represented reality somehow in a symbolic way.[44] Stordalen stresses further that at the heart of linguistic symbolism of primeval tales is the connection between crucial conditions of daily

---

35. Blocher, *Beginning*, 174.
36. Adar, *Genesis*, 24–25.
37. Sherlock, *Humanity*, 42; Barr, *Immortality*, 62–66; White, *Narration*, 128, 137; Dijk-Hemmes, "Metaphorization": sexual infidelity; Gorham and Leal, "Naturism," 6.
38. Wilcox, "English," 287; Aquinas' assertion of God's full knowledge (*Summa Theologica*, Ia. XIV. 9), in Gilby, *Thomas Aquinas*, 107; Shuster, *Fall*, 62.
39. Westermann, *Commentary*, 253.
40. Colwell, "Sin," 641.
41. Schaeffer, *Genesis*, 92.
42. Blocher, *Original*, 85.
43. Ibid., 96–97.
44. McKenzie, "Myth and the Old Testament," 270, as quoted by Stordalen, *Echoes*, 67.

human life and the mythic realm, which makes the story significant to everyday human experience.[45] Since the cultural notion of shame in nakedness can portray a change from one relational existence to another[46] there is no reason why the notion of sin cannot be expressed alongside or through such a notion of shame. Additionally, Wilcox suggests that embarrassment in nakedness can be seen as a metaphor for the more fundamental failing of disobedience (through pride) and the shame that acknowledges that disobedience.[47] Ericksen also affirms that nakedness functions both literally and metaphorically to dramatize the result of sin and the need for confession and penance.[48]

However, an important question that needs answering is *how* does the notion of shame demonstrate the brokenness of sin? Blocher proposes that the claim to know good and evil divides the inner self of a person: the ego sets up an unhealthy hyper-conscience, which arrogantly credits humanity's own initiative in the "pretended self-creation." If human beings recognized the whole self, including liberty, as *given* by the Creator, they would remain in peace, but because they rejected it, they also hid the *given-ness* of their beings. The self that sets itself up as autonomous resents the *given* self (as something given), and considers it something alien. Consequently, there is inner division; there is *shame*. The sense of shame here is the mark of dependence that belies the assertion of self-sufficiency.[49] This notion of shame echoes that of Bonhoeffer: it is only in shame that humans acknowledge their limits, and because humans hate limits they live in a divided and reluctant acknowledgment of revelation, of limit, of the others and of God.[50] Therefore, if nakedness is interpreted as "defenselessness" and "helplessness,"[51] then the shame created by nakedness is the result of the rejection of that limit—remorsefulness to reality. This interpretation of "limit" also occurs in White's view: any

45. Stordalen, *Echoes*, 67.
46. White, *Narration*, 140.
47. Wilcox, "English," 293.
48. Ericksen, "Penitential," 261; Ericksen proposes that if the fall from purity to sin cannot be fully imagined in a postlapsarian world then the shift from clothing to unprotected nakedness can (especially in a British climate), 262.
49. Blocher, *Beginning*, 174; this explanation is compatible with the proposal of "pride," or Ambrose's interpretation of claiming equality with God (Bray, "Original Sin in Patristic Thought," 40).
50. Bonhoeffer, *Creation*, 80.
51. Magonet, "Themes," 43.

objective limits stemming from inescapable differences become a source of acute shame.[52] The "inner division" should be considered central to the shame of the fall narrative. Even if the sense of nakedness is interpreted as "shame, guilt, and punishment,"[53] the sense of "punishment" must be "*self*-focused." The narrative highlights a grievous disruption that governs the whole being of humanity from the lowest level of corporeality.[54]

Adam-Christ Typology and the Universal Brokenness in Hamartology

So far, attention has been given to the significance of the metaphor of nakedness in conveying the brokenness of sin in a relational aspect. Accordingly, the metaphor of nakedness is crucial to hamartology and soteriology, especially the universality of sin in Adam and the solution in Christ, i.e., the Adam-Christ typology.[55] The metaphorical values of nakedness and clothing can signify contrasting conditions: corrupted vs. restored and broken vs. wholeness.

In the discourse of original sin, the anecdote is expressed through nakedness, a cultural symbol and representation of shame, which communicates the broken state caused by sin through the complex nature of shame. Furthermore, not only does the symbol of nakedness connote a depraved state or a corrupted condition, it also represents a condition that implies punishment, shame and vulnerability. It is clear that there is a link between embarrassment and the exposure of the body.[56] Within the universality of shame, the language of nakedness operates within the "conceal-reveal" and "object-containment" models, and implies a spiritual shame that urges the need to hide.[57] However, the awkwardness of shame can also be associated with the "clothing of shame" in the Psalms or with the inappropriate dressing of Matthew 22:1–14, or the mockery of the purple cloak that Jesus wore in his trial.[58] These

---

52. White, *Narration*, 133.
53. Ryken et al., *Imagery*, 582.
54. Rad, *Genesis*, 91.
55. Fee, *The First Epistle to the Corinthians*, 750; Dunn, *Romans*, 285, 297; Goulder, "Exegesis of Genesis 1–3 in the New Testament," 226–27; Parker, "Original Sin: A Fresh Approach," 228–45.
56. Paster, *Embarrassment*, 144–47; Wilcox, "English," 287.
57. Blocher, *Beginning*, 173.
58. John 19:2; Wilcox, "English," 298n.47.

examples of shame project a model where there is concealment, reveal, and a viewer. On that account, shame before an omniscient God (the viewer in the Eden narrative)[59] implies identical "conceal-reveal" and "object-containment" models for sin. Most importantly, in these models the viewer *must* obtain a moral value that is capable of passing judgment for shame to fully function.

Theologically, the concept of "original sin" is often thought of in terms of *transmission* or *inheritance* of both blameworthiness and liability of punishment.[60] For instance, Tertullian—a traducianist—suggested that sin transmitted with the soul was derived from the parents.[61] In contrast, Origen found that transmission does not happen since each individual soul had fallen before entering the world. However, neither of these views earned the favor of the consensus by the fourth century.[62] Interestingly, Irenaeus' view of sin's transmission is that we share in Adam's guilt because we caused offense to God with Adam while we were within his loin;[63] therefore, the essence of our inheritance from Adam is the loss of the gift of life.[64] This teaching has a close connection with the concept of birth, both physically and spiritually, and as a result, the Christian church taught that sexual intercourse was the transmitter of sin.[65]

However, the above hypotheses display a number of shortcomings. First, sin is placed within the "object-containment" model, which allows sin to be "transmitted" or "taken away." The notion of "removal" of original sin in the sanctification and glorification process, which Parker mentions,[66] is in fact restricted to the "spiritual influence" model wherein sanctification and the process of "removal" of sin are the work of the Holy Spirit. Secondly, the "sin transmission" model overlooks an important collective aspect. If the corrupted nature and deprived state of humanity is itself sinful,[67] then the ethical decisions made individually are insig-

---

59. Ibid., 287.

60. Parker, "Original," 239; Carter, *A Contemporary Wesleyan Theology*, 263; Wiley, *Christian Theology*, Vol. 2, 126; Field, *Student's Handbook of Christian Theology*, 124.

61. Bray, "Original," 42.

62. Ibid., 42.

63. Irenaeus, *AH* V.16.3.

64. Ibid., III.18.7.

65. Culpability of transmission of sin through sex was started by Anthanasius (*Contra gentes* 3), then this concept spread throughout the church, Bray, "Original," 43.

66. Parker, "Original," 236.

67. Hodge, *Systematic Theology*, Vol. 2, 230; Buswell, *A Systematic Theology of the*

nificant in the light of the collective and representative concepts of sin and fall.[68] Indeed, as Lane suggests, if the essence of the fall is to live as autonomous moral agents rather than depending upon the Spirit of God, then *by definition* its consequence must be the loss of the moral integration that is the consequence of turning away from God.[69] Therefore, the consequence of human sin is not to be seen as an arbitrarily imposed penalty but rather as an inevitable outworking of the implications of sin. In other words, the effects of the fall upon human nature can be seen both as the judgment of God and as the outworking of the choice that was made.[70]

As a result, the universality and the solidarity that humanity shares with Adam has been more and more emphasized than the concept of transmission or inheritance of sin.[71] With special reference to the metaphor of shame in nakedness, the centrality of "original sin" should remain focused on the "brokenness" both individually and collectively. Consequently, the transmission of sin in this sense must be retained within a notion of "influential" transmission; the transmission from Adam to his posterity must take into account the fact that Eve gave the fruit to Adam in the first place.[72] Therefore, unlike the complete dismissal of the concept[73] "original sin" should be maintained within the representative model.[74]

Christian Religion, 286; Berkhof, *Systematic Theology*, 246; Wiley, *Theology*, Vol. 2, 123; Strong, *Systematic Theology*, 549, 577.

68. Bloesch, *Essentials of Evangelical Theology*, Vol. 1, 106–7; Erickson, *Christian Theology*, 639; Strong, *Systematic*, 596.

69. Lane, "Lust," 35.

70. Ibid., 35. Alternatively, Hendrikus Berkhof claims that sin "is not a fall from a higher form of existence, but the refusal to rise to the higher form of existence of loving fellowship with God" (*Christian Faith*, 212). Yet, any view on sin must take into account the consequence and the condition of a sinful humanity.

71. To the extent where Parker even holds that the term "Original Sin" can be discarded without bringing much loss, Parker, "Original," 245.

72. This universal import is built upon Ricoeur's postulation that the fall spreads over several moments (Ricoeur, *The Symbolism of Evil*, 252–53); Blocher, *Original*, 51.

73. Parker, "Original," 245 (built upon Thomas, *The Principles of Christian Theology*, 158, and Brunner, *The Christian Doctrine of Creation and Redemption*, 103).

74. See "Interchange" and "From Adam to Christ" in Hooker, *From Adam to Christ*, 73–87.

Representative Motif and the Adam-Christ Typology

The representative value of brokenness and restoration in the phrase (*eph'hen/in quo*) "in whom,"[75] which is fully applied to the Adam-Christ typology,[76] should not be overlooked. This representative motif is coherent with the fundamental interpretation of Paul and Augustine, which focuses on the representation of Adam and Christ in the interpretation of sin and of the cross.[77] The universality of "sin" represented in Adam as head of humanity is expressed with the phrase "through one man" in Romans 5:12,[78] and 1 Corinthians 15:21.[79] The first individual act of sin gives rise to the corruption of human nature; and in turn, the corruption of human nature gives rise to all individual acts of sin.[80] This representative motif is also supported by other biblical evidence such as Psalm 51:5; Ephesians 2:3; 1 Corinthians 40:22; Job 14:4–5; and John 3.[81]

The expression of this representative motif through the metaphor of nakedness is recognized by many early church fathers. For instance, Ambrose, in *De Paradiso*, makes the metaphor of nakedness more direct: "When, therefore, they saw that they had been despoiled of the purity and simplicity of their untainted nature, they began to look for objects made by the hand of man wherewith to cover the nakedness of their minds and hearts."[82] Ambrose's formulation of nakedness, like the homilies and the

---

75. Parker, "Original," 230; but for Bray ("Original," 43), this phrase in Rom 5:12 was mistaken by the Ambrosiaster, as "in whom" instead of "because," obviously this must be a reading in the light of the traditional idea of the mystical union of all humanity with Adam.

76. This is according to Augustine (Fisher, *History of Christian Doctrine*, 186). Wolde argues: "Even without the sin of the first human being, Christ would have come on earth; in other words, sin is not necessary to make the redemption by Christ meaningful" (*Stories*, 71); however it is notable that Wolde has mistakenly omitted Jesus' emphatic statement in John 8:24.

77. For example, Morris, "Guilt and Forgiveness," in Ferguson and Wright, *New Dictionary of Theology*, 285; Barth, *CD*, II.2, 739; Barth's "first of all" powerfully expresses his bold and decisive reversal of the Adam-Christ order (ibid., 740).

78. Reformed theologians such as Berkhof, Buswell and Hodge adopt this representative or federal mode (Parker, "Original," 235); cf. Rom 3, see Hughes, "Adam and His Posterity," 164–65; Eddy, "The Proofs of Original Sin: An Eighteenth Century Critique," 286.

79. Blocher, *Original*, 48.

80. Hughes, "Adam," 168–69; Eddy, "Proofs," 287.

81. Hughes, "Adam," 172; Eddy, "Proofs," 286.

82. Ambrose, *Sancti Ambrosii Opera* 13.63, *FOC*, Vol. 42, 343; Ericksen, "Penitential," 268.

penitential, also pushes its application from the original sin to all sinners: "Whoever . . . violates the command of God has become naked and despoiled, a reproach to himself."[83] Alternatively, Augustine also employs the metaphor but reverses its emphasis by describing the prelapsarian Adam as "naked of dissimulation" and "clothed with the divine light."[84] Interestingly, Irenaeus suggests that through disobedience Adam lost the robe of sanctity, which he previously had from the Spirit.[85]

The anecdote of sin through Adam has clearly been portrayed through the figurative language of nakedness; however, this is only one part of the Adam-Christ typology. The question remains: what is the symbol for the antidote of Christ? The clothing dialogue between Adam and the Messiah in the Midrashic sources can provide some answers.[86] Ruben and Kosman note that the vestment that Adam lost has been spoken of as "the garment of the Messiah" which implies a process of total rectification and an ultimate return to Edenic innocence.[87] The Adam-Christ typology is supported by the representative motif, opening with the corruption started by Adam and finishing with the restoration in Christ. The universality of the *broken state* in the metaphor of nakedness clearly communicates the spoiled condition of humanity. Although the metaphor does not go as far as authorizing or nullifying a concept of "inheritance" or "transmission" of sin, it does depict a universally corrupted state that humanity shares in Adam, which is to be resolved in Christ.

Prophetic Covenantal Theology and Metaphors of Nakedness and Clothing

So far, we have seen the theological association between the metaphors of nakedness, sin and shame in the fall narrative. We have also seen, in chapter 4, that nakedness expresses the human state of physical vulnerability. Interestingly, the prophetic language of covenant employs a metaphorical language of nakedness in which similar and consistent notions of sin, shame and vulnerability are mixed altogether. In fact, the interplay

---

83. Ambrose, *De Paradiso* 13.65, FOC, Vol. 42, 343; Ericksen, "Penitential," 269n.21.

84. Augustine, *De Genesi contra manichaeos* 2.16.24, FOC, Vol. 84, 120; Ericksen, "Penitential," 269n.21.

85. Irenaeus, *AH* III.23.5, ANF, Vol. 1, 457; Lane, "Lust," 34–35.

86. Rubin and Kosman, "Clothing," 169–74.

87. Ibid., 174.

of nakedness and clothing is employed frequently enough to construct a systematic comprehension of covenantal theology of its own.

Often in the prophetic passages, the emotive metaphors of nakedness and clothing complement the metaphor of a woman, which altogether symbolize the condition of a country, a city, or even the church.[88] At times, that metaphorical woman is turned into a "porno-prophetic" imagery, accompanied by scandalous ideas of sexual unfaithfulness,[89] and public exposure of nudity;[90] at other times, the woman is clothed with love and glamor in the analogy of a marriage contract.[91] In fact, it is said that the language has been taken for granted.[92] However, the compatibility is objectively undeniable in ancient Jewish sexual laws and social traditions of ancient Near Eastern societies where it was customary for a jealous husband to strip his wife naked in public to humiliate her sexual unfaithfulness.[93] The use of nakedness and clothing, however, can be divided into three basic categories: (1) literal nakedness (natural vulnerability, simplicity and emptiness), (2) adulterous nakedness (sinful and sexual), and (3) judgmental nakedness (shameful and judgmental).[94]

---

88. Isa 47; Jer 2–3; Ezek 16, 23; Hos 2; Amos 5; Nah 3; Zeph 3; and Rev 17, 19, 21–22; see Ruiz, *Ezekiel*, 370–72; DeRoche, "Israel's 'Two Evils' in Jeremiah II 13," 369–71; Fensham, "The Marriage Metaphor in Hosea for the Covenant Relationship Between the Lord and His People (Hos. 1:2–9)," 71–78; Weems, *Battered*, 44; Berlin, *Lamentations*, 3; Schaab, "I Will Love Them Freely," 3–4: The Function of Metaphor as Religious Language.

89. An unfaithful woman as Israel (Klawans, *Impurity and Sin in ancient Judaism*, 32–36). Interestingly, Israel can also be depicted as an unfaithful husband (DeRoche, "Israel's," 371); Trible, "The Gift of a Poem," 271–80: other places where Jeremiah uses female imagery in his portrayal of YHWH.

90. Guest, "Hiding," 413–48; Berlin, *Lamentations*, 8: Stripping naked as a measure-for-measure punishment. These sexual images are really part of the paradigm of impurity; cf. O'Connor, "Jeremiah," 178–86, 179: opposing the female imagery.

91. Fensham, "Marriage," 77; McCarthy, *Covenant*, 33.

92. Exum, "The Ethics of Biblical Violence against Women," 249.

93. Epstein, *Customs*, 26; Kruger, "The Hem of the Garment in Marriage," 79; Greengus, "The Old Babylonian Marriage Contract," 515n.40; for gestures connected with marriage, see Greengus, "Old Babylonian Marriage Ceremonies and Rites," 55–57.

94. For prophetic imageries in the context of covenantal theology, see Johnson, "Judgement."

Literal Nakedness as Dependency, Clothing as Intimacy, Provision and Establishment of Covenant

The image of nudity in Ezekiel 16:7–8 depicts the found condition of a vulnerable baby girl. The physical state of her vulnerability is expressed through her nakedness until the time she receives a robe from a man.[95] It is important to note the folklore overtone in this marital imagery.[96]

In Mesopotamian culture, the relationship between a husband and his wife is not only a matter of ethics, but also of economics. A married woman is considered more or less "a possession" to her husband, and the husband, in return, has to provide his wife substantially for her essential needs, i.e. clothing, food, shelter, etc.[97] In this passage, Israel is symbolically referred to as a young girl growing up and being taken care of by God in a relationship with him.[98] However, that young woman submits herself to sexual promiscuity and thus is exposed to humiliation in front of her lovers. The flow of the narrative is consistent to an ancient customary procedure: when a wife commits adultery she has committed a severe infringement on her husband's rights.[99] The husband then can bring the mentioned economical "contract" to an end,[100] through the disrobing of her clothes,[101] and leave the responsibility to take care of her needs and vulnerability. The intensity of this physical vulnerability can be found in other forms of punishment and judgment.[102] Therefore, within the one notion of literal nakedness, a relationship can either be established by covering nakedness, or terminated by exposing nakedness.

---

95. Brownlee suggests that the phrase "spread my robe over you and covered your nakedness" refers to sexual intercourse (Brownlee, *Ezekiel*, 225).

96. Shields, "Multiple Exposures," 5; Carley, *The Book of the Prophet Ezekiel*, 95; Eichrodt, *Ezekiel*, 202.

97. Kruger, "Hem," 81–82; however, Setel argues that this economic relationship is a reversal of the social reality of the female role (Setel, "Pornography," 92).

98. Schöpflin, "The Composition of Metaphorical Oracles within the Book of Ezekiel," 109.

99. Heger, "Source of law in the Biblical and Mesopotamian Law Collections," 339.

100. Shemesh, "Punishment of the Offending Organ in Biblical Literature," 357; Kruger, "Hem," 79–83.

101. Clothing also has profound symbolic marital meanings (Ruth 3:9; Ezek 16:8); Kruger, "Hem," 80–83, 79.

102. Shields, "Exposures," 6; turning into whoring in ungratefulness (Gowan, *Ezekiel*, 67); punished by gang rape (Weems, *Battered*, 60).

Adulterous Nakedness as Sin and Abruption of Covenant

The image of adulterous nakedness appears not only in Ezekiel 16:36, but also in Isaiah 57:8.[103] This image is accompanied by such phrases as "pour out your wealth," "expose your nakedness," "uncover your bed," "make a pact with those whose beds you love," and "look on their nakedness." These passages contain clear associations between nakedness and adultery: from door and doorpost to the bed, then uncovering the bed, open it wide, climb in, and "make a pact," then "look on their nakedness."[104] Because of this adulterous nakedness most people associate nakedness with indecency and sex. Such an assumption is understandable due to the sexual connotation of nakedness in the Mosaic sexual laws. However, this image of sexual immorality and adulterous nakedness serves as a metaphor for the insult, disobedience, and unfaithfulness that Israel commits against God.[105] Therefore, the formation of this prophetic covenantal theology depends on the consistency of a metaphorical phenomenon.[106] First, the notions of fidelity and faithfulness, which are fundamental to marriage, are borrowed to express spiritual fidelity.[107] Secondly, the actions of exposing and viewing nakedness, between a married person and people that are outside of that marriage bond, are considered breaking the fidelity of sexual intimacy. In short, metaphorical nakedness in adulterous relationships provides the prophetic covenantal theology with an immense power, expressing the relational aspect more fully in a way that provokes thoughts.

Judgmental Nakedness as Termination of Covenant

When the prophets use the metaphor of an adulterous woman to depict a broken relationship between Israel and God, such a relationship is

---

103. Schöpflin, "Ezekiel," 110; Exum, "Ethics," 251–53.

104. Although commentators have highlighted how differently this passage could be interpreted. Motyer argues that there is no evidence for the word "nakedness" in this passage and therefore, the sexual connotation is denied (Motyer, *Isaiah*, 355). Keil and Delitzsch (*Isaiah*, 546) argue that the sexual connotation is also clear in Ezek 16:26 (promiscuity) and Ezek 23:20 (reference to genital size).

105. McKenna, *Isaiah*, 193; Berlin, *Lamentations*, 20; Klawans, *Impurity*, 32–36: purity/impurity paradigm.

106. Shields, "Exposures," 5.

107. Here borrowing Marks' term "religious apostasy" (in Dijk-Hemmes, "Metaphorization," 167).

understood in a covenantal and contract-like fashion.[108] God—the loving husband who provides everything for his people—has every right to stop the supply when those he loves betray him.[109] Often the end of the relationship, which is expressed through the metaphor of the woman's nakedness, is perfectly understandable and consistent with the customary concepts of disrobing and public exposure.[110] In fact, these are extremely violent images but one can understand it as an extension of the ancient principle of "measure for measure."[111]

The "measure for measure" principle can be applied further to the extent that the sexual organs will be punished for the sin of adultery.[112] This means not only the vulva, but also the breasts, stomach, belly, and thigh, etc., suffer the punishment (including self-loathing and self-injury, tearing one's breasts, etc.).[113] Numbers 5:11–31 records how the woman who commits adultery should be brought to the priest, before God. This passage points out clearly that the punishment for an adulterous woman is the damage of her reproductive organ, or her loss of fertility.[114] The adulterous figures end up suffering pain and death with great shame by gang rape,[115] for their lust and unfaithfulness under the hand of those they had previously lusted after.

When we apply this principle of covenantal punishment in the prophetic writings to the husband-wife relationship under investigation, we can see that the effect of the antithesis (nakedness versus clothing) is

---

108. Hos 1–2; Jer 31; Ezek 16 (Fekkes III, "His Bride Has Prepared Herself," 283n.34); Berlin suggests that these metaphors were used simply because they were thoroughly understood and accepted (Berlin, *Lamentations*, 21).

109. Eslinger ("Perception," 151–52) also refers to the relationship between Judah/Jerusalem and God.

110. For a study on the severe punishment and suffering of Zion/Woman, see Guest, "Hiding," 413–48.

111. Berlin, *Lamentations*, 8; Shemesh, "Punishment," 343.

112. Shemesh, "Punishment," 352; Shemesh argues that circumcision was applied to the offending sexual organs in Gen 34:13–26 (ibid., 350), but the narrative appears to be more about a revenge than a "punishment." Besides, capital punishment such as stoning (Lev 20:10) is a consequence of sexual misconducts (Heger, "Source," 330, 337–38).

113. Shemesh, "Punishment," 350, 356–57.

114. Ibid., 352–53; Frymer-Kensky, "The Strange Case of the Suspected Sotah," 18–24.

115. Weems, *Battered*, 60; Duguid, *Ezekiel*, 302–4; Brownlee, *Ezekiel*, 236; Ogilvie, *Hosea*, 46; Renkema, *Lamentations*, 134.

powerful.[116] The correlation between nakedness and judgment raises an important question for an understanding of the theology of judgment. Judgment seems to cause infliction, pain and suffering. Therefore, nakedness is employed in the context of judgment because of its capability of expressing suffering and agony. Nakedness signifies the forcing and exposing of sinners to utter condemnation, not simply *passive* vulnerability to suffering or a factual dependence on the protection of clothes. Nakedness in this sense is understood as *active* harm, humiliation and infliction. The metaphor of nakedness therefore depicts most effectively punishment and judgment. The anguishing and tormenting punishment of public degradation[117] expresses thoroughly through the vulnerability and scorning shame of the offender, and creates a mixture of emotive feelings within the readers.[118] This is the occasion where the three themes of vulnerability, shame and sexuality in the concept of nakedness provide a complementary metaphor of exaggerating punishment for the analogy of husband-wife relationship, which respectively reflects the connection between YHWH and Israel.[119]

Non-Covenant Judgmental Nakedness as Punishment for the Ungodly

It is important, however, to note that this prophetic image of nakedness is spoken not only against Israel (Ezek 16:6–39; 23:9–30; Hos 2:2–10;[120] and Lam 1:8),[121] but also toward other nations. The destiny of the naked harlot—an image that often represents other nations—is not treated with any difference. Lamentations 4:21, Nahum 3:5, Isaiah 47:2–3, and Revelation 17:16 adopt a similar treatment as Ezekiel 16 and 23.[122] As Babylon

---

116. See emotive metaphors in chapter 3; see also the purity/impurity paradigm in Carley, *Ezekiel*, 95; Eichrodt, *Ezekiel*, 202.

117. Eslinger, "Perception," 151–52.

118. Strong feelings of horror and outrage, immorality and shame, suffering and pity create a mixture of reactions for the crucial part of the poet's message (Berlin, *Lamentations*, 9).

119. Berlin, *Lamentations*, 9.

120. Nakedness is also associated with shame and hunger under divine punishments (4Q166= 4QHosea Pesher 2:12–13, as quoted in Aune, *Revelation 6–16*, 897).

121. Berlin, *Lamentations*, 3.

122. Renkema, *Lamentations*, 564; Aune, *Revelation 17–22*, 957.

loses its dignity in its downfall,[123] and is treated like a slave girl,[124] so the future Babylon will be ruined by similar punishment.[125] Only this image of disgrace and exposure could fully depict the horrific situation before the judgment of God.[126]

The Glamorous Bride of Christ as a Result of a New and Restored Covenant

Contrary to the imagery of nakedness and the judgmental theme of ruin and damnation, the nuptial imagery of the bride of Christ is the Christian hope for the eternal bliss.[127] While God's enemy, the harlot Babylon, is scorned in punishment and nakedness, the Bride of Christ prepares herself, clothed in her wedding garment of bright, clean and fine linen (Rev 19:8).[128] This bridal image has a strong link to eschatology:[129] the Bride of Christ not only escapes the horrific eternal judgment but also is clothed in the wedding garment of righteousness. There is, as it seems, a theological coherence behind the concept of the bride in both the Old and New Testaments.[130] The nuptial imagery in Revelation seems to resonate not only the husband-wife metaphor in the Old Testament prophetic writings, but also the punishment of nudity derived from it.

Accordingly, the antithesis between nakedness and clothing has been employed to bring about an effective contrast between the condemnation for the evilness of other nations, and the restored covenant between YHWH and Israel. Moreover, the resonance of these Old Testament prophetic imageries within the concept of eschatological punishment

---

123. Childs, *Isaiah*, 366.

124. Motyer, *Isaiah*, 297; Watts, *Isaiah*, 171; McKenna, *Isaiah*, 105.

125. Wall, *Revelation*, 209.

126. Ryken et al., *Imagery*, 582; Renkema, *Lamentations*, 134.

127. As it is rightly pointed out, the bride of Christ rejoices while the harlot Babylon is doomed to damnation (Rev 17–18, 19–22) (Fekkes III, "Revelation," 269).

128. Fekkes III, "Revelation," 269–70: comparison between Isa 61:10 and Rev 19–21.

129. Muirhead, "Bride," 183–84; Batey, "Bride," 176–78, 180–82: Paul's bridal image; Batey, *New Testament Nuptial Imagery*, 55–57: the contrast between the church (Christ's bride awaiting the supper) and the drunken harlot Babylon.

130. The Old Testament background goes back as far as YHWH's covenant with Israel, while the New Testament background continues with Jesus' claim in Mark 2:19, Matt 9:14–17 and Luke 5:33–35 (see Muirhead, "Bride," 176–83); Batey, "Bride," 176–78, 180–82; Fung, "Pictures," 97–100 and Martin, "Bride, Bridegroom," 148.

informs us of their continual power in portraying the Christian hope of the glamorous Bride of Christ.

Nakedness and Clothing in Eschatology

If the notions of nakedness and clothing in prophetic language give expression to the contrast between judgment and blessing, in eschatology, heavier weight is placed on the aspects of shame and honor. As we recall John's eschatological language of nakedness and clothing, apart from the condemnation of the whore Babylon that reflects the prophetic fashion, we can find another two incidents: spiritual poverty and watchman.

First, Revelation 3:17–18 adopts the economic connotation of nakedness to express spiritual poverty. Contrasting with what the church thinks about itself (wealthy and luxurious), the epistle reveals the underlying state of spiritual poverty (ill, poor, and naked).[131] This is a warning that calls the church to put on the true garment of salvation provided by Christ or they too will face judgment.[132] When we compare this to Calvin's twofold concept of clothing,[133] we find somewhat of a resonance of justification in Christ.

Similarly, the concept of nakedness is mentioned again in Revelation 16:15 with the depiction of shame at the *parousia*.[134] It is important to note that the term "nakedness" here is the Greek αἰσχυνη, meaning "shame/disgrace," not γυμνοτη, meaning "naked/genitalia."[135] The state of "staying awake" and "keeping the clothes" at the coming of Christ implies a deep vigilance and alertness on the part of Christians,[136] whereas nakedness refers to a state of judgment or death,[137] and the shame of exposing sexual organs like the evil whore.[138]

---

131. Hemer, *Letters*, 191, 201.

132. Thomas, *Revelation*, 312–15; the motif of shame and Judgment Day in Ericksen, "Penitential," 269–70, 272, see nn.23, 26 and particularly n.28, quoting Napier; Healey, *The Old English Vision of St. Paul*, 43, 51–54.

133. Calvin, *CC—Corinthians*, Vol. 2, 218.

134. Neyrey, "Nudity," 122–23.

135. Aune, *Revelation 6–16*, 897; Osei-Bonsu, "Resurrection," 89.

136. Rockel, "Nudity"; Aune, *Revelation 6–16*, 897: arguably guarding against neglect of the commandment.

137. Johnson, "Judgement"; Knight, *Revelation*, 113.

138. Thompson, *Revelation*, 156.

Wenham echoes Ellis' view of judgmental nakedness in his view on this concept of being "found" or being "seen" on the day of Judgment.[139] This exposure is traced back to Jesus' eschatological teaching in Luke 12:36–38 and Mark 13:34–36 (where the servants are not waiting for the master with alertness). While the difference in this judgmental scenario is the sleeping of the servants, not their nakedness, the story does imply a state of spiritual laxness.

The heart of the matter, however, is what actually led to the employment of the antithesis of nakedness and clothing in eschatology? The answer might be the involvement of cultural elements, for example, the borrowing of the watchman imagery,[140] or the philosophical concept of a naked state of the soul.[141] We now carry out an examination.

The Philosophical Concept of Naked Soul in Theology

The relationship between the human body and the soul is an interesting topic that arouses the curiosity of many scientists.[142] The origin of the soul, and its relation to the body are also extensively discussed in philosophy and theology.[143] The body-soul relation is not only found in the Old Testament but also in the New Testament, in Greek philosophy, in the teachings of the church fathers, as well as in some recent theological texts.[144]

---

139. Wenham, "Being 'Found' on the Last Day," 478; 1 Corinthians 4:2, 9:27; Matt 24:45–46; Luke 12:42–43; Phil 3:11; Ellis, "II Corinthians V.1–10 in Pauline Eschatology," 219–21; Neyrey, "Nudity," 122.

140. Aune, *Revelation 6–16*, 897; Mishnah Middoth 1:2 (Danby, *Mishnah*, 5th division *Kodashim* ["Hallowed things"], 590); Witherington III, *Revelation*, 210; Smalley, *The Revelation of John*, 412.

141. The fifteenth-century painter Roger Van de Weyden said that not only the damned go to hell naked but the saved go to heaven in the same condition (Pattison, *Shame*, 311–12). Rev 6:11, however, uses the clothing language of white robes probably to depict the state of purity and blessedness.

142. Peters, "Resurrection: What Kind of Body?" 60–64; Edwards, *After Death?* 47–57; "Near-Death Experiences and the Afterlife"; International Association for Near-Death Studies, www.iands.org/.

143. For an extended discussion see Yates, "The Origin of the Soul: New Light on an Old Question," 121–40: the most famous Christian traditional view is attributed to Tertullian, which holds that all souls are from Adam (ibid., 122); the other view, which holds that God created every soul *ex nihilo*, belongs to the Roman Catholic church (ibid., 126).

144. Copleston, *Aquinas*, 156–58, 161, 168; Peters, "Resurrection," 69–73.

The Antithesis of Nakedness and Clothing in Theology and Liturgy 139

Greek philosophy and Platonism understood the body to be an outer clothing of the soul.[145] Plato used the term "naked" to describe the bodiless soul as well as to describe the condition of the unrighteous in Sheol.[146] While Aristotle understood the soul and the body as essentially related,[147] he viewed the soul as a prison, a house, or a mortal tomb.[148]

The church fathers also developed this notion.[149] Tertullian thought that the soul had an astral body (Luke 16:23–24).[150] For Augustine, the soul is like God, and incorporeal without a body;[151] moreover, the body and the soul are of one unity.[152] Aquinas shared this view, that the soul is not complete on its own,[153] but rejected the idea that the soul uses or controls the body,[154] believing that the soul will be united with the body again at resurrection.[155] However, if the soul has to be detached from the body (not forever) it can exist without the body as an independent, complete, and incorruptible substance.[156] Although it might be suggested that few apart from Plato have rightly affirmed the soul's immortal substance,[157] the Christian view on the body and soul does not hold that humans enjoy the fullness of being apart from the body. The existence of the soul in

---

145. Copleston, *Aquinas*, 161. The soul is contaminated by the desires of the body, and as such, when the body dies, the soul is "released" and separated from the body. This view contrasts that of Augustine, which holds that sin is from the soul (Flew, *Body*, 43–45; Augustine, *City*, 14.3–5).

146. Hettlinger, "Corinthians," 180; the word *oikia* was understood as a body and 2 Cor 5:3 is tangentially connected with Greek thought (Kim, *Clothing*, 211).

147. Flew, *Body*, 76–80.

148. The majority of theologians and Christians believe that the body is inferior to the soul (e.g., Athanasius and Aquinas; Copleston, *Aquinas*, 156; Pettersen, *Athanasius and the Human Body*, 20–21), as far as the soul is trapped in the weakness of the body but not to the extent of a prison or a mortal tomb from which it is to be liberated.

149. For a comparative study see Cooper, *Body, Soul, & Life Everlasting*, 10–13.

150. Flew, *Body*, 91; cf. Reicke, "Body and Soul in the New Testament," 208.

151. Flew, *Body*, 96–98.

152. Augustine uses the concept of the horseman and the cup with the drink to speak of the unity in the body-soul relation (Augustine, *City*, 19.3).

153. Aquinas, *Summa Theologica*, I.75.5; Cooper, *Body*, 12.

154. Copleston, *Aquinas*, 158, 161; Flew, *Body*, 101–2.

155. Copleston, *Aquinas*, 168; cf. Flew, *Body*, 106. Ephrem suggests that without the body, the soul would not be able to perceive or be conscious in Paradise (Harvey, "Embodiment in Time and Eternity," 121, 123–24).

156. Aquinas, *Summa Theologica*, I.76.1 and I.75.6; Cooper, *Body*, 12.

157. Calvin, *Institutes* 1.15.6.

the after-world (Luke 16:19–31)[158] and the distinction between the body and the soul (Matt 10:28;[159] Heb 4:12;[160] 1 Thess 5:23)[161] are generally acknowledged by scholars. In contrast to the Greeks who looked forward to the immortality of the soul, Christians anticipate the resurrection body with which God will clothe his people at Christ's appearing.[162] However, the Bible remains ambiguous about the state of the soul when it is detached from the body, what it looks like, and what it is fully capable of.

The Interim State in Theology

Our discussion of body-soul relation, in fact, starts from the Bible's ambiguous eschatological analogy of nakedness in 2 Corinthians 5:3, in correlation with nakedness in Revelation 16:15. The use of nakedness in 2 Corinthians 5:1–3 generates an interesting discussion on a form of "nakedness" after death, a state of disembodiment and the nakedness of the soul in the interim state.[163]

For some scholars, the idea of nakedness here is a punishment, through which Paul expressed his fear.[164] What is this fear? The argument holds that Paul is expressing a general dread for the state of spiritual nakedness before God, i.e., the wicked souls will be in a judgmental naked state. For example, as Calvin points out, the wicked will appear before God in disgraceful nakedness because they are not clothed with a glorious body.[165] Hettlinger and Oepke also content themselves with the view of this *final* and *eternal* nakedness, a symbol of defenselessness before the condemning judgment of God.[166] However, why is there such fear?

---

158. It is argued that this passage implies an intermediate state (Cooper, *Body*, 136–37).

159. Hagner, *Matthew 1–13*, 285–86; France, *The Gospel of Matthew*, 403.

160. Koester, *Hebrews*, 274; Ellingworth, *The Epistle to the Hebrews*, 263.

161. Witherington III, *1 and 2 Thessalonians*, 172–73; Williams, *1 and 2 Thessalonians*, 103; Bruce, *1 and 2 Thessalonians*, 130.

162. Milne, *Truth*, 327–28.

163. Osei-Bonsu, "Resurrection," 89–90; Glasson, "Corinthians," 146; Craig, "Dilemma," 145–47; Cassidy, "Death," 215–17.

164. Cassidy, "Death," 214; Ellis, *Paul and His Recent Interpreters*, 44–45: reference to Old Testament notion of shame; Hettlinger, "Corinthians," 176; Sevenster, *Studia Paulina*, 204; Plummer, *Second Epistle of St. Paul to the Corinthians*, 160–64.

165. Calvin, *CC—Corinthians*, Vol. 2, 218.

166. Hettlinger, "Corinthians," 180; Ryken et al., *Imagery*, 582; some disagree with this view, such as Whitely who, without any further evidence, asserts that Paul does

Some say the "fear" might be closely connected to the Old Testament's fear of nakedness, which is mainly based on Genesis 3 and the prophetic writings.[167] But this "fear" of nakedness, Glasson points out, is not to be understood as the nakedness of a physical body because the soul does not have sexual organs by which to feel ashamed.[168]

Alternatively, others have often referred to the involvement of Platonism and Greek thought in Paul's use of "naked" metaphor,[169] hinting at an overlap in Hebrew and Greek concepts.[170] However, suppose the idea of the soul being separated from the body[171] and the idea of a "naked soul"[172] are overlaps between Hebraic and Greek thoughts, the heart of the matter is the question of why Paul used such a metaphor? Some suggest that Paul was repudiating the Greek hope of nakedness as opposed to the Christian one.[173] Bultmann holds that Paul simply polemicized against the Gnostic hope[174] or an idealization of disembodiment that may have been advocated by gnosticizing Christians.[175] Others such as Ellis and Kim establish this metaphorical nakedness more concretely, arguing

---

not appear to have said this (Whiteley, *The Theology of St. Paul*, 257).

167. Ellis, *Recent*, 44–45.

168. Glasson, "Corinthians," 146.

169. Hettlinger, "Corinthians," 180; see chapter 2 for a Platonist and Greek view of the body; Osei-Bonsu, "Resurrection," 90; Cassidy, "Death," 215; Glasson, "Corinthians," 145–46.

170. As pointed out by Ellis, *Recent*, 35: Even scholars who normally oppose a Greek dualism in Pauline anthropology tend toward it when interpreting 2 Cor 5:8; Robinson (*The Body*, 17, 29, 77) contends to equate "absent from the body" with the "naked" interim state; Cullmann, *Christ and Time*, 238; Cullmann, *Immortality of the Soul or Resurrection of the Dead?* 52; Schweitzer, *The Mysticism of Paul the Apostle*, 131; Kennedy, *St Paul's Conception of Last Things*, 266–70.

171. Whiteley, *Paul*, 256; see a clearer Old Testament understanding of death in Cooper, *Body*, 58–66.

172. Both pneuma and psyche mean "a free soul," that is, a disembodied soul and were translated from Hebrew terms (Reicke, "Body," 207–10). Osei-Bonsu argues that Paul was aware of both concepts—a disembodied soul (using the anthropological concept of nakedness) and the intermediate state (Osei-Bonsu, "Resurrection," 89–90; Cassidy, "Death," 215). This view is taken by many others such as Lucian, Hoffmann, Gundry, Weiss, Plummer, Robertson, Sevenster, Cullmann, Hughes (Craig, "Dilemma," 145; Cooper, *Body*, 156).

173. Belleville, *Corinthians*, 134; Osei-Bonsu, "Resurrection," 95; Hettlinger, "Corinthians," 176.

174. Bultmann, *Corinthians*, 137; cf. Harris, *Corinthians*, 386; Glasson, "Corinthians," 155; Osei-Bonsu, "Resurrection," 91.

175. Harris, *Corinthians*, 385–86.

that it refers to a person who is not clothed with Christ, but remains in the Adamic garment of sin and shame.[176] This Adam-Christ typology suggests that nakedness in this sense is also associated with a notion of an eternal punishment[177] for example the lack of the wedding garment.[178] In this case, whereas the believers in Christ will be extra-clothed with a resurrection body,[179] the Adamic body of unbelievers at the *parousia* will fail to change into the heavenly body.[180]

Accordingly, in the light of Pauline metaphorical language, especially his language of baptism, the new man, resurrection body and putting on Christ,[181] the use of nakedness in 2 Corinthians 5:3 has to take into account its theological role within a wider soteriological context. Nakedness in this context can also imply a spiritual, shameful naked state of the condemned before God. Therefore, the analogy of nakedness refers not only to a dreadful spiritual state without the resurrection body but also to the shameful condition of the unrighteous before God at the *parousia*.

Nude Baptism: Old Versus New

It is notable that the body is a significant religious and spiritual metaphor.[182] Paul refers to the body as the temple of God's Spirit (1 Cor

176. Ellis, *Recent*, 45; Kim, *Clothing*, 222.

177. Kim, *Clothing*, 218–19.

178. Irenaeus associates 2 Cor 5:4 with the wedding garment (Matt 22:11–14) in *AH* IV.36:6 and similarly Apocalypse (7:9, 14): the saints are clothed, the unrighteous unclothed, but further, Rev 3:18, they have washed their robes as well (Kim, *Clothing*, 222; cf. Lloyd-Jones, "The Wedding Garment," 11–18; Cullmann, *Time*, 240–41).

179. Augustine thinks that the new body will be spiritual yet not changed into spirits (Augustine, *City*, Vol. 2: 18–19); Kim, *Clothing*, 222; Hettlinger, "Corinthians," 193; Harris thinks that Christians get the resurrection bodies at death (*Corinthians*, 390–91).

180. Kim, *Clothing*, 217n.128. Schweitzer argues that the one and only resurrection of Late-Jewish time can be found in the Apocalypse of Baruch (ibid., xlix–li), where all the dead rise first in their original form, they may recognize each other, then after the Judgment, some turn into angelic beings and others into repulsive ones (Schweitzer, *Mysticism*, 131–32).

181. Robinson, *Body*, 79; Eph 5:26; 1 Cor 6:17; Gal 3:27; Eph 4:24; and Col 3:10.

182. See Coakley, *Religion*, 1997; McGuire, "Religion and the Body," 283–97. For a brief social theory of the body see Raine, "Reconceptualising the Human Body," 100–101. For body theology in terms of critical reflections on bodily experience as a fundamental realm of the experience of God, see Nelson, *Body Theology*, 43. For the body as a symbol and social relationship, see Gager, "Body-Symbols and Social Reality," 347.

6:19),[183] a member of Christ (1 Cor 6:15), and a living sacrifice (Rom 12:1). A naked body, however, has a different degree of significance, particularly in the practice of nude baptism of the early church.[184]

However, we begin our discussion of nude baptism in the early centuries with an interesting fact that nudity was banned in Old Testament liturgy. Surprisingly, Exodus 20:26 records an ambiguous prohibition for nakedness. It has been suggested that this prohibition is connected to a set of rules about priestly garments in Exodus 28:42–43, but no explanation for the prohibition of such exposure is provided.[185] As it is clearly impossible for God to hate human nakedness, which he created, there is an opinion that this prohibition might prevent a priest from going up to the altar with pride,[186] while others suggest that nakedness is linked to uncleanness and bodily excrement, which defiles the altar.[187] The most persuasive suggestion, however, comes from the aspect of idol worship. It has been pointed out that nakedness associated with sexual sins and harlotry in idol worship, was prohibited in the worship of YHWH.[188] As a result, the prohibition consecrates Israel from their idolatrous neighbors.[189] This religious-based conclusion makes much sense of the Hebrew concept of nakedness and national identity, as opposed to that of Gentiles.[190]

If nakedness was an issue in Old Testament liturgy, then what made the early Christians celebrate nude baptism? Perhaps this matter needs to be viewed from different perspectives. First, while God's prohibition seems to be against nakedness at the altar, there is no other evidence that attests to God detesting nakedness. On the contrary, in 2 Samuel 6:14–20, David was semi-naked when he danced before God but he was not killed or condemned.[191] It seems that David's genuine dance and his humility

---

183. Punt, "Paul, Body Theology, and Morality: Parameters for a Discussion," 379.

184. Miles, *Carnal*, chapter 1.

185. Durham, *Exodus*, 389.

186. Rockel, "Nudity."

187. Rushdoony, *Institutes*, 405.

188. Jordan, *Law*, 62.

189. Fretheim, *Exodus*, 243.

190. Cf. *Jubilees* 3:31; cf. Jewish view of male nakedness and God's presence in chapter 2.

191. Johnson, "Law"; Robinson, *Samuel*, 183. Perhaps David was naked because he was having a wild dance in such a short ephod (Evans, *Samuel*, 163; Anderson, *Samuel*, 105).

in worship were what mattered,[192] thus, theologically his semi-nakedness was not problematic.[193] Secondly, since the early church emerged from within Greco-Roman culture where nudity was common in public[194] the liturgy of nude baptism became prevalent.

Admittedly, nudity and clothing have traditionally been associated with the story of the fall, with shame and the legal prohibitions of sexual misconduct. Nakedness became marred with the stain of disobedience and a disrupted relationship with God. Consequently, this is an important point for the rituals of nude baptism because nakedness symbolizes the prevalent theme of Christian Theology: "old" versus "new"; similarly, "flesh" versus "spirit," "Adam" versus "Christ." If nakedness is seen otherwise, the contrast between nakedness and clothing will lose its effectiveness as metaphors when it is fabricated into the theological foundation of nude baptism.

Early Christianity and Nude Baptism

Christians in the fourth century found no contradiction between nakedness and holiness, so they practiced naked baptism.[195] In fact, an active tradition can be traced back to the latter half of second century, when Hippolytus[196] gave the following baptismal instructions: "Then, after these things, let him give him over to the presbyter who baptizes, and let the candidates stand in the water, naked, a deacon going with them likewise."[197] Also, "of Christ in the Song of Songs, *I have put off my coat, how shall I put it on?* O wondrous thing! ye were naked in the sight of all, and were not ashamed; for truly ye bore the likeness of the first-formed Adam, who was naked in the garden, and was not ashamed. . . . Then, when ye were stripped, ye were anointed with exorcized oil, from the

---

192. Brueggemann, *Samuel*, 250.

193. Some suggest that the purpose of the story was to explain Michal's barrenness (Conroy, *1–2 Samuel, 1–2 Kings*, 104; Robinson, *Samuel*, 183).

194. See chapter 2.

195. Christiansen, "Women and Baptism," 3–5; Beasley-Murray, *Baptism in the New Testament*, 148; Kim, *Clothing*, chapter 7; Moule, *Worship in the New Testament*, 52–53; Martin, *Worship in the Early Church*, 101. Christ was depicted naked at baptism, although as a boy before puberty, not as an adult (Tinsley, "Coming," 33).

196. Knight, "St. Hippolytus."

197. Hippolytus, in Easton, *The Apostolic Tradition of Hippolytus*, 46, perhaps the presbyteris also naked (n.2).

very hairs of your head, to your feet, and were made partakers of the good olive-tree, Jesus Christ."[198]

Interestingly, Cyril of Jerusalem (c.315–386)[199] also gave similar instructions:

> As soon, therefore, as ye enter in, ye put off your garment; and this was an image of *putting off the old man with his deeds.* Having stripped yourselves, ye were naked; in this also imitating Christ, who hung naked on the Cross, and by His nakedness *spoiled principalities and powers, and openly triumphed over them on the tree.* For since the powers of the enemy made their lair in your members, ye may no longer wear that old vestment; I do not at all mean this visible one, but that *old man, which its corrupt according to the deceitful lusts.*[200]

There is a theological foundation hidden behind these liturgical instructions for nude baptism.[201] In particular, commentators have pointed out the interaction between nudity and theological concepts such as covenant, putting on and off,[202] contrasting of death and life, purification, renunciation, surrender, and sanctification.[203] Most interestingly, this nudity was involved in the whole social aspect of the church, i.e. the involvement of a community, *witnessing* and *affirmation* of the third party (a congregation, a priest, a household, a leader, etc.).[204]

---

198. Cyril of Jerusalem, *Mystagogical Catechesis II—On the Rites of Baptism*, 60.

199. Knight, "St. Cyril of Jerusalem."

200. Cyril of Jerusalem, *Mystagogical*, 59; Miles, *Carnal*, 33–35.

201. For the implementation of the practice, see Christiansen, "Women," 1–8; Miles, *Carnal*, chapter 1; Wilson, "'Nakedness,'" 44; Kim, *Clothing*, 112–28; Smith, "Garments."

202. See Beasley-Murray, *Baptism*, 148; Christiansen ("Women," 2, 4–5) has given much attention to the putting on and off of garments before and after baptism; however, baptism that has a stronger focus on conversion than on the cleansing of the body might, in some cases, result in people not taking their clothes off.

203. It is worth remembering that nudity is also present in other rituals such as circumcision and other rites of purification (Church of Scotland, *The Biblical Doctrine of Baptism*, 11–14).

204. Miles, *Carnal*, 35–36; Kim, *Clothing*, 96–101; Christiansen, "Women," 4: Christiansen suggests that there may have been a separation between men and women and some restrictions; for example, when a woman was baptized, she was out of sight of the men that were present at the baptism, because baptism was by total immersion and unclothed and immorality was not accepted. Baptism was probably self-administered, 1–4; Corrigan, "Text and Image on an Icon of the Crucifixion at Mount Sinai," 49.

In her investigation Miles points out that, while religious ritual would not require literal nakedness to reinforce the symbolic meaning, naked baptism became a central feature of Christian initiation because of an "interweaving of intellectual, psychological, and physical experience in the extended preparation for baptism."[205] As a result, a new integration of the body in religious commitment was produced.[206] To an extent, nudity in baptism became the nexus where theology meets the practicality of liturgy in a communal setting.[207]

The Old-Versus-New Motif of Baptismal Nudity

Wilson asserts that the arguments for baptismal nudity were "explicitly and powerfully theological, speaking to us critically of our obsession with the body-perfect, and the connectedness of nakedness, bodiliness, sexuality and sin."[208] Indeed, the theology of the practice of nude baptism appears to resonate strongest with the classic motif of conversion—old-versus-new. Why is this so?

First, it is obvious that the New Testament gives baptism a place of great importance, especially the washing and cleansing away of sins, which is closely connected with the Old Testament rites of atonement that require the bloodshed of covenant.[209] So, although baptism is linked to many theological concepts,[210] the practical application of baptism is fundamentally expressed through water, i.e., purifying and washing. This perhaps is where nakedness is considered appropriate. In order to have a good wash, it is appropriate and necessary for *every part* of the body to touch the water.[211] Nudity, in this context, reinforces the ritual: the baptisand brings to Christ the unhidden and uncovered self to receive forgiveness and purification—a sense of newness, freshness, and revitalization.

Additionally, from a viewpoint of biblical metaphor, baptismal nudity and re-clothing signifies the contrast images in conversion: die to self

---

205. Miles, *Carnal*, 36.

206. Ibid., 45.

207. Nelson, *Body*, 43; cf. theology of the senses, Gorringe, *The Education of Desire*, 4, 13–27.

208. Wilson, "Nakedness," 44.

209. In the New Testament the washing away of sins and cleansing in the blood is through the death of Christ, Church of Scotland, *Baptism*, 22.

210. Church of Scotland, *Baptism*, 22–25.

211. Beasley-Murray, *Baptism*, 148.

and resurrect with Christ, putting off the old self and putting on Christ (Gal 3:27), confession and forgiveness, cleansing of sins and regeneration of new life, etc.[212] The concept of putting on and off in Colossians 3:9–10 and Ephesians 4:22–24 is significant to the rite of baptism.[213] Accordingly, in nude baptism, the literal stripping off of old clothes and the putting on of new white robes,[214] are within the actualization of the biblical clothing metaphor.

Alternatively, the theological old-versus-new motif can be justified through the perspective of renunciation (as such, in this fashion stripping the old self is imitating the naked Christ).[215] This stripping of the "old self" can be expressed through a renunciation of materials, for which clothes represent and thus echo the *naked birth* and *naked death* in Job 1:21. A new life in Christ is a life dependent on Christ in life and in death, as opposed to the old life in the flesh preoccupied with the material pleasures, which are to be stripped.

Furthermore, the old-versus-new theme can be expressed through Adam's nakedness, as "the first-formed Adam."[216] In this manner, shameless nakedness is about "undoing the damage of the fall" (Cyril).[217] The baptisands receive a baptismal birth[218] that enables them to look forward to the shameless nakedness before God on the last day.[219] The new Adam in Christ replaces the old Adam.

---

212. Church of Scotland, *Baptism*, 22–25.

213. Kim, *Clothing*, 96; Whiteley, *Paul*, 166; Scroggs and Groff, "Baptism in Mark," 537–38; although baptism is also related to the baptized and resurrected Christ (Phil 3:20–21; 1 John 3:2; 2 Cor 3:18), 539. For the concept of exchange of garments and "robe of glory" at baptism see Brock, "Robe," 250–55. As argued from Paul's writings, it is Christ that Christians are called to put on (Davis, "Fashioning a Divine Body," 355).

214. Christiansen, "Women," 4–5; cf. Jackson, "Youth," 275–76; Smith, "Clement of Alexandria and Secret Mark," 457n.19; Beasley-Murray, *Baptism*, 148: Beasley-Murray points out that the sequence of thought of putting on Christ and the literal stripping off and putting on of clothes, thus establishes the practices of baptismal nudity and the putting on of the white robe after baptism.

215. Cyril of Jerusalem, *Mystagogical*; Tinsley, "Coming," 26–27, 32–34; Augustine, *City*, 16:2; Miles, *Carnal*, 35.

216. Miles, *Carnal*, 33.

217. Wilson, "Nakedness," 45–46; Kim, *Clothing*, 99; in Theodore of Mopsuestia's words, becoming naked and unashamed like Gen 2:25 (Smith, "Garments"; Miles, *Carnal*, 33).

218. Augustine, *Sermon* 228:1 (Miles, *Carnal*, 35).

219. Wilson, "Nakedness," 43–46.

Finally the old-versus-new motif can be found in a covenantal context. This recalls the *old* bodily covenant of circumcision—to which Kline refers to as an oath of allegiance and an act of consecration to YHWH[220] versus baptism as the oath-sign of the Christian to the *new* covenant and their allegiance to Christ.[221]

In evaluating the significance of nudity in baptism it is important to note the purificatory nature of this ritual, although it also has an ethical significance in John's baptism.[222] However, baptism in the Holy Spirit is more emphasized (Acts 19:1–6). Nude baptism appeared to have lost the weight of baptism in the Holy Spirit in its own echo of the old-versus-new motif.

Summary

This chapter has conducted a brief survey of some of the theological uses of nakedness. Although not every word for "nakedness" is derived from the "*arôm*" of Genesis 3:7, and some cases are even regarded as "semi-nakedness," the general understanding remains: nakedness is associated with shame, vulnerability, and sexuality.

Apart from some instances where the literal meaning of nakedness is expressed, the remaining occurrences fall into the category of metaphorical language. In some places, this imagery of nakedness can be a euphemism for sexuality (in Leviticus and in some prophetic writings). In others, for instance, the *parousia*, it can be employed to refer to the "naked" state of the soul after death. In the liturgy of baptism, the antithesis of nakedness and clothing is a powerful metaphor, not only for the hope of being clothed with Christ's righteousness, but also for the resurrection body at the *parousia*.[223]

---

220. Kline, *By Oath Consigned*, 43–44, 48, 62, 81. This bodily ritual, whose origins are said to be irretrievable, has more than a close association with the Jewish identity (Kline, *Oath*, 48; Hall, "Circumcision," 1025). In the Bible, this practice was bound with covenants: Abraham and YHWH (Gen 17), Moses and YHWHh (Exod 4), and Joshua and YHWH (Josh 5), not even Moses' own son is safe apart from the covenant of circumcision; how much less Pharaoh's (Hall, "Circumcision," 1027). Circumcision was then developed into many powerful metaphors with other bodily organs: lips (Exod 6:12, 30), ears (Jer 6:10) and the heart (Jer 9:25–26; Deut 10:16).

221. Kline, *Oath*, 62, 81.

222. Lampe, *The Seal of the Spirit*, 24.

223. The Christian hope for resurrection is clearly different from Greek thought (Kim, *Clothing*, 108).

6

The Antithesis of Nakedness and Clothing in Crucifixion

IN PREVIOUS CHAPTERS, WE have explored the notion of physical vulnerability, shame and sexuality as possible meanings and ways of understanding nakedness. We have also seen the association between nudity in baptism and the motto "follow the naked Christ." In this chapter, nakedness and the three themes of vulnerability, shame, and sexuality continue to be addressed in relation to Christ's nakedness at the crucifixion. We will explore the origin of crucifixion and the cruelty of Roman crucifixion to shed more light on the naked death of Christ.

History has witnessed enough human cruelty throughout all ages.[1] Daniel-Rops similarly points out that humankind has improvized various ways of execution whereby fellow human beings could be broken on the wheel, torn asunder by horses, eviscerated, thrown into pits of Serpents, boiled in oil, drowned in slime, or buried alive.[2] Dowling's list is no less impressive: decapitation, gouging out of eyes, the cutting of throats, mutilation, stoning, spiking of men through the torso then placing them in public view as they slowly die, etc.[3] More evidences can be found,[4]

---

1. From Roman punishment (Edgerton, *The Balance of Human Kindness and Cruelty*, 13–14) to medieval forms (Baraz, *Medieval Cruelty*), to more modern method of mass genocide, or cruelty in crimes (Hyatt-Williams, *Cruelty, Violence, and Murder*), or cruelty to animals and women (Steintrager, *Cruel Delight*); Scott, *The History of Corporal Punishment*, 3.

2. Daniel-Rops, *Jesus in His Time*, 424.

3. Dowling, *Clemency & Cruelty in the Roman World*, 1.

4. Edgerton, *Balance*, 13. In early Rome, victims of civil or military oppression were tied into sacks filled with poisonous vipers, then thrown into the Tiber, or dragged

not only in historical writings but also in archaeological paintings and inscriptions of executions that involve the hanging of naked corpses.[5]

Why would humans be so cruel? Perhaps the human experience of pain has a greater impression, persists far longer and more distinctly than others, for instance, the feeling of pleasure.[6] Consequently, physical and even psychological pains were developed from a passive-survival perspective,[7] to an active perspective, i.e., inflicting pain in order to achieve aims and even to fulfil desires such as greed and vengeance. Eventually, the active way of inflicting pain becomes a socially accepted form of punishment, through which cruelty is expressed in the name of "justice." This raises the question as to how far cruelty may be applied in punishment. The answer varies according to country and society around the world.

Our focal concern is the cruelty of condemnation and punishment, particularly in Roman times. Seneca addressed this issue in the first century with a definition that specifically referred to the "mind's intemperance in exacting punishment," holding that being violent without any cause or purpose is not cruelty.[8] However, Roman rulers showed their cruelty through ill founded, groundless, or arbitrary punishment, which in turn evidenced a lack of education and erudition, even barbaric characteristics.[9] For that reason, pagan writers including Tacitus, Suetonius, and Valerius Maximus leave us with the impression of a Roman empire characterized by inventiveness in devising painful modes of torture and

---

to death behind a chariot. They were also flogged, scourged, burned, beheaded, and crucified. Some prisoners were hung by their genitals or tied while a trained eagle bit and clawed them to death. Martyrs were slowly burned to death, or boiled in cauldrons or put in frying pans. More inventive tortures such as submersing men in a freezing pond until their extremities froze and could be shattered by blows. Girls were sewn naked into the belly of a freshly killed ass with only their head protruding; then the ass was exposed to the hot sun until it rotted. The practice of torment that involves nudity is common, one of which involves tying up a honey-smeared naked body for ants and bees to gnaw at the flesh (Mannix, *The History of Torture*, 26, 38; Scott, *Corporal*, 4–5).

5. King, "Circumcision," 52–53; "Destruction of Judean Fortress Portrayed in Dramatic Eight Century B.C. Pictures," 62–63. This hanging was probably a form of exhibition that displayed trophies and victories, partly associated with the earlier hunting culture.

6. Scott, *Corporal*, 3–4.

7. I.e., to destroy or injure any human being or animal that might conceivably be an injury or threat, Scott, *Corporal*, 4–5.

8. Baraz, *Medieval*, 15.

9. Timonen, *Cruelty and Death*, 8.

execution.[10] The punishment of crucifixion, in fact, is one of the best examples.

The Origins and Development of Crucifixion

A Barbaric Origin

While it is commonly agreed that crucifixion had a barbaric origin,[11] it is worth noting that crucifixion itself originated from a religious background. In particular, victims of crucifixion were lifted from the ground so they would not defile the earth, which was the sacred property of the god Ormuzd.[12] Unlike Jewish forms of capital punishment,[13] and at times mistakenly assumed to be a Roman invention, crucifixion was actually practiced by the Assyrians, Carthaginians, Phoenicians, and Persians.[14] In fact, it was passed on from Persia to Carthage, where it was subsequently developed into an exclusive form of punishment that the Romans applied to rebels, runaway slaves, and the lowest type of criminal, but not Roman citizens.[15]

Primary Form of Crucifixion and Slaves

When the Romans adopted crucifixion they only used it on slaves, mainly as a form of punishment to instil fear[16] and not as a method of execution. It was not meant to kill,[17] but to punish the hands and the feet that had

---

10. Baraz, *Medieval*, 30–31; for Seneca and violence in Roman time see Futrell, *The Roman Games*, 22. Scott uses the phrase "exercised their brains" to describe how the Romans intensified the severity of their whippings, *Corporal*, 67.

11. Mounce, *Matthew*, 257; Evans, *Saint Luke*, 867. It is likely that the practice was abolished by Constantine (Godet, *The Gospel of St. Luke*, Vol. 2, 327–28).

12. Barclay, *Matthew*, Vol. 2, 364; Klausner, *Jesus*, 349.

13. This is probably because an impaled body is an affront to God (Tzaferis, "Crucifixion," 48; Blinzler, *Jesus*, 246–48), but there is also a distinction between hanging a dead corpse and killing a person by hanging, Hengel, *Crucifixion*, 24.

14. Tzaferis, "Crucifixion," 48; Daniel-Rops, *Jesus*, 425; Edersheim, *Jesus*, 584.

15. Barclay, *Matthew*, 364.

16. Garnsey, *Social Status and Legal Privilege in the Roman Empire*, 127; Hengel, *Crucifixion*, 34–35, chapter 8: 51–53, 62.

17. Tzaferis, "Crucifixion," 48.

not been properly used.[18] The slave first had to march through the neighborhood proclaiming his offense in humiliation; then he was stripped and scourged. He would then be tied to a vertical stake and punished, frightened and humiliated, but not killed.[19]

However, there appears to be a missing link. If it is true that the primary form of crucifixion was not with the intention to kill, then how did such a form of punishment become a horrendous form of execution? The most plausible argument would suggest an increase of cruelty supported by a desire to discourage revolt and disloyalty.[20] This increase of cruelty fits perfectly well with the existing general cruel attitudes toward slaves and particularly in the Roman flagellation—the emblem of slavery:

> The owner of a slave was vested with the power that does with absolute possession. He owned the slave body and soul. The human creature ranked with the horse, the cow, or the dog, to be kicked and beaten at the whim of its master. Slave he was from birth to death. He was whipped for any and every crime or misdemeanour; he was whipped for the sins of omission as well as commission; he was whipped often enough to provide amusement for his master's guests. Frequently, very frequently, the slave died, either under the whip, or as a direct result of the punishment inflicted.[21]

So far, the origin and primary form of crucifixion have demonstrated the particular nature and development of cruelty in Roman crucifixion. We now embark on an examination of Roman flogging, which was initially used on slaves, and subsequently developed into the flogging that preceded crucifixion.

Roman Flogging and Slaves

It has been assumed that flogging was a form of corporal punishment that may have existed in all primitive ages and savage races.[22] In Roman times, however, flogging was developed into a brutal form of punishment. The victim was stripped, his hands tied up to a post exposing the back for the lash. The lash itself was a long leather thong, studded with sharpened

18. Daniel-Rops, *Jesus*, 425.
19. Tzaferis, "Crucifixion," 48.
20. Auguet, *The Roman Games*, 11.
21. Scott, *Corporal*, 67.
22. Ibid., 33–34.

pieces of bone and pellets of lead; thus, it reduced the naked body to strips of raw lacerated flesh with inflamed and bleeding weals.[23] Hendriksen describes this more succinctly: "Generally two men were employed to administer this punishment, one lashing the victim from one side, one from the other side, with the result that the flesh was at times lacerated to such an extent that deep-seated veins and arteries, sometimes even entrails and inner organs, were exposed. Such flogging, from which Roman citizens were exempt (cf. Acts 16:37), often resulted in death."[24]

Indeed, historical sources evidence that this kind of flogging was associated with some kind of cross or wooden post. For instance, Dionysius of Halicarnassus testifies about a naked slave being torn to death (in *Roman Anitiquities* 7.69): "The men ordered to lead the slave to his punishment, having stretched out both his arms and fastened them to a piece of wood which extended across his breast and shoulders as far as his wrists, followed him, tearing his naked body with whips."[25]

Furthermore, scourging became a brutal business in itself. This method of punishment and coercion during the time of Jesus became something of an "art."[26] Josephus recorded that Jesus, son of Ananias, was "flayed to the bone with scourges";[27] Eusebius depicts how certain martyrs at the time of Polycarp "were torn by scourges down to deep-seated veins and arteries, so that the hidden content of the recesses of their bodies, their entrails and organs, were exposed to sight."[28] Indeed, flogging was regarded as a cruel form of punishment, under which many people died,[29] or at least were crippled for life.[30]

---

23. Barclay, *Matthew*, 363.

24. Hendriksen, *Matthew*, 957.

25. Dionysius of Halicarnassus, in Thayer, "Dionysius of Halicarnassus: Roman Antiquities"; cf. Cary, *The Roman Antiquitites of Dionysius of Halicarnassus*, Vol. 4, 355.

26. Scott, *Corporal*, 36.

27. Josephus, *The Jewish War*, 6:304, in *Josephus: In Nine Volumes*, Vol. 3: The Jewish War, Books IV–IV, 465.

28. Morris, *The Gospel according to John*, 699.

29. Morris, *The Gospel according To Matthew*, 708.

30. Scott, *Corporal*, 66–67.

Improvization of Cruelty

Clearly, this terrific flogging was brought about by some element of improvization of cruelty, particularly from a punishment of a threatening nature to a death sentence for some petty offense. In the light of scholarly evidence attesting the updating of new punishments,[31] the coming of slave flogging caused by improvization is still shocking in its nature, yet imaginable. The horrifying collection of entertaining punishments, namely the *summum supplicium* (such as crucifixion, burning alive and condemning to the beasts),[32] shows that there would have been no limits to Roman cruelty.

Admittedly, in the improvization of cruelty, infliction of pain does not necessarily stop at the physical level but it extends to any level that could cause the most pain, including the psychological. "Pain, physical or mental, is the essence of punishment. Every form of punishment that has been devised has had for its object the infliction of pain or suffering upon the individual; physical pain in some cases, psychical suffering in others, a combination of physical pain and mental suffering in most."[33]

The psychological infliction of the Romans was well known. Alexander, for example, in his revenge ordered eight hundred Jews to be crucified while he was feasting with his concubines. Even more barbarous and inhuman, he ordered the throats of the victim's children and wives to be cut before their eyes, while they were being crucified.[34] The intensity of psychological infliction was obvious.

Therefore, if exposing the victims' nakedness could increase the severity of the punishment (both physical injury[35] and psychological shame),[36] it would not be excluded simply because it transgressed some

---

31. Baraz, *Medieval*, 31; Dowling, *Cruelty*, 222n.4, 331, Dowling echoes Suetonius' (*V. Dom.*) description of new tortures created by Domitian to investigate a supposed conspiracy: the torturer scorched the genitals of the accused until they talked, or cut off their hands; Neyrey, "Cross," 114.

32. Garnsey, *Privilege*, 124; Stewart, "Judicial Procedure in New Testament Times," 105; Auguet, *Games*, 96–99, 105–7.

33. Scott, *Corporal*, 165.

34. Josephus, *The Antiquities of the Jews* 13.14.2: "The Work of Flavius Josephus."

35. The flogging can inflict legs, thighs, buttocks, back and also genitals (Neyrey, *Honor*, 166).

36. McIlroy, "Honour," 3. In Jewish and Mediterranean cultures, being stripped naked is being put to shame (Bourdieu, "The Sentiment of Honour in Kabyle Society," 234n.2 and 241n.32; cf. chapters 2 and 4 of this book).

sense of decency. After all, improvization of cruelty is an exhibition of the superiority of the Roman Empire.

Crucifixion: A Naked death

After it was adopted by the Roman Empire, crucifixion reached its peak of cruelty. As Steward points out: "Truly man, in the most depraved excesses of his cruelty, never devised a more fiendish capital punishment."[37] By this time, crucifixion was not only a common expression of cruelty toward slaves, but was also a useful political tool in the hands of the Roman militants.

Crucifixion as an Inhumane Political Tool

It was not until the first century B.C. that crucifixion evolved into a method of execution, especially for criminals, foreign captives, fugitives, and rebels during times of war and uprisings.[38] It is clear that, in Roman times, slaves and non-Roman citizens were subject to lingering and painful executions.[39] Crucifixion was an effective tool used for ascertaining political goals, and preserving public order in all the provinces.[40] As indicated, under Roman rule it was illegal to crucify a Roman citizen, as crucifixion was a method of death exclusively for slaves, rebels, common thieves, provincials, and aliens.[41] Therefore, this death penalty was a political execution.

Admittedly, this political tool was so powerful and famously feared because of its cruelty. Crucifixion was used in the Jewish War to terrify the Jews into surrender, and mass crucifixion was not uncommon.[42] Crucifixion developed such levels of cruelty that the descriptions of this

---

37. Stewart, "Procedure," 105.

38. Tzaferis, "Crucifixion," 48; Mann, *Mark*, 607; Cunningham, *Jesus and the Evangelists*, 187.

39. Dowling, *Cruelty*, 1–2.

40. Lane, *The Gospel according to Mark*, 561–62; de Lacey and Turner, *Discovering the Bible: Jesus and the Gospels*, 75; Dowling, *Cruelty*, 224; Goodacre, "Scripturalization in Mark's Crucifixion Narrative," 34–47.

41. Daniel-Rops, *Jesus*, 425.

42. Iersel, *Mark: A Reader-Response Commentary*, 471; Crossan, *Who Killed Jesus?* 166: 2,000 were crucified by Varus in 4 B.C.E., 3,600 were crucified by Florus in 66 C.E., and 500 a day were crucified by Titus in 70 C.E.

barbaric form of execution with its utmost cruelty[43] became an obscenity to the ear.[44] Blinzler points out: "Even the mere word, cross, must remain far not only from the lips of the citizens of Rome, but also from their thoughts, their eyes, their ears, Rome's most famous orator, Marcus Tullius Cicero, had once exclaimed."[45]

Throughout the Roman Empire, crucifixion involved shocking torments such as stripping, flogging, being hung with nails, being exposed to the scorching heat of the sun, then perhaps more impaling, or breaking the legs (*crurifragium*) to quicken death,[46] or a spear thrust or a shattering blow.[47]

Crucifixion as a Perverted Physical Torment

Crucifixion was barbaric, savage and inhuman, not because it was simply about nailing a living person to a cross, but because the whole process was associated with an array of methods to inflict torment and disgust. In Dowling's words, it is pain of the fiercest nature.[48] Before marching to the place of crucifixion, a victim was stripped for flogging.[49] Records show that sometimes the naked victim was flogged while he carried the cross.[50] The purpose of this flogging was to weaken the prisoner prior to crucifixion.[51] It was even held that this flogging was merciful because it hastened death on the cross;[52] otherwise the victim could possibly still be alive on the cross for almost a week.[53] This flogging, however, was carried out with care by not killing the victim too soon,[54] because such cruel flogging could cause death before reaching the moment of hanging on

---

43. Hengel, *Crucifixion*, 24; Torrance, "Cross, Crucifixion," 246.
44. Hengel, *Crucifixion*, 10, 22.
45. Blinzler, *Jesus*, 246.
46. John 19:31–32 (Torrance, "Crucifixion," 245–46).
47. Taylor, *Mark*, 589.
48. Dowling, *Cruelty*, 231.
49. Tzaferis, "Crucifixion," 49; Klausner, *Jesus*, 350; Bucher, "Crucifixion in the Ancient World."
50. Brown, *The Death of The Messiah*, 870.
51. Mounce, *Matthew*, 256.
52. Keener, *John*, 1119–20.
53. Cunningham, *Jesus*, 187.
54. Tzaferis, "Crucifixion," 49.

the cross.⁵⁵ The flogging mentioned here, which was prior to crucifixion, was more humiliating than just a punishment or simply to inflict physical pain.⁵⁶ It was actually designed to strip the victim's skin, lacerate bits of flesh off, and cause open wounds to the whole surface of the body so that the raw flesh may become bait, attracting flies, insects or possibly even wild beasts. It would have been unreasonable not to strip the clothes off, since in this kind of flogging the skin was ripped open and the raw flesh exposed. Hanging on the cross is nothing less than bloody naked bait.⁵⁷

Consequently, the pain and irritation would increase once the victim was already nailed on the cross,⁵⁸ as he would be unable to move. As a result, every time the victim tried to move, the pain would increase, literally at excruciating levels. All this was done in order to cause a death as painful as possible.⁵⁹ Therefore, to have the body stripped naked throughout this process was nothing less than a rule of thumb.⁶⁰ For a convicted man to die while being flogged and before reaching the cross was considered fortunate,⁶¹ because if the victim was alive, he would also have to be hung with nails thrust through his wrists.⁶² This torment would then last for hours, in some cases even days while the victim went through unspeakable torture, suffering from his lacerated flesh, organ displacement, hunger, thirst, cramp, scorching heat, flies, and so on.⁶³

Crucifixion as Dehumanization

Crucifixion was designed to degrade and humiliate.⁶⁴ It is important to note that crucifixion was a penalty for the lower class (*humiliores*), while the upper class (*honestiores*) were given more "humane" punishments.⁶⁵ It is not overstating the case to say that the victim was psychologically

55. Keener, *Matthew* (1999), 672n.191.
56. Neyrey, "Cross," 113; *Mishnah Makkoth* ("Stripes") 3:12, 3:14 in Danby, *Mishnah*, 407–8.
57. A "slab of unused meat" (Jakes, *Naked and Not Ashamed*, 113).
58. Klausner, *Jesus*, 350.
59. Brooks, *Mark*, 258.
60. Keener, *Matthew* (1999), 679; Mounce, *Matthew*, 256.
61. Stewart, "Procedure," 105.
62. Clinic, "Crucifixion"; Charlesworth, "Jesus and Jehohanan," 148–49.
63. Stewart, "Procedure," 105; Bucher, "Crucifixion."
64. Hengel, *Crucifixion*, 10, 22–24.
65. Ibid., 34, 51–53; Torrance, "Crucifixion," 245–46.

inflicted beyond the limit of human dignity, i.e., the human victim was turned into a despised object. Koester rightly points out that other forms of execution might allow the victims to retain some measure of dignity, but crucifixion did not.[66] The fact that crucifixion was an extreme degradation,[67] a torment and an inhumane death,[68] and the most shameful death man can suffer,[69] could not be overemphasized. The victim was normally denuded,[70] and insulted physically to the very private parts in the flogging.[71] Then, he would be led naked to the sight of execution.[72] The victim was deprived of his dignity, being turned from a living human being into a feast for scavenging birds,[73] and not to be removed or buried,[74] unless an exception of mercy was granted.[75] While nakedness was the norm for crucifixion,[76] the helpless and agonizing victim could not move, swat flies, or even breathe. Often, victims befouled themselves with their own urine or excrement.[77] Being crucified in different positions,[78] the criminals suffered a death of pain, irritation, itches, painful and humiliating genital mutilations with sadistic mockery in the middle of a public place.[79] In Cunningham's words, "The whole point of Roman crucifixion

---

66. Koester, *Symbolism in the Fourth Gospel*, 188.

67. Mounce, *Matthew*, 257; Neyrey, *Honor*, 64–65.

68. Green, *Matthew*, 296; Fitzmyer, "Crucifixion," 498. Apart from being crucified naked, the body suffered jagged iron nails driven through the most sensitive nerve centers of the wrists and ankles. This is why ancient writers did not dwell on this shameful death (Morris, *Matthew*, 708). Josephus (*The Jewish War*, 389) records in *The Jewish War* 5.11.1 §451 how "[t]he soldiers, out of rage and hatred, amused themselves by nailing prisoners in various attitudes until no space could be found for the crosses due to their vast number, nor crosses for the bodies ." Green, "Death of Jesus," 147.

69. Trilling, *The Gospel according to St. Matthew*, 255–56.

70. Rapske, *The Book of Acts in Its First Century Setting*, Vol. 3, 297.

71. Neyrey, "Cross," 113, 117; Hengel, *Crucifixion*, 25; Dowling, *Cruelty*, 222.

72. Brown, *Messiah*, 870, 952.

73. Artemidorus, *Oneirocritica*, 127; Green, "Kaleidoscopic View," 159.

74. Hurtado, *Mark*, 270; Painter, *Mark's Gospel*, 203; Stock, *The Method and Message of Mark*, 399; Green, "Death," 147.

75. Crossan, *Jesus*, 167: quoting Josephus in *Life* 420–21; John 19:31: Jews might request the removal of corpses on sacred festivals.

76. Tinsley, "Coming," 32.

77. Neyrey, "Cross," 113–14; Keener, *John*, 1136; Cunningham, *Jesus*, 188.

78. Ibid., 114.

79. Hengel, *Crucifixion*, 87; Anderson, *The Gospel of Mark*, 341; Nineham, *Saint Mark*, 423–24; Summers, *Commentary on Luke*, 303.

was to reduce the victim to the status of a thing, stripping him of every vestige of human dignity, in order to discourage any challenging of the might of Rome."[80]

Crucifixion: A Public Affair and Sadistic Entertainment

Although in the Roman Empire crucifixion was a much more common and horrendous punishment, it was only one of many creative "popular entertainments" available, such as throwing the victims to the wild beasts, being torn apart, etc., (*crux, bestiae, ignis*).[81] These terrifying means of execution were regarded as forms of live "entertainments," possibly for two reasons: (1) the involvement of the public was crucial for the political purpose, just as in a political campaign, and (2) the audience could increase the degree of humiliation and ridicule during the process of carrying out the penalty. The participating public (the witnesses) would normally be the very community that the victim had probably always been a part of.[82]

Crucifixion was improvised with an intention to create entertainment for public display.[83] Having been stripped naked and flogged,[84] the criminal had to be publicly shamed all the way from marching through the town to the place of crucifixion. Hanging around his neck was the crime he committed,[85] which was written on a tablet that would then be attached to the cross on which he was to be crucified.[86] Furthermore, the criminal was subjected to the degradation, taunts, and derision of the passer-by.[87] It was in the public places, in Dowling's words, that "the observers could rejoice in the punishment of the condemned and learn from their agony not to follow their example."[88]

Yet, besides all the public humiliation, crucifixion was a sadistic horror. It was a death with the full rein of sadism and perversion of

---

80. Cunningham, *Jesus*, 187.
81. Hengel, *Crucifixion*, 35.
82. Bornhaeuser, *The Death and Resurrection of Jesus Christ*, 150.
83. Nolland, *Luke 18:35—24:53*, 1145.
84. Rapske, *Acts*, 297; Artemidorus, *Oneirocritica*, 127; Kohler and Hirsch, "Crucifixion."
85. Bornhaeuser, *Jesus*, 144; Blinzler, *Jesus*, 244.
86. Gundry, *Matthew*, 569–70; de Lacey and Turner, *Jesus*, 75.
87. Cunningham, *Jesus*, 187.
88. Dowling, *Cruelty*, 224.

the executioners,[89] who found some sickening pleasure at the sight of a miserable humanity reduced to the last degree of impotence, suffering, and degradation.[90] The sadistic nature of crucifixion was expressed not only through the stripping off of clothes, the horrendous flogging of the naked body, but also through the impalement and insult of the victim's sexual organs,[91] and finally the enlargement of the genitals[92] of the helpless victim.

The Death of the Naked Christ

Archaeological evidence shows a clearer perspective of Roman crucifixion, but admittedly, the Passion narrative in the Gospels does not reveal much detail of Christ's nakedness. What is the reason for this lack of description?

The Gospels and the Naked Christ

The Gospels record the disrobing and clothing of Jesus in the Passion narrative, generally to express the physical insult and shame that Jesus endured:[93] the flogging (Matt 27:26; Mark 15:15; John 19:1); the stripping (Matt 27:28; Mark 15:17; John 19:2); the mocking scarlet robe and the return of his own clothes (Matt 27:31; Mark 15:20), and finally the dividing of his clothes at the crucifixion (Matt 27:35; Mark 15:24; Luke 23:33–34; John 15:23). We may not know exactly how many times the clothing and undressing happened,[94] but what we can be certain of is that Christ was disrobed at the scourging and once again at the cross, when his clothes were divided.[95] The naked scourging was meant to be shameful,[96] and the confiscation of property indicates that Jesus' clothes were totally

---

89. Stock, *Mark*, 399; Wallace, *The Gospel of John*, 289; Keener, *Matthew* (1999), 678; Keener, *John*, 1135.

90. Morris, *John*, 712.

91. Hengel, *Crucifixion*, 25; Seneca's *Dialogue 6 (De consolatione ad Marciam)* 20.3 ("To Marcia on Consolation"), in *Moral Essays*, Vol. 2, 69; Plass, *The Game of Death in Ancient Rome*, 60.

92. Neyrey, "Cross," 114.

93. Ibid., 117.

94. He was stripped and clothed with different clothing during the mockery (Neyrey, *Honor*, 64).

95. Filson, *Commentary on the Gospel according to St. Matthew*, 33–39.

96. Neyrey, *Honor*, 64.

removed.⁹⁷ Therefore, he suffered shame,⁹⁸ as Neyrey comments on the flogging: "His body, however, was also ashamed. His enemies seize him, 'laying their hands on him' and thus restricting his power (26:50). Roman soldiers flog his body, and it is only our piety that does not allow us to imagine that they flogged his legs, thighs, and buttocks as well as his back. Humiliation and shame in this situation hurt worse than the physical pain."⁹⁹

However, a very important question is why have the Gospels missed out these brutal descriptions? It is clear that the writers of the Synoptic Gospels allotted a considerable amount of effort in depicting the passion of Jesus Christ, but they did not focus on the little details of how the flogging was actually carried out.

Generally, commentators agree that all the Gospels portray the crucifixion of Jesus with a minimum of words,¹⁰⁰ or even more precisely, none of them go on to describe the terrible details of the Roman crucifixion.¹⁰¹ This is probably because the main focus of the Gospel writers was the significance of Christ's death rather than the suffering *per se*.¹⁰² Additionally, crucifixion was too famous for its abhorrent and painful death, even in the eyes of the pagan world,¹⁰³ to be discussed in detail.¹⁰⁴ In other words, such descriptions are rare in the literature of antiquity not because of the infrequency of the practice, but rather due to the literary aesthetic consideration.¹⁰⁵ Nolland sums up this substantial argument, perhaps, most adequately:

> It is striking that none of the Gospel accounts provides any description of the actual crucifixion. There is likely a number of reasons for this: (a) in the world for which the Gospels were written this barbaric punishment was well known, and the mere mention of it would evoke powerful images; (b) given the

97. Kruse, *John. Tyndale New Testament Commentaries*, 367.
98. Bock, *Jesus according to Scripture*, 386.
99. Neyrey, *Honor*, 66.
100. Cranfield, *The Gospel according to Saint Mark*, 455; Lane, *Mark*, 564; Schmid, *The Gospel according to Mark*, 289.
101. Augsburger, *Matthew*, 290; Morris, *Matthew*, 708.
102. Morris, *The Gospel according to St. Luke*, 326; Cunningham, *Jesus*, 187.
103. Lane, *Mark*, 561; Blinzler, *Jesus*, 246.
104. Brooks, *Mark*, 225–26; Hendriksen, *Luke*, 1026–27.
105. Green, "Death," 147; Stanton, *The Gospels and Jesus*, 286. It was so barbarous and inhumane that polite Romans did not talk about it.

limited descriptions in the secular sources and the tenor of some comments, it would seem that educated Romans considered the subject so unsavoury as to be avoided as much as possible in conversation; (c) the one who had been crucified in this case was the beloved Lord, so to dwell on his agony on the cross felt wrong; and (d) the focus of interest of the Gospel accounts is not on the crucifixion as such, except as having happened, but on the larger pattern of significance within which the crucifixion finds its place.[106]

Patristic Thoughts and the Naked Christ

Whereas the Passion narrative of the Gospels does not reveal so much detail of Christ's nakedness, patristic studies provide a considerable amount of evidence. The public confession of the scandalous paradox of the crucifixion was not only in the earliest hymns about Christ but also in preaching, for instance, the *Homily on the Passion* by Melito (died c.180):

> He who hung the earth *in its place* is hanged, he who fixed the heavens is fixed *upon the cross*, he who made all things fast is made fast upon the tree, the Master has been insulted, God has been murdered, the King of Israel has been slain by an Israelitish hand. Of strange murder, strange crime! The Master has been treated in unseemly wise, with his body naked, and has not even been deemed worthy of a covering, that he might not be seen. For this reason the lights of *heaven* turned away, and the day darkened, that it might hide him who was stripped upon the cross, shrouding not the body of the Lord, but the eyes of men.[107]

Melito implies that Christ was crucified totally naked. This view was also held by other early church fathers. For example, according to Augustine, Christ's nakedness can be paralleled with Noah's nakedness.[108] In this interpretation, the focus is, metaphorically, on Christ's suffering and the stripping of power and glory. More interestingly, Christ's nudity on the cross is one among many reasons for the liturgical practice of nude baptism in early Christianity, especially in the words of Cyril of Jerusalem:

---

106. Nolland, *The Gospel of Matthew*, 1191–92.
107. Melito, *Passion*, 179; Hengel, *Crucifixion*, 21.
108. Tinsley, "Coming," 32; Augustine, *City*, 16.2.

The Antithesis of Nakedness and Clothing in Crucifixion   163

imitating Christ who hung naked on the cross.[109] Finally, Christ's nakedness at the crucifixion was reflected not only in the Christian liturgy and theology of baptism,[110] but also as a motto for a Christian lifestyle. Jerome's famous adage, "*nudus nudum Jesum sequi*" (naked to follow a naked Christ) repeated here,[111] signifies "innocence and purity" or the "willing self-deprivation."[112] Surely, Christ's nakedness on the cross must have influenced, to some extent, the traditional interpretation of nakedness in homiletics, the Christian baptismal rituals and the early Christian philanthropic lifestyle.

The Loincloth and the Naked Christ

In the light of evidences thus far, the naked Christ has increasingly become more than a probability. However, the depiction of Christ on crucifixes and in the Arts varies in a complicated fashion,[113] mostly with a loincloth and at times with total nudity.[114] This loincloth is the existing division among modern scholars and commentators regarding the nudity of Christ on the cross. While many say that Jesus was nailed to the cross naked,[115] others insist that he was hung, at least, with a loincloth.[116] Certainly this division has existed from the earliest times: one side (Saint Ambrose,[117] Saint Augustine,[118] and Saint Cyprian[119]) agreed that Jesus

---

109. Cyril, *Baptism*, in Cross, *Cyril*, 59; Hippolytus, in Easton, *Hippolytus*, 46; Miles, *Carnal*, 33–35.

110. Miles, *Carnal*, 35; Tinsley, "Coming," 24–36.

111. Miles, *Carnal*, 63.

112. Walters, *Male*, 82–83.

113. Tinsley, "Coming."

114. Walters, *Nude*, 66, 73.

115. Malina and Rohrbaugh, *Social-Science Commentary on the Synoptic Gospels*, 164–65, 276, 409; McIlroy, "Honour," 3; Keener, *John*, 1138; Kruse, *John*, 367; Milne, *The Message of John*, 278; Keener, *Matthew* (1997), 679; Neyrey, "Cross," 125, 131; Senior, *The Passion of Jesus in the Gospel of Luke*, 129; Neyrey, *Honor*, 64–65.

116. Thoby [*Histoire du Crucifix*, 191, 6] cites Leclerq's comments (*Dictionnaire d' Archéologie chrétienne*) and Barbé (*La Passion de N-S Jésus-Christ selon le chirugien*), as quoted in Tinsley, "Coming," 32–33.

117. Jacobus de Voragine, *The Golden Legend: Readings on the Saints*, Vol. 1: The Passion of our Lord, 77.

118. Augustine, *City*, 16.2, Vol. 2, 99–101; Tinsley, "Coming," 32.

119. Cyprian, in Davies, *Born*, 49; Cyprian, ANCL8-2, 26–27.

was stripped naked; the other side, (the Jewish doctors)[120] differed on this matter, unclear whether men should be entirely naked or that there should be some frontal covering.[121]

On the one hand, we know it was the norm to degrade by nakedness.[122] Moreover, since Christ's clothes were confiscated, it is commonly believed that Christ was naked on the cross.[123] "The ideas of disgrace and exposure combine in the biblical metaphor for shame, which is the lifting of a woman skirts or the cutting of a man's clothing, especially so as to expose his buttocks. Such was the utter disgrace that Jesus endured when crucified naked on a Roman cross. He endured the shame of the cross and was honoured by God raising him from the dead and exalting him."[124]

On the other hand, some scholars carefully acknowledge that while it was the norm for the crucified to be stripped naked, there is a possibility of a loincloth in Jesus' case,[125] although their "arguments" are of varied quality. Some believe that the loincloth existed but they have no further explanation,[126] or leave it with uncertainty.[127] Commentators like Brown and Witherington, while agreeing with the possibility of Jewish sensitivity resulting in the presence of a loincloth,[128] do not reject the view that under the control of Roman soldiers it is more likely for Jesus to have been totally naked.[129]

There are two questions at hand: (1) was there a loincloth in the customary clothing? and (2) could there possibly be a concession between the Jewish sensitivity and the Roman soldiers?

---

120. See *Mishnah: Sanhebrin*, 6.3 (Neusner, *Mishnah*, 594).

121. Daniel-Rops, *Jesus*, 429.

122. Note that this interpretation is considered in the same context of Rev 3:17 and 16:15, *Sipre* on Deut 32:21 (Davies and Allison, *Matthew*, 614).

123. Bruner, *Matthew*, Vol. 2, 734; Wright, *Matthew for Everyone*, Part 2, 183.

124. McIlroy, "Honour," 3.

125. Edwards, *Mark*, 468–69; Tinsley, "Coming," 33; Morris, *John*, 715; Daniel-Rops, *Daily Life in Palestine at the Time of Christ*, 211–18.

126. Jones, *The Gospel according to St Mark*, 239; Barclay, *Matthew*, 366–67.

127. Blomberg, *Matthew*, 415.

128. Witherington III, *John's Wisdom*, 305; Brown, *The Gospel according to John*, Vol. 2, 902.

129. Witherington III, *The Gospel of Mark*, 395; Brown, *The Gospel according to John* (xiii–xxi), 902.

Customary Clothing

Some scholars argue that among the customary clothing of early Palestinian people, the loincloth did exist.[130] For instance, Bock[131] flags up the Jewish abhorrence of nakedness in the book of *Jubilees*,[132] and suggests that John may have implied the outer garments at the division of Jesus' clothes. However, biblical commentators are more diverse in their focus. Some keep their focus on emphasizing the importance of the seamless tunic. Fredrickson adds that this tunic was a priestly garment worn next to the body like the one being worn by Aaron in the holy place.[133] Other commentators give few or no comment regarding the loincloth in their collections of items: an outer garment, a tunic, a belt, sandals, and maybe a head covering;[134] or, a four parts turban, outer cloak, a girdle, sandals, or an undershirt.[135] The only[136] ancient source where a loincloth is mentioned is the pseudepigrapha Gospel of Nicodemus 7.2.[137] Nevertheless, the reality of the loincloth at the cross is tentative. Even if it had existed, commentators agree that all other items were taken away and divided.[138]

A Questionable Concession

What about the possibility of a concession made between Roman soldiers and Jewish sensibility toward nudity and scruples about public nakedness,[139] which in turn resulted in the loincloth of Jesus? The proposed answers to this question are diverse.

---

130. Edwards, "Dress and Ornamentation," 236.
131. Bock, *Jesus*, 386.
132. *Jubilees* 3:30–32, 7:20.
133. Lev 16:4 (Fredrickson, *John*, 247).
134. Beasley-Murray, *John*, 347.
135. Edwards, *John*, 180–81. If they ever existed, the undergarments of Jesus' time are not equivalent to ours and all items were divided (Carson, *The Gospel according to John*, 611–12).
136. Blinzler, *Jesus*, 253.
137. *The Gospel of Nicodemus*, or *Acts of Pilate*, 60. This description, however, appears to have mixed the sequences altogether; Corrigan, "Crucifixion," 48; Schiller, *Iconography of Christian Art*, translated by Janet Seligman, Vol. 2: The Passion of Jesus Christ, 88–97.
138. Carson, *The Gospel according to John*, 611–12.
139. *Jubilees* 3:30–31; Gen 9:20–27.

Based on the fact that Jesus retained his clothes on the march to Golgotha,[140] some scholars such as Brown, Lagrange, and Dalman establish a link with a point made in *Mishnah Sanhedrin* 6:3 and 6:4,[141] about the values of decency in the Jewish death. However, notwithstanding the values of decency in the context of *Mishnah*, even the sages considered that a man could be stoned naked.[142] Moreover, the context of Jewish stoning is very different from the Roman execution, which is the hanging of a living person as a criminal penalty. Even if Jesus had been allowed to wear clothes on the march, France believes he would not have been allowed to wear clothes on the cross, considering the brutality of the previous scourging and mocking.[143] However, the counter-argument holds that although the Roman practice of crucifixion may have required the stripping of clothes, this should not imply that the condemned person was without a loincloth—*subligaculum*.[144] Nonetheless, could such a concession possibly have been made? Evidences suggest the opposite.

First, evidence for the existence of the concession is clearly not traceable. Lane suggests that it is unknown whether Romans would make such a concession.[145] Edersheim unfortunately has not provided any evidence to support his view for this concession. Besides, while he suggests that Jesus' loincloth was a reality due to the concession, he agrees that most rabbinic sources do not share the "decency theory."[146] Lagrange shares this view,[147] believing that the soldiers, who allowed someone else to carry the cross for Christ and gave him a drink to dull the pain, must have allowed him a covering; or Jesus' friends would have asked for this

---

140. France, *Matthew* (2007), 1063; France, *The Gospel of Mark*, 639.

141. Brown, *John*, 902; Dalman, *Jesus—Jeshua*, 185–86.

142. *Mishnah Sanhedrin* (Danby, *Mishnah*, 390).

143. France, *Matthew* (2007), 1066–67.

144. *Subligaculum* is a linen tape wrapped around the loins and waist, normally worn under the outer clothes. It was kept on by gladiators while fighting, and those who were condemned and thrown to the beasts in the circus. Consequently, Thoby articulates that victims of crucifixion must also have worn it and suggests this is in fact a feature of the earliest representation of the crucifixion. Thoby [*Crucifix*, 191–96] cites the comments of Leclerq (*Dictionnaire*) and Barbé (*Passion*, 1950), quoted in Tinsley, "Coming," 32–33.

145. Lane, *Mark*, 566.

146. Edersheim, *Jesus*, 584; *Sanhedrin* 6.3–4, Danby, *Mishnah*, n.2.

147. Lagrange, *Mark*, 168. This view of a Jewish death is shared with Edersheim, *Jesus*, 589.

favor.¹⁴⁸ However, the reality of Roman contempt for Jews suggests that this concession is not only untraceable, but also critically questionable.

Secondly, the concession seems to be a methodological mistake. Recently Viladesau, following Thoby and evidences in the *Mishnah* and the *Jubilees*, argues that the loincloth was allowed on the grounds that Roman gladiators wore them.¹⁴⁹ Thoby is correct in saying that the gladiators wore loincloths, because nakedness in the Roman arenas was not a rule.¹⁵⁰ However, it is a mistake to confuse crucifixion, a matter Romans never discussed, with the entertaining culture of gladiators. Furthermore, it is another mistake to ignore how commonly naked punishment was associated with sadistic behaviors and sexual manners in the Roman culture of stadium, arena, and circus.¹⁵¹

Thirdly, the strongest and most interesting argument for the concession is a result of misinterpretation. The argument for the concession was founded on the returning of Jesus' clothes before the march to Golgotha:¹⁵² "It was normal for criminals to be led to the cross naked. The return of Jesus' clothes perhaps reflects a Roman concession to the Jews because of the special shame they attached to appearing naked in public."¹⁵³

Why is this argument a misinterpretation? Clearly, the returning of Jesus' clothes was against the normal practice of a naked march in the city of the executed,¹⁵⁴ but Christ's clothes were returned not because of the concession. Rather, the re-clothing of Jesus after the flogging indicates that he was not condemned to be flogged for crucifixion. He was to be flogged and then released (Luke 23:16, 22; John 19:1, 12).¹⁵⁵ This makes better sense as Jesus' scourging was a decision made arbitrarily

---

148. Lagrange, (*Études*, 427–28), quoted in Tinsley, "Coming," 32.

149. Viladesau, *Cross*, 22.

150. Auguet, *Games*, 96–99, 106–7.

151. Wistrand, *Entertainment and Violence in Ancient Rome*, 55–59; Plass, *Game*, 56, 60, 210–12, 206n.2.

152. Nolland, *Matthew*, 1185, 1193.

153. Blomberg, *Matthew*, 415; France, *Matthew* (1985), 394; France, *Matthew* (2007), 1063; and France, *Mark*, 639.

154. Dionysius of Halicarnassus 7.69.2 (Thayer, "Dionysius"); Cary, *Dionysius*, 355; Josephus, *Jewish Antiquities*, 19:270 in Book 18–20, 339; Davies and Allison, *Matthew*, 605.

155. De Lacey and Turner, *Jesus*, 75; Bultmann, *The Gospel of John*, 658n.2; Fenton, *The Gospel according to John*, 189.

by Pilate without any formal judgment and separate from crucifixion,[156] unlike the normal procedure of the court.[157] Dodd points out that Pilate's phrase "*Ecco Homo*" was associated with his attempts to manipulate the trial toward an acquittal of Jesus; therefore the scourging he suffered was not the customary preliminary to crucifixion, and certainly without the context of a death sentence.[158] Therefore, the guards must have dressed Jesus, not leaving him naked, because it was Pilate's intention to release Jesus. This strengthens Blinzler's argument, which suggests that Jesus was scourged only once and not twice,[159] and thus when Jesus' death sentence was passed, he still had his clothes on.[160] Accordingly, the returning of Christ's clothes has nothing to do with the concession made by the Roman soldiers who, allegedly, may have had some regard for the customary Jewish abhorrence for public nakedness.

In conclusion, the weight of the evidence means that a plausible argument for an exception in Jesus' case, which would have been against the norm of naked crucifixion, is less likely. The case for the Naked Christ remains the highest probability.

A Conclusion

According to the evidence, the existence of a loincloth is unlikely: the concession of a loincloth, as a result of Jewish sensitivity, creates a blatant contradiction to the sadistic nature of the Roman rulers and crucifixion.[161] We summarize the main points:

---

156. Westcott, *The Gospel According to St John*, 268; Ridderbos, *The Gospel of John—A Theological Commentary*, 599; Blinzler, *Jesus*, 223–24.

157. Blinzler, *Jesus*, 234; Lagrange, *Mark*, 165–66.

158. Dodd, *History Tradition in the Fourth Gospel*, 102; Waetjen, *The Gospel of the Beloved Disciple*, 389; Blinzler, *Jesus*, 225.

159. Blinzler, *Jesus*, 234; although Carson (*John*, 597) believes that Jesus was flogged twice. However, if Jesus was flogged twice, then during the second time his clothes must have been removed completely following the norm, and Pilate should not have been surprised at why he died very soon after that.

160. Blinzler, *Jesus*, 244, although Blinzler still had a second thought about the Roman avoidance of complete nakedness in Judea as indecent in Jewish eyes.

161. Clearly in scourging and mocking, France, *Matthew* (2007), 1066–67.

1. Roman soldiers so despised the Jews[162] that they would do their best to humiliate and shock the Palestinians—the lower class and the oppressed.[163]

2. Jewish sensitivity toward nakedness may have been a reality, but it was inconsistent. On the one hand, it was a thrilling opportunity for Romans soldiers to manifest their hatred toward the Jews.[164] Yet, on the other, if the Jews knew the norm of naked crucifixion,[165] they could have stoned Jesus,[166] but they did not! This suggests that their cultural sensitivity had been neglected.

3. The fact that mass crucifixion of thousands of people was carried out in various ways, including the impalement and nailing of the genitals, tells us two things: (a) there was probably no tolerance toward Jewish values, and (b) Christ's crucifixion was no different from a normal death for criminals.[167] Christ's death was even considered unimportant during that time. "So unimportant was the crucifixion of Jesus of Nazareth from a Roman point of view that Tacitus, in his review of the trouble in Judea, comments, 'Under Tiberius nothing happened' (*History* V. 9, *sub Tiberio quies*)."[168]

4. Roman soldiers seldom made an exception or were considerate to the values and customs of the lower class citizens, i.e., the provincials and the slaves whose country they invaded and colonized. They came from a culture of nude public baths, thus, it would have been more probable for Roman soldiers to provoke Jewish offense than tolerate local customs. More importantly, to Romans soldiers, being cruel was the normal inclination of their society.[169] They were trained and

---

162. Keener, *John*, 1122.

163. Keener, *Matthew* (1997), 388; Keener, *John*, 1138.

164. Josephus recorded how the Roman soldiers showed their buttocks and created a riot (Neyrey, *Honor*, 24).

165. Morris, *Matthew*, 715; Cranfield, *Mark*, 455; Hargreaves, *A Guide to St Mark's Gospel*, 269; Hooker, *The Gospel according to St Mark*, 371; Lane, *Mark*, 564; Painter, *Gospel*, 203; de Lacey and Turner, *Jesus*, 74.

166. Davies, *Matthew*, 196; Spong, *Liberating the Gospels*, 259, 276.

167. He was crucified as a criminal between two malefactors (Anderson, *Mark*, 342).

168. Lane, *Mark*, 561–62.

169. Wistrand, *Entertainment*, 59; Auguet, *Games*, 96–99, 11–12; Plass, *Game*, 56–60.

paid to be cruel: in the Roman army, the cruelty of corporal punishments was deeply rooted.[170] Therefore, Roman scourging and the horror of crucifixion did not originate from military protocols, but sprung from the nature of cruelty. The soldiers involved in the task of crucifixion had a different psyche through which they not only kept calm and at ease, but also considered inflicting the victims as entertainment. They were soldiers of blood, torn flesh, of screaming and cursing in rage and anger. Therefore, considering the Roman attitudes toward slaves and the foreign provincial peasants, it is most probable that when Jesus died like a slave, he would have received one of the worst death penalties.

At this stage, in the light of this study, it is appropriate to conclude that there is little need for more convincing and plausible evidence for the nakedness of Christ on the cross.[171] What is more important is the implication and interpretation of Christ's nakedness in the context of the cross.[172]

---

170. The forms of punishment varied widely from decimation, "clubbed or stoned to death," or being fed upon barley instead of wheat; from corporal punishment (*castigatio*) to being discharged with ignominy (*missio ignominiosa*). If corporal punishments were inappropriate in some cases, even more humiliating substitutes could be found (Watson, *The Roman Soldier*, 118–19, 121–25).

171. Rather, the existence of the loincloth indicates a reluctance to show Christ's nude body, because of the shame attached to nudity (Kartsonis, *Anastasis*, 143).

172. For example, Calvin, *CC—John*, Vol. 2, 230.

PART 3

Nakedness and Clothing in
a Model of Atonement

7

The Making of the *Christus Nudus* Model

THE FOCUS OF THIS chapter is to examine the origin and inspiration of *Christus nudus* in a process that will substantiate the content of the subsequent soteriological model. In chapter 6, *Christus nudus* was revealed as the icon of shame and suffering. Such a powerful image has been an inspiration for Christian traditions such as the famous motto "naked to follow the naked Christ"—a philanthropic and mimetic effect of atonement;[1] or alternatively, the practice of nude baptism as an imitation of Christ's death and resurrection.[2] Such an interpretation of the naked cross warrants the identification of *Christus nudus* as a foundation for the philosophical and theological interpretation of the concept of a naked soul in eschatology, which accordingly distinguishes the eschatology of the elect.[3]

As a result, one may conclude that a *Christus nudus* soteriological model depends heavily on the semantics and semiotics of *the* icon of Christianity—the cross of a crucified Messiah and a risen Christ. Yet, the nakedness of Christ on the cross has much more to offer at a theological level, especially a soteriological model. This chapter will show that the notion of *Christus nudus* moves beyond the historical nakedness of crucifixion into a trinitarian and christological perspective of cosmological nakedness. We shall explore three areas: (1) the origin of *Christus nudus*

---

1. Francis of Assisi, *Little Flowers of St. Francis of Assisi*, chapter 36; Jerome, *NPNF2-6*, 287; Tulloch, *Luther and Other Leaders of the Reformation*, 10–11.

2. Beasley-Murray, *Baptism*, 1973, 148–53, built upon Cyril's imitation of Christ, Chrysostom's association of the baptisand's nakedness and Adam's nakedness in Eden; Rowley, "Jewish Proselyte Baptism," 322–23.

3. The wedding garment in Augustine, *NPNF1-6*, 408.

among Christian traditions, teachings and liturgy, (2) the divine face of nakedness, *Deus nudus, Christus nudus,* and the cross: a soteriology through a conceal-reveal model; and (3) the clothing of *theosis* through the self-emptying Christ as a result of the restorative and reconciliatory work of the cross.

Christus Nudus and Interpretation

The idea of portraying a naked Christ has been an artistic inspiration and a symbol for his dual existence; his humanity and divinity. Not long ago Maev Kennedy reported on the discovery of a stone-carved statue of a naked, suffering Christ in the Netherlands, which is estimated to be 500 years old.[4] More recently, an artistic expression of a naked chocolate Christ received much opposition,[5] for being one of the worst assaults on Christian sensibility.[6] Some interpret such an expression of *Christus nudus* as an attempt to attain notoriety or attention,[7] but such an accusation is both naïve and an indication of poor scholasticism. Clearly the notion of *Christus nudus* in crucifixion has never been completely ignored;[8] in fact, referring to the crucifixion of Christ, John of Ruysbroeck (1293–1381) claims: "He was stripped stark naked. So fair a body neither man nor woman ever saw so cruelly ill-used. He suffered shame, and anguish, and cold, before all the world: for He was naked, and it was cold, and a searching wind cut into His wounds. . . . Christ our Bridegroom, wounded to the death, forsaken of God and of all creatures, dying on the cross, hanging like a log for which no one cared, save Mary, His poor mother, who could not help Him!"[9]

More importantly, a notion that has been omitted and gradually forgotten is a cosmological *Christus nudus*, which has been circulating among various theologians throughout history. This cosmological notion of *Christus nudus*, which must be understood as derived from Christ's nakedness on the cross, is embedded within certain theological themes:

4. Kennedy, "Christ Portrayed as Naked, Human and Divine."

5. Cones, "Sweet Jesus!" 50; BBC News, "My Sweet Lord"; Parry, "Statue of Christ Made from Chocolate."

6. BBC News, "Chocolate Jesus Exhibit Cancelled."

7. Blake, "Outrage at Naked Chocolate Jesus in New York Gallery."

8. "The Body is Sacred: Naked Woman, Nudity and Sin"; Wijngaards, "Naked Without Shame"; Anderson, "Naked Christs and Balaam's Ass."

9. John of Ruysbroeck, *The Adornment of the Spiritual Marriage*, 15.

(1) the Adam-Christ typology, (2) mimesis of Christ through nude baptism, and (3) philanthropist developments of the Naked Christ built upon the first two themes. These three themes, as will be argued later, are interwoven and construct a unique soteriology that employs nakedness and clothing.

The Naked Christ and Adam-Christ Typology

Christ's nakedness is repeatedly alluded in religious and theological literatures, especially those that describe his crucifixion;[10] for example, meditating on Christ's crucifixion, Louis of Blois referred to Gertrude's vision of a Naked Christ.[11] More importantly, such description becomes a foundation for a theological development that is associated with Christ's nakedness. For instant, Calvin connects Christ's nakedness to an important theological imagery: the clothing of righteousness and justification.[12] However, there is nothing new in such theological comments, for the patristic sources evidence earlier developments. In fact, after Melito (died c. 180), who preached the nakedness of a crucified Lord,[13] Cyprian of Carthage (died c. 258) employed imageries of nakedness and clothing for a mimetic-philanthropist soteriological model. He proposed two aspects: (1) Christ clothes sinners and (2) Christians clothe others. In the former, Cyprian emphasized the Adam-Christ typology in that sinners must "buy" Christ's clothes,[14] because Christ clothes sinners with the robe of immortality.[15] In the latter, he proposed a philanthropic soteriology.

In Adam, according to Cyprian, all are naked no matter how many garments and jewels are worn; for without Christ's beauty, sinners are unsightly.[16] Consequently, Christ's nakedness is theologically significant within a soteriological model that alludes to Adam's nakedness.

---

10. Chrysostom, *NPNF1-13*, 24: Homilies on Gal 3:1; John of Ruysbroeck, *Adornment*, chapter 5; Ryle, "The Cross"; Spurgeon, *Spurgeon's Sermon Volume 4: 1858*, Sermon 212—The New Heart.

11. Louis of Blois, *Spiritual Works of Louis of Blois*, 1903, chapter 1—The Immense Mercy of God, and the Benignity of the Mother of God towards Sinners Demonstrated by Various Revelations, 207; Louis of Blois, *Oratory of the Faithful Soul; or, Devotions to the Most Holy Sacrament, and to Our Blessed Lady*, 1848: Friday Morning, 53–54.

12. Calvin, *Institutes* 4:17:2; *CC—John*, Vol. 2, 230.

13. Melito, *Passion*, 179; Hengel, *Crucifixion*, 21.

14. Cyprian, in Davies, *Born*, 87; *ANCL13*, 11.

15. Cyprian, *ANCL13-2*, 26–27, Treatise IX—On the advantage of Patience.

16. Cyprian, *Lapsis*, Bévenot, 45–47n.30.

As the Adam-Christ typology is employed, there are two elements: continuity and contrast. Adam and Christ are both naked, but the Last Adam brought about the "clothing of righteousness," which the First Adam lost. Jacobus de Voragine points out that this continuity-contrast motif was also picked up by other church fathers such as Augustine, Ambrose, and Gregory.[17] Furthermore, in his development of this typology, Chrysostom establishes the connection between sin, nakedness, and Christ's victory, as he puts Christ's nakedness in a soteriological context of the Adam-Christ typology:

> There, it was slave with master, here, it is friend with friend: there, it is said, "In the day that thou eatest thereof thou shalt die" (Gen. ii. 17); an immediate threatening; but here is nothing of the kind. God arrives, and here is nakedness, and there was nakedness; there, however, one that had sinned was made naked, because he sinned, but here, one is made naked, that he may be set free. Then, man put off the glory which he had; now, he puts off the old man; and before going up (to the contest), puts him off as easily, as it were his garments.[18]

Similar to Chrysostom and Cyprian's Adam-Christ typology,[19] John Tauler clarifies further that the dialogue of nakedness and clothing should be associated with Adam's disobedience and Christ's victory. In particular, Adam's defeat is found in his lack of clothing whereas victory over sin is found in Christ's nakedness.[20] Ironically, Christ's nakedness signifies shame, but he suffered shame in order to preserve the purity of innocence.[21]

> [F]or His greater shame and dishonour, He was hung up thus naked in the sight of His bitterest enemies and mockers. For it was not the custom to crucify naked those who were guilty of death, unless they were notorious malefactors, who, as an example for others, were obliged to suffer a horrible death. Adam also, when he had lost his innocence, hastened to clothe himself with garments: but Christ was stripped naked that He might

---

17. Jacobus, *Golden*, 77.

18. Chrysostom, *NPNF1-13*, 287, Colossians 2:6–7—Homily VI.

19. Tauler, *Meditations on the Life and Passion of Our Lord Jesus Christ*, chapter 33: 262, 264–65.

20. Ibid., 262.

21. Ibid., 266–67.

preserve the purity of innocence whole and unhurt; nor had He need of any covering.[22]

Clearly, the soteriology in this Adam-Christ typology maintains the similarity of nakedness, but contrasts Christ's victory to Adam's defeat. This is a valuable point to the recapitulating work of Christ.[23]

Soteriological Mimesis of the Naked Christ in Nude Baptism

Another interpretation of *Christus nudus* is built upon the union between believers and Christ in nude baptism. In this practice, a baptisand imitates Christ's nakedness,[24] and a robe, given after emerging from the water, reflects participation and a soteriological mimesis of Christ's naked death and glorious resurrection.[25] Yet, also hidden in this symbolic language is the resonance of Adam-Christ typology: an old versus new motif. Cyril of Jerusalem is lucid about such a motif in this particular liturgy.[26] It is noticeable that more than a thousand years after Cyprian, Francis of Sales resounded the Adam-Christ typology in a soteriological context, but at that time, the focus was on the transformation between the putting off of "the garments of the old Adam" and the putting on of "the habits of the new man"—Jesus Christ.[27] The metaphors of "putting off" and "putting on" are employed to signify the imitation and participation in Christ's renunciation, death and resurrection: "die with Our Saviour naked upon the cross, and rise again with him in newness of life."[28]

Cyril's contemporary, Ambrose, was also sympathetic to the baptismal clothing image of righteousness.[29] Similarly, Jerome employs nakedness and clothing to refer to the importance of being clothed with

22. Ibid., 263–64.

23. Irenaeus' Adam-Christ typology and recapitulation in *Adversus Haeresies* are an important foundation for the establishment of *Christus nudus*.

24. Schaff, *History of the Christian Church*, Vol. 2, The Celebration of Baptism §70.

25. Nakedness at baptism is a mimetic symbol of the atoning act of Christ (Mazza, *Mystagogy*, 157).

26. Cyril of Jerusalem, *NPNF2-7*, Lecture XX: On the Mysteries II: Of Baptism; Chapter IV—Ceremonies of Baptism and Chrism; see chapter 5 of this book.

27. Francis of Sales, *Treatise on the Love of God*, book 9, chapter 16, 408.

28. Ibid., 409.

29. Ambrose, *Theological and Dogmatic Works*, 17; *The Mysteries*, chapter 7, 34: in baptism, the white garment of Christ symbolizes that sinners are washed and made whiter than snow.

Christ, as opposed to being naked, to make a distinction between the righteous and the unrighteous.³⁰ In fact, Ambrose had a clearer use of the naked-clothed dialogue, particularly in terms of the spiritual state and the cleansing of sins:

> After this you received white garments. As an indication that you were stripped of the covering of your sins you put on the chaste of clothing of innocence, of which the prophet said: "Sprinkle me with hyssop and I shall be cleansed, wash me and I shall be whiter than snow" (Ps. 51:7).

> [The color of the garment is] according to the Gospel because the garments of Christ were white as snow when, in the Gospel, he manifested the glory of his resurrection (cf. Matt. 17:2). He whose sin is forgiven is whiter than snow. Hence the Lord says through Isaiah: "If your sins are like purple, I will make them white as snow" (Isa. 1:18).³¹

Compared to Cyprian of Carthage, who emphasizes the contrast between Christ's nakedness and that of Adam, Cyril's soteriological mimesis takes Cyprian's notion of clothing as far as the robe of immortality,³² but narrows the focus of Christ's nakedness to his self-renunciation while at the same time adding slightly to that mixture a *victorious Christ*. As a result, not only does *Christus nudus* become an important exemplar for the Christian notion of renunciation and the subsequent philanthropic teaching of almsgiving, it is also a significant basis for the *moral influence* of atonement. Accordingly, a Christian follows Christ in his nakedness,³³ unclothed to be clothed,³⁴ stripped off of the old and clothed with the new. This imitation of nakedness for Calvin is the act of admitting the sinful naked state and coming to Christ in that bare state.³⁵ Therefore, underlying this baptismal symbolism is a Christian lifestyle of renuncia-

---

30. Jerome, *NPNF2–6*, The Life of Paulus the First Hermit: 302–3.
31. Ramsey, *Ambrose*, 153: on the Mysteries 7.34.
32. Cyprian, *Born*, 49.
33. Francis of Assisi, *Flowers*, chapter 36; Jerome, *NPNF2–6*, 287; Tulloch, *Luther*, 10–11.
34. Miguel de Molinos, *Spiritual Guide which Disentangles the Soul*, chapter 22; Tauler, *Meditations*, chapter 39: 308.
35. Calvin, *CC—Philippians*, 97; Augustus Toplady, "Rock of Ages": "Nothing in my hand I bring, Simply to thy cross I cling; Naked come to Thee for dress; Helpless, look to Thee for grace; Foul, I to the fountain fly: Wash me, Saviour, or I die," quoted in Derek Tidball, "Penal Substitution: a Pastoral Apologetic," 352.

tion and partaking in Christ's humility and hospitality. John Wesley and Whitefield specifically associated a Christian's imitation of Christ's nakedness, in the "purchase" of the "clothes of Christ," with partaking in his nakedness.[36] "Then go and learn what thou hast so often taught, 'By grace ye are saved through faith': 'Not by works of righteousness which we have done, but of his own mercy he saveth us.' Learn to hang naked upon the cross of Christ, counting all thou hast done but dung and dross."[37]

From a general examination of this soteriological mimesis we can see that there are important practical implications of *Christus nudus*: (1) a mimesis of Adam-Christ typology in a Christian's baptismal renunciation of the old and the establishment of the new; and (2) a lifestyle of renunciation and imitation of Christ's hospitality. As a result, the latter implication becomes foundational to the philanthropic development of *Christus nudus*.

Philanthropic Development of the Naked Christ

Building upon the baptismal mimesis of *Christus nudus*, a philanthropic perspective encourages self-renunciation through good deeds and almsgiving; not as a personal endeavor, but as the outcome and inspiration of Christ's atoning work. According to this development, Christ's nakedness on the cross is the exemplar of humility and self-abnegation,[38] which inspires the fruit of good deeds and almsgiving—the outcome and the security of redemption. In particular, Cyprian taught that those who have been clothed with Christ must show true repentance, refusing all other raiment and being girt with good deeds awaiting eternal life.[39] Building upon Proverbs 16:6, Cyprian went as far as suggesting that through clothing others, sins are purged.[40] This point, however, is totally dependent on the first: "Nor would the infirmity and weakness of human frailty have any resource, unless the divine mercy, coming once more in aid, should open some way of securing salvation by pointing out works of justice and

---

36. Whitefield, *Sermons on Important Subjects*, 600: Sermon 55: Persecution Every Christian's Lot.

37. Wesley, *Sermons*, Sermon 33: 51, 56; Sermon 43: 219–23.

38. MacLaren, *Expositions of Holy Scripture: St John Chs. XV to XXI*, An Eyewitness's Account of the Crucifixion.

39. Cyprian, *Lapsis*, 51–53, 99.

40. Cyprian, *ANCL13-2*, 2: The treatise VIII—On work and alms; Cyprian, *Lapsis*, 51–53.

mercy, so that by almsgiving we may wash away whatever foulness we subsequently contract."[41]

Cyprian's philanthropic soteriology is clear: "Let us give clothes to Christ on earth so that we may receive the clothing of heaven."[42] In fact, he emphasizes: "[H]aving once been clothed with Christ, refuse all other raiment now; having supped with the devil, choose rather now to fast; apply yourself to good deeds which can wash away your sins, be constant and generous in giving alms, whereby souls are freed from death."[43]

While Cyprian even goes as far as to suggest that by almsgiving and faith sins are purged,[44] Jerome equates failing to clothe others with rejection of Christ himself and leaving him lie "at the door naked and dying."[45] Alternatively, Augustine does not go as far as to affirm that almsgiving can wash away sin, but concurs to the point that by clothing others Christians are clothed themselves. Christ's "wedding garment," in his view, is associated with believers' good works and the sanctifying work of God.[46] Furthermore, John Wesley also relates to this association between almsgiving and sanctification, and claims that this is the way wherein God has appointed his children for complete salvation.[47] Philanthropic soteriology, thus, is built upon a renunciation of worldly possession as a practical imitation of Christ's self-abnegation.[48] In other words, philanthropic soteriology is an active implication taken from the mimesis of Christ's atoning work—follow and imitate Christ who is the exemplar of renunciation and poverty.[49]

In their development, each of the above three interpretations of *Christus nudus* employs the common "conceal-reveal" linguistic model and the "putting on—putting off" motif. This is a significant observation that contributes considerably to the christological development of the early church fathers. Ambrose, for example, employs the metaphors "conceal" and "taking on" to convey his understanding of the incarnation

---

41. Ibid..

42. Cyprian, *Born*, 97; Cyprian, *ANCL13-2*, 19.

43. Cyprian, *Lapsis*, 51–53, 99: to do penance is to follow the naked Christ, to shine light in good works: pray assiduously and clothed in sackcloth.

44. Cyprian, *ANCL13-2*, 2: The treatise VIII—On work and alms; cf. Prov 16:6.

45. Jerome, *NPNF2-6*, 36 (Letter XXII—To Eustochium).

46. Augustine, *NPNF1-6*, 408.

47. Wesley, *Sermons*, Sermon 43: 219–23.

48. Tauler, *Meditations*, chapter 33: 262–63, 266.

49. Ibid., chapter 33: 264–65.

and the work of Christ: Christ redeemed humanity by concealing what he was and taking on what he was not, so that he might call humanity to that which he was through what he was not.[50] This proposal of a pre-existent Christ is supported by Adam-Christ typology,[51] where Ambrose states that through incarnation, Christ took on flesh and became the sin of all humanity in order to wash away the sins of the entire race.[52] Similarly, this motif of Christ becoming human so that we might become divine is also found in the works of other church fathers such as Irenaeus,[53] Clement of Alexandria,[54] and Gregory of Nazianzus.[55]

Consequently, one may conclude that underlying the above interpretations of *Christus nudus* is a Christology that points toward a cosmological Naked Christ whose incarnation and redemptive work resolves the sin of humanity and puts right the First Adam's wrongs. As George Herbert (1593–1633) puts it:

> Hast thou not heard, that my Lord Jesus di'd?
> Then let me tell thee a strange storie.
> The God of power, as he did ride
> In his majestick robes of glorie,
> Resolv'd to light; and so one day
> He did descend, undressing all the way.
> The starres his tire of light and rings obtain'd.
> The cloud his bow, the fire his spear,
> The sky his azure mantle gain'd.
> And when they ask'd, what he would wear;
> He smil'd, and said as he did go,
> He had new clothes a making here below.
> When he was come, as travellers are wont,
> He did repair unto an inne.
> Both then, and after, many a brunt

---

50. Ambrose, *Works*, 74: *The Holy Spirit*, chapter 9:107: 240–41: chapter 6:56.

51. Jacobus, *Golden*, 77.

52. Ambrose, *Works*, 233: *The Sacrament of the Incarnation of Our Lord*, chapter 5:39: 244, chapter 7:65.

53. Irenaeus, *AH* V: preface, ANCL9, 55: The Word of God, Jesus Christ became what we are in order to make us what he himself is. For Bakken ("Holy Spirit and Theosis," 415), Irenaeus' *theosis* corresponds to the "man-becoming" of God. Negrut, "Orthodox Soteriology: *Theosis*," 155n.4; Beck, "Divine Initiative: Salvation in Orthodox Theology," 106.

54. Quoted in Bakken, "Theosis," 415.

55. Gregory of Nazianzus, *Orations* 38:13; 45:9, *NPNF2-7*, 349, 426; Nellas, *Deification in Christ*.

> He did endure to cancell finne:
> And having giv'n the rest before,
> Here he gave up his life to pay our score.[56]

Surely, this notion of a cosmological *Christus nudus* has opened up new questions regarding atonement that require a robust understanding of the Incarnation, Christology, and trinitarianism. It appears that to some extent this notion of cosmological *Christus nudus* addresses both the divine and the human dimensions of atonement. Yet, in order to outline these dimensions some questions must first be answered. In particular, one may wonder how to best understand this cosmological *Christus nudus*, especially, an appropriate way to understand a cosmological renunciation? Moreover, this cosmological *Christus nudus* also raises new soteriological questions: Is there more to this "moral influence" exemplar of Christian renunciation and philanthropy? In what way should *Christus nudus* be seen as substitutionary?[57] And most importantly, how is *Christus nudus* connected to the robe of righteousness?

Christus Nudus and the Divine Face of Nakedness

Previously, the notion of *Christus nudus* has been referred to in the context of the great exchange from nakedness to clothing: nakedness represents sin, shame, and rejection, whereas clothing represents justification, glory, and acceptance. In this fashion, the *Christus nudus* model concentrates on the transformation of a sinner before and after the cross. In a cosmological sense, however, this transition is the result of Christ's humility and his act of self-emptying, suffering the consequences of humanity's sin and shame.[58] This act of self-emptying (*kenosis*) can be seen as *becoming naked*. On that account, *Christus nudus* should not be restricted to the historical nakedness of a suffering Messiah; rather, there is space for it to express a cosmological revelation of God within the master

---

56. From "The Bag" in Herbert, *The Temple*, 157–58.

57. In particular, Christ suffered a naked penalty to appease the Father's divine wrath (Thomas à Kempis, *Imitation of Christ*, chapter 8, 231–32: The Offering of Christ on the Cross; Our Offering, The Voice of Christ. Similarly, see Taylor, *The Rules and Exercises of Holy Living*, 398: A Form of Prayer recording all the parts, chapter 4, section 10).

58. Phil 2:6–11; Fee, *Paul's Letter to the Philippians*, 211–18; Martin, *Philippians*, 97–100; Silva, *Philippians*, 105–7; Thielman, *Philippians*, 118–19; Fowl, *Philippians*, 99–100.

plan of atonement. One may then ask the "what" and the "how" questions regarding this *Christus nudus*: What is *Christus nudus*? How does *Christus nudus* come to exist? And so what is the connection of such a notion within the big picture of the Cross?

Deus Nudus:
The Self-Revealing God and the "What" of Christus Nudus

Nakedness, clothing and the linguistic "conceal-reveal" model were employed in Luther's concept of *Deus nudus* as he elaborated on the nature of a self-revealing God.[59] For Luther, the concept of *Deus nudus* is built upon a tension between his understanding of transcendence (which is the sharp contrast between God and humanity),[60] and condescendence.[61] In the dissociation of transcendence,[62] according to Luther, God is a *Deus nudus* (naked God), i.e., God "in his absolute majesty," "the absolute God" (*Deus absolutus*).[63] In fact, Hölderlin asserts that in this myth of the dress of God *Deus nudus* reveals himself as *Deus vestitus*.[64] Unlike

---

59. No earlier source before Luther's concept of *Deus nudus* has been found. The reason that Luther's lens of *Deus nudus* is taken into account here is because of his christological discourse of *Deus nudus*, *Deus absconditus*, and *Deus revelatus*. There is a hermeneutical value in Luther's *Deus nudus* that connects the concept of a "hidden God" with the concepts of revelation and incarnation in *Christus nudus*.

60. Luther, WA 40 II, 328–85, in Bayer, "Martin Luther (1483–1546)," 1, 9, 53.

61. Berkhof, *Faith*, 118; Bayer, "Luther," 52; Nilsson, "Martin Luther," 6.

62. Hayden-Roy, "Hermeneutica Gloriae vs. Hermeneutica Crucis," 66.

63. In fact, Luther insists in *On the Bondage of the Will*: "To the extent, therefore, that God hides himself and wills to be unknown to us, it is no business of ours" (*LW*, Vol. 33, 139; Vol. 12, 312). According to Clark, both Luther and Calvin derided it as a quest for the vision of God (*visio Dei*) . . . the desire to see God "naked" (*Deus nudus*) (Clark, *Recovering the Reformed Confession*, 71). The electing God of Calvin is a *Deus nudus absconditus*, and the same is true of the Canons. "Jesus Christ is not in any sense the *fundamentum electionis* . . . but at very best He is only the *fundamentum salutis*"; Calvin, *Institutes* 3.11.2–3. Berkouwer does not deny that Calvin did not always state the matter clearly and adequately, but at the same time adds that "t a decisive point he rejected precisely the penetration into *deus nudus* (the Father alone, as Calvin puts it) by saying that the heart of the Father rests in Christ" (Berkouwer, *Divine Election*, 156). Unfortunately this cannot be said of all later theologians, for example Boettner (*The Reformed Doctrine of Predestination*, 1932), who completely omits the "in Christ"—dimension of election, yet it cannot be denied that his presentation often gives the impression of speaking of a *deus nudus*.

64. Bottici, *A Philosophical Political Myth*, 78.

Deus nudus, a concept of divine secrets and hiddenness,[65] *Deus vestitus* is God clothed in his word and promise.[66] Moreover, *Deus abscontidus* ("the hidden God") is a notion that, according to Bloesch, Protestant Reformers sometimes describe as the unknown, inscrutable God behind the revelation in Jesus, because humans are incapable of perceiving the very essence of God,[67] and only know what he chooses to reveal in Christ. As a result, in Christ he is love, but outside Christ he is judgement and wrath.[68] Cosmologically speaking, therefore, the notion of *Christus nudus* has a significant position in this perspective of the self-revealing God.

The conception of *Deus absconditus* gives some indication to the way in which God ought not to be found,[69] unlike the *Deus revelatus* ("the revealed God") who reveals himself.[70] Although at times God acts directly and absolutely, for Luther, God is *Deus revelatus* who wants us to act in accordance with *potentia ordinata* rather than *potentia absoluta*.[71] The one who finds God beyond what is revealed will find, instead of the God of grace, the *Deus absconditus* or *Deus nudus*—a sinister force of devouring consummation rather than enlightenment.[72]

Consequently, on the one hand, it is impossible to approach God without his initiative to self-reveal. On the other hand, not only is there a somewhat *limited* revelation of *Deus nudus* in Jesus Christ—the image of the invisible God, but also there appears to be a separation between *Deus nudus* and *Christus nudus*. It follows that tensions occur in both Christology and the doctrine of predestination. Concerning this very matter, Barth criticized Calvin's doctrine of predestination for separating the electing God and Jesus Christ, arguing that Calvin's God is a *Deus nudus*

---

65. Luther prefers the term *Deus absconditus* suggested by Isa 45:15, or sometimes *Deus nudus*, to the *Deus ignotus* (hidden God) found in Acts 17:23 (Davies and Turner, *Silence and the Word*, 99).

66. Luther, *LW*, Vol. 12, 312–13; Bayer, "Luther," 53.

67. God exists within an ontological time and space that is distinct from ours (Barth, *CD*, I.1, 490).

68. Bloesch, *God, the Almighty*, 63.

69. In Trigg's words, it is a self-chosen form of worship (Trigg, *Baptism in the Theology of Martin Luther*, 26).

70. Luther (*WA* 43:457–59 [especially 459:7–20], Trigg, *Baptism*, 26); *LW*, Vol. 5, 42–44; Clark, *Recovering*, 71–72.

71. Luther (*WA* 43:71, 25–28, Trigg, *Baptism*, 26); *LW*, Vol. 3, 274, on Gen 19:14; Hayden-Roy, "Hermeneutica," 61.

72. Frei et al., *Theology and Narrative*, 163; Schroeder, "Using Luther's Concept of *Deus absconditus* for Christian Mission to Muslims," 3; Barth, *CD*, II.1, 18–19.

absconditus, not *Deus revelatus*, who must be sought in Jesus Christ.[73] Besides, as Redding points out, although the hidden divine decree that exists apart from God's self-disclosure in Jesus Christ appears to preserve God's freedom and sovereignty, it introduces a dichotomy into the Godhead that questions Christ's deity and his equality with God.[74]

A sense of "separation" is apparent in the different ways that *Deus nudus* and *Christus nudus* relate to humanity: particularly, to the *Deus nudus* humanity is enemy,[75] but to the *Christus nudus*, humanity is that which he represents. Accordingly, while the former concept of divine nakedness is about "concealing," the latter is about "revealing." Even to Luther, this contrast is so clear that he urged to flee from the angry God to the gracious God.[76] However, such a sense of "separation" should not be mistaken. For Luther, God becomes open to human perception through revelation under the form of contrariety: in the naked, broken figure of the crucified.[77] Consequently, such a separation can be deceptive and is especially capable of misleading the content of atonement when it omits the essentially complementary connection between the two notions of *Deus nudus* and *Christus nudus*. *Christus nudus* is the image of the invisible God—*Deus absconditus*; he is *de facto* the representation of *Deus revelatus*.[78] According to Barth, God reveals himself indirectly through his Son Jesus, and we can truly know God: to know the *Deus revelatus* is to know *Deus absconditus*.[79] As such, it follows that through incarnation *Christus nudus* becomes the actualization of *Deus revelatus*, revealing

---

73. Barth, *CD*, II.2, 111.

74. Building upon Barth and Reid, see Redding, *Prayer and the Priesthood of Christ in the Reformed Tradition*, 97; Reid, "The Office of Christ in Predestination," 9; cf. Gunton, "Karl Barth's Doctrine of Election as Part of His Doctrine of God," 382.

75. Bayer, *Theology the Lutheran Way*, 18–19; Nilsson, "Luther," 6.

76. Berkhof, *Faith*, 136.

77. Luther (WA 5:176, 32–33; 605:11, 16–17) in Gibson, "The Absurdity and Sublimity of Christ: Christology in the Films of Ingmar Bergman."

78. Atkinson claims that Luther's *Deus nudus* was *Deus incognitus*, and humanity cannot get access into a living relationship with him. In Christ humanity can learn God's heart, mind and will, and how God looks at humanity—the saving knowledge. And although it is true that in Christ God had shown his hand, and real knowledge of God, it was the *Deus Revelatus* only of whom Luther spoke and wrote, and never the *Deus Nudus* (Atkinson, "The Significance of Martin Luther").

79. Bloesch, *Almighty*, 63, 49: God in the Bible is both *Deus revelatus* and *Deus absconditus*.

God to humanity,[80] according to the will of God.[81] This revelation of God, in which he identifies himself on the cross of Jesus, is grasped as the mystery of the world.[82] A God who in his aseity and impassibility remains untouched by human vulnerability and suffering is far easier to grasp than the God who in his infinite power makes himself vulnerable to pain and crucifixion.[83] Similarly, Nilsson deepens the connection between the *Deus nudus* and the *Christus nudus* by stating that the *Deus nudus* has, as it were, stepped out of his own secret and entered the world, revealing himself through Jesus Christ—*Christus nudus*.[84] Bayer, therefore, rightly sums up Luther's thought that the office and the work of Christ are to abolish the clash of the *Deus nudus* and the *Homo nudus*.[85] Accordingly, *Christus nudus* remains a mystery in its revelation and hiddenness of God while it is, at the same time, a stumbling block:[86] he is God who leaves his majesty to freely identify with the human predicament, even to death on a cross.[87]

Consequently, there are three points to be established: (1) The contrast between *Deus nudus* (Creator) and *Homo nudus* (Creation) is far too great for a direct revelation or encounter without a mediator. This follows that (2) *Christus nudus* is the only mediator through whom *Deus nudus* reveals himself to *Homo nudus*.[88] Therefore, (3) *Deus vestitus* self-undresses, as it were, in the "*Word becomes flesh*," in order to reveal himself. In other words, *Christus nudus* is *de facto* the presentation of the great mystery of *Deus nudus*,[89] to which Paul refers (Eph 3:3; Gal 1:12). As a result, Gerrish rightly puts it: "In Christ God works in a paradoxical mode *sub contraiis*. His wisdom is hidden under folly, his strength

---

80. John 6:38; 14:6, 9: "I am the way and the truth and the life. No one comes to the Father except through me.... Anyone who has seen me has seen the Father."

81. John 6:65: "No one can come to me unless the Father has enabled him."

82. Jüngel, *God as the Mystery of the World*, 378.

83. Bloesch, *Almighty*, 64; cf. Mertens, *Not the Cross, but the Crucified*, 111.

84. Nilsson, "Luther," 6.

85. Luther (*WA* 6:516, 30–32; *LW*, Vol. 36) in Bayer, "Luther," 42, 54.

86. Berkhof, *Faith*, 61–62; Moltmann remarks that God's hiddenness is the revelation of his grace, not affliction (Moltmann, *Experiences of God*, 67).

87. Melito, *Passion*, in Lake and Lake; Westhelle, *The Scandalous God*, 2; Hegel, *The Christian Religion*, 70.

88. Bloesch, *Almighty*, 61.

89. Ibid., 64.

under abject weakness. He gives life through death, righteousness to the unrighteous; he saves by judging and damning."[90]

Accordingly, *Christus nudus* is of both historical and theological significance. On the one hand, it recovers the scandalous icon of Christianity—the cross with a Naked Christ viewed in horror by people in Roman times—as opposed to a domesticated cross.[91] On the other, the notion of *Christus nudus* has a theological significance in its relation to *Deus nudus* and the revelation of God. As such, a foundation has been established on the "what" of *Christus nudus* within the master plan of salvation, we now turn to explore the question "how."

Nakedness as Kenosis: Incarnation and the "How" of Christus Nudus

The Creator-created contrast is so great that in patristic understanding, which corresponds with the Pauline corpus,[92] revelation through incarnation only makes sense in the act of divine self-emptying (*kenosis*). On that account, Irenaeus claims that the Word of God became what we are in order to make us what he is.[93] Similarly, Clement of Alexandria[94] and Gregory of Nazianzus link this exemplar of humility to the hope for immortality of the elect.[95] The notion of *kenosis* is also important in Cyril's Christology.[96] As such, just as revelation assumes hiddenness,[97] so the divine disclosure of Christ the Logos—the image of the invisible God—assumes the notion of a preexistent Christ, and his act of self-emptying (*kenosis*). Accordingly, the concept of self-emptying is well accepted in early Christian theology, as Harvey puts it:

> in becoming man, Christ, who had previously lived in glory with the Father, emptied . . . himself of his pre-existent divinity, and took on full humanity, thus becoming like unto us men

---

90. Gerrish, "'To the Unknown God': Luther and Calvin on the Hiddenness of God," 268.

91. Westhelle, *Scandalous*, xi, 10; Schmidt, *A Scandalous Beauty*, 8.

92. Gregory of Nazianzus relates *kenosis* with *theosis* (Phil 2 and 2 Cor 8:9; Norris, "Deification: Consensual and Cogent," 415.

93. Irenaeus, *AH* V. preface.

94. Bakken, "Theosis," 415.

95. Gregory of Nazianzus, *Orations*, 45.9; 38.13 (Daley, *Gregory of Nazianzus*, 124).

96. Cyril of Alexandria, c. Nest 63C, cited by Prestige, *Father and Heretics*, 165.

97. Berkhof, *Faith*, 60–61.

in every way. . . . All modern commentators on this passage, from Lightfoot to Barth, have laid great stress on the humility of Christ in this act of self-emptying, and none of them seems to have found any difficulty in accepting the idea of Christ as being "pre-existent," and thus being *able* to empty himself of the divinity he once shared with the Father in glory.[98]

However, it must be noted that not only does this notion of *kenosis* refer to the self-emptying of Christ in the incarnation but also his conscious obedience to the divine will that leads to his death on the cross.[99] As such, *kenosis* and atonement go together hand in hand: *Deus nudus* reveals himself through *Christus nudus*—a "Godhead veiled in flesh" and "an incarnate deity."[100] Yet, the self-emptying of that Deity goes beyond the revelation of the Word made flesh, into the revelation of God's ultimate love through the cross. Incarnation and atonement are indeed interwoven. As a result, this understanding of divine self-emptying begs the question as to what Christ self-emptied from?

In its earliest formulation, the sixteenth-century Formula of Concord opposed the idea of divestment of attributes.[101] The nineteenth-century German thinkers, however, constructed a kenotic Christology that referred to the incarnation as the self-emptying of the pre-existent and eternal Son to become the human Jesus.[102] Yet, their interpretations proved difficult in regard to the extent of this self-emptying: complete

---

98. Harvey, "A New Look at the Christ Hymn in Philippians 26–11," 337. Preexistence is found both in Paul (Phil 2), John (John 8:58) and Hebrews (MacQuarrie, "The Pre-existence of Jesus Christ," 200).

99. The founder of Kenotic Christology—Thomasius—points out that there is a distinction between the humiliation, which Christ undergoes in his earthly life and that act of self-limitation by which the divine Logos assumes humanity (Thomasius, *Beiträge zur kirchlichen Christologie*, 1845; *Christi Person und Werk*, 1853 in MacQuarrie, "Kenoticism Reconsidered," 120, 123).

100. McFarlane, "Atonement, Creation and Trinity," 198, 200: there is no unmediated contact between Creator and Creation, thus Jesus plays the mediating role of Wisdom; he is the wisdom of God, and is involved in the genesis of creation. Dawe uses the phrase "veiling of divine in human flesh" (Dawe, "A Fresh Look of the Kenotic Christologies," 341).

101. McCormack, "Karl Barth's Christology as a Resource for a Reformed Version of Kenoticism," 245.

102. Lawton, "Books on the Person of Christ," 47.

emptying,[103] "partial emptying,"[104] or a temporary choice not to "give up" the exercise of certain prerogatives and powers that belong to Jesus by virtue of his divine nature.[105] It has been argued that in becoming human the Son divested himself temporarily of some of the divine attributes,[106] such as omnipotence, omniscience, and omnipresence for incarnation to happen; thus the subsequent implication follows that the essence of God is his self-giving love that freely limits itself to allow some autonomy to his creation.[107] However, Baillie argues that if the Son divested himself of his attributes, then the result is not a genuine incarnation but only a theophany.[108] As such, kenotic theology often receives much criticism, especially given its apparent christological implication regarding the nature of the God-man.[109]

Thomasius provided a way of asserting the sense in which Jesus could be both divine and human; however, he could not provide a way of conceiving how the Logos could be both limited (whether by dropping

103. Godet, *Commentary on the Gospel according to St. John*, Vol. 1, 243–53; Vine suggests that it is the divine nature (*The Epistles to the Philippians and Colossians*, 56); Gess ("Nature or God?" and "Christ's Atonement for Sin," 27–28, 134–35) suggests the laying aside of Godhead, building upon Bruce and Hodge (Bruce, *The Humiliation of Christ*, 144–52; Hodge, *Systematic*, Vol. 2, 235–37).

104. This self-emptying involves the setting aside of certain divine attributes, or at least the independent exercise of his divine powers (Gore, *The Incarnation of the Son of God*, 171; Farrbairn, *The Place of Christ in Modern Theology*, 476–77; Grenz et al., "Kenosis, Kenoticism," 70). Thomasius makes the distinction between *relational* attributes and retaining *immanent* attributes, in order to make Incarnation possible (Dawe, "Kenotic," 343; Patzia and Petrotta, "Kenosis," 69).

105. Strong, *Systematic Theology*, Vol. 1, 703; Patzia and Petrotta, "Kenosis," 69.

106. The Greek *morphe* is argued to be divine attributes, which Christ emptied himself of (Lightfoot, *Saint Paul's Epistle the Philippians*, 100–132); Müller, *The Epistles of Paul to the Philippians and Philemon*, 78. Müller claims that to say that Christ divested himself of his glory "is no legitimate deduction from the phrase in question, but a bold conclusion based on the subsequent statement that He took the form of a servant" (ibid., 81).

107. Evans, "Kenotic Theories," 65.

108. Baillie, *God was in Christ*, 94–97.

109. For a list of objections to the *kenosis* doctrine, see Berkhof, *Theology*, 328–29; Carmody, "Kenosis," Vol. 8: Jud-Lyt, 154: for the kenotic school of theology there is no other way of reconciling a really human experience in Jesus with belief in his divinity, in all Christian antiquity there is no trace of kenoticism and it is metaphysically impossible for God to change; Dorner, *A System of Christian Doctrine*, Vol. 3, 283–39. Dorner was one of the first and greatest opponents of the *kenosis* doctrine, yet he proposed progressive and gradual incarnation, which logically leads to Nestorianism and is utterly subversive of the real pre-existence of Christ.

attributes or modifying them) and world-ruling.[110] Following a similar line of thought, Gore and Forsyth contend that Jesus was limited in his knowledge.[111] Surely *kenosis* refers to a phenomenon wherein Christ became so susceptible to passibility and suffering that even Satan thought Jesus would sin and give in to temptation,[112] but the patristic understanding, such as that of both Melito and Irenaeus, speaks clearly of Christ as being both God and man in his work of redemption and revelation.[113] Augustine also holds that Christ concealed his divine radiance and became tangible to meet humanity in a dark and fallen world.[114] Therefore, Dawe warns against making the Logos a limited form, for although there may have been a temporary limitation of knowledge in Christ, the directive center of Jesus' person was really divine.[115]

Alternatively, Barth has offered some light on this question: "for God it is just as natural to be lowly as to be high."[116] God does not cease to be God in becoming human,[117] but by adding on "the form of a servant" he puts off the "form of God" and enters into "unrecognizability, into the *incognito*."[118] It is the utter self-outpouring that constitutes Christ's glory; therefore, the paradox of personal existence is that his abasement

---

110. Dawe, "Kenotic," 344–45.

111. Gore claims that "[i]t was really because the future was not clear that Jesus could pray 'O my Father, if it be possible, let this cup pass from me.'" (Gore, *Dissertations on Subjects Connected with the Incarnation*, 83). Forsyth's reliance upon the notion of *kenosis* led him to the view that Christ did not fully understand the purpose of his sufferings and the significance it would have for God and the world (*God the Holy Father*, 21–22; *The Church and the Sacraments*, 256); for discussions on Matt 24:36; Mark 13:32; and Luke 2:52 see Wallace, "When Did Jesus Know?"

112. For Irving, at the incarnation, the Son did not assume the perfect, unfallen, flesh of Adam, but our fallen human nature (Irving, in G. Carlyle [ed.], *The Collected Writings of Edward Irving in Five Volumes*, Vol. 5, 115–16: "Christ took our fallen nature is most manifest, because there is no other existence to take"). This is a point Barth makes favorable reference to (Barth, *CD*, I.2, 154); Gunton, "Two Dogmas Revisited: Edward Irving's Christology," 365.

113. Wallace, "Christology," 224.

114. Smith, "Kenosis, Kenotic Theology," 602; Thomas, "Kenosis Question," 146: *morphe* is understood as the effulgence of his glory, or the visible expression of the inner essence.

115. Dawe, "Kenotic," 346.

116. Barth, *CD*, IV.1, 192; Dawe, "Kenotic," 348.

117. This is Barth's understanding of "holy mutability" in the fulfilment of God's immutable purpose of redemption (Barth, *CD*, II.1, 496).

118. Barth, *The Epistle to the Philippians*, 63; McCormack, "Barth," 248. Thus no divestment of anything proper to deity is entailed (ibid., 250).

is also his exaltation, and emptying is his fulfilment. This resonates with the paradoxical fashion wherein God demonstrates strength in weakness, and wisdom in foolishness.

As a result, *kenosis* is not a proposal to solve or to unlock the mystery of God's condescension in the incarnation,[119] but it is a metaphor explaining the act of self-effacement, humility, and self-renunciation,[120] describing the complete freedom of God, wherein the acceptance of the limitations of a human life does not make him unlike himself or lose his divinity.[121] Hence, the focal point of *kenosis* should be Christ's humility and obedience, who freely exchanges equality with God for the form of a slave, moving from the world of eternity to the world of time, making himself open and vulnerable to death, even death on the cross.[122] As such, *kenosis* is understood as the expression of the inner dynamic of the Trinity; not as the casting off of certain attributes,[123] but as an expression of the very heart of God in the provision of the means of salvation.[124] By putting on the fallen human form,[125] the Word became susceptible to suffering and sinning, even to the point of a god-forsaken cross, in order to bring the clothing of redemption.[126] Consequently, *kenosis* and incarnation can be seen as the divine face of nakedness;[127] and therefore, systematically speaking, through *kenosis* the condescension of *Christus nudus* through incarnation is a "divine exposure" and a revelation of *Deus nudus*. Yet through this lens, *kenosis* is understood in a mixed setting of Christology and soteriology:[128] not only does this "stripping" refer to Christ's humility

---

119. Smith, "Kenosis," 601: kenotic theology is not intended to be an *ad hoc* device for making sense of the Christ-event, but the Christ-event is the historic expression of the eternal dialectic within the triune God; Martin, *Philippians*, 121.

120. Horan, "The Apostolic Kerygma in Philippians ii. 6–9," 60–61.

121. Dawe, "Kenotic," 348; Chauncy, *The Duty of Ministers*, 12–13; Gibbs and Gibbs, "'In Our Nature': The Kenotic Christology of Chales Chauncy," 228, 233.

122. Allchin, "Kenosis," 367; Wesley: "Empty himself of all but love" (Smith, "Kenosis," 602); Irving, *Writings*, 126, 161.

123. Gunton, "Dogmas," 364; Thomas, "Kenosis," 151.

124. Müller, *Christ and the Decree*, 173.

125. Irving, in Carlyle (ed.), *Writings*, 115–16; Barth, *CD*, I.2, 154; Gunton, "Dogmas," 365.

126. Rom 5; Phil 3:21; Rev 3:5; Isa 6:8; 57:17–20.

127. Both "reveal" and "conceal" are simultaneously at work (Calvin, *CC—Philippians*, 57).

128. As a result of a return to the Chalcedonian doctrine of the two natures (Wallace, "Christology," 226); Gorman, *Inhabiting the Cruciform God*: building upon his

in the divine face of nakedness, but it also refers to his cruciform face of nakedness;[129] because it is in the light of the human self-emptying of Christ that one can venture to speak of a self-emptying of the eternal Logos as a clue to the meaning of incarnation.[130] Accordingly, we now turn to explore the soteriological language of nakedness and clothing.

Christus Nudus and the Cruciform Face of Nakedness

As Irenaeus points out in his theory of recapitulation,[131] the cross of *Christus nudus* has two faces: (1) the *correcting* face wherein Christ corrects where humanity has gone wrong, and (2) the *perfecting* face of the cross, which brings humanity into a relationship with God. We shall argue that through the *correcting* face of the cross, Christ's nakedness justifies the elect and clothes them with the "robe of righteousness," and through the *perfecting* face of the cross, as a result of being clothed with Christ, the redeemed have the hope of sanctification into Christ-likeness, resurrection and eternal life with God in glory.

Recapitulation: The Correcting and Perfecting Faces of the Cross

The idea of recapitulation, which means "summing up,"[132] dominates the theology of the second century: adumbrated by Justin, expounded by Irenaeus, and given a decisive place in Tertullian.[133] This patristic understanding of recapitulation is widely recognized.[134] As for Irenaeus,

---

former influential *Cruciformity: Paul's Narrative Spirituality of the Cross*, 9–18, and *Apostle of the Crucified Lord*, Gorman argues that cruciformity is, at its heart, theoformity—what Christian tradition has labelled "theosis" (ibid., 4). Gorman begins by showing that Paul viewed Christ's cross as the definitive theophany of the kenotic God, and presents a new interpretation of justification as theosis. One can see a connection between Gorman and Thomasius' distinction between revelatory *kenosis* and cruciform *kenosis*.

129. Jones, *Soul Shaper*, 161.

130. Macquarrie, "Kenoticism," 123.

131. Osborn, *Irenaeus of Lyons*, 97–116.

132. Ibid., 97; Hardy and Richardson, who translated the Library of Christian Classics version of Irenaeus, chose to use the word "renew" (or "renew and reverse") to convey the idea of recapitulation (*The Library of Christian Classics*, Vol. 1, 386–89).

133. Osborn, *Irenaeus*, 97.

134. McKnight, *Community*, 100–101; Johnson and Webber, *What Christians*

redemption and perfection are never separate.[135] His idea of recapitulation has been associated with the *kenosis-theosis* motif, for he sees *theosis* as the ultimate goal of redemption.[136]

Nevertheless, the idea of the *correcting* face of the cross did not belong to Irenaeus alone. In fact, Cyril of Jerusalem also spoke about Christ's victorious nakedness,[137] and this *correcting* effect underlies the phrase "undoing the damage of the Fall" in nude baptism of early Christianity.[138] Also, following Pauline thought, Irenaeus utilizes the theme of the First and Second Adam (1 Cor 15; Rom 5).[139] He holds that humanity was represented federally and covenantally in Adam, and that Eden was eschatologically alluding to the reality of the Last Adam.[140] At the fall, Adam—the representative of humanity—disobeyed God, but salvation is brought through the obedient work of the eschatological Adam—Jesus Christ.[141] Irenaeus' soteriology, thus, holds that at the culmination

---

Believe, 257–58; Webber, *Ancient-future Faith*, chapter 6; Grenz, *Theology for the Community of God*, 341: Irenaeus "never intended that his theory be viewed as a description of a transaction in the history of creation. It was merely a picture of the meaning of the victory of Christ." However, although Irenaeus is the first to draw comparisons between Eve and Mary, contrasting the faithlessness of the former with the faithfulness of the latter, misinterpreting Irenaeus' doctrine of recapitulation can lead to tainting the works of the church fathers (Steenberg, "The Role of Mary as Co-recapitulator in St Irenaeus of Lyons," 117–37: Steenberg has pressed the concept of the recapitulation of Christ into a Roman Catholic Mariology).

135. Osborn, *Irenaeus*, 98.

136. As to the question "For what purpose did Christ come down from Heaven?" Irenaeus (*AH* III.18.7, *ANCL*5, 343) answers, "For it behoved Him who was to destroy sin, and redeem man under the power of death, that He should Himself be made that very same thing which he was, that is, man; who had been drawn by sin into bondage, but was held by death, so that sin should be destroyed by man, and man should go forth from death." Aulén, *Christus Victor*, 19; Mertens, *Cross*, 65; Willems, *The Reality of Redemption*, 41–60; The Eastern Orthodox mysticism emphasizes imitation of Christ: the *kenosis* of the Word makes *theosis* possible (Pomazansky, "The Oneness of Essence, the Equality of Divinity, and the Equality of Honor of God the Son with the God the Father," 92–95).

137. Cyril of Jerusalem, *Mystagogical Catecheses*, II.2 (Cross [ed.], *Cyril*, 1951, 59); Miles, *Carnal*, 33–35.

138. Wilson, "Nakedness," 45–46; Kim, *Clothing*, 99, or in Theodore of Mopsuestia's words, becoming naked and unashamed like Genesis 2:25 (Smith, "Garments," 12; Miles, *Carnal*, 33).

139. Hooker, *Adam*, 22, 42, 59. Osborn remarks that Irenaeus learned from Paul *correction* and from John *perfection* (Osborn, *Irenaeus*, 117).

140. *AH* V.12.

141. He sees Christ as the new Adam, who systematically undoes what Adam did;

of redemptive history, the incarnate Son of God recovered what was lost in the First Adam.[142] Recapitulation, therefore is the "summing up" of all history and humanity in Christ Jesus as the conclusion of the drama of redemption (Eph 1:10).[143] In Irenaeus' theory of recapitulation, however, one can sense a strong impression of "battlefield" victory,[144] nevertheless the parallel between Christ and the promised seed of Adam and Eve in the book of Genesis puts across a clear idea that the summing up of all things is the fulfilling victory of Christ, the reverse of the curse, and the salvation for those who are in Christ.[145]

What is especially distinctive of Irenaeus, however, is that he extends the *correcting* face into a *perfecting* face. According to Irenaeus, the high point of salvation history is the advent of Jesus; thus, he understands the atonement of Christ occurring through his incarnation[146] rather than his crucifixion, although the latter event is an integral part of the former.[147] Irenaeus characterizes the penalty for sin as death and corruption; however, God is immortal and incorruptible, thus, simply by becoming united to human nature Christ conveys his qualities to us: they spread, as it were, like a benign infection. As a result, Irenaeus concludes that the Son of God determined that he would become the Son of man "that man also might become the Son of God."[148] This connects recapitulation to *theosis*,[149] as the ultimate achievement in Christ's *kenosis*.

---

therefore, where Adam was disobedient concerning the Tree of Knowledge, Christ was obedient even to death on the wood of a tree. *AH* V.19.1; V.17.3 (*ANCL9*, 102–7); Osborn, *Irenaeus*, 102.

142. Some theologians erroneously declare that Irenaeus is articulating a view of universalism in his doctrine of recapitulation; cf. Bingham and Rompay, *Irenaeus' Use of Matthew's Gospel*, 182.

143. *AH* V.20.

144. In particular, Irenaeus holds that the elect are justified through Christ's eschatological work as he is "both waging war against our enemy, and crushing him who had at the beginning led us captives in Adam, and trampled upon his head." (*AH* V.21); Osborn, *Irenaeus*, 101.

145. *AH* III.18.7; III.21.9–10; III.22.3; V.21.1 (*ANCL5*, 342–43, 357–61; *ANCL9*, 110–11); Klager, "Retaining and Reclaiming the Divine," 462n.158.

146. *AH* V.1.1; Mertens, *Cross*, 65; Willems, *Reality*, 41–60.

147. As will be made clear by his association of the tree of knowledge and the cross as a tree, Irenaeus has implied the importance of the cross to an extent. McKnight suggests that Irenaeus does not say it is the incarnation *per se* that redeems (McKnight, *Community*, 104).

148. *AH* III.10.2.

149. Ibid., III.19.1 (*ANCL5*, 344–45): the corruptible had to be united to the

Nakedness as Necessary to the Correcting Face of the Cross

Irenaeus' idea of the *correcting* effect of Christ's incarnation is very important for an understanding of *kenosis*.[150] However, although Irenaeus saw the *correcting* effect as he made the connection between the tree of knowledge and the cross (a cruciform *kenosis*),[151] he did not see the connection regarding nakedness between Adam and Christ as Ambrose later made.[152] Accordingly, in this section we will focus on the cruciformity of nakedness, a metaphor for Christ's self-emptying in his suffering to correct and recapitulate Adam.[153] The focal question is "in what way should Christ's nakedness be seen as *correcting*?"

As we take Irenaeus' recapitulation as our framework, we shall mention the *correcting* aspect of Christ's nakedness in the Adam-Christ typology first. Adam-Christ typology in Irenaeus refers to the ultimate reversion: What has been lost in Adam is now recovered in Christ. Therefore, the *correcting* aspect of Christ's nakedness is closely connected to the concept of "victory" and "battle."[154] According to this perspective of Christ's *correcting* nakedness, correction is established in victory through obedience and submission. Consequently, Christ repeats (recapitulates) and defeats, correcting what the First Adam did wrong through his victorious nakedness.[155]

Alternatively, one of the clearest and most immediate ways is the exchange motif,[156] wherein Christ corrects by exchanging with human-

---

incorruptible so that mortality might be swallowed up in immortality.

150. Osborn, *Irenaeus*, 99.

151. Ibid., 100, 102; *AH* V.19.1, V.17.3: the tree of the cross amends the disobedience of the tree of paradise.

152. Jacobus, *Golden*, 77.

153. This is the prominent theme of mimesis in nude baptism, see chapter 5 of this book.

154. *AH* V.21; Osborn, *Irenaeus*, 101. For Chrysostom, Adam was naked because of his sin whereas Christ was naked to conquer sin. (*NPNF1–13*: Colossians 2:6–7—Homily VI).

155. In contrast to Adam's attempt to make himself like God, Christ's self-emptying expresses his complete humility and unconcern about himself when he pours out and becomes a slave to other people (Harvey, "Look," 338; Klager, "Retaining," 462n.158; Bandstra, "Adam and the Servant in Philippians 2:5ff," 213–16: connection between Phil 2:5 and Rom 5:19).

156. Hooker, *Adam*, part I.

ity; but what is involved in this exchange? Luther proposes that at the cross, the "wondrous exchange" takes place, whereby through the union of Christ with human nature, his righteousness becomes ours, and our sins become his.[157] In this sense, justification happens at the moment the exchange is complete. If the metaphor of clothing is employed ("clothing" as "vehicle" and "righteousness" as "target"),[158] in a similar fashion to early Christian nude baptism, then one can see an exchange motif in Calvin's comment: Jesus' nakedness brings about the clothing of righteousness.[159] The notion of "robe of righteousness," as Calvin distinguishes from another "robe" in his *twofold* notion of clothing,[160] refers to justification—the *correcting* face of the cross. It follows that justification is the immediate result of Christ's *correcting* nakedness whereby Christ brings poverty to riches, shame to honor, nakedness to clothing, tattered garments to boldness, and defeat to victory. This notion of *correcting* nakedness is *exclusive*—something that only Christ can do,[161] because only Christ is righteous and able to provide the clothing of righteousness. As a result, one might understand that the redeemed receive that which has been stripped from Christ.

A third way of seeing the *correcting* aspect is to view Christ's nakedness as an example. Accordingly, by following and imitating his nakedness humanity participates in a union with Christ. *Christus nudus* is approachable and loving. He is the Logos whose *kenosis* is a cosmological nakedness pointing to a divine disclosure of *Deus nudus*. He is God Incarnate, whose humility is expressed in his self-emptying as he stooped down into created humanity even to death on the cross.[162] However, not only does the "conceal-reveal" linguistic model of nakedness and clothing put forth a sense of correction in the human understanding of *Deus nudus* (as opposed to complete unawareness), but Christ's nakedness is shown to be a true example of sacrificial love, especially in his naked

---

157. Wallace, "Christology," 225; Osborn, *Irenaeus*, 111.
158. See linguistic metaphorical language in chapter 3.
159. Calvin, *CC—John*, Vol. 2, 230; *CC—Matthew, Mark, Luke*, Vol. 3, 298–99.
160. Calvin, *CC—Corinthians*, Vol. 2, 218.
161. McKnight, *Community*, 101.

162. Thielman, *Philippians*, 115. However, unlike Thielman, many scholars suggest that in his self-emptying Christ did not literally empty himself of any divine attribute; instead, he metaphorically emptied himself by revealing the form of God in the form of a slave and in human likeness (Bruce, *Philippians*, 46; O'Brien, *The Epistle to the Philippians*, 218).

death. As we have examined in chapter 6, crucifixion is a kind of death that was used for slaves and rebels in Greco-Roman society, which deprived them of their most basic human rights. Yet, Christ refused to take advantage of the privilege of his deity and, giving up that right, became a slave,[163] even a "suffering" servant, as the connection between *kenosis* and Isaiah 53:23 is established.[164] Therefore, Augustine's philanthropic model is completely compatible with this line of thought. For Westhelle also, a theology of the cross is not a theological articulation of some objective truth; rather, "it is a practice [a journey] of solidarity with the pain of the world, which follows the encounter with Christ crucified."[165] This resonates with the philanthropic soteriology discussed earlier.[166]

The various perspectives of Christ's *correcting* nakedness, however, have not offered any light on the *correcting* face of the cross from God's perspective. In Moltmann's words, "*What does the cross mean to God?*" one could ask "Why was Christ's nakedness *correcting*?" Or, mirroring Anselm's question "*Cur Deus Homo?*," we now ask "*Cur Christus nudus?*" What constitutes the *correcting* factor in Christ's nakedness: is it the fact that Christ was undeservedly stripped on behalf of naked sinners in some form of a "scapegoat"[167] mechanism, or is it the stripping and clothing metaphors that construct a "transactional" understanding of sin wherein Christ "swaps" places with sinners and becomes a "sacrifice"?

It is appropriate, therefore, to have a robust understanding of sin in order to understand the *correcting* face of the cross; in particular, how the death of *Christus nudus* deals with sin and restores the human-God relationship. For Luther, sin infuriates *Deus nudus*—a strict and distant God,[168] who "crushes us under the law";[169] hence, sin is understood with the help of the law.[170] However, an understanding of sin must start with

---

163. Moule, "Further Reflection on Philippians 2:5–11," 268–69.

164. Bandstra points out that for Jeremias, the phrase "he emptied himself" is a precise rendering of the Hebrew phrase translated "he poured out his soul unto death" in Isa 53:12; the same meaning occurs in Ps 141:8 without "unto death" (Bandstra, "Philippians," 213–16; Jeremias, "Zu Phil ii 7: ΕΑΥΤΟΝ ΕΚΕΝΩΣΕΝ," 182–88).

165. Westhelle, *Scandalous*, 112.

166. *AH* IV.36.6; Balthasar, *Incarnation*, 98–99.

167. Girard, *The Scapegoats*.

168. Gerrish, "Hiddenness," 263–92.

169. Berkhof, *Faith*, 200.

170. Barth, following Calvin's thought, argues that humans come to know sin exclusively through the confrontation with Christ's humility (Berkhof, *Faith*, 201).

a corporate perspective. For Calvin, hereditary depravity and corruption of the human nature makes humanity liable to God's wrath.[171] Consequently, Christ's atoning death—the *correcting* face of the cross—requires a "collective" and "corporate" concept of sin.[172] From Irenaeus[173] to the Cappadocian Fathers this "representative" model is recognized: in order to redeem the human will from bondage, the Son must "take up into Himself the very conditions of a human will . . ."[174] This fullness of humanity is a necessary means to a positive understanding of the atonement not as a bargain, but as the restoration of the corporate life of humanity to its true end: we stand or fall together.[175] As a result, sin is not the accumulation of all the sins of the elect, but the power of sin diffused throughout the substance of the flesh of fallen human nature.[176] This view of sin makes it possible to develop a corporate conception of salvation.[177] Hence, the cross can be seen as the moral influence in identifying with the human situation, yet at the same time it is the revelation about *Deus nudus* through the Emmanuel *Christus nudus*. Christ's genuine humanity, passibility and vulnerability are expressed in his nakedness and for

---

Pannenberg (*Systematic Theology*, Vol. 2, 252n.258), however, criticizes Barth's method in that "he did not see that uncovering sin in the light of the revelation in Christ relates to something that is more universal by nature and that precedes the revelation. Failure to see this means making the fact of sin a mere postulate of the Christian faith."

171. Calvin, *Institutes* 2.1.8.

172. As argued in chapters 4 and 5, sin is a state of brokenness that affects the both human condition and relation.

173. Osborn, *Irenaeus*, 99; *AH* III.1.6.6–1.6.7.

174. Irving, *Writings*, 23.

175. Gunton, "Dogmas," 367.

176. Irving, *Writings*, 217; Calvin, *Institutes* 2.1.8.

177. Gunton, "Dogmas," 368. For example, a satisfaction view of atonement holds that: "it is a matter of justice for God to grant eternal life to his obedient image-bearers. Failure to recognize this element of the system of truth contained in the Scriptures leads to a defective understanding of the atonement, specifically the necessity of Christ's atoning death as means of satisfying divine justice." (Karlberg, "The Original State of Adam," 306); Hodge, *The Atonement*, and Morris, *The Apostolic Preaching of the Cross*, for classic treatments of the Reformed position, contrasting Aulén (*Victor*). However, Gunton remarks: "The dominance of Western discussion of atonement by notions of legal satisfaction has been gravely distorting. But the fundamental assertion that human ill is radical, and yet is revealed and healed by God in Christ, is not endangered by the correction of the place where stress is laid in the doctrine of the atonement (see, in particular, Aulén and Whale)" (Gunton, *Yesterday and Today*, 182).

that reason it is legitimate for recapitulation language to speak of Christ's achievement in a corporate scope!

While, on the one hand, the *Christus nudus* model concentrates on the revelation of *Deus nudus*; on the other, it must connect Christ's nakedness to his separation from the Father. Following Moltmann's attempt, the *Christus nudus* model also seeks to understand God in the light of the God-forsakenness of Jesus on the cross.[178] Moltmann remarks, "Not until we understand his abandonment by the God and Father whose imminence and closeness he had proclaimed in a unique, gracious and festive way, can we understand what was distinctive about his death. Just as there was a unique fellowship with God in his life and preaching, so in his death there was a unique abandonment by God."[179]

What needs to be established, therefore, is a connection between Christ's *kenosis* and the "cup" that Jesus must drink and the cross Jesus claimed he must take up and the separation from God the Father that he must undergo, as Barth powerfully puts: "He is the man whom God in His eternal counsel, giving Him the command, treated as its transgressor, thus rejecting Him in His righteous wrath, and actually threatening Him with that final dereliction. That this was true of Adam, and is true of us, is the case only because in God's counsel, and in the event of Golgotha, it became true first of all in Jesus Christ."[180]

Traditionally, the cup in Jesus' prayer is interpreted as the cup of the Father's wrath.[181] Hence, that "cup" is easily associated with the Father's abandonment, which was "part of the putting away of sin."[182] Moltmann suggests that the plea expresses his fear of being separated from God and the horror in the face of the "death of God"; thus, this *unanswered prayer* is the beginning of Jesus' passion.[183] Therefore, Christ's nakedness is the symbol of Christ's submission: he who knew no sin, was made sin for us,[184] as he accepted God-forsakenness as part of the "cup."[185]

---

178. Moltmann, *The Crucified God*, 200; Letham, *The Work of Christ*, 172–73.

179. Moltmann, *The Crucified God*, 149.

180. Barth, *CD*, II.2, 739–40.

181. Ryken et al., *Imagery*, 186; Marshall, "The Theology of the Atonement," 52: the cup is a metaphor for suffering, especially suffering imposed by God.

182. Morris, *Matthew*, 721; Peterson, "Atonement in the New Testament," 28: "divine judgement for sin."

183. Moltmann, *The Trinity and the Kingdom of God*, 76.

184. 2 Cor 5:21.

185. Carroll and Green, *The Death of Jesus in Early Christianity*, 33: "If the death

Protestants associate the *Deus absconditus* with God's secret will and his wrathful judgement on sin and his revealed will in the love and mercy of Jesus Christ.[186] This raises the question whether it is correct to view *Deus nudus* as a God of wrath, who punishes *Christus nudus* according to justice. If what God is in himself is identical to that which is revealed in Jesus Christ, and if love is God's innermost nature (including his wrath and judgement),[187] then the original concept of a wrathful *Deus nudus* must be replaced. Consequently, the way Christ's nakedness is viewed in relation to the "cup" is also altered: it is not a punishment by which the Father is satisfied by seeing the Son being naked on the cross.[188] Rather, the Father is with *Christus nudus* in his suffering, not in a "psychological" on-looking sympathetic way,[189] but in the deadly separation between *Deus nudus* and *Christus nudus*—a "trinitarian split" at the cost of restoring the dysfunctional human-God relation.[190] As a result, in this dereliction *Christus nudus* passes through the full *recapitulatio*, including God-forsakenness,[191] in order to become the high priest.[192] Within this scope, the *correcting* face of the naked crucified God-Man[193] makes sense from both divine and human perspectives: atonement is achieved collectively and corporately. Yet, important and necessary as it is, nakedness is only the start of an atonement that leads to the ultimate clothing—the promise of glory in the union with God (*theosis*). Accord-

---

of Jesus is the climax of the passion account, the scene of Jesus' struggle in prayer ([Mark] 14:32–34) is clearly its turning point. Here Jesus discerns and submits to the will of God."

186. Bloesch, *Almighty*, 63.

187. God's wrath and judgement must be seen in the light of his love (Barth, *CD*, I.1, 204–5; McKnight, *Community*, 68–69: God's wrath as jealousy; Terry, *Justifying*, 120: punishment, not rage; Stott, *The Cross of Christ*, 125: God's wrath is never uncontrollable; Forsyth, *The Work of Christ*, 119). However, Cottrell opposes the idea of wrath as an expression of his love, and argues it is rather an expression of the *holiness* of God (*The Faith Once for All*, 95).

188. Constable, "Nudus," 83–91; Strunks, "The Metaphors of Clothing and Nudity in the 'Essais' of Montaigne," 83–89.

189. McCormack, "Barth," 247.

190. Jesus' nakedness represents the "cup" of separation—a death naked of God, upon which Moltmann refers to as "Jesus died 'without God'—godlessly" (Moltmann, *Trinity*, 82); Letham, *Work*, 172–73.

191. Gunton, "Dogmas," 371.

192. Irving holds that in Jesus' agony of death the Spirit left him so that "he might know the hour and the power of darkness," (Irving, *Writings*, 133).

193. Moltmann, *Crucified*, 51.

ingly, we now explore the *perfecting* face of the cross—the vindication of Christ's righteousness at his resurrection.[194]

Atonement as Clothing: The Perfecting Face of the Cross

Redemption should not be restricted to dealing with the problem of sin but should extend to the transformation of humanity and its union with God; not only does Christ take upon himself humanity's iniquity and clothes the elect with his righteousness, he also makes them partakers of his divine immortality.[195] Accordingly, the purpose of salvation is not only about Christ getting right humanity's wrongs, but also to bring humanity to perfection in Christ,[196] in God's initial intention to be his image-bearers.[197] As such, not only is salvation identified with a personal conversion, but also with a collective and corporate concept of personhood.[198] As Adam's failure eliminated the potential God intended for humanity, Jesus Christ provides the example of what true humanity is, not to the potential of the first humanity, but to complete that potential:[199] *theosis*—the union between humanity and God.[200] It follows that Christ's act of *kenosis* is imperative to the *theosis* of Christians.[201] Athanasius, in his famous statement, declares that the Son of God became man "that he might deify us in himself."[202] From this teaching originates the idea of *theosis*, also known as deification, divinization, or participation in

---

194. "Therefore God has clothed Him with the robes of imperial majesty." (MacLaren, *Expositions*).

195. Calvin, *Institutes* 4:17:4; Mosser, "The Greatest Possible Blessing: Calvin and Deification," 44–45; Lossky, *In the Image and Likeness of God*, 103.

196. Osborn, *Irenaeus*, 105, 116.

197. Ignatius of Antioch, in Bakken, "Theosis," 415.

198. Zizioulas, *Being as Communion*, 50.

199. "The condition which we obtain through Christ is far superior to the lot of the first man," says Calvin (*CC—Corinthians*, Vol. 2, 53); Gorman, *Inhabiting*, 5; Christensen and Wittung, *Partakers of the Divine Nature*, 253–57; Finlan and Kharlamov, *Theosis*.

200. *AH* III.18:7; Aulén, *Victor*, 19; Mertens, *Cross*, 65; Willems, *Redemption*, 41–60; St. Hilary of Poitiers, *On the Trinity*, IX.38, X.7, *NPNF2-9*, 167, 183–84; Lossky, *Image*, 103; Wesche, "Eastern Orthodox Spirituality," 29.

201. Lossky, *Image*, 97–98.

202. Athanasius, *Letter 60, To Adelphius*, 4, section 3 and 8, *NPNF2-4*, 575–78. On the Incarnation, he wrote similarly that Christ "was made man that we might be made God," (*On the Incarnation*, 54, *NPNF2-4*, 65).

God.²⁰³ This line of thought finds a common ground among other patristic teachings such as those of Irenaeus,²⁰⁴ Clement of Alexandria,²⁰⁵ Augustine,²⁰⁶ Chrysostom,²⁰⁷ Athanasius, Gregory of Nazianzus, Gregory of Nyssa,²⁰⁸ and Hilary of Poitiers.²⁰⁹ Gregory of Nazianzus connected *kenosis* (Christ's self-emptying and taking on human poverty) with *theosis* (humanity's becoming gods) in his interpretation of 2 Corinthians 8 and Philippians 2.²¹⁰

> The one who was rich also became poor, for he took on the poverty of my flesh in order that I might share the richness of his Godhead. The one who was full also emptied himself, for he laid aside his own glory for a short time in order that I might share in that fullness. What is the wealth of this goodness? What is this mystery concerning me? I participate in the image [of God], but I did not guard it. He participated in my flesh in order that he might also save the image and make the flesh immortal.²¹¹

---

203. Ayres, "Deification and the Dynamics of Nicene Theology," 375–94: being "like" God (377), or "imitate" God (379); Allchin, *Participation in God*, 63.

204. *AH* V. preface. For Bakken ("Theosis," 415), Irenaeus' *theosis* corresponds to the "man-becoming" of God; Negrut, "Soteriology," 155n.4; Beck, "Initiative," 106. Osborn (*Irenaeus*, 126) remarks "the term may fall into well-deserved neglect by interpreters of Irenaeus."

205. Bakken, "Theosis," 415.

206. Mosser, "Greatest," 38; Harnack admits that Augustine taught deification at one point, but brought the doctrine to an end in the West (*History of Dogma*, Vol. 3, 165). However, not only did Augustine not bring deification to an end, but deification also played an important role in his mature theology (Mosser, "Greatest," 38; Balás, "Divinization," 339; Bonner, "Augustine's Conception of Deification," 369–86; "Deification, Divinization," 265–66; Chadwick, *Augustine*, 54; Rist, *Augustine*, 259–60.

207. McCormich, "Theosis in Chrysostom and Wesley," 38–103.

208. Athanasius, *De incarnatione verbi Dei* 54, 142: "Christ became human that humans might become divine"; Gregory of Nazianzus, *Poema dogmatica* 10.5–9 and Gregory of Nyssa, *Oratio catechetica magna* 25 (quoted by Negrut, "Soteriology," 155: footnote 4); Beck, "Initiative," 106.

209. Hilary of Poitiers, *Trinity*, 156: Christ sought "to raise humanity to divinity. While on earth, Jesus taught his disciples to believe Him the Son of God, and exhorted [them] to preach him the Son of Man; man saying and doing all that belongs to God; God saying and doing all that belongs to man."

210. Norris, "Deification," 415.

211. Gregory of Nazianzus, *Orations*, 38.13; 45.9; Nellas, *Deification*, 205.

The Making of the Christus Nudus Model 203

The scriptural basis for *theosis* varies widely.[212] However, to Western ears that are unaccustomed to the Eastern Orthodox writers, the bold terminology of *theosis* can sound blasphemous; yet it is completely erroneous to assume that *theosis* belongs to Eastern Orthodox teachings alone.[213] *Theosis* is also found in the writings of Western theologians such as Aquinas[214] and Luther,[215] and in the ecclesiastical traditions such as Anglican,[216] Methodist (both Arminian and Calvinistic),[217] and among figures such as Jonathan Edwards,[218] Augustus Hopkins Strong,[219] C. S. Lewis,[220] and Evangelicals from different confessional backgrounds.[221]

The question now is *how* should *theosis* be understood? Jerome's notion of "gods by grace"[222] surely points out that Christian *theosis* is not "invented deification" or "false deification" of the kind found in pagan teachings on deification of creatures.[223] What it implies exactly is the possession of certain "divine" attributes through union with

---

212. Studer, "Divinization," 242; Rakestraw, "Becoming Like God," 257-69.

213. Mosser, "Greatest," 36; Balás, "Divinization," 339.

214. Mosser, "Greatest," 38; Williams, *The Ground of Union*, chapters 2-3: 168-69.

215. Mosser, "Greatest," 38; Braaten and Jenson, *Union with Christ*, 1-20; Mannermaa, "Theosis as a Subject of Finnish Luther Research," 37-47; Bakken, "Theosis," 409-23.

216. Allchin, *Participation*, 63; Edwards, "Deification and the Anglican Doctrine of Human Nature," 196-212; Doctrine Commission of the Church of England, *The Mystery of Salvation*, 29, 189, 206.

217. Allchin, *Participation*, 24-44; Christensen, "Theosis and Sanctification," 71-94; McCormich, "Theosis," 38-103.

218. Jenson, "Theosis," 111.

219. Strong, *Systematic Theology*, 793-809; *Union with Christ*; Rakestraw, "Becoming," 257-69.

220. Lewis, *Mere Christianity*, Vol. 4, 174-75; *The Weight of Glory and Other Addresses*, 18.

221. Hughes (Episcopalian), *The True Image*, 281-86; Oden (Wesleyan), *Life in the Spirit*, 207-12; Torrance (Reformed), *Theology in Reconstruction*, 243-44; Rakestraw (Baptist), "Becoming," 257-69.

222. Jerome, *Homilies of St Jerome*, 106-7.

223. Calvin, *CC—Isaiah*, 28:29, Vol. 2, 306; *Institutes* 2.8.26; Norris, "Deification," 415: philosophers Iamblichus and Proclus, poet Callimachus and Julian the Apostate (Callimachus, *Hymn to Diana*, 159; Iamblichus, *Concerning the Life of Pythagoras*, 23.103; Proclus, *Commentary on Plato's Parmenides*, 149S; Julian, *Or*.5.178b); Koester, "The Divine Human Being," 243, the subsequent Hellenistic and Roman cult of the divine emperor (ibid., 244).

God.[224] For Maximus, and for early writers such as Gregory of Nyssa, deification meant taking on God's modes of activity, such as compassion and self-surrender, rather than simply sharing a set of abstract and static attributes. Shared attributes are only significant as a dimension of shared activities, or else deification means fusion directly with the transcendent divine nature.[225] Therefore, deification is usually referred to as assimilation and union with God "in so far as the condition of this life allows."[226] This means the elect are *not becoming God* in his *essence*, but are partaking in his *energies* (and Christ's suffering),[227] through grace accepted by faith[228]—a union that, as Barth points out, does not happen without the Mediator.[229] Accordingly, as it appears for Calvin, *theosis* can be more about sanctification than deification,[230] because Christ was God in a way that believers would never be, no matter how much they share in the life of God.[231] As a result, this union bars any concept of infusion in *theosis*, whether *krasis* (blending) or *mixis* (mixing).[232]

---

224. Mosser, "Greatest," 37: Creatures can never become the kind of being that the uncreated Creator is; Schurr, "On the Logic of Ante-Nicene Affirmations of the 'Deification' of the Christian," 99, 103–5; Frede, "Monotheism and Pagan Antiquity," 58–62.

225. Williams, "Deification," 107; Oden notes that there is no possibility of finite creatures being made infinite, invisible pure spirit, etc. (*Life*, 208–9); Corduan, "A Hair's Breadth from Pantheism," 269–71.

226. John of the Cross, *Dark Night of the Soul*, II.24 (*The Complete Works of Saint John of the Cross*, Vol. 1, 454); Dionysius the Areopagite also suggests deification to be a certain assimilation and unification with God in so far as it is possible (Dionysius the Pseudo-Areopagite, *The Ecclesiastical Hierarchy*, 16–21); Calvin's trinitarian union with God through union with Christ by the power of the Holy Spirit can be called deification, if deification is defined *not* as becoming God but becoming like God *as far as it is possible* (Partee, *The Theology of John Calvin*, 173, 177–78; Habets, "Reforming Theosis," 146–48).

227. Cyprian, *Ep.* 58.6.3, in Clarke, *The Letters of St. Cyprian of Carthage*, Vol. 3, "Ancient Christian Writers, No.46," 65.

228. Norris, "Deification," 428.

229. Barth, *CD*, IV.2, 57.

230. Partee, *Calvin*, 178.

231. Athanasius, *Discourse Against the Arians*, 3.1, 17–19, 24–25, in Bright, *The Orations of St. Athanasius against the Arians*.

232. Alexander of Aphrodisias, *On Mixtur*, 216.14–218.6: Chrysippus's view on mixing; Arnim, *SVF*, 2.473 (Long and Sedley, *The Hellenistic Philosophers*, Vol. 1, 290–94; Vol. 2, 287–91); Sambusky, *Physics of the Stoics*, 11–17.

Believers are one with Christ, not in a mixture or infusion of essence but by the secret power of his Spirit.[233]

The concept of *theosis* is described under a number of theological rubrics that include adoption to divine sonship, participation in God, sharing of divine life, impartation of immortality, restoration of the *imago dei*, glorification, and consummation.[234] For Calvin, the excellence of the promises is that the elect are made partakers of the divine nature,[235] but this "divine nature" implies being raised up to God and united with him, not to his essence or equality, but to his "kind" or "quality."[236] For Karl Barth, it is through practical fellowship with God that Christians conform their actions to the divine nature.[237] Besides, the prayer of Jesus in John 17:11, 21–23 is frequently utilized as the Pauline theme of the Christian life being a life "in Christ."[238] As Christians put on the image of the heavenly man, they are renewed and transformed into the likeness of God as a result of the work of divine grace.[239]

It is commonly understood that, ultimately, patristic teaching of *theosis* cannot be expressed on a christological basis alone, but demands a pneumatological development as well.[240] Similarly, to the Greek fathers, the Christian life is best conceived as the restoration of the lost likeness to the redeemed in Christ, through the work of the Holy Spirit, who communicates the energies of God so that they may become partakers of the divine nature.[241] For Calvin, the impartation of the divine nature takes

---

233. Luther in Mannermaa, "Theosis," 43; Calvin, *Institutes* 3.11.5; Williams, "Deification," 107; Wendel, *Calvin*, 239.

234. Mosser, "Greatest," 36.

235. Calvin, *CC—Peter*, 370–71; Calvin, *CC—Romans*, 223.

236. The elect are made to conform to God by the grace and power of the Spirit, not by an inflowing of substance and without rendering them consubstantial with him (Calvin, *Institutes* 1.15.5); *CC—I John*, 205–6.

237. Barth, *CD*, IV.4, 28.

238. Ware, *The Orthodox Church*, 231; Williams, "Deification," 106.

239. 1 Cor 15:49, Eph 3:16–19; 4:13–15; Gal 2:20; and 1 John 4:16 (Nellas, *Deification*, 23–25, 35–39, 127, 139); Leech, *Experiencing God*, 258; cf. The concept of *glory* in Lossky, *The Vision of God*, 129–37; Ware, "The Hesychasts," 251–53.

240. Bakken, "Theosis," 417; Osborn, *Irenaeus*, 132–36; *AH* V.9.4, V.12.4, (*ANCL9*, 77–78, 84–85); Calvin, *The Bondage and Liberation of the Will*, 119–20; 193–94, 232; *Johannis Calvini opera quae supersunt omnia, Corpus Reformatorum*, 6.314–15; 6.367–68, 396, (as quoted in Billings, "United to God through Christ," 319), with the voluntary will of the believer and not with coercion; Zizioulas, *Communion*, 111.

241. Bray, "Deification," 189.

place when union takes place,[242] whereby through his role as the Mediator, Christ adopts the elect as his brothers;[243] thus, both exchange and adoption happen at the same time.[244] As such, in trinitarian language, the union between believers and God is a *trinitarian participation* since it involves all three members of the Godhead, following the example of the hypostatic union and the communication of properties between Christ's divinity and humanity.[245] Consequently, we are one with Christ not because of transfusion of substance but because of the power of his Spirit through whom he communicates to us life and blessings from the Father.[246] In other words, the Holy Spirit breathes divine life into us and is the bond by which Christ effectually unites us to himself, and to the Father, whose love we partake and in whose image we are reformed.[247]

Another important aspect of *theosis* is its eschatological language: when Christ returns he will shine upon the godly with his glory and they may partake in it: glorification and union with Christ are directly associated.[248] Clearly, Calvin's adaptation of Anselm's definition of God, "*quo nihil maius cogitari potest*,"[249] suggests that Calvin interprets the meaning of the phrase "partakers of the divine nature" in a very literal way: a peak of honor and a blessing no mind can fully grasp.[250]

---

242. Not only in his death and resurrection, but also in all of his blessings, Calvin, *Institutes* 4.17.4, 4.15.6; Willis-Watkins, "The Unio Mystica and the Assurance of Faith according to Calvin," 78.

243. Calvin, *Institutes* 3.1.1, 2.12.2, 1.13.24.

244. Augustine also taught that Christ's death on the cross enables humans to be adopted members the family of God (Augustine, *On John's Gospel*, Tractates 1.4, 2.13, 23.5, 48.9, in *NPNF1–7*); Bonner, "Augustine," 369–86.

245. Calvin, *Institutes* 2:13–14; *CC—John*, Vol. 2, 185.

246. Calvin, *CC—John*, Vol. 2, 184. In the 1545 edition of the *Institutes*, Calvin says that we are "made of one substance with him" and "daily he more and more unites himself to us in one, same substance" (Willis-Watkins, "Unio," 80: Calvin does not always use *substantia* consistently). This was later removed in the 1559 edition to avoid the appearance of contradiction (Weis, "Calvin Versus Osiander on Justification," 31–47; Gamble, *Calvin's Opponents*, Vol. 5 of *Articles on Calvin and Calvinism*, 353–69].

247. Calvin, *Institutes* 3.1.1–3, 1.15.4; *CC—John*, Vol. 2, 112–13, 188–89.

248. Calvin, *CC—Romans*, 189; *CC—Thessalonians*, 318–19; Calvin, *Institutes* 3.25.10; John of the Cross proposes the "candle and sun" analogy [*Spiritual Canticle* 27, (*Works*, Vol. 2, 133)].

249. Meaning "that than which nothing greater can be conceived," Anselm, *Proslogion*, chapter 2 (Charlesworth, *St. Anselm's Proslogion*, 116).

250. Calvin, *CC—Peter*, 370–71. One might see this *telos* as being a result of the work of the Spirit; Grenz, *The Social God and the Relational Self*, 325–26: the identity

With such an understanding of *theosis* we can now explore the soteriological implications of the extent the metaphor of clothing represents the *perfecting* face of the cross. Due to the fact that "God became man, so that man may become like God," salvation is not a positive result for a legalistic dilemma; rather, it is a healing process bringing humanity to perfection by an incorruptible inheritance.[251] Therefore, the inclination to sin is seen as a symptom of a malady that needs treatment, not just a transgression that requires retribution. Consequently, the human-God association is not merely legal but relational. For Paul, the cross goes on in life-giving power; it is never an episode in the story of the resurrection; the resurrection is an episode in the story of the cross.[252] Yet, the cross should not be isolated, because without the resurrection it remains a tragedy.[253] As a result, in Moltmann' words, rebirth cannot be fulfilled in this world except through the resurrection: "What is experienced in the Spirit as God's love is only the beginning of what will be experienced then as God's glory. Sanctification is the beginning of glorification; glorification is the consummation of sanctification."[254]

"Being clothed with Christ" or "putting on Christ" are concepts that refer to the transformation of a Christian into the likeness of Christ,[255] which can be expressed through the metaphor of clothing[256] (valid biblical metaphors for the *Christus nudus* model: "clothing of salvation,"[257]

---

of participants in the new humanity is co-heir with Christ; the Father bestows on them by virtue of their being "in Christ" what he eternally lavishes on the Son; Boersma, *Violence*, 259–61: Irenaeus also holds that God's eschatological hospitality introduces a mystery in the phrase "pass into God."

251. Osborn, *Irenaeus*, 113; *AH* III.4.2, III.18.7, V.1.1 (union), III.20.2 (participation), IV.11.1.

252. Käsemann, *Perspectives on Paul*, 59.

253. Mertens, *Cross*, 115; Moltmann, *Experience*, 41–42.

254. Moltmann, *The Spirit of Life*, 164.

255. Bakken, "Theosis," 411; Gorman, *Inhabiting*, 4.

256. Luther (*WA* I, 28, 25–32), in Mannermaa, "Theosis," 37–47; Anastos, "Gregory Palamas's Radicalization of the Essence, Energies, and Hypostasis Model of God," 344, 347.

257. "Clothe with salvation" (Ps 132:16); "crown with salvation" (Ps 149:4); "helmet of salvation" (Isa 59:17); "garment of salvation" (Isa 61:10); "righteousness as clothes" (Job 29:14); "helmet of salvation" (Eph 6:17); "salvation as a helmet" (1 Thess 5:8).

or "robes of righteousness,"²⁵⁸ and "clothed with Christ"²⁵⁹). "To put on Christ," therefore, is not only about being justified, it is also about being sanctified and glorified. Consequently, divine clothing can be a metaphor for *theosis*—an act of putting on God and becoming like him.

(1) *Clothing of justification:* There is a necessity for putting off the flesh before putting on Christ, especially in the context of baptism.²⁶⁰ Gregory, however, contended that *theosis* does not imply the destruction or absorption of the self, but its transformation, its purification, its illumination and restoration to the purity of its "primary substance," the "being made in the icon of God."²⁶¹ *Theosis* unites a person with divine grace resulting in a reunion with God thus transcending and detaching oneself from the world and becoming like God.²⁶² This justification may be described as an exclusive clothing, for which there is no bargain, no reduction, no purchase, and no achievement;²⁶³ and as Irenaeus taught, this adoption only takes place when the corruptible is swallowed up by the incorruptible and immortal.²⁶⁴ In justification Christ's righteousness becomes ours.²⁶⁵ Whereas at the *correcting* face of the cross Christ was stripped and poured out for our clothing of righteousness, at the *perfecting* face of the cross the elect is clothed with Christ in union with him.²⁶⁶

(2) *Clothing of sanctification:* According to Bakken, *theosis* entails participation in Christ's nature and can be seen in the concept of *imitatio*

---

258. "Righteous acts like filthy rags" (Isa 64:6); "clothed with righteousness" (Ps 132:9); "righteousness as breastplate" (Isa 59:17); "robe of righteousness" (Isa 61:10); "white robes"/"have washed their robes" (Rev 7:13–14).

259. "Clothed with the Lord Jesus" (Rom 13:14); "clothed with Christ" (Gal 3:27); "become the righteousness of God" (2 Cor 5:21); "crown of righteousness" (2 Tim 4:8).

260. Beasley-Murray, *Baptism*, 149; Quasten, "The Garment of Immortality," 391–401: Jerome's letter to Fabiola.

261. Wesche, "Spirituality," 41; Gregory of Nazianzus, "Epistle 101 ad Cledonium," *NPNF2-7*, 441.

262. Gregory of Nyssa, *Sermon against Those Who Put off Their Baptism*, PG 46:420C (quoted in Daniélou, *The Bible and the Liturgy*, 38); Riley, *Christian Initiation*, 423–31; Lampe, *A Patristic Greek Lexicon*, 1261–62.

263. Cyril of Jerusalem, *Mystagogical*, Cross, *Lectures*, 18, 59; McCauley and Stephenson, *The Works of Saint Cyril of Jerusalem*, Vol. 2, FOC, Vol. 64: 143–51; on the administration of baptism, see Taft, "Baptism," 251.

264. Irenaeus, *AH* III.19.1.

265. Built upon Luther (*WA* 10 I, 1, 157, 1–4; *WA* 17 I, 438, 14–28) (Mannermaa, "Theosis," 40, 46–47; Mannermaa, "Justification and Theosis in Lutheran-Orthodox Perspective," 26).

266. Corrigan, "Crucifixion" 54.

Christi.²⁶⁷ For Luther, however, the "divine nature" of the believer is Christ himself and *theosis* is *Christianus Christus proximi* (the Christian has become the Christ of his neighbour). Therefore, Christians live not by themselves, but Christ and the miserable neighbour live in the life that they live.²⁶⁸ Interestingly, the patristic view of justification contends that the elect "put on" the clothing of good deeds; as such, the "clothing of justification" is associated with "putting on" the lifestyle of Jesus Christ. It is within such a framework that one can connect the moral influence of "naked to follow the naked Christ" to Christ's total kenotic self-giving,²⁶⁹ and to do so by the inspiration of his Spirit and remaining in him.

(3) *Clothing of glorification:* No denominator can be established between "becoming Christ-like" in character and divinization because *theosis* must also be seen eschatologically as a progression from justification to sanctification (becoming Christ-like),²⁷⁰ and ending with "deification."²⁷¹ At the consummation of creation, the elect are clothed with glory to cherish their union with Christ and share his inheritance.²⁷² This, for Calvin, is eschatological *theosis*—a blessing no mind can imagine.²⁷³

Conclusion

Building upon the discussion on imageries and symbolic language in chapter 3, this chapter has argued that the particular case of the Naked Christ revisits both the humanness of Jesus' naked body and the cosmological notion of *Christus nudus*. *Christus nudus* represents divine

---

267. Bakken, "Theosis," 413.

268. Built upon Luther (*WA* 40 I, 283, 7–9) (Mannermaa, "Theosis," 48).

269. Calvin takes the images of vine and branches to speak of the way God produces fruit through the human faculties (Calvin, *Bondage*, 199–331; *Corpus Reformatorum*, 6:393–95).

270. *Epistle to Diognetus*, X, ANF, Vol. 1, 29; John of the Cross, *Living Flame* I (1st and 2nd redaction, in *Works*, Vol. 3, 17–36, 106–26); *Spiritual Canticle* 28, 37 (2nd redaction, Vol. 2, 324–27, 365–68).

271. Christians' reintegration into the life of God (Rakestraw, "Becoming," 257–69; Clendenin, "Partakers of Divinity," 365–79); Clendenin, *Eastern Orthodox Christianity*, 120.

272. For spiritual marriage, see Hart, "The Bright Morning of the Soul: John of the Cross on *Theosis*," 328; Garrigou-Lagrange, *Christian Perception and Contemplation*, 153.

273. For Calvin, "deification is the eschatological goal and blessing greater than which nothing can be imagined." (Mosser, "Greatest," 36).

nakedness in the act of self-emptying. This understanding contributes a considerable development to the soteriology of the Naked Christ: the Word of God, out of love, self-emptied and stooped down into the created order to recapitulate humanity; and his separation from God is somehow depicted in his nakedness on the cross. This *kenosis* is a necessity and the reason for the subsequent achievement of the cross—the union between the redeemed and God.

Theosis, therefore, is understood with Christ's *kenosis* at its foundation. As a result of being "justified" and "becoming like Christ," the elect are called into the perfection of sonship and, thereof, being co-heirs with Christ. As such, the "clothing of justification" is a necessity for the "clothing of glory": not only does justification transform the elect into the lifestyle that imitates Christ's personhood; it also gives them hope for an eschatological perfection of redemption. Hence, while the *correcting* aspect of the cross grants the redeemed the robe of justification, the *perfecting* aspect of the cross maximizes the restored human-God relationship into a complete and fulfilled union, wherein the elect participate in God with the ultimate meaning of co-inheritance.

As such, to describe atonement through the metaphors of nakedness and clothing, referring to both the *correcting* and the *perfecting* faces of the cross and what God achieves in Christ's humility and self-emptying, is a legitimate and historically rich way to convey the death of Christ.

8

The Legitimacy of the *Christus Nudus* Model

THIS CHAPTER DEFINES THE contribution of *Christus nudus* and examines its compatibility with the "community called atonement."[1] The aim of this chapter is not to give a detailed survey of a Christian doctrine of atonement;[2] rather, it is to answer the hermeneutical question of how to interpret the contribution of *Christus nudus* in accordance with the contribution of other traditional models in a kaleidoscopic fashion.[3]

We shall set the parameters for our discussion first and foremost according to the current kaleidoscopic fashion of soteriology. Subsequently, we shall look at three classic models while constructing the correspondent contribution of *Christus nudus*.[4] Finally, we shall gather some con-

1. This is done in a mimetic response to McKnight's question: "Which is the fairest of them all?" (McKnight, *Community*, 107–14).

2. The limitations of this chapter are an acknowledgement of recent contributions in this field. On sacrificial language of atonement, see Heim, *Saved from Sacrifice*. On soteriology and the influence of a historical Jesus, see McKnight, *Jesus and His Death*. Schmiechen has presented ten models (*Saving*). Shelton's covenantal language of the cross has also proposed an excellent survey of atonement theories (*Covenant*, especially chapters 9–11).

3. This book applies Irenaeus' method, which combines the various atonement models by means of his understanding of recapitulation (Boersma, "Redemptive Hospitality in Irenaeus," 207–26). Developed from Green's definition, the term "kaleidoscopic fashion," used in this book, borrows certain features of a kaleidoscope, especially its multi-perspective and yet at the same time viewing the same material. *Christus nudus* model, therefore, will interpret the Naked Christ under three classic models: *Christus Victor*, *satisfaction*, and *moral example*.

4. The construction of this chapter is heavily indebted to Boersma, especially the

cluding remarks regarding the distinctive contribution of *Christus nudus* among the community called atonement.

Kaleidoscopic Atonement and Christus Nudus

Every cultural period and theological school, and every generation of Christians more or less forms and develops its own soteriology,[5] but no model is universally valid or capable of answering every question.[6] Consequently, although New Testament writers sought to communicate the same fundamental belief that the death and resurrection of Christ is the great redemptive act by which God has brought a new community into being, it is correct to claim that all attempts to explain the inexplicable must inevitably be inadequate.[7] A theology of the cross, therefore, is comparable to a tent pitched by a nomadic tribe that wanders from one situation to another, adapting to the culture in which it finds itself.[8] Or similarly in McKnight's analogy of golf clubs,[9] an atonement model, with its own strengths and weaknesses, offers a specific and unique contribution. Therefore, by considering the many facets of the atonement "diamond,"[10] a theology of the cross employs a kaleidoscopic view of atonement.[11] This implies an arguable existing mutual relationship between metaphors.[12] Nonetheless, the matters at stake are how to define

interplay between violence and hospitality (Boersma, *Violence*); victory, satisfaction and regeneration (Forsyth, *Work*, 150–51; *Positive Preaching and the Modern Mind*, 224).

5. Dillistone, *The Christian Understanding of the Atonement*, 25–26.
6. Mertens, *Cross*, 63–84, 101; Marshall, *Aspects of the Atonement*, 128.
7. Hooker, *Not Ashamed of the Gospel*, 138–39.
8. McGrath, *The Enigma of the Cross*, 80.
9. McKnight, *Community*, 38–42.
10. Gumbel, *Question of Life*, 49; Terry, *Justifying*, 7–9.
11. Green, "Kaleidoscopic," 164, 166: five spheres of public life. Such a kaleidoscopic fashion implies that our understanding of the cross circulates or rotates around a "center" (Niesel, *The Theology of Calvin*, 247; Partee, "Calvin's Central Dogma Again," 192–93). The hermeneutical method of employing one central concept to hold other soteriological concepts has been widely used: for reconciliation, see Martin, *Reconciliation*, 46–47; for peace see Yarbrough, in Alexander and Rosner, *New Dictionary of Biblical Theology*, 498–503; Porter, "Peace, Reconciliation," 695–99.
12. This particular perspective might appear relativistic, but it has been formulated within the effect of the metaphorical factor. Gunton, for example, argues that victory, justice and sacrifice should not be treated as theories, or vaguely as images or ideas, but as metaphors (*Actuality*, 42–45). This treatment allows the possibility of a combined

this kaleidoscopic view of atonement and subsequently how differently such a kaleidoscopic view shapes the *Christus nudus* model.

Kaleidoscopic Fashion

In a kaleidoscopic fashion every model has a distinctive nature, logic, function, and validity to the audience that it serves.[13] Twenty-first-century mentality can easily misconstrue the intention of New Testament metaphors.[14] Images such as "ransom" and "sacrifice" may be more valuable for a culture impacted by commercial values. "Exchange," "substitutionary," and "representational" are better fitted in a forensic context; whereas "victor and liberator" and "recapitulation" might be more valuable and better accepted according to a view of oppression, whether social-politically or spiritually.[15]

While a kaleidoscopic view of atonement emphasizes the necessity of diversity in one's view of the cross,[16] this does not deny that some models can be more attractive than others, to certain people at certain times, and some might be more problematic.[17] Therefore, there is a tension in its construction: a tension between singularity and plurality.[18] On the one hand, methodologically speaking, a kaleidoscopic model endeavors

and complementary metaphorical understanding of atonement (Terry, *Justifying*, 66), which a kaleidoscopic fashion is designed to be. Forsyth also implies a unification of the triumphant, satisfactory and regenerative aspects could be depicted in the phrase "threefold cord" (*Work*, 199–201); Hart, "Redemption and Fall," 190: metaphors are not to be understood as exchangeable, but complementary, directing to distinct elements in and consequences of the fullness of God's saving action in Christ and the Spirit.

13. Green, "Kaleidoscopic," 170.

14. Green and Baker, *Recovering*, 88.

15. This does not deny human conditions as a factor that also shapes an atonement model. Chapter 9 will touch on shame and guilt in the general picture of human condition. In this chapter, however, in order to relate to the historical aspect of the three classical models, more emphasis is given to an anthropological and sociological perspective of model formulation.

16. Green, "Kaleidoscopic," 170; Thiselton, *The Hermeneutics of Doctrine*, 318–19.

17. Green, "Kaleidoscopic," 185; Asselt, "Christ's Atonement," 64: Follow L. J. Van den Brom, Asselt argues that a more highly developed model includes the other less complicated models, and together they contribute to the richness of the whole. Therefore, all the models together constitute, as it were, an extended chain or family from which one cannot isolate or eliminate a single model.

18. I.e., between one view being more foundational than others and many views contributing to a big picture.

to cover the theological content of the doctrine of salvation with a variety of views. On the other hand, there is a continual check between the first-century historical reality anchor metaphors and the metaphors proposed by different individuals and groups at different times.[19]

Boyd argues that we are logically forced to debate the merits of competing ways of arranging the biblical material on the basis of the biblical material itself, because it is logically impossible for all theories to be, at the same time, equally right and equally wrong.[20] Boyd makes an important point, but by accepting the competing nature of models, we run the risk of assuming that all models undertake identical tasks; yet in reality, each model might serve a different task. Actually, a kaleidoscopic view serves to hold necessary tensions.

At one level, in order to make sense of the scandal of the cross, some might suspend the resurrection in order that the full impact of the cross may be experienced.[21] This evidences a tension: on the one hand, the cross symbolizes Christ's atoning death, on the other, an understanding of the cross should not be achieved at the expense of his life and teaching,[22] not to mention his resurrection.[23] Indeed, apart from Jesus' life we have little on which to base any claim regarding the soteriological significance of his death.[24] Similarly, we have also established in chapter 7 that the *correcting* face of the cross should not be limited to Christ' death alone; rather, his incarnation recapitulates humanity and sets the example of a humanity according to God's creational intention.

At another level, the *correcting* face of the cross, although depicted in many ways, refers to one action—the bringing together of two parties, who have become estranged, into at-one-ment,[25] also known as "reconciliation."[26] Nonetheless, there is a tension in the way reconciliation is achieved. On the one hand, "reconciliation and restoration" refer to a human-God relationship, i.e., God in Christ reconciles the world to

---

19. Boyd, "Christus Victor Response," 187.
20. Boyd, "Response," 189; Spence, *The Promise of Peace*, 3–4, 13.
21. Dillistone, *Atonement*, 155; Hooker, *Ashamed*, 13.
22. Heim, *Sacrifice*, 2.
23. Grayston, *Dying, We Live*; Stanley, *Christ's Resurrection in Pauline Soteriology*.
24. Green, "Kaleidoscopic," 164: especially n.15.
25. Grant, "The Abandonment of Atonement," 3; Dillistone, "Atonement," 50; Atkinson, "Atonement," 18.
26. Paul, *The Atonement and the Sacraments*, 20–21.

himself,[27] having paid the cost of forgiveness.[28] On the other hand, "reconciliation and restoration" has a greater scope of impact: self-God, self-self, self-others, and self-cosmos.[29] As a result, this tension challenges our concept of sin.

A kaleidoscopic explanation of reconciliation is problematic if it does not also have a kaleidoscopic conception of sin: at times sin is understood as relational;[30] other times sin is described as *objects* or *dirt*,[31] being removable and transferable.[32] Clearly, different views on the problem of sin might infer different interpretations of "reconciliation." For example, if original sin is understood not as an ancestral inheritance that human beings are born with, but as an external and environmental entity that human beings are born into—an enemy,[33] then salvation begins with being released "from the bondage of the enemy."[34] Reconciliation is achieved when sin is defeated. If, however, sin is understood as dishonoring God,[35] or primarily something that God punishes us for,[36] then reconciliation is achieved through the (substitutionary) merit that Christ satisfies God's justice. Otherwise, in a moral influence view, if sin is that from which Jesus exemplarily shows us how to turn away, then

---

27. The world is estranged from God rather than God is estranged from the world (Green, "Kaleidoscopic," 168); Hooker, *Ashamed*, 27.

28. Brümmer, *Atonement, Christology and the Trinity*, 49.

29. McKnight, *Community*, 20–24.

30. Shelton, *Covenant*, 27–28; Brümmer, *Atonement*, 49.

31. Goldingay, "Your Iniquities Have Made a Separation between You and God," 51; Goldingay, "Old Testament Sacrifice and the Death of Christ," 3–20.

32. Shelton holds that sin is not a *thing* to be removed (Shelton, *Covenant*, 122–23). His point is valuable to the covenant and relational motif, but it totally dismisses the biblical linguistic model of "object-containment" of sin in sacrificial rituals and in biblical poetry (e.g. Pss 51:2, 7, 9; 103:12). There is no danger of relativism here necessarily. The fact that different linguistic-cognitive frameworks can be employed in different biblical texts implies that sin must not be understood in a simplified norm, rather it can be understood in multiple metaphorical frameworks.

33. Cronk, *The Message of the Bible*, 45; Hopko, *The Lenten Spring*, 30; Davies, *Beginning Now*, 204–6.

34. Hayes, *The IViyo loFakazi bakaKristu and the KwaNdebele Mission of the Anglican Diocese of Pretoria*, 168.

35. Take Anselm's view on sin for example, Anselm asks, "Is sin anything else than not rendering to God what is his due? But what is God's due? It is summed up in the one word, honor." (*CDH*, 1:11, 216).

36. Rodger, "The Soteriology of Anselm of Canterbury," 28.

reconciliation is love in response.[37] All in all, these conceptions of sin endeavor to depict the different relational aspects: human-God, human-human, human-self and human-cosmos. A view of sin is inadequate if it only considers sin as an *external* problem that affects *outwardly*, and therefore fails to deal with the *internal* conflict of shame and guilt. It is also inadequate to view sin as an impersonal forensic debt, or merely an imperfection that can be overcome by moral influence, because the concept of relational restoration seems to be neglected.[38] Rather, sin is better understood as a relational dysfunction that causes damage to both the offender and the offended and thus reconciliation is needed.[39] To respond to such a multidimensional view of sin, a kaleidoscopic view of atonement—a synthesis of many views of the cross[40]—is needed in order to address sin as a relational problem both from within and without.[41]

Overall, the forensic language of atonement might logically expound sin through metaphors such as defending, advocating, and justifying, but it runs short of a relational dimension between a defendant and the Judge.[42] Victory language expounds deliverance, liberation, rescue, and ransom, but consequently lacks an attention to forgiveness and participation.[43] In sum, trivializing metaphors can threaten to turn the doctrine of atonement into a simplistic and inadequate model.[44] When faced with the problem of sin, a model cannot only focus on placating God's anger; neither can it focus on victory or an example and omit how reconciliation happens between humanity, God, and creation, which is a result of the gracious activity of God at work through Christ.

---

37. Abelard, *Exposition of the Epistle to the Romans*, in Fairweather, *A Scholastic Miscellany*, 283.

38. Fiddes, *Tracks and Traces*, 243. Settling a forensic debt does not automatically imply an interest in a relationship, and moral mimesis assumes an ability to love and imitate.

39. Shelton, *Covenant*, 27–28; Brümmer, *Atonement*, 49.

40. Robbins, "Atonement in Contemporary Culture," 329.

41. Reichenbach, "Healing View," 129–30. It must be stressed, however, that a therapeutic view of atonement should also pay attention to the innate healing.

42. Gunton, *Actuality*, chapter 1, 93–94.

43. Schreiner, "Penal Substitution Response," 50–52.

44. Terry, *Justifying*, 10–15.

Christus Nudus in the Light of Kaleidoscopic Fashion

The *Christus nudus* model emerges from the fact that the earliest depictions of the cross and crucifixion lacked realism;[45] however, the focus of the *Christus nudus* model must extend beyond the horrific punishment of a dead and naked Messiah,[46] to communicate the hope of the robe of righteousness and the restoration achieved by his self-outpouring. Therefore, within a kaleidoscopic view, the challenge for the *Christus nudus* model is, on the one hand, to preserve a faithful theological content while on the other to project compatibility between different views of atonement within a kaleidoscopic fashion.

How should the *Christus nudus* model do this? First, the dialogue between clothing and nakedness, in the work of Christ, should not be restricted to cruciformity alone; rather, nakedness and clothing also represent *kenosis* and *theosis* in soteriology.[47] Just as Christ emptied himself in the death of his naked body, revealed God and reconciled humanity into a union with God, so must the cruciform face of the cross lead to theoformity. Secondly, nakedness and clothing must be flexible enough to project concepts from different models. The metaphor of nakedness can recall the Eden narrative,[48] to connect sin[49] and the victory in obedience achieved by *Christus nudus*, which consequently sets humanity free from the bondage of sin. Alternatively, nakedness and clothing can carry connotations of legal language in relation to "wrath"[50] and "judgement."[51]

---

45. A.D. 400 and A.D. 430 (Pocknee, *Cross and Crucifix*, 19–20). West points out that when Christ was first portrayed on the cross, he was shown fully vested in an alb-like garment reflecting the Eastern distaste for naked men, but nakedness is historically accurate (West, *Outward Signs*, 22). Artists have shrunk from portraying the nakedness of Christ and added a loincloth to conceal shame—an integral part of the cross [Corrigan, "Crucifixion," 49, 54; Hooker, *Ashamed*, 10; Jordan, "Body," 284].

46. Hooker, *Ashamed*, 9–12.

47. Calvin's exchange, Irenaeus' recapitulation, Augustine and Chrysostom's victory, Abelard and Cyril of Jerusalem's moral influence can compatibly refer to restoration through the lens of *kenosis* and *theosis*.

48. See chapter 4 of this book; the traditional interpretation of failure, defeat, and helplessness, etc., is useful especially to the Adam-Christ typology.

49. "Loss of glory," "loss of the robe of glory," "loss of the chance of being immortal," or "falling short of God's glory" (Brock, "Robe," 247).

50. E.g., Morris, *The Epistle to the Romans*, 225; Morris, *The Cross in the New Testament*, 226.

51. In chapter 5 of this book, according to Kim and Ellis, Paul's concept of nakedness refers to the lack of a resurrection body, (a point that Murray Harris further

Christus Nudus in a Community Of Atonement

In chapter 7, we have mentioned briefly that the interpretations of *Christus nudus* have varied from a victory motif to satisfaction and moral example motifs. We now turn to explore how *Christus nudus* contributes to these models and how it must depend on their support in order to form a kaleidoscopic view.[52]

Christus Nudus and Christus Victor

The classic or dramatic theory starts with the idea that atonement is brought about through Christ's victory over the power of evil, releasing humanity and bringing it into a relationship with God.[53] This view understands sin as enslavement under evil powers[54]—an environmental spectrum that human beings are born into, rather than being born with.[55] On this account, the necessity of liberation from sin is reinstated: reconciliation only happens after humanity has been released or liberated from the captivity of sin.[56] Ray claims that salvation is freedom *from* sin and evil; and this liberation is the necessary precondition for a right relationship with God, with self, and with others.[57] Boyd also offers a similar

---

interprets as the intermediate state of the Greek bodiless ideology, but in either way, it is an *unwanted* and *undesirable* state). The contrast between nakedness and clothing employed in Revelation speaks powerfully about judgment and destruction.

52. The three commonly recognized as classical models of atonement are satisfaction, moral influence and victory (Green, "Kaleidoscopic," 169; Asselt, "Multi-dimensional," 54). Within a kaleidoscopic approach, there are notions in one model that can be placed under the lens of other models, for example, exchange (substitution and satisfaction, ransom and *Christus Victor*), vicarious representation (*Christus Victor*, satisfaction and moral influence), and recapitulation (satisfaction, *Christus Victor* and moral influence). For example, substitutionary can be seen as an overarching model (Asselt, "Multi-Dimensional," 52–67).

53. Aulén, *Victor*, 4; Boersma, *Violence*, chapter 8, 181: *Christus Victor* "is, in a real sense, the most significant model of the atonement."

54. Boyd, "Christus Victor View," 28–29.

55. Orthodox soteriology considers sin as an entity separate from relational beings: an enemy, a bondage (Hayes, *IViyo*, 168; Cronk, *Message*, 45; Hopko, *Spring*, 30; Davies, *Beginning*, 205–15).

56. The baptismal candidate is not free to voluntarily renounce Satan until he or she has been prized from Satan's clutches by the exorcism, i.e., liberation precedes renunciation in a similar fashion to Israel's liberation from the clutches of Pharaoh at the Red Sea (Hayes, "Evangelism and Liberation," 55).

57. Ray, *Deceiving the Devil*, 53.

point, suggesting that forgiveness is itself rooted in a person being freed from Satan's grip.[58]

The question of how liberation is achieved has been answered in three ways: recapitulation, ransom and *Christus Victor*.[59] Irenaeus claims that in God's reasonable nature, he gave himself as a ransom for those who had been led into captivity,[60] but his understanding of victory is closely connected to the human-God union,[61] therefore, Christ conquered Satan in his obedience to the Father.[62] Recapitulation of humanity's disobedience is also affirmed by other Greek fathers, such as Athanasius and Cyril of Alexandria.[63] Alternatively, the "ransom" view of the Eastern fathers offers a connection to "liberation." Origen and Augustine also understood the death of Christ, as the ransom paid to the devil for the souls of the lost, yet at times Christ was also a priest offering a propitiatory sacrifice to the Father.[64] Gregory of Nyssa held the view that Christ was the "ransom" paid to the devil,[65] even to the extent that Jesus' soul was "bait" to deceive Satan in an exchange for humanity.[66] However, unlike his contemporaries, Gregory of Nazianzus rejected the view that Christ's blood was shed as an expiation for sin, nor as a ransom to the devil in exchange for the release of captive humanity, because the devil has no such right over humanity;[67] rather, Christ is *Christus Victor* who offers his life in order that humanity could be set free from death.[68]

---

58. Boyd, "Victor," 32.

59. Shelton, *Covenant*, 160.

60. *AH* V.1.1, ANCL9, 56.

61. Letham, *Work*, 159.

62. *AH* V.21.2, ANCL9, 113.

63. Athanasius, *Discourse against the Arians*, I.43–44; Cyril of Alexandria, *Passover Homilies* XVII, MPG, 77: 785–87; *Against the Nestorians* I, MPG, 76.17; *Commentary on the Gospel of John*, MPG, 73.161; 74.432 (quoted in Letham, *Work*, 161).

64. McIntyre, *Shape*, 4–6; Augustine, *de Trinitate* 4.13.17 and 13.15.19, NPNF1–3, 78, 178; Grensted, *A Short History of the Doctrine of the Atonement*, 37–38. However, Letham argues that Origen understood victory in terms of a conquest rather than a transaction with the devil (Letham, *Work*, 161).

65. Gregory of Nyssa, NPNF2–5, 495: 26: "He who first deceived man by the bait of sensual pleasure is himself deceived by the presentment of the human form."

66. Gregory of Nyssa, NPNF2–5, 495: 22–26; Ambrose, *Letters*, 41:7–8, 72.8, NPNF2–10, 446–47.

67. Gregory of Nazianzus, *Oratio* 45.22, NPNF2–7, 431.

68. Ibid., 431; Harrison, "Theosis as Salvation," 437.

Similarly, in the *Christus nudus* model, the Adam-Christ typology and recapitulation are also apparent: Chrysostom had established the connection between sin, nakedness and Christ's victory: one was naked because of sin, the other was made naked to set free.[69] This victory motif in Adam-Christ typology had already been observed by the early church fathers such as Augustine, Ambrose, and Gregory.[70] The advantage of this motif is that it connects Christ's victory to humanity's failure, namely the origin of sin in the Eden narrative. The victory in Christ's obedience that liberates sinners from the bondage caused by their disobedience is a compatible contribution that *Christus nudus* has established with *Christus Victor*.

Nonetheless, the *Christus nudus* model maintains certain differences from *Christus Victor*. First, the "battlefield" between God and Satan has been reduced to a battle between obedience and disobedience. Nevertheless, this has become an advantage for *Christus nudus*. Unlike *Christus Victor*,[71] *Christus nudus* offers a provision for human participation in atonement, i.e., atonement is not only about God's liberation, but Christ also recapitulates where humanity fails. Criticism against *Christus Victor*, especially regarding the unclear connection with human sin,[72] must reconsider the victory motif in *Christus nudus*. The resonance of the Eden narrative, as a backdrop to Christ's obedience, contrasts the previous defeat caused by human sin to the victory humanity shares in Christ: the victory of the "woman's offspring" is the fulfilment of the curse against the devil. By recollecting the obedience motif, *Christus nudus* effectively creates a connection between Christ's solidarity and humanity's participation: repentance and rectification of wrongs before receiving forgiveness and reconciliation.

In addition, since the "battlefield" motif has been reduced, there is no such notion of "captive," "captor," or "ransom" in *Christus nudus*. Rather, Christ is the representative who identifies with humanity in the

---

69. Chrysostom, *NPNF1-13*: Colossians 2:6–7—Homily VI, 287. This was also Tauler's point (Tauler, *Meditations*, chapter 33: 262, 264–67).

70. Jacobus, *Golden*, 77.

71. *Christus Victor* can mistakenly reduce redemption to a purely cosmic affair without the participation or even knowledge of human beings and thus fails to take seriously human responsibility for evil (e.g., Ray, *Deceiving*, 127–28). Boyd ("Victor," 35) remarks that *Christus Victor* "is a cosmic reality before it is an anthropological reality, and it is the latter because it is the former."

72. Letham, *Work*, 163.

consequence of their sin and overthrows evil in the victory of his obedience, whereby sinners in him can gain victory over temptation. There are two advantages to this interpretation: first, whereas it is difficult to see why incarnation was necessary in *Christus Victor*,[73] in *Christus nudus* it is necessary for God to achieve the victory of obedience *for* humanity *in* humanity. Hence, by using the metaphor of nakedness *Christus nudus* successfully secures the reason why Christ's victory is relevant to human sin. The second advantage is that there is no hint of divine trickery in *Christus nudus*. Victory over the devil can be achieved *without* the notion of deceptive "ransom."

A counter argument to the *Christus nudus* model regarding "divine trickery" might take Ray's safeguard of God's wisdom over violence,[74] to indicate how God's deception of the devil explains God's defeat of evil[75] using his unfathomable wisdom.[76] However, to employ divine trickery in order to explain victory is totally unnecessary. Not only does this trickery run the risk of either being a manipulative model (i.e., God is manipulatable) or an indication of an unnecessary "fair-play" cosmic law that even God must respect,[77] it also misses two important points: (1) In Jesus' ministry and victory over the devil and demons—the foundation for *Christus Victor*—there is no hint of this trickery. And (2) the wisdom of God, which overturns evil powers, can be explained by the paradoxical nature of God's work: strength in weakness, wisdom in foolishness, victory in defeat and life in death.[78] The Naked Cross projects the mysterious nature of God's wisdom: it truly is a stumbling block for many.[79] There is nakedness in Adam's defeat but the seemingly defeated nakedness of the cross of Christ returns with victory. As Christ is the first fruit of resurrection (Rom 4:25) and the robe of righteousness (1 Cor 15:17), atonement is secured.

---

73. Brümmer, *Atonement*, 72.

74. Ray, *Deceiving*, 138–39.

75. Ibid., 121; however, this assigns a sense of duplicity to God, which makes the argument seriously untenable, (Letham, *Work*, 162; Ray, *Deceiving*, 126); cf. Boyd, "Victor," 37.

76. Augustine, *On the Trinity* 4.13.18, in *NPNF1-3*, 79.

77. Ray, *Deceiving*, 121–22, 138, although Ray also recognizes that Irenaeus argues against the notion that the devil had any right (Irenaeus, *AH* III.23.3, *ANCL5*, 364–65).

78. Weston, "Proclaiming Christ Crucified Today," 155.

79. Chan, "The Gospel and the Achievement of the Cross," 24.

So far, like the victory motif in *Christus Victor*, not only does *Christus nudus* have a strong universal sense of sin and a corporate conception of Christ's humanity,[80] it also offers a concept of participation as a personal yet corporate response to atonement,[81] particularly the participation expressed in baptism.[82] Yet, it is interesting that the *Christus nudus* model does not have the notions of bondage and oppression expressed in the *Christus Victor* model. In particular, the "bondage" and "oppression" of shame and a body enslaved to sin are a result of the inherent brokenness of humanity—an ontological and relational dilemma.[83] In this way, as humanity renounces evil in obedience to God, liberation and restoration from ontological flaws and the plague of shame can be claimed in Christ's victory. Therefore, *Christus nudus* contributes to the victory motif a notion of oppression that is closer to human ontology and relation. In sum, despite the fact that *Christus Victor* might be construed as more fundamental than other aspects due to its strong biblical foundation,[84] the *Christus nudus* model can still offer a victory that restores the humanity of the First Adam through obedience. In this way, victory is made meaningful to the reconciliation of a broken relationship between God and humanity.

Christus Nudus and Satisfaction

The language of God's satisfaction is an attempt to give an account of atonement with metaphors drawn from the world of law and feudal society.[85] Anselm argued that a holy and just God will not let sin go unpunished; either punishment has to be executed, or satisfaction must be achieved.[86] However, in Anselm's view, punishment of sin is inadequate because it only deals with what has been taken from God, but not with

---

80. Wiles, *The Making of Christian Doctrine*, chapter 5.

81. Brümmer, *Atonement*, 69–73; Owen, *The Death of Death in the Death of Christ*, Vol. 10, 173, 214.

82. Boyd, "Victor," 32–33; also mentioned in nude baptism (chapters 5 and 7 of this book).

83. See chapters 4 and 5 of this book.

84. Boyd, "Victor," 24–27. Christ's blood sets humanity free from sins (1 Cor 5:7; John 1:29; 2:13–22; 1 Pet 1:18) (Hooker, *Ashamed*, 135).

85. Gunton, *Actuality*, 89: satisfaction depends on a particular conception of justice; Weaver, *The Nonviolent Atonement*, 16; Shelton, *Covenant*, 175.

86. Anselm, *CDH*, 1.15.

the restoration of creation according to God's original intentions.[87] What is needed, rather, is for satisfaction to be offered to God.[88] Human beings cannot achieve God's "satisfaction"; therefore, Anselm proposed that it was necessary for the God-Man to achieve it:[89] a divine action must be done on behalf of humanity to set right what has been wronged by human sin.[90] Jesus offers his life as a gift to the Father, a gift that outweighs the accumulated weight of sin.[91] However, Anselm insisted that this gift was not to be understood in the language of cosmic legality nor out of necessity, but of willingness.[92]

Consequently, satisfaction language understands Christ's death as substitutionary.[93] On the one hand, Christ's substitution is *exclusive*: he is "in our place"—the "ransom for many,"[94] and the servant who bears sin and dies *for* others: as Christ takes on the sin of the world, he takes on the rejection and the brokenness of the world.[95] On the other hand, substitution is *inclusive*: Christ is a representative on sinners' behalf.[96] In a mysterious way, Christians participate in Christ's vicarious suffering, his shame, his death and his triumph.[97] Accordingly, substitution simultaneously implies a "swap" between Christ and believers,[98] and a sense of

---

87. Deme, *The Christology of Anselm of Canterbury*, 88.

88. McIntyre, *St Anselm and His Critics*, 86–88; Balthasar, *The Glory of the Lord: A Theological Aesthetics—II Studies in Theological Styles: Clerical Styles*, 249; Asselt, "Multi-Dimensional," 60.

89. Anselm, *CDH*, 2.7.

90. Ibid., 2:18; Gunton, *Actuality*, 91–92.

91. Anselm, *CDH*, 1.21, 2.4, 16; with perfect obedience, Dillistone, *Atonement*, 193.

92. Anselm, *CDH*, 1.10, 2.10.

93. Barth, *CD*, III.2, 144, 211–12; Morris, *The Atonement*; Morris, *Cross*, 225–26; Buren, *Christ in Our Place*, 51–52; Asselt, "Multi-Dimensional," 59–61; Jeffery et al., *Pierced for Our Transgressions*; McKnight, *Jesus*, 347.

94. Peterson, "Atonement," 29.

95. France, *Jesus and the Old Testament*, 121: Isa 53: incidental illustration, Jesus' quotes Isaiah in Luke 22:37; Mark 10:45; 14:24 and parallels; and Mark 9:12; Matt 3:15; and Luke 11:22, thus inclined to the impending imputation of guilt to one who did not deserve it, 116; Cf. Epistle of Peter (Hooker, *Ashamed*, 127–28); Green, "Kaleidoscopic," 166.

96. McIntyre, *Shape*, 89–92, 97: especially in the light of Isa 52:13—53:12; Pannenberg, *Jesus-God and Man*, 236–39.

97. Hooker, *Ashamed*, 140.

98. For Hooker, substitution does not always mean swapping, not "instead" but "representative"; however, sometimes substitution does mean "swapping," e.g., Jesus

solidarity with Christ's death: believers *in him* might die and rise to life *with him*.[99] Yet, most importantly, Christ succeeds where humanity fails, as Gunton puts it: "[W]e have to say that Jesus is our substitute because he does for us what we cannot do for ourselves. That includes undergoing the judgement of God, because were we to undergo it without him, it would mean our destruction."[100]

One of the weaknesses of satisfaction language is, however, that it employs a certain notion of justice that subsequently depicts atonement as a result of something done *to* God rather than something done *by* God.[101] In fact, Gunton also points out that Anselm's satisfaction places too much weight on Jesus' action toward the Father and too little involvement of the triune God in human history, thus making the whole affair appear to be more an exercise of power than love.[102] Rashdall even goes as far as to criticize Anselm's use of "justice" of being an ancient barbaric ideal.[103] As a result, satisfaction, which is achieved through substitution and representation, must not be an end in itself; rather, its objectives are for the sake of a relationship. In this way, satisfaction language can aim at the reconciliation of the human-God relationship—the same point New Testament writers sought to express.[104] Consequently, substitution and representation must be understood as two sides of the one relationship: Jesus takes our place so that we may become reconciled before God.[105]

---

in the place of Barabbas (ibid., 36, 88; Hooker, *Adam*, 26–27). McIntyre suggests that there is a blurred distinction between "substitution" and "representation" (McIntyre, *Shape*, 99). Gunton also suggests the two concepts to be correlative; he argues that because Jesus is our substitute, it is also right to call him our representative (Gunton, *Actuality*, 166).

99. Hooker, *Ashamed*, 29–31, 35–36.

100. Gunton, *Actuality*, 165.

101. Brümmer argues that it is true that God is the initiator and author of atonement but he is not the one who carries it out; rather the agent of atonement is Christ in his humanity (*Atonement*, 77).

102. Gunton, *Actuality*, 93–94: the other two are: (1) it appears almost as if God is as much concerned to achieve a correct balance of numbers in heaven as to realize his love towards the creation (2) Anselm appears to equate salvation with the remission of penalty, thus relatively little emphasis is given to the atonement as the place where reconciliation, in the sense of a renewed personal walk with God, is made real. Therefore, the cross is understood in a way that seems rather external—a transaction that takes place in a different space and time from ours.

103. Rashdall, *The Idea of the Atonement in Christian Theology*, 355.

104. Hooker, *Ashamed*, 139.

105. Gunton, *Actuality*, 167.

This means that "satisfaction" is a satisfaction designed by God in his own providence—a grace-initiated satisfaction, the agent and chief author of which is the whole Trinity.[106]

Critics of satisfaction language accuse it of (a) separating God from his character of love; (b) reducing God's ability to forgive freely without retribution;[107] (c) binding God to the demands of justice,[108] and worse, (d) of separating the Father and the Son.[109] However, such accusations can, perhaps, be redressed by Irving's trinitarian argument: for Irving, Jesus' substitution must be seen in the agency of the Spirit as well as an expression of the Father's love in the Son's sufferings and death.[110] Therefore, any satisfaction language that depicts God as a satisfaction-oriented agent concerned more about justice than repentance and reconciliation misses the point completely because God's justice is *personalized*, not *depersonalized*.[111] Few, if any, evangelical scholars hold to such a view of satisfaction wherein the Father punishes the Son.[112] Rather, Stott goes as far as to effectively unite the Father and Son in the redemptive "self-substitution."[113] If God demands from himself the satisfaction, then forgiveness truly is unconditional. Such a demand is consistent with a trinitarian view of redemption, which holds that the agent and the chief author is the entire Trinity.[114] Admittedly, no forensic language in itself can speak adequately of God's satisfaction, but if "satisfaction" is an attempt to depict the way in which sin is dealt with as well as reveal the

---

106. Owen, *Death*, 163.

107. Aberlard (in Schmiechen, *Saving*, 293–95); Rashdall, *Atonement*, 355; see more below.

108. Nonetheless, justice is never an independent entity but always an expression of the character of a loving and Holy God. It is a mistake therefore to think of the moral law of God in terms of a contemporary statute law, where a judge rules on behalf of an impersonal entity called the state and has no personal stake in the issues before him (Tidball, "Pastoral," 350–52: "He demands nothing that he does not first provide.") See also chapter 7 of this book.

109. Brock, "And a Little Child Will Lead Us," 52–53; Spaulding, "Milbank's Trinitarian Ontology and a Re-Narration of Wesleyan-Holiness Theology," 146–59; Shelton, *Covenant*, 22; Gray, "Postmodernism," 36–44; Weaver, *Nonviolent*, chapter 5—"Feminist Theology on Atonement," 122–56.

110. Irving, *Writings*, 234, 147.

111. Tidball, "Pastoral," 350.

112. Marshall, "Atonement," 63n.53, 68; Williams, "Penal Substitution," 178.

113. Stott, *Cross*, 133–63; Campbell, *Atonement*, 136.

114. Owen, *Death*, 163.

cost of forgiveness, then it retains validity as long as God pays the price for forgiveness.[115]

In response to satisfaction, what does *Christus nudus* have to offer? As mentioned in chapter 7 of this book, to understand atonement according to the notion of "clothing of righteousness" is to grant to the metaphors of clothing and nakedness forensic validity and therefore they become compatible with satisfaction language. A person who is righteous or justified has no legal liability for any crime. Therefore, linguistically speaking, the phrases "clothing of righteousness" and "clothed with righteousness," especially with regards to "clothing of salvation," connote a notion of "justification," i.e., claiming or declaring a person, who previously was not righteous, to be righteous.[116] As clothing nullifies the effect of nakedness, so does Christ's righteousness nullify the effect of sin. The robe of righteousness signifies that sinners are invited into a relationship with *Deus revelatus* who reveals himself in the nakedness of Jesus.[117] This notion of solidarity and justification is compatible to Pauline thought: in Christ's solidarity with humanity, and our solidarity with him, justification is dependent upon both death and resurrection.[118] We are accounted righteous in Christ: if Christ's death deals with sin then his resurrection is the basis for our righteousness.[119]

How can the "clothing of righteousness" (justification in participation) explain the "removal of sin" in relation to God's wrath and his satisfaction? First, *Christus nudus* must understand that God's wrath is not impersonal but as an expression of God's jealous love.[120] What seems to be the pitting of one member of the Trinity against the other must be understood in the context of a grace-initiated satisfaction. As mentioned previously, humanity cannot approach *Deus nudus*, therefore *Christus nudus* is the only way through which the human-God relationship can be restored.[121] In the Son's self-emptying and humility, even in the naked-

---

115. Brümmer, *Atonement*, 46, 78.

116. Building upon our linguistic analysis in chapter 3, this is comprehensible. "Object-containment" and "conceal-reveal" models allow us to make sense of the antithesis between righteousness and unrighteousness, as well as between clothing and nakedness.

117. See the correcting face of the cross in chapter 7 of this book.

118. Hooker, *Adam*, 27, 31–35.

119. Hooker, *Interchange and Atonement*, 477.

120. McKnight, *Community*, 68–69; Gunton, *Actuality*, 102.

121. This point is established in chapter 7.

ness of the cross, the Father experienced separation as much as the Son did in order to reconcile the world to himself, in a "union of will."[122] If nakedness represents the broken state of the human-God relation, then Christ's nakedness signifies the stripping of his sinlessness and holiness when he identifies with our sins.[123] As a result, by becoming naked for us Christ effectively creates a bridge where sinners can approach his righteousness, like a transaction in participation.[124] Consequently, the Father looks at sinners through Jesus' righteousness and is satisfied because his righteousness counters sinfulness just as clothing covers nakedness.[125] In this way Jesus' effective removal of wrath through satisfaction and his liberation of sinners from a state of rejection and separation makes more sense.

So far, the *Christus nudus* model has not explained how sin is dealt with in relation to justice and punishment for sin,[126] in the light of satisfaction. It is true that the *Christus nudus* model begins with the historical naked punishment of crucifixion and therefore this image of "punishment" might be more appealing to the satisfaction model.[127] Nonetheless, it is unnecessary for *Christus nudus* to be restricted to such a punitive interpretation due to the fact that *Christus nudus* does not simply become a man to die;[128] rather through the *correcting* face of his death sinners are brought to a *perfecting* face—being clothed with righteousness. Therefore, nakedness and clothing are connected to the notion of satisfaction, not through the "cost" in punishment but the "cost" in Christ's self-emptying. In this way, satisfaction is safeguarded within the bigger picture of the transforming power of the robe of righteousness.[129]

---

122. Bernard of Clairvaux, *On the Song of Songs IV*, sermon 71; Fiddes, *Past Event and Present Salvation*, 143.

123. In this way, hospitality is more preeminent than violence (Boersma, *Violence*, 49).

124. Jeffery et al., *Pierced*, 243.

125. This makes perfect sense in light of the concept of *theosis*—participation and union with God—discussed in chapter 7 in the language of clothing.

126. Cp. Barth, *CD*, IV.1, 553; cf. Owen, *Death*, 269–70.

127. Vanhoozer claims that other models may not exclude penal substitution without committing a totalizing violence on its proponents (Vanhoozer, "The Atonement in Postmodernity," 370–71).

128. Green, "Must We Imagine the Atonement in Penal Substitutionary Terms?," 156; McKnight, *Jesus*, 336: Jesus was aware that he was not merely on a mission to die; Heim, *Sacrifice*, 301; Weston, "Proclaiming," 153.

129. This coincides with the early church fathers' emphasis on *kenosis*.

In sum, the *Christus nudus* model offers an alternative notion of "satisfaction" that is conventional and conditional and is founded upon the need for restoration. God's satisfaction is not simply the clothing of naked sinners; rather, his satisfaction is found in the reconciliation between him and sinners through Christ. Hence, the *Christus nudus* model does not merely focus on how much sin offends God but more importantly on how the damage caused by sin can be reverted so that the human-God relation can be restored. In the *Christus nudus* model the exchange from nakedness to clothing, which refers directly to a relational restoration and reconciliation, is equally important as the Father's satisfaction. According to this perspective, as humanity is restored by the robe of righteousness, Christ's nakedness achieved God's ultimate satisfaction—the reconciliation of the human-God relationship.[130]

Christus Nudus and Moral Influence

Abelard rejected the notion that the devil has any power over God because God is sovereign and is free to remit sins.[131] The purpose of sending the Son, however, was to show God's love and through this to inspire sinners to respond to him in love.[132] Moreover, for Abelard, the death of Christ brings about redemption by setting us free and winning for us the liberty of becoming God's children,[133] so he rejects the notion of justice by the blood of an innocent person.[134] In response to Abelard's view, Bernard of Clairvaux argues that righteousness and love cannot be merely taught or revealed; rather bestowed and infused.[135] In fact, many interpreters would endorse Franks' summary that Abelard had reduced the whole process of redemption to one single principle, namely the manifestation of God's love, which awakens an answering love in us.[136] However, McGrath suggests it would be a misinterpretation to claim that Abelard reduced the significance of Christ's death wholly to an example.[137] Fiddes

---

130. Forsyth, *Work*, 202: regeneration is the condition of God's satisfaction.

131. Abelard, *Romans*, 281; Schmiechen, *Saving*, 292.

132. Ibid., 283.

133. Ibid., 284.

134. Ibid., 283.

135. Bernard of Clairvaux, *Letters*, 190, quoted in Fiddes, *Salvation*, 144.

136. Out of this principle Abelard endeavored to explain all other points of view (Franks, *The Work of Christ*, 146); Thiselton, *Hermeneutics*, 367.

137. McGrath, *Christian Theology*, 355; Asselt, "Multi-Dimensional," 62: Abelard

also points out that for Abelard, the demonstration of God's love is at the same time restorative and so an objective act.[138] In that sense, for Abelard, the salvation of sinners is an act of divine love, which woos us to love rather than fear him.[139]

Nonetheless, by misunderstanding Anselm in thinking that he downplayed the love of God[140] the Abelardian School failed to comprehend that punishment does not have to be vengeful; but it can also be discipline in love. This creates a situation where moral influence is incapable of answering why Jesus must die for God to show his love. In fact, to an extent, not only does such a view of God's love ignore the cost of atonement,[141] it also infers a sentimentalization of love.[142] Moreover, moral influence lacks a definition of what the example involves and what it is to be imitated; it also presupposes that humans have the capability to imitate such divine love,[143] which is a liberal pitfall.[144]

In response, the *Christus nudus* model correlates with moral influence at the "inspiration" of love, but differs at two points: imitation and participation. The *Christus nudus* model proposes that the love of God exhibited at the cross inspires sinners not only to love him in return but also to partake in Christ's death and resurrection and therefore to be in union with him.[145] In this sense, imitation and participation go hand in hand. The *Christus nudus* model refers to a mimetic atonement, yet one that is followed by a transformation from "the garments of the old Adam" to "the habits of the new man"—Jesus Christ.[146] Furthermore, the sote-

---

also speaks about sacrifice as a persuasive proof of God's love that inspires us to return that love, by which our sins are forgiven.

138. Fiddes, *Salvation*, 144.

139. Abelard, *Romans*, 284.

140. Schmiechen, *Saving*, 293–95.

141. At least, it is not clear how Christ's unsightly offering on the cross is able to evoke a reciprocation of love on our part (Asselt, "Multi-Dimensional," 62).

142. MacKinnon, "Subjective and Objective Conceptions of Atonement," 171–72.

143. Asselt, "Multi-dimensional," 62.

144. Personal experience is so emphasized that atonement appears to have no effect outside the believer. Rashdall remarks that the chief meaning of atonement is to be found in its effects in us (Rashdall, *Atonement*, 81–83, 88–89, 436–37); Terry, *Justifying*, 22–23.

145. Chapters 5 and 7 have established the union between believers and Christ in the practice of nude baptism—an act of imitating Christ's self-emptying love (Mazza, *Mystagogy*, 157; Hooker, *Ashamed*, 137).

146. Francis of Sales, *Treatise*, 408.

riological transformation expressed in baptism allows the *Christus nudus* model to connect moral influence and satisfaction models together using the notion of the "clothing of righteousness."[147]

It is important to observe that according to first century thinking, Jesus' calling to take up the cross was a suicidal call.[148] "Naked to follow the naked Christ,"[149] therefore, was scandalous talk, for it implied that those who wished to follow Christ should take up the cross and march naked to the crucifixion site with Christ. Accordingly, the good news could have been about how to escape such punishment, rather than a summons to embrace it.[150] As a result, Christ's exemplar becomes much more "challenging" rather than "inspiring," but this is the point Abelard tried to achieve: God's love inspires us to do anything for him.[151] Yet the inspiring love in moral influence could have offered much more. The *Christus nudus* model proposes that atonement must free Christians to respond, not only to God with love, but also to multiply Christ's love to others.[152] Unlike Moltmann's dismissal of the moral imitation and overstatement of the eschatological imitation of Jesus,[153] the *Christus nudus* model proposes that Christians who are saved must have both Godward and humanward love. Hence, not only do Christians follow Christ in his death and resurrection, they also follow his humility and self-emptying

---

147. Ambrose, *Works*, 17: *The Mysteries*, chapter 7: 34: in baptism, the white garment of Christ symbolizes that sinners are washed and made whiter than snow; Ambrose, in Ramsey, *Ambrose*, 153: on the Mysteries 7.34: The white garment represents a person whose sin is forgiven; Jerome, *NPNF2-6*, The Life of Paulus the First Hermit: 302–3.

148. Robbins, "Contemporary," 338. Crucifixion is an ideal expression of the anomalously frightful, violent and abrupt end of mortal life (Geyer, *Fear, Anomaly and Uncertainty in the Gospel of Mark*, 10).

149. Ambrose, *Expositio euangelii secundum Lucam*, PL 15:1830, cited by Fleming, "*The Dream of the Rood* and Anglo-Saxon Monasticism," 53.

150. Hooker, *Ashamed*, 9.

151. Abelard, *Romans*, 283.

152. Luther's Christ for the neighbor (Mannermaa, "Theosis," 48; Luther, *LW*, Vol. 31, 300, 371).

153. Moltmann, *Crucified*, 55; Koester points out that a different concept of the imitation of Christ had been more influential in the formation of the early Christian communities, namely the concept of the imitation of Jesus' humanity rather than of his divinity (Koester, "Divine," 246).

love,[154] in a lifestyle of renunciation and hospitality.[155] In fact, certain patristic thoughts even went as far as to assert that sins are purged through such hospitality.[156] As a result, moral influence can be expressed through a philanthropic development of *Christus nudus*.

Another important point *Christus nudus* argues for, in response to moral influence, is that Christians cannot imitate Christ's love unless they remain in Christ. Harrison's Orthodox interpretation of *theosis* in the fall narrative helpfully offers a similar point: the Serpent distorts and misdirects human desire toward a false sense of *theosis*—a notion of deification apart from God, and thus disconnects human beings from the genuine source of life, God himself.[157] As a result, by disobedience, humanity disconnects from God, and through that disconnection, humanity is incapable of becoming like him.[158] It follows that without Christ's crucial role and his divine help, sinners are incapable of following Christ's example. In the *Christus nudus* model, the connection between the imitation of Christ and union with Christ is vital:[159] one cannot become like Christ without being united with him.[160]

Lastly, a problem: even if moral influence inspires love from humanity to God, it cannot resolve the sin that humanity committed against God: while it might change a life, it does not rid that person's sin.[161] *Christus nudus* proposes that through participation in Christ's death and resurrection, a connection can be established between the exemplar of love and the exemplar of repentance: repentance and forgiveness bring about reconciliation.[162] In this way, the *Christus nudus* model redefines moral

---

154. Imitation of Christ: as with Christ Jesus in 2:9–11, Christians' faithfulness amid hardship and their humble obedience will one day be transformed into glorification (Hooker, "Philippians 2:6–11," 155–57).

155. Cyprian, *Lapsis*, 51–53, 99; MacLaren, *Expositions*.

156. Cyprian, *ANCL*13-2, 2: The treatise VIII—On work and alms; Cyprian, *Lapsis*, 51–53: "apply yourself to good deeds which can wash away your sins, be constant and generous in giving alms, whereby souls are freed from death"; Augustine, *NPNF*1-6, 408.

157. Harrison, "Theosis," 432–33.

158. Robbins, "Contemporary," 333.

159. Yates, "From Christology to Soteriology," 269–70; Allchin, "Kenosis," 366–67.

160. John of the Cross, *Ascent* II.5-7, in *Works*, Vol. 1, 74–88; Hart, "Morning," 341–42.

161. McKnight, *Community*, 114; Schmiechen, *Saving*, 296: the moral exemplar model ignores the importance of sin, death and evil.

162. Campbell, *The Nature of the Atonement*, 136–37; Brümmer, *Atonement*, 78.

exemplary language as identification with Christ's vicarious repentance. Christ identifies with humanity so that we might take up the cross and follow him, to die with him, to be raised with him and to share in his glory. Surely if the centrality of exemplary atonement is Christ calling us to take up our cross and follow him,[163] then the motto "naked to follow the Naked Christ" should receive more attention. In this way, the imitation of Christ is merged into participation and union with him:[164] "It is no longer I who live but Christ who lives in me" (Gal 2:20).

Weaknesses and Contribution of the Christus Nudus Model: A Conclusion

We now reach some concluding remarks regarding the theological formulation of the *Christus nudus* model as well as its communicative contribution. In a kaleidoscopic fashion, this chapter has highlighted the compatibility between the *Christus nudus* model and three classical models: *Christus Victor*, satisfaction, and moral example. The three spectrums of victory, satisfaction, and imitation in the *Christus nudus* model are held together with a common goal for "reconciliation" and "restoration" of the human-God relationship.[165] With this kaleidoscopic arrangement, the concepts of repentance and forgiveness and the solution for sin alternately play their roles, albeit under different depictions.

Methodologically, *Christus nudus* is constructed in a way that allows the concepts of the three classical models to interpret and refine the soteriological content of its own. This is not to say that any contribution from any atonement model will fit the *Christus nudus* model. Therefore, the intention of testing the compatibility between the contributions offered by the three classical models and the *Christus nudus* model is to assess the distinctiveness and contribution of *Christus nudus* among the diversity of atonement models.

---

163. Mark 8:34–35.

164. Wesche, "Spirituality," 30.

165. Marshall, *Aspects*, 98–137. Spence also rightly points out that the concept of reconciliation implies a prior relational estrangement and hostility or personal conflict or antagonism between the two parties (Spence, "A Unified Theory of the Atonement," 417).

Three Major Weaknesses of the Christus Nudus Model

Although we have demonstrated that the *Christus nudus* model is compatibile with three classical models of atonement, such achievement is not without some difficulties or problems.

First, it has been stated in chapter 6 that the symbol of *Christus nudus* has not been recorded in the biblical texts for cultural reasons, but also, the cosmological notion of *Christus nudus* is not recorded in the Bible and might appear to lack a fundamental biblical support.[166] It follows that the *Christus nudus* model is best articulated in conjunction with patristic writings. As a result, this symbol depends on the theological content of the classical interpretations than on textual witness. However this reliance on theological content is the most appropriate methodological approach to interpret the symbol of *Christus nudus*. This is an apparent methodological issue due to the fact that the *Christus nudus* model is designed within a kaleidoscopic fashion and originates from the question of how to make sense of the atonement, brought about by a naked body on a crucifix, to a body-obsessed culture.

Secondly, although the *Christus nudus* model employs a historical symbol, its interaction with the historical Jesus is only marginal while its structure depends heavily on semantic and semiotic interpretation. It follows that metaphors of nakedness and clothing are employed to target several abstract concepts. As a result, the soteriological content of this model might be accused of stretching words into different ideas to justify its semantic symbolism.[167] For example, there is obscurity in the identity of what is being clothed: sin, death, or God's wrath. However, this is not an internal contradiction, but a result of the fluid nature of metaphors. In order for the *Christus nudus* model to work, metaphors of nakedness and clothing must be abstract and flexible enough for the theological content to be read in the light of other traditional models. As a result, each time *Christus nudus* moves under the scope of a different model, new vehicles arrive to accommodate new targets. Nonetheless, this does not imply that *Christus nudus* can be interpreted with *any* model; rather, only models with which it is compatible.

166. Hooker (tradition, reason and biblical witness) compared with Rashdall (*Atonement*, 48), in Terry, *Justifying*, 51.

167. Schmiechen, *Saving*, 328–29: Lack of precision in the use of the basic images or key words leads to great misunderstanding; but it is difficult to achieve precision in the use of basic images, language and logic, due to the tendency to mix theories together and use key words in different ways.

Thirdly, the *Christus nudus* model employs anachronistic and interdisciplinary concepts. In particular, patristic interpretations of *Christus nudus* have rarely been mentioned elsewhere. In addition, the philosophical link between *Christus nudus* and Luther's *Deus nudus* might sound foreign and unnecessary. Moreover, although concepts of *kenosis* and *theosis* have been mentioned in recent scholarship,[168] Western readers might find it difficult to accept or negotiate. As a result, the *Christus nudus* model might not be as "culturally-friendly" as it is intended to be. However, these anachronistic and inter-disciplinary concepts illuminate self-emptying and participation and were chosen as a platform for the *correcting* and *perfecting* faces of the cross. Without them, the *Christus nudus* model is merely a creative interpretation of an atrocious punishment in first-century Palestine. All in all, by employing these anachronistic and cross-tradition concepts we have raised an awareness of the unnecessary omission of traditions.

Systematic Contribution of Christus Nudus

The *Christus nudus* model is the first attempt to hold together three aspects of atonement using the metaphors of nakedness and clothing. The first systematic contribution of the *Christus nudus* model, therefore, is a symbol that holds together victory, satisfaction, and imitation within the combination of incarnation and soteriology. Concepts such as recapitulation and identification need the symbol of *Christus nudus*, through which the model at the same time relates to various concepts (representation of humanity, self-emptying, revelation of God, and the horrible punishment of the cross) to simultaneously depict the atonement picture. This multi-dimensional symbol is important for soteriology because it can be a nexus for multiple theories, which in turn emphasizes the importance of a kaleidoscopic view of the cross.

Secondly, the *Christus nudus* model acts as an overarching axis, upon which the idea of atonement rotates from one model to the other. This requires it to be compatible and negotiable both in content and semiotics. Methodologically, the *Christus nudus* model has adopted a kaleidoscopic way of being; yet at the same time appreciates the contribution of existing models in its symbolism.

---

168. Sanders, *Paul and Palestinian Judaism*, 548–52; Barton, *The Biblical World*, Vol. 2, 264.

Admittedly, it would be foolhardy to overstate the contribution of *Christus nudus*. While the historical perspective of *Christus nudus* encourages subsequent theological and liturgical implications, it has a limitation in terms of biblical depth. The richness of the sacrificial metaphor is replaced by *kenosis* and self-emptying. The victory motif remains only as an echo of the Eden narrative. The satisfaction model only retains "justification in participation" through the metaphor "clothing of righteousness." Yet, the reduction and incompleteness in the *Christus nudus* model is evidence of the fact that no single model is adequate to explain the inexplicable. Therefore, the contribution of the *Christus nudus* model only makes sense in the light of other models.

Conclusion

If the reconciliation of the creation-Creator relationship is the core of at-one-ment, then the restoration of human-God relationship should be addressed as the focal point. In this way, soteriology holds together a network of concepts (revelation, repentance, forgiveness, restoration, reconciliation, regeneration, justification, union, healing, example, and victory). Models that seek to explain the "how" of the cross cannot escape this network of concepts. Every model must make relevant Jesus' life, death, and resurrection to the human-God relationship, to the new anthropology and creation: mediation is Christ's office and restoration is Christ's achievement. In its construction, the *Christus nudus* employs a kaleidoscopic fashion to present the cross in a rather collective interpretation, resonating the soteriological correlation and contribution of the three classical models and securing a faithful theological content (to that of the biblical witness). Despite its weaknesses, the *Christus nudus* model makes a significant contribution as a collective symbol.

In the Christian life, however, atonement is more than theoretical logic: forgiveness, freedom, victory, and participation in divine economy are personal experiences. These experiences can be beneficially heightened when reflected in new ways, new symbols, and new languages. Moreover, in order to maintain the freshness and excitement of the atonement narrative, especially in a way that encourages a body-obsessed culture to engage with the message of the cross, the *Christus nudus* model proposes that an innovative impact on the interpretation of a naked cross in general is need. This is what the *Christus nudus* model hopes to achieve. Therefore, the next chapter will draw our attention to the impact that the

Christus nudus model has on a body-obsessed culture that is plagued by shame and guilt.

9

The Effect of the *Christus Nudus* Model
A Conclusion

It has been said that theological discourse must take seriously the social and cultural presuppositions that determine whether it merits a hearing.[1] This approach has received much attention recently, especially with regard to theological engagement with postmodern thinking.[2] As previously mentioned in the introduction, with the rise of secularization and privatization, the Christian faith can become less real, and reduced to a mere matter of personal preference, or just one of many competing worldviews.[3] While it is important to understand a postmodern culture's rejection of a concept of absolute truth,[4] it is equally dangerous to omit

---

1. Green and Baker, *Recovering*, 217; Newbigin, *The Gospel in a Pluralist Society*, 141–42; Newbigin, *Foolishness to the Greeks*, 21–64; Grenz and Franke, *Beyond Foundationalism*, 150–66.

2. Wright, "Future Trends in Mission," 161; White, "Evangelism in a Postmodern World," 366. For related works on communicating the Gospel to a postmodern culture, see Ward, *The Blackwell Companion to Postmodern Theology*; Connor, *Postmodernist*. For more on the context of postmodernism and evangelical theology, see Bartholomew et al., *The Futures of Evangelicalism*; On the implications for biblical theology and hermeneutics, see Bartholomew et al., *After Pentecost*; Allen, *Christian Belief in a Postmodern World*; Dockery, *The Challenge of Postmodernism*; McCallum, *The Death of Truth*.

3. White, "Evangelism," 360–62; Newbigin, *Pluralist*, 15; Walker, "Sectarian Reactions: Pluralism and the Privatization of Religion," 46–64; Aldridge, *Religion in the Contemporary World*, 190–222; Beckford, *Social Theory & Religion*, 30–102; Berger, *A Far Glory*, chapters 1–3.

4. Gunton calls such a rejection "the rootless will" (*The One, the Three, and the Many*, 101–2).

the church's mandate to preach the truth of the gospel.[5] After all, the mission of the church is to seek and to save the lost.[6] Grenz, therefore, is correct in his protest against the postmodern rejection of the metanarrative,[7] and his argument for a new ethos through which the church articulates and embodies the gospel in the context of culture.[8] Moreover, one might consider White's suggestion: rather than telling people what to believe, they should be led to discover the truth for themselves through practical assistance.[9] However, how does an atonement model such as *Christus nudus* provide such a practical assistance in order to communicate the message of the cross to a postmodern culture? Will it again be dismissed by postmodernism,[10] or will its effect prove that the message behind the symbol of a naked cross still has more to offer?

In the course of its construction and testing, the *Christus nudus* model has denoted a historical, anthropological, and cultural compatibility that arrests the attention of its audience. As previously mentioned in the introduction of this book, the domestication of the cross has resulted in the loss of the tension of its scandal. For a body-obsessed culture, within its current media entertainment, the naked body of Christ has become more commonly viewed as an icon that portrays a cruel and sadistic execution.[11] Some contemporary depictions of the cross in movies and the arts appear scandalous and even offensive to their audience, but these expressions are blurred with artistic expressions,[12]

---

5. Litfin, in Crouch, "Emergent Evangelicalism," 43.

6. Bosch, *Transforming Mission*, 10; White, "Evangelism," 370; McKnight, *Community*, 134: "Missional work is *atoning*."

7. Grenz, *Postmodernism*, 165.

8. Ibid., 167–69; Newbigin, *Pluralist*, 141–42; Newbigin, *Foolishness*, 21–64.

9. White, "Evangelism," 369–70: Rather than declaring something to be truth because it works, we would maintain that it works because it is true; Banks, *Redeeming the Routines*.

10. McLaren, in Crouch, "Emergent," 42–43. For McLaren, Christianity backfires when it uses arguments that pit absolutism against relativism, as they "prove meaningless or absurd to postmodern people . . ." (ibid., 43); Weston, "Proclaiming," 145.

11. Incidentally and ironically, such an attitude expressed by Roman soldiers towards crucifixion has been mentioned earlier in chapter 6.

12. In a body-obsessed culture, where the body is the center of the entertainment industry, the body of Christ is commercialized. For example, the chocolate naked Christ statue "My sweet Lord" in Manhattan (Cones, "Sweet," 50); Mel Gibson's sanguinary film *The Passion of Christ*, and a fictional portrayal in the film *The Last Temptation of Christ*, and Dan Brown's *The Da Vinci Code*, etc., where Christ's life-story is given fictional details. Segal, "The Da Vinci Code and The Passion of the Christ—What

rather than attempts at pursuing historical correctness. Consequently, these depictions result in the domestication and misinterpretation of the naked body of Christ.[13] Therefore, the *Christus nudus* model seeks to distinguish its notion of the naked Christ from the religious-based-yet-artistically-modified trend that postmodern artists and filmsmakers have fabricated, which makes Christ's body meaningless to a body-obsessed notion of salvation, shame, or guilt.[14]

Consequently, by employing the language of nakedness and clothing along with the image of a naked Christ, the *Christus nudus* model offers its distinctive effect to a soteriological dialogue with a postmodern body-obsessed culture, which can be systematized into three particular aspects: anthropology, soteriology, and methodology. (1) An anthropological effect of the *Christus nudus* model readdresses shame, guilt, and an obscure notion of atonement, (2) a soteriological effect endeavors to maintain the *modus operandus* of the cross and the *telos* of a humanity that is "in Christ"; and (3) a methodological effect reconsolidates the integrity of the dialogue between biblical witness, theology and a body-obsessed culture.

Anthropological Effect: Shame, Guilt, and Sin in a Body-Obsessed Culture

In a body-obsessed culture, the problem of chronic shame is not simple. A therapeutic approach that perceives shame as a result of a broken concept of self diagnoses a much more complicated form of separation—an innate alienation and division.[15] This shame can be more pervasive and

---

They Tell Us about American Religion Today," 213; Paul Fryer's Gorilla-crucifix at an art installation in Marylebone, London (Jury, "Artist Apes the Crucifixion to Save Threatened Gorillas").

13. E.g. feminist theologian Williams, quoted in Cyer, "Fallout Escalates Over 'Goddess' Sophia Worship," 74.

14. With a deep awareness of Weston's warning of being too quick to look for the *contemporary* connections and forgetting that *biblical* connections are more important (Weston, "Proclaiming," 150, 160), there is still a need to recognize connections creatively, in order to arrest the attention of a postmodern pluralistic mentality before diverting the conversation into a biblical dialogue of atonement. In this way, the social environment is taken seriously but the forms of communication would be shaped within but not wholly determined by that environment (Green and Baker, *Recovering*, 214).

15. While Kohut's bipolar self (grandiose and idealized) can be applied here (Kohut, *Analysis*, 1971, 24–34; Morrison, "The Eye Turned Inward: Shame and the Self,"

more destructive because it does not have an audience.[16] Therefore, from a relational perspective, the characteristic of self-focused shame reflects an ontological dysfunction: the self downplays its relationality in its self-centeredness. Compared with the previously discussed cognitive "conceal-reveal" model, which opens a scope through which both external guilt and shame can be understood in relational terms as a "gaze,"[17] there is a shift of the "gazer" and the object. When shame diverts inwardly, the model for alienation that nakedness and clothing provides only works if the self is its own audience. In this sense, the self seeks inner wholeness—a complication that requires reconciliation within oneself.[18]

In chapter one, a body-obsessed culture, which has a bipolar shame-narcissism mechanism,[19] traps the self in an obsession for body-appearance[20] and mistakes instant bodily change as "salvation"; in fact, it has deceptively and exploitively convinced society that clothes indeed make people. Therapeutic approaches to this notion of shame include diets, makeovers and fashion,[21] plastic surgery and the cosmetics industry, all of which attempt to offer "changes" in order to find reconciliation and recovery from this notion of shame.[22] However, these image-dominant attempts only heighten and subsequently maximize shame-sensitivity

---

271–91), Watts suggests that shame arising from falling short of our ideals is more likely to be constructive (Watts, "Shame," 65). However, in this particular "brokenness of self" it is probably correct that shame, as a result of falling short of our ideals, can also be destructive, depending on the components and construction of these ideals (Mann, "Sinless," 38–39; Capps, *The Depleted Self*, 72).

16. Mann, *Sinless*, 21, 31–34; Pattison, *Shame*, 42.

17. Pattison, *Shame*, 193–95: some feel that the gaze of God deepens their shame; Frank, "Naked," 128–30; Watts et al., *Psychology for Christian Ministry*, 12: It is particularly appropriate for people to feel shame before God, but we are not shamed by him. When feeling ashamed, we sense that people can see through us and there is no defense against their critical gaze. God sees through us, but his gaze is benevolent and his critical gaze has a different effect (Watts, "Shame," 64).

18. This concept of shame after guilt can adopt the framework used to analyze "moral taint" in Oshana, "Taint," 363–64.

19. Willard mentions this bipolarity (*Renovation of the Heart*, 135).

20. Chapter 1 has raised the complexity and ambiguity of post-modern concepts of beauty: subjective concepts of beauty are driven by conventional cultural concepts. To an extent the body has become a *courtroom* for the verdict of acceptance or rejection (Lasch, *Narcissism*, 1978). Watts is not convinced that shame is as ubiquitous as Lasch claims (Watts, "Shame," 59).

21. Wan, *Naked*, 2007; Wan and Porter, "Naked?"

22. Elshtain, "The Body and Projects of Self-Possession," 150.

rather than resolve it; so much so, that clothes become an impediment rather than an ally, a hindrance rather than a complement of beauty.[23] As a result, a body-obsessed culture understands deeply the metaphorical significance of clothing: it is almost ontological, if not totally, a works-righteousness notion of atonement.

Accordingly, a body-obsessed culture and its distorted concept of atonement (one that is *creatable, purchasable* and autonomous) implies the inadmissibility for a savior's victory or liberation,[24] substitution or justification, sacrifice or example because the self can achieve salvation and atonement all by itself through the body.[25] Its dilemma, however, is twofold: on the one hand, a constant search for what happens beyond death, and, on the other, an attempt to rescue and renew the current body.[26] Yet the more serious underlying problem is the lack of a *telos* for the human body.

So far, recent scholarship has highlighted the need for atonement models to deal with shame rather than guilt;[27] therefore, a distinction between shame and guilt is considered to be important.[28] It is also correct to point out that the absence of an "other"[29] causes the concept of sin to be replaced by the concept of guilt,[30] consequently, sin is treated lightly.[31] Therefore, placing shame, guilt, and sin under the scope of relational dysfunction,[32] and offering a wider relational perspective on this

---

23. Cumming, "The Body in Clothing of Delight," 217.

24. A nudist perspective of reconciliation, for example, claims that nakedness reconciles the body to the wider cosmos as it brings liberation, gives joy to the living, and de-eroticizes the body (Ross, *Germany*, 136–43).

25. This includes genome mutation, due to a possible genetic dictate on personal traits and, therefore, relationship.

26. Elshtain, "Self-possession," 149–50.

27. Mann, *Sinless*, 33; Capps, *Depleted*: we need a theology of sin that addresses itself to a culture of shame rather than of guilt. Albers, *Shame*: a theology of the cross as "God's shame-bearing symbol"; Watts, "Shame," 54–55; Green and Baker, *Recovering*, 153–70.

28. Watt, "Shame," 55; Watts et al., *Psychology*, 12; Pattison, *Shame*, 73.

29. Mann, *Sinless*, 20–23.

30. Green suggests it is not totally true to say that there is no sense of sin. There is a disguised sense of sin, which is not taken to the clergyman, but to the doctor or psychiatrist (Green, *The Meaning of Salvation*, 237); Capps, *Depleted*, 4–5.

31. Tidball, "Pastoral," 346–47.

32. As discussed in chapters 3 and 5; Watts, "Shame," 66; Scheff, *Microsociology*, 15, 18: Shame signals a state of alienation in social relationships.

treatment,[33] is essential. However, in order for atonement to confront a body-obsessed culture with a vertical reconciliation,[34] and a hope in an anthropology that is rooted in union with Christ,[35] it is imperative to take into account the false hope of an alternative atonement through body-modification and show how dangerous it is. An earnable notion of atonement, which starts with body-modification, implies that atonement or salvation is unlimited; forgiveness is autonomous. Worse still, is the implication that self-forgiveness can be equated to atonement. Yet, this sense of atonement depends on the body perpetually keeping up with the demands of consumerism. As a result, consumerism has virtually become a judge determining those who can "afford" the clothing of salvation to be the "elect" and others to be "damned." Such a notion is not an alternative human ontology but dehumanization.[36]

What is needed, therefore, is to maintain the tension of the cross: salvation does not come from a pursuit of body-perfection, but from a tattered, mangled, and naked body. Only with this tension in view can a model of atonement point to a humanity that reflects God-likeness,[37] rather than allowing its identity to be restricted in the definition and confinement of bodily conditions.[38] As a result, the *Christus nudus* model is anthropologically effective: on the one hand, it critiques the body-obsessed pursuit of another human ontology for perpetuating shame and guilt;[39] and on the other, it makes sense of the hope for a *telos* of humanity according to God's initial intention.

33. Grenz, *Postmodernism*, 172: postmodern Christian holism must put the human person back into the social and environmental context; McKnight, *Community*, 117–18.

34. Boersma, *Violence*, 209; Brümmer, *Atonement*, 52; Green and Baker, *Recovering*, 213–14.

35. See identification and incorporation in Christ through baptism (McKnight, *Community*, 150–55).

36. See Sorokin's glorification-degradation dualism (*The Crisis of Our Age*, 198–99).

37. Cyril of Jerusalem, quoted by Harakas, *Health and Medicine in the Eastern Orthodox Tradition*, 33–34; Bakken, "Theosis," 416.

38. Harrison, "Theosis," 434.

39. In the future development of a body-obsessed culture another model of atonement will be needed if genetic mutation becomes applicable to the body, intelligence, personality and relationship becomes commercialized and commodified. For now, if modification of the external look of the body is believed to be capable of providing any sense of "salvation" then it is predictable that with the same body-obsession and the quest for another ontology, humanity is not far from believing that it can be free from any need for atonement. New Age movements and fantasies of incredible supernatural

Soteriological Effect: The Modus Operandus of a Christus Nudus

In chapters 7 and 8, the *correcting* and *perfecting* faces of the cross are closely connected to the incarnation. As a result, atonement maintains a tension: *Christus nudus* is a cosmological notion that refers to the self-emptying of God; yet at the same time, in that naked body of Christ dwells the fullness of God (Col 1:15–20). Consequently, the cross of a naked Christ rightly emphasizes God's *modus operandi* of salvation: victory is gained through a shameful and mangled body;[40] and the hope for a *telos* of the restored humanity comes from Christ's renunciation, even to the point of distortion and disfigurement, evidences that God is wildly and scandalously *for* us.[41]

As this tension is maintained, there is a subsequent subversion in the link between shame and the psychological: salvation is not about being rescued from shame, but suffering in shame. Through participation in Christ, the redeemed also renounce and suffer in shame in order to be clothed with acceptance in God.[42] Atonement, therefore, comes from renunciation, not consumption, as proven in the death and resurrection of Christ—the firstborn from among the dead (Col 1:15–18). On this account, the "perfection" of human ontology depends on its relationship with God.[43] Since Christ is the Head of the church, the restored humanity found in him is one that does not pursue the perfect body, but renounces it as he did,[44] and in doing so put on his resurrection body[45]—the *eschaton* of the promise of a wholesome and glorious humanity in God.[46]

---

abilities through genetic mutation (see TV series such as *Heroes*, *X-Men*, etc.) are expressions of a thirst for another human ontology that no longer needs to be atoned.

40. Gunton, *Actuality*, 119.

41. Frank, "Naked," 133.

42. More precisely, we participate in the Son's act of eternal response to the Father (Grenz, *Social*, 326–27).

43. Barth, *CD*, IV.4, 28: Christian *theosis*—through practical fellowship with God and conformation of action with the divine nature.

44. Rev 16:5 (see chapter 5 of this book); Webber, *Ancient-Future*, 144, 150: to be baptized into Christ is to identity with him in his suffering, to enter death and be raised in new life; this is to participate in Christ's victory over evil, not only individually but also corporately.

45. Green, *Body*, 21–23, 38–46, 170–77.

46. See chapter 7; Shelton, *Covenant*, 225.

In a body-obsessed culture, it is the paradoxical nature of the *modus operandi* of atonement that marks the distinctiveness of the life and activities of the church.[47] With regard to a postmodern culture, where the body is idolized and woven into the commercial values of consumerism,[48] the *Christus nudus* model has proposed an ecclesiological reshaping that challenges its lifestyle and philosophy. In response to the current popular view of church as organized religion,[49] which downplays Christ-centeredness by the accentuation of individualistic and community comfort, the tension of the *modus operandi* of an atonement model is the distinctiveness that marks the church's rootedness in Christ and his robe of righteousness.

This *modus operandi* of atonement also makes sense of the cost of discipleship—a life of obedience to God by faith.[50] Nude baptism as a re-enactment of this public renunciation,[51]—a lifestyle of repentance and participation in Christ's suffering and anticipating the glory of his resurrection—reflects the transformation inspired by the example of Christ's life.[52] To the people of his age, Jesus' calling to take up one's cross and follow him was nothing less than a statement of a suicidal lunatic.[53] Yet, to be naked and follow Christ on that humiliating march[54] is to embrace life and anticipate the robe of righteousness in Christ.

---

47. Green and Baker, *Recovering*, 210–11.

48. Jennings, "The Desire of the Church," 248; Wolf, *The Beauty Myth*, 144.

49. Worricker, "You and Yours."

50. Shelton, *Covenant*, 223–24; Webber, *Ancient-Future*, 145–49: the cost of discipleship—God's absolute claim over our entire life, our obedience and belonging to an alternative culture shaped by the kingdom; obedience to Christ versus obedience to the Christian culture: giving up bad habits is one thing, taking up new habits such as reading the Word, praying, witnessing, attending church, tithing, etc. is another. Bonhoeffer, *The Cost of Discipleship*, 77–79.

51. See also chapters 5 and 7; Guy, "'Naked' Baptism in the Early Church," 133–42; Chrysostom (in Riley, *Initiation*, 423; Lampe, *Patristic*, 1261–62) says: "We put off the old garment which has been made filthy with the abundance of our sins; we put on the new one which is free from every stain." Webber, *Ancient-Future*, 144: baptism is not a once-off event but an initiation of a lifelong pursuit of holiness taking place in the accountability of God's community on earth—the church.

52. McDonald notes that what we have in Christ is not a pleasing impression but the reality of a changed life, not a personal feeling that might pass but a fact of moral newness that is eternal (McDonald, *The Atonement of the Death of Christ*, 46–47); Sherman, "Toward a Trinitarian Theology of the Atonement," 373.

53. Robbins, "Contemporary," 338.

54. See chapter 6 of this book.

This is a reflection of the paradoxical nature of atonement in traditional liturgy that has been lost.

Consequently, while it is important that recent scholarship has given high opinion to the Eucharist as a public face of atonement and hospitality[55] there is an equally great need to recover the paradoxical nature of atonement. The accomplishment of atonement is the human-God reconciliation and the actualization of the hope for a redeemed human ontology,[56] where the problem of chronic shame and guilt is dealt with in light of the promise of peace.[57] However, this accomplishment is the result of a mystery and a deeper tension in the *modus operandus* of salvation that should never be lost.

Methodological Effect: Reconsolidating the Christus Nudus Model

In the construction of the *Christus nudus* model, this book has undertaken investigations into the meaning of nakedness and clothing in an anthropological analysis of a body-obsessed culture, a semantic assessment of biblical symbolism and theological imagery, and explored the historical reality of Roman crucifixion. The relational dimension in metaphors of nakedness and clothing, especially in the wider biblical context of shame and guilt, is a useful utility that facilitates a soteriological model.

A cosmological interpretation of *Christus nudus*, within christological and trinitarian perspectives, allows the cross to be interpreted using the two concepts *kenosis* and *theosis*. On that account, *Christus nudus* is both the *representation* and *substitution* of humanity who addresses both the divine and the human dimensions of atonement. Here, the

---

55. Mann, *Sinless*, 152–55; Boersma, *Violence*, 207–8. McIntyre suggests that the Eucharist was the centrality of soteriology in the early centuries of the Christian era (McIntyre, *Shape*, 20).

56. Hardy, "Created and Redeemed Sociality," 22; Schmiechen, *Saving*, 355: ecclesial patterns understood as the natural and inevitable outgrowth of interpretations of Jesus' life, death and resurrection.

57. McKnight, *Community*, 129; Boersma, *Violence*, 207; Spence, *Promise*, 116–18: Any presentation of the gospel must be faithful to "peace" and "reconciliation" with God. The accomplished fact must be emphasized: Christ died so that we do not have to die the death that our sin deserves. This is God's promise of peace. To "be reconciled" is to "believe." The corporate aspects of salvation are also intensely relevant to a world, which is passionately concerned with *belonging* (Dillistone, *The Christian Faith*); Self, *Struggling with Forgiveness*, 165.

metaphorical linguistic "conceal-reveal" model is especially valuable to an articulation of the mystery of the cross: the fullness of God dwells in the self-emptying *Christus nudus* who offered himself for the human-God reconciliation. This cosmological understanding of *Christus nudus* connects both *kenosis* and *theosis* to the effects of the cross and rightly sets atonement toward an ultimate eschatological *telos*—the union of the redeemed in God.[58]

Although the *Christus nudus* model collaborates with other traditional models in a kaleidoscopic fashion, its distinctiveness is reserved for its anthropological and soteriological implications. The *Christus nudus* model recovers the tension of the scandal of the cross—the *modus operandus* of atonement: glory and a hope for a *telos* are found in a shameful death. As a result, the *Christus nudus* model rightly addresses a body-obsessed notion of self-seeking atonement: salvation indeed comes, not from the body-perfect, but from a tattered, mangled and naked body.

Therefore, the *Christus nudus* model secures two grounds: (1) it recovers the historical evidence that has been buried in the negligence of cultural propriety and postmodern artistic expressions, and (2) challenges the ignorance toward a tattered body, wherein the fullness of God dwells. In this way, the *Christus nudus* model safeguards both the attractiveness of the cross and its theological richness for both the church and the unchurched.[59]

Over the course of the construction of the *Christus nudus* model, metaphors of nakedness and clothing have been employed to challenge the misleading body-obsessed notion of atonement and highlight a serious omission of some important theological implications of a naked cross. Using the symbol of a Naked Christ does not imply that Christianity is a product of experiences or manipulation by stirring feelings.[60] Rather, the cross does not appear to have been explained away rationally and noeticentrically but leaves room for the element of "mystery."[61] Accordingly, the *Christus nudus* model maintains both biblical and theological integrity, placing correct emphasis on the self-emptying love of God in the tension of the cross.

---

58. Russell, "The Doctrine of Deification in the Greek Patristic Tradition," 227–31.

59. Adopted intention from Terry, *Justifying*, 212–13.

60. McDonald, *Atonement*, 53–54. Cf. McLaren, "The Cross as Prophetic Action," 112.

61. Grenz, *Postmodernism*, 169.

The symbol of a Naked Christ is an attractive starting point for an atonement dialogue with a body-obsessed culture[62] and a stepping-stone to an apologetic dialogue of the cross. Having arrested the attention of a body-obsessed culture, the *Christus nudus* model points to a self-emptying God who resolves human sin and shame and restores dysfunctional relations. As a result, a community is created wherein sin, shame and dysfunctional relations are dealt with and whose members share a renewed human ontology that is transformed into Christ's likeness in a union with him. The missing *telos* in the current body-obsessed culture can be found in Christ's resurrection and victory.

Therefore, *Christus nudus* is a historically and theologically rich symbol that can touch base with its audience in their stories and day-to-day living. It does not stop at replacing a body-obsessed notion of alternative humanity; rather, it places perpetual chronic shame within the bigger picture of the human-God reconciliation with the *telos* of being clothed with Christ, in union with God. This is the glory of *Christus nudus*.

---

62. Cf. Webber, *Ancient-Future*, 152.

Bibliography

Aaron, David H. "Shedding Light on God's Body in Rabbinic Midrashim: Reflections on the Theory of a Luminous Adam." *HTR* 90 (1997) 303–9.
Abelard. *Exposition of the Epistle to the Romans*. In *A Scholastic Miscellany: Anselm to Ockham, Library of Christian Classics X*, translated and edited by E. R. Fairweather, 276–87. London: SCM, 1956.
Abi-Hashem, N. "Self-Esteem." In *Baker Encyclopedia of Psychological & Counseling*, edited by David G. Benner and Peter C. Hill, 1085. Grand Rapids: Baker, 1985.
Ableman, Paul. *Anatomy of Nakedness*. London: Orbis, 1982.
Achtemeier, Elizabeth. *Minor Prophets I*. Peabody, MA: Hendrickson, 1996.
Adams, J. Donald. *Naked We Came: A More or Less Lighthearted Look at the Past, Present, and Future of Clothes*. New York: Rinehart and Winston, 1967.
Adamson, Peter, and Richard C. Taylor. *The Cambridge Companion to Arabic Philosophy*. Cambridge: Cambridge University Press, 2005.
Adar, Zvi. *The book of Genesis*. Jerusalem: Magnes, 1990.
Adorno, Theodor W., and Max Horkheimer. *Dialectic of Enlightenment*. Translated by John Cumming. London: Verso, 1979.
Albers, Robert H. *Shame: A Faith Perspective*. New York: Haworth, 1995.
Aldridge, Alan. *Religion in the Contemporary World: A Sociological Introduction*. 2nd ed. Cambridge: Polity, 2007.
Allchin, A. M. "Kenosis." In *The Oxford Companion to Christian Thought*, edited by Adrian Hastings et al., 366–67. Oxford: Oxford University Press, 2000.
Allchin, A. M. *Participation in God: A Forgotten Strand in Anglican Tradition*. London: Darton, Longman & Todd, 1988.
Allen, Boyd. "Christian Naturism." No pages. Online: http://www.geocities.com/boydallen/.
Allen, Diogenes. *Christian Belief in a Postmodern World*. Louisville, KY: Westminster John Knox, 1989.
Ambrose, Saint. *Theological and Dogmatic Works*. Translated by Roy J. Deferrari. Washington, DC: The Catholic University of America Press, 1963.
American Psychiatric Association. *Diagnostic and Statistical Manual of Mental Disorders*. Washington, DC: Author, 2000.
Anastos, T. L. "Gregory Palamas's Radicalization of the Essence, Energies, and Hypostasis Model of God." *GOTR* 38 (1993) 335–49.
Andersen, Francis I. *Job*. Leicester, UK: InterVarsity, 1976.
Anderson, A. A. *2 Samuel*. Dallas: Word, 1989.

———. *The Book of Psalms*. Vol. 2, *Psalms 73–150*. London: Oliphants, 1972.
Anderson, Hugh. *The Gospel of Mark*. London: Oliphants, 1976.
Anderson, James F. *The Bond of Being*. St. Louis, MO: Herder, 1949.
Anderson, Joshua S. "Naked Christs and Balaam's Ass: A Blueprint toward a Renewed Christian Aesthetic." No pages. Online: http://www.rutherford.org/Oldspeak/Articles/Religion/oldspeak-christ2.asp.
Anderson, Ray S. *On Being Human*. Grand Rapids: Eerdmans, 1982.
Andrews, Bernice. "Body Shame and Abuse in Childhood." In *Body Shame*, edited by Paul Gilbert and Jeremy Miles, 256–65. New York: Brunner-Routledge, 2002.
Andro-Medical. No pages. Online: http://www.maxhim.co.uk.
Anselm. *Cur Deus Homo*. In *St. Anselm: Basic Writings*, translated by S. N. Deane. La Salle, IL: Open Court, 1962.
———. *St. Anselm's Proslogion*. Translated and edited by M. J. Charlesworth. Notre Dame, IN: University of Notre Dame Press, 1979.
Aquinas, Thomas. *Summa Theologiae*, and *Summa Contra Gentiles*. Bk. 1. Translated by Anton C. Pegis. London: Notre Dame Press, 1955.
Aristotle. *De Anima* (On the Soul). In *The Complete Words of Aristotle: The Revised Oxford Translation*, Vol. 1, revised by J. A. Smith, edited by Jonathan Barnes. Princeton: Princeton University Press, 1984.
———. *The Nicomachean Ethics*. Translated by David Ross, revised by J. L. Ackrill and J. O. Urmson. Oxford: Oxford University Press, 1988.
———. *Poetics*. 1459a. In *The Complete Works of Aristotle: The Revised Oxford Translation*, Vol. 2, translated by I. Bywater, edited by Jonathan Barnes. Princeton: Princeton University Press, 1984.
Artemidorus. *Oneirocritica*. Translated by Robert J. White. Park Ridge, NJ: Noyes, 1975.
Asselt, W. J. van. "Christ's Atonement: A Multi-Dimensional Approach." *CTJ* 38 (2003) 52–67.
Athanasius. *De incarnatione verbi Dei*. In *Athanasius on the Incarnation of the Word of God*, 2nd ed., translated by T. Herbert Bindley. London: The Religious Tract Society, 1903.
———. *Discourse against the Arians*. In *The Orations of St. Athanasius against the Arians*, 2nd ed., edited by William Bright. Oxford: Clarendon, 1884.
Atkinson, Canon James. "The Significance of Martin Luther." *Churchman* 78.2 (1964). Online: http://www.churchsociety.org/churchman/documents/Cman_078_2_Atkinson.pdf.
Atkinson, David. *The Message of Job*. Leicester, UK: InterVarsity, 1991.
Atkinson, James. "Atonement." In *A Dictionary of Christian Theology*, edited by Alan Richardson, 18–24. London: SCM, 1969.
Attenborough, David. *Life on Earth: A Natural History*. DVD. Executive Producer: Christopher Parsons, Film editors: Ron Martin and Alec Brown. BBC Bristol, UK, 1978.
Augsburger, Myron S. *Matthew*. Nashville, TN: Thomas Nelson, 1982.
Augustine. *The City of God*. Edited by R. V. G. Tasker and Ernest Rhys. London: Dent & Sons, 1945.
Auguet, Roland. *The Roman Games*. Hertforshire, UK: Panther, 1975.
Aulén, Gustaf. *Christus Victor: An Historical Study of the Three Main Types of the Idea of the Atonement*. London: SPCK, 1931.
Aune, David E. *Revelation 6–16*. WBC. Nashville, TN: Thomas Nelson, 1998.

———. *Revelation 17–22*. WBC. Nashville, TN: Thomas Nelson, 1998.
Ayres, Lewis. "Deification and the Dynamics of Nicene Theology: The Contribution of Gregory of Nyssa." *SVTQ* 49 (2005) 375–94.
Baillie, D. M. *God was in Christ*. London: Faber & Faber, 1948.
Baird, Forrest E., and W. Kaufmann. *Philosophic Classics: From Plato to Derrida*. 5th ed. Upper Saddle River, NJ: Pearson Prentice Hall, 2008.
Baker, John. "The Myth of Man's 'Fall'—A Reappraisal." *ExpT* 92 (1981) 235–37.
Bakken, Kenneth L. "Holy Spirit and Theosis: Toward a Lutheran Theology of Healing." *SVTQ* 38 (1994) 409–23.
Balás, David. "Divinization." In *Encyclopedia of Early Christianity*, edited by E. Fugerson, 338–40. New York: Garland, 1997.
Balentine, Samuel E. *Leviticus*. Interpretation. Louisville, KY: John Knox, 2002.
Balsdon, J. P. V. D. *Romans and Aliens*. London: Duckworth, 1979.
Balthasar, Hans Urs von. *The Glory of the Lord: A Theological Aesthetics—II Studies in Theological Styles: Clerical Styles*. 1969. Reprint. Translated by Andrew Louth et al. Edinburgh: T. & T. Clark, 1984.
Balz, H. "γυμνός, γυμνότης." In *Exegetical Dictionary of the New Testament*, Vol. 1, edited by H. Balz and Gerhard Schneider, 265–66. Grand Rapids: Eerdmans, 1990.
Bandstra, A. J. "Adam and the Servant in Philippians 2:5ff." *CTJ* 1 (1966) 214.
Banks, R. *Redeeming the Routines*. Grand Rapids: Baker Academic, 2001.
Baraz, Daniel. *Medieval Cruelty: Changing Perceptions, Late Antiquity to the Early Modern World*. New York: Cornell University Press, 2003.
Barbour, Ian G. *Myths, Models and Paradigms: The Nature of Scientific and Religious Language*. London: SCM, 1974.
Barclay, William. *Matthew*. Vol. 2. Edinburgh: Saint Andrew, 1975.
Barnard, Malcolm. *Fashion as Communication*. London: Routledge, 1996.
Barnett, Paul. *The Second Epistle to the Corinthians*. Grand Rapids: Eerdmans, 1997.
Barney, Sydney D. *Clothes and the Man*. London: Pitman & Sons, 1951.
Barr, James. *The Garden of Eden and The Hope of Immortality*. London: SCM, 1992.
Barrett, K. C. et al. "Avoiders versus amenders: Implications for the Investigation of Shame and Guilt during Toddlerhood?" *Cognition and Emotion* 7 (1993) 481–505.
Barth, Karl. *The Epistle to the Philippians*. Richmond, VA: John Knox, 1962.
Bartholomew, Craig et al. *After Pentecost: Language and Biblical Interpretation*. Grand Rapids: Zondervan, 2001.
———. et al. *The Futures of Evangelicalism: Issues and Prospects*. Grand Rapids: Kregel, 2004.
Barton, John. *The Biblical World*. Vol. 2. London: Routledge, 2002.
———. "Historical-Critical Approaches." In *The Cambridge Companion to Biblical Interpretation*, edited by John Barton, 9–11. Cambridge: Cambridge University Press, 1998.
Bassett, Frederick. "Noah's Nakedness and the Curse of Canaan a Case of Incest?" *VT* 21 (1971) 232–35.
Bastian, Misty L. "The Naked and the Nude." In *Dirt, Undress, and Difference*, edited by Adeline Masquelier, 34–60. Bloomington, IN: Indiana University Press, 2005.
Batey, Richard A. *New Testament Nuptial Imagery*. Leiden: Brill, 1971.
———. "Paul's Bride Image: A Symbol of Realistic Eschatology." *Interpretation* 17 (1963) 176–82.

Baudrillard, Jean. *Symbolic Exchange and Death*. Translated by Iain Hamilton Grant. 1976. Reprint. London: SAGE, 1993.
Bauman, Zygmunt. *The Individualized Society*. Cambridge: Polity, 2001.
———. *Intimations of Postmodernism*. London: Routledge, 1992.
———. *Liquid Life*. Cambridge: Polity, 2005.
———. *Liquid Modernity*. Cambridge: Polity, 2000.
———. *Modernity and Ambivalence*. Cambridge: Polity, 1991.
———. *Postmodernity and Its Discontents*. Cambridge: Polity, 1997.
———. *Postmodern Ethics*. Oxford: Blackwell, 1993.
Bayer, Oswald. "Martin Luther (1483-1546)." In *The Reformation Theologians: An Introduction to Theology in the Early Modern Period*, edited by Carter Lindberg, 51–66. Oxford: Blackwell, 2002.
———. *Theology the Lutheran Way*. Edited and translated by Jeffrey G. Silcock and Mark C. Mattes. Grand Rapids: Eerdmans, 2007.
BBC Broadcasting Standards Commission and Independent Television Commission. *Briefing Update*. No. 11. July 2003.
BBC News. "Cosimo Cavallaro's Naked Chocolate Christ 'My Sweet Lord.'" No pages. Online: http://news.bbc.co.uk/2/hi/americas/6509127.stm.
BBC. "Chocolate Jesus Exhibit Cancelled." No pages. Online: http://news.bbc.co.uk/2/hi/americas/6513155.stm.
Beasley-Murray, George. *Baptism in the New Testament*. London: Macmillan, 1962.
———. *John*. Waco, TX: Word, 1987.
Beattie, D. R. G. "What is Genesis 2–3 About?" *ExpT* 92 (1980) 9.
Beaudoin, Tom. *Virtual Faith: The Irreverent Spiritual Quest of Generation X*. San Francisco: Jossey-Bass, 1998.
Bechtel, Lyn M. "Rethinking the Interpretation of Genesis 2.4B-3.24." In *A Feminist Companion to Genesis*, edited by Athalya Brenner, 77–177. Sheffield, UK: Sheffield Academic, 1993.
Beck, J. "Divine Initiative: Salvation in Orthodox Theology." In *Salvation in Christ*, edited by J. Meyendorff and R. Tobias, 105–20. Minneapolis: Augsburg, 1992.
Beckford, J. A. *Social Theory & Religion*. Cambridge: Cambridge University Press, 2003.
Belleville, Linda L. *2 Corinthians*. Leicester, UK: InterVarsity, 1996.
Benedict, Ruth. "Dress" In *Fashion Foundations: Early Writings on Fashion and Dress*, edited by Kim K. P. Johnson et al., 29–34. Oxford: Berg, 2003.
Benner, David G., and Peter C. Hill. *Baker Encyclopedia of Psychological & Counseling*. Grand Rapids: Baker, 1985.
Berger, P. L. *A Far Glory: The Quest for Faith in an Age of Credulity*. Oxford: Macmillan, 1992.
Bergsma, John Sietze and Scott Walker Hahn. "Noah's Nakedness and the Curse on Canaan (Genesis 9:20–27)." *JBL* 124 (2005) 25–40.
Berkhof, Hendrikus. *Christian Faith: An Introduction of the Study of Faith*. Translated by Sierd Woudstra. Rev. ed. Grand Rapids: Eerdmans, 1986.
Berkhof, L. *Systematic Theology*. Edinburgh: Banner of Truth, 1939.
Berkouwer, G. C. *Divine Election*. Grand Rapids: Eerdmans, 1960.
Berlin, Adele. *Lamentations: A Commentary*. Louisville, KY: Westminster John Knox, 2004.
Bernard of Clairvaux. *On the Song of Songs IV*. Translated by Irene M. Edmonds. Cistercian Fathers Series 40. Kalamazoo, MI: Cistercian, 1980.

Bernard, Jami. *Total Exposure*. New York: Carol, 1995.
Best, Ernest. *Second Corinthians*. Louisville, KY: John Knox, 1987.
Bhagchandra. "Contribution of Jainism to the development of Buddhism." In *Contribution of Jainism to Indian Culture*, edited by R. C. Dwivedi, 162–66. Delhi: Motilal Banarsidass, 1975.
Billings, Todd J. "United to God through Christ: Assessing Calvin on the Question of Deification." *HTR* 98 (2005) 315–34.
Bingham, D. Jeffrey, and L. van Rompay. *Irenaeus' Use of Matthew's Gospel in Adversus Haereses*. Leuven: Peeters: 1998.
Black, Max. "How Metaphors Work: A Reply to Donald Davidson." In *On Metaphor*, edited by Sheldon Sacks, 181–92. Chicago: University of Chicago Press, 1979.
———. *Models and Metaphors: Studies in Language and Philosophy*. New York: Cornell University Press, 1962.
———. "Metaphor." In *Models and Metaphors: Studies in Language and Philosophy*, edited by M. Black, 24–27. Ithaca, NY: Cornell University Press, 1962.
———. "More About Metaphor." In *Metaphor and Thought*, edited by A. Ortony, 19–43. Cambridge: Cambridge University Press, 1984.
Blake, Daniel. "Outrage at Naked Chocolate Jesus in New York Gallery." No pages. Online: http://www.christiantoday.com/article/outrage.at.naked.chocolate.jesus.in.new.york.gallery/10172.htm.
Blenkinsopp, Joseph. *Isaiah 1–39: A New Translation with Introduction and Commentary*. London: Doubleday, 2000.
Blinzler, Josef. *The Trial of Jesus*. Translated by Isabel McHugh and Florence McHugh. Cork, Ireland: Mercier, 1959.
Bloch, Iwan. *Anthropological Studies on the Strange Sexual Practices of All Races and All Ages*. Honolulu: University Press of the Pacific, 2001.
Blocher, Henri. *In the Beginning*. Downers Grove, IL: InterVarsity, 1984.
———. *Original Sin: Illuminating the Riddle*. Leicester, UK: Apollos, 1997.
Bloesch, Donald. *Essentials of Evangelical Theology*. Vol. 1. New York: Harper & Row, 1978.
———. *God, the Almighty: Power, Wisdom, Holiness, Love*. Carlisle, UK: Paternoster, 1995.
Blomberg, Craig L. *Matthew*. Nashville: Broadman, 1992.
Bock, Darrell L. *Jesus according to Scripture*. Grand Rapids: Baker Academic, 2002.
"The Body is Sacred." No pages. Online: http://www.thebodyissacred.org/body/naked.asp.
Boersma, Hans. "Redemptive Hospitality in Irenaeus: A Model for Ecumenicity in a Violent World." *Pro Ecclesia* 11 (2002) 207–26.
———. *Violence, Hospitality, and the Cross*. Grand Rapids: Baker, 2004.
Boettner, L. *The Reformed Doctrine of Predestination*. Grand Rapids: Eerdmans, 1932.
Bolt, M. "Interpersonal Attraction." In *Baker Encyclopedia of Psychological & Counseling*, edited by David G. Benner and Peter C. Hill, 642–43. Grand Rapids: Baker, 1985.
Boman, Thorlief. *Hebrew Thought Compared with Greek*. London: SCM, 1960.
Bonar, Andrew A. *A Commentary on Leviticus*. Carlisle, UK: Banner of Truth, 1846.
Bonhoeffer, Dietrich. *The Cost of Discipleship*. Translated by C. Kaiser. 1937. Reprint. London: SCM, 1959.
———. *Creation and Fall: A Theological Interpretation of Genesis 1–3*. London: SCM, 1959.

Bonner, Gerald. "Augustine's Conception of Deification." *JTS* 37 (1986) 369–86.

———. "Deification, Divinization." In *Augustine through the Ages: An Encyclopedia*, edited by Alan D. Fitzgerald, 265–66. Grand Rapids: Eerdmans, 1999.

Boomershine, Thomas E. "The Structure of Narrative Rhetoric in Genesis 2–3." *Semeia* 18 (1980) 113–29.

Bordo, Susan. "The Body and the Reproduction of Femininity: A Feminist Appropriation of Foucault." In *Gender/Body/Knowledge: Feminist Reconstructions of Being and Knowing*, edited by Alison M. Jaggar and Susan Bordo, 13–33. New Brunswick, NJ: Rutgers University Press, 1989.

———. *The Male Body: A New Look at Men in Public and in Private*. New York: Farrar, Straus and Giroux, 1999.

———. *Twilight Zones: The Hidden Life of Cultural Images from Plato to O. J.* Berkeley: University of California, 1997.

———. *Unbearable Weight: Feminism, Western Culture, and the Body*. Berkeley: University of California, 1993.

Bornhaeuser, Karl. *The Death and Resurrection of Jesus Christ*. Translated by A. Rumpus. Bangalore: C. L. S., 1958.

Bosch, David J. *Transforming Mission: Paradigm Shifts in Theology of Mission*. Maryknoll, NY: Orbis, 1991.

Bottici, Chiara. *A Philosophical Political Myth*. Cambridge: Cambridge University Press, 2007.

Bottomley, Frank. *Attitudes to the Body in Western Christendom*. London: Lepus, 1979.

Boudon, Raymond, and François Bourricaud. *A Critical Dictionary of Sociology*. Translated by Peter Hamilton. London: Routledge, 1989.

Bourdieu, Pierre. "The Sentiment of Honour in Kabyle Society." Translated by Philip Sherrard. In *Honour and Shame: The Value of Mediterranean Society*, edited by J. G. Peristiany, 191–241. Chicago: University of Chicago Press, 1966.

Boyd, Gregory A. "Christus Victor Response." In *The Nature of the Atonement: Four Views*, edited by James Beilby and Paul R. Eddy, 186–91. Downers Grove, IL: InterVarsity Academic, 2006.

———. "Christus Victor View." In *The Nature of the Atonement: Four Views*, edited by James Beilby and Paul R. Eddy, 23–49. Downers Grove, IL: InterVarsity Academic, 2006.

Braaten, Carl E., and Robert W. Jenson. *Union with Christ: The New Finnish Interpretation of Luther*. Grand Rapids: Eerdmans, 1998.

Braine, David. *The Human Person: Animal and Spirit*. London: Duckworth, 1993.

Bray, G. L. "Deification." In *New Dictionary of Theology*, edited by Sinclair B. Ferguson et al., 189. Downers Grove, IL: InterVarsity, 1988.

Bray, Gerald. "Original Sin in Patristic Thought." *Churchman* 108 (1994) 37–47.

Brettler, M. *God is King: Understanding an Israelite Metaphor*. JSOTSup 76. Sheffield, UK: JSOT, 1989.

Brettschneider, Marla. "Jewish Feminism, Sexuality, and a Sexual Justice Agenda." In *New Jewish Feminism: Probing the Past, Forging the Future*, edited by Elyse Goldstein, 241–50. Woodstock, VT: Jewish Lights, 2009.

Brichto, Herbert Chanan. *The Names of God: Poetics Readings in Biblical Beginnings*. Oxford: Oxford University Press, 1998.

Briggs, Charles Augustus, and Emilie Grace Briggs. *A Critical and Exegetical Commentary on the Book of Psalms*. Vol. 2. Edinburgh: T. & T. Clark, 1907.

Briscoe, D. Stuart. *The Preacher's Commentary: Genesis*. Nashville: Thomas Nelson, 1987.
Brock, Rita N. "And a Little Child Will Lead Us: Christology and Child Abuse." In *Christianity, Patriarchy, and Abuse: A Feminist Critique*, edited by Joanne Carlson Brown and Carole R. Bohn, 52–53. New York: Pilgrim, 1989.
Brock, Sebastian. "The Robe of Glory: A Biblical Image in the Syriac Tradition." *The Way* 39 (1999) 247–55.
Brooks, James A. *Mark*. NAC. Nashville: Broadman, 1991.
Brown, Callum G. *The Death of Christian Britain: Understanding Secularisation 1800–2000*. 2nd ed. London: Routledge, 2009.
Brown, Dan. *The Da Vinci Code: A Novel*. London: Bantam, 2003.
Brown, Peter. *The Body and Society: Men, Women, and Sexual Renunciation in Early Christianity*. New York: Columbia University Press, 1988.
Brown, Raymond. *The Death of the Messiah*. London: Chapman, 1994.
———. *The Message of Deuteronomy*. Leicester, UK: InterVarsity, 1993.
———. *The Gospel according to John (1–12)*. Vol. 1. London: Chapman, 1966.
———. *The Gospel according to John (13–21)*. Vol. 2. London: Chapman, 1971.
Brown, William P. *Ecclesiastes*. Louisville, KY: John Knox, 2000.
Brownlee, William H. *Ezekiel 1–19*. Waco, TX: Word, 1986.
Bruce, A. B. *The Humiliation of Christ*. Edinburgh: T. & T. Clark, 1905.
Bruce, F. F. *Philippians*. Good News Commentary. New York: Harper & Row, 1983.
———. *1 and 2 Thessalonians*. WBC. Waco, TX: Word, 1982.
Brueggemann, Walter. *First and Second Samuel*. Louisville, KY: John Knox, 1990.
———. *Genesis: A Bible Commentary for Teaching and Preaching*. Atlanta: John Knox, 1982.
———. *Isaiah 1–39*. Louisville, KY: Westminster John Knox, 1998.
———. *Isaiah 40–66*. Louisville, KY: Westminster John Knox, 1998.
Brümmer, Vincent. *Atonement, Christology and the Trinity: Making Sense of Christian Doctrine*. Aldershot, UK: Ashgate, 2005.
———. *The Model of Love: A Study in Philosophical Theology*. Cambridge: Cambridge University Press, 1993.
Brunner, E. *The Christian Doctrine of Creation and Redemption*. London: Lutterworth, 1952.
Bruner, Frederick Dale. *Matthew*, Vol. 2. Cambridge: Eerdmans, 1990.
Bucher, Richard P. "Crucifixion in the Ancient World." No pages. Online: http://www.orlutheran.com/html/crucify.html.
Bultmann, Rudolf. *The Gospel of John: A Commentary*. Edited by G. R. Beasley-Murray. Philadelphia: Westminster, 1971.
———. *The Second Letter to the Corinthians*. 1976. Reprint. Minneapolis: Augsburg, 1985.
Buchanan, George. *A Critical and Exegetical Commentary on the Book of Isaiah: 1–39*. Edinburgh: T. & T. Clark, 1912.
Buren, Paul van. *Christ in Our Place*. London: Oliver and Boyd, 1957.
Buss, David. *The Evolution of Desire*. 2nd ed. New York: Basic, 2003.
Buswell, J. Oliver. *A Systematic Theology of the Christian Religion*. 2 vols. Grand Rapids: Zondervan, 1962–63.
Bynum, C. W. *Fragmentation and Redemption: Essays on Gender and the Human Body in Medieval Religion*. New York: Zone, 1991.

Caird, C. B. *The Language and Imagery of the Bible*, London: Duckworth, 1980.
Calvin, John. *The Bondage and Liberation of the Will*. Translated by Graham I. Davies, edited by A. N. S. Lane. Grand Rapids: Baker, 1996.
Campbell, James I. *The Language of Religion*. New York: Bruce, 1971.
Campbell, John McLeod. *The Nature of the Atonement*. Grand Rapids: Eerdmans, 1996.
Capps, Donald. *The Depleted Self: Sin in a Narcissistic Age*. Minneapolis: Fortress, 1993.
Carey, George. *I Believe in Man*. London: Hodder and Stoughton, 1977.
Cargal, Timothy B. "Nakedness." In *Dictionary of the Bible*, edited by David Noel Freedman, 944. Grand Rapids: Eerdmans, 2000.
Carley, Keith W. *The Book of the Prophet Ezekiel*. Cambridge Bible Commentary, Cambridge: Cambridge University Press, 1974.
Carmichael, Calum M. "The Paradise Myth: Interpreting Without Jewish and Christian Spectacles." In *A Walk in the Garden*, edited by Paul Morris and Deborah Sawyer, 47–63. Sheffield, UK: Sheffield Academic, 1992.
Carmody, J. M. "Kenosis." In *New Catholic Encyclopedia*, Vol. 8, edited by T. Carson et al., 143. New York: McGraw-Hill, 1967.
Carr, Anthony T. "Body Shame." In *Body Shame*, edited by Paul Gilbert and Jeremy Miles, 90–102. New York: Brunner-Routledge, 2002.
Carroll, Daniel. "Introduction: Issues of 'Context' within Social Science Approaches to Biblical Studies." In *Rethinking Contexts, Rereading Texts*, edited by Daniel Carroll, 13–21. Sheffield, UK: Sheffield Academic, 2000.
Carroll, D. *Psychology of Language*. Pacific Grove, CA: Cole, 1986.
Carroll, John T., and Joel B. Green. *The Death of Jesus in Early Christianity*. Peabody, MA: Hendrickson, 1995.
Carruthers, Peter. *Introducing Persons: Theories and Arguments in the Philosophy of Mind*. London: Croom Helm, 1986.
Carson, D. A. *The Gospel according to John*. Leicester, UK: InterVarsity, 1991.
Carter, Charles W. *A Contemporary Wesleyan Theology*. Vol. 1, Grand Rapids: Zondervan, 1983.
Cary, Earnest. *The Roman Antiquitites of Dionysius of Halicarnassus*. Vol. 4. London: Heinemann, 1937.
Cash, T. F. et al. "Sexism and 'Beautyism' in Personnel Consultant Decision Making." *JAP* 62 (1977) 301–10.
Cassidy, Ronald. "Paul's Attitude to Death in II Corinthians 5:1–10." *EQ* (1971) 215–17.
Cassuto, U. *A Commentary on the Book of Genesis*. Part 1: From Adam to Noah: Genesis 1–5.8. Translated by Israel Abrahams. Jerusalem: Magnes, 1944.
Chadwick, Henry. *Augustine*. Oxford: Oxford University Press, 1986.
Chafin, Kenneth L. *1 & 2 Samuel*. Nashville: Thomas Nelson, 1989.
Chan, Mark L. Y. "The Gospel and the Achievement of the Cross." *ERT* 33 (2009) 19–31.
Chapman, Cynthia R. *The Gendered Language of Warfare in the Israel-Assyrian Encounter*. Winona Lake, IN: Eisenbrauns, 2004.
Charlesworth, J. H. "Jesus and Jehohanan: An Archaeological Note on Crucifixion." *ExpT* 84 (1972–1973) 147–50.
Chauncy, Charles. *The Duty of Ministers: A Sermon Preached at the Ordination of the Rev. Mr. Penuel Bowen*. Boston: Edes and Gill, 1766.
Childs, Brevard S. *Isaiah*. Louisville, KY: Westminster John Knox, 2001.
Chrétien, Jean-Louis. *Hand to Hand*. Translated by Stephen E. Lewis. New York: Fordham University Press, 2003.

Christensen, Michael J. "Theosis and Sanctification: John Wesley's Reformulation of a Patristic Doctrine." *WTJ* 31 (1996) 71–94.
Christensen, Michael J., and Jeffrey A. Wittung. *Partakers of the Divine Nature: The History and Development of Deification in the Christian Traditions*. Grand Rapids: Baker, 2007.
Christiansen, Ellen Juhl. "Women and Baptism" *Studia Theologica* 35 (1981) 3–5.
Church of Scotland. *The Biblical Doctrine of Baptism*. With introductory note by T. F. Torrance and John Heron. Edinburgh: Saint Andrew, 1958.
Churchland, P. *Scientific Realism and Plasticity of Mind*. Cambridge: Cambridge University Press, 1979.
Clammer, J. "Aesthetics of the Self: Shopping and Social Being in Contemporary Urban Japan." In *Lifestyle Shopping: The Subject of Consumption*, edited by R. Shields, 197–216. London: Routledge, 1992.
Clark, M. S., and J. Mills. "Interpersonal Attraction in Exchange and Communal Relationships." *Journal of Personality and Social Psychology* 37 (1979) 12–24.
Clark, R. Scott. *Recovering the Reformed Confession*. Phillipsburg. NJ: Presbyterian & Reformed, 2008.
Clements, R. E. *Isaiah 1–39*. New Century Bible Commentary. Grand Rapids: Eerdmans, 1980.
Clendenin, Daniel B. *Eastern Orthodox Christianity: A Western Perspective*. Grand Rapids: Baker, 1994.
———. "Partakers of Divinity: The Orthodox Doctrine of Theosis." *JETS* 37 (1994) 365–379.
Clines, D. J. A. "The Tree of Knowledge and the Law of Yahweh." *VT* 24 (1974) 11.
Coakley, Sarah. "Introduction: Religion and the Body." In *Religion and the Body*, edited by Sarah Coakley, 2–3. Cambridge: Cambridge University Press, 1997.
———. *Religion and the Body*. Cambridge: Cambridge University Press, 1997.
Cohen, A. *The Minor Tractates of the Talmud*. Vol. 2. London: Soncino, 1965.
Cole, R. Alan. *Mark*. Tyndale Commentary. Leicester, UK: InterVarsity, 1989.
Coleridge, Samuel Taylor. *Collected Letters of Samuel Taylor Coleridge*. Edited by E. L. Griggs. Vol. 2. Oxford: Clarendon, 1956–71.
———. *The Notebooks of Samuel Taylor Coleridge*. Edited by K. Coburn. London: Routledge, 1957.
Colwell, John E. "Sin." In *New Dictionary of Theology*, edited by Sinclair B. Ferguson and David F. Wright, 641–43. Leicester, UK: InterVarsity, 1988.
Cones, Bryan. "Sweet Jesus!" *U.S. Catholic* 72.6 (2007) 50.
Connor, Steven. *Postmodernist Culture: An Introduction to Theories of the Contemporary*. Oxford: Blackwell, 1989.
Conrad, Edgar W. *Reading Isaiah*. Minneapolis: Fortress, 1991.
Conroy, Charles. *1–2 Samuel, 1–2 Kings*. Wilmington, KY: Glazier, 1983.
Constable, Giles. "*Nudus Nudum Christum Sequi* and Parallel Formulas in the Twelfth Century." In *Continuity and Discontinuity in Church History: Essays Presented to George Hunston Williams*, edited by F. Forrester Church and Timothy George, 83–91. Leiden: Brill, 1979.
Cooke, Edward, translator. *A Just and Seasonable Reprehension of Naked Breasts and Shoulders*. Written by a Grave and Learned Papist. London: The Three Roses, Ludgate-street, 1678.
Cooper, John W. *Body, Soul, & Life Everlasting*. Grand Rapids: Eerdmans, 1989.

Copleston, F. C. *Aquinas*. Harmondsworth, UK: Penguin, 1955.
Corduan, Winfried. "A Hair's Breadth from Pantheism: Meister Eckhart's God-Centered Spirituality." *JETS* 37 (1994) 263–74.
Corrigan, Kathleen. "Text and Image on an Icon of the Crucifixion at Mount Sinai." In *The Sacred Image East and West*, edited by Robert G. Ousterhout and Leslie Brubaker, 48–54. Chicago: University of Illinois Press, 1995.
Cottrell, Jack. *The Faith Once for All: Bible Doctrine for Today*. Joplin, MO: College Press, 2002.
Coughlan, Geraldine, and Alex Clarke. "Shame and Burns." In *Body Shame*, edited by Paul Gilbert and Jeremy Miles, 155–70. New York: Brunner-Routledge, 2002.
Court, J. H. "Pornography." In *Baker Encyclopedia of Psychology*, edited by David G. Benner, 854–55. Grand Rapids: Baker, 1985.
Cox, David. "Psychology and Symbolism." In *Myth and Symbol*, edited by F. W. Dillistone, 51–66. London: SPCK, 1966.
Craig, W. L. "Paul's Dilemma in 2 Corinthians 5.1–10: A 'Catch-22'?" *NTS* 34 (1988) 145–47.
Craik, Jennifer. *The Face of Fashion: Cultural Studies in Fashion*. London: Routledge, 1994.
Cranfield, C. E. B. *The Gospel according to Saint Mark*. Cambridge: Cambridge University Press, 1959.
———. *Romans: A Short Commentary*. Edinburgh: T. & T. Clark, 1985.
Crawley, Ernest. "The Sexual Background of Dress." In *Dress, Adornment and Social Order*, edited by Mary Ellen Roach and Joanne Bubolz Eicher, 72–76. New York: Wiley & Sons, 1965.
Cregan, Kate. *The Sociology of the Body: Mapping the Abstraction of Embodiment*. London: SAGE, 2006.
Crenshaw, James L. *Ecclesiastes*. London: SCM, 1988.
Croft, William, and D. Alan Cruse. *Cognitive Linguistics*. Cambridge: Cambridge University Press, 2004.
Cronk, George. *The Message of the Bible: An Orthodox Christian Perspective*. Crestwood, NY: St Vladimir's Seminary Press, 1982.
Cross, Gary. *Time and Money: The Making of Consumer Culture*. London: Routledge, 1993.
Crossan, John Dominic. *Who Killed Jesus?* New York: HarperCollins, 1995.
Crouch, Andy. "Emergent Evangelicalism: The Place of Absolute Truths in a Postmodern World: Two Views." *Christianity Today* 48.11 (2004) 42–43.
Cullmann, Oscar. *Christ and Time: The Primitive Christian Conception of Time and History*. Translated by Floyd V. Filson. London: SCM, 1962.
———. *Immortality of the Soul or Resurrection of the Dead?* London: Epworth, 1958.
Cumming, Valerie. "The Body in Clothing of Delight." *The Way* 39.3 (1999) 215–25.
Cunningham, Philip A. *Jesus and The Evangelists*. New York: Paulist, 1988.
Cyer, Susan. "Fallout Escalates Over 'Goddess' Sophia Worship." *Christianity Today* 38.4 (1994) 74.
Cyprian of Carthage. *Born to New Life*. Translated by Tim Witherow, edited by Oliver Davies. London: New City, 1991.
Cyprian. *De Lapsis and De Ecclesiae Catholicae Unitate*. Translated by S. T. Maurice Bévenot. Oxford: Clarendon, 1971.

———. *Ep.* 58.6.3. Translated by G. W. Clarke. In *The Letters of St. Cyprian of Carthage*. Vol. 3: "Ancient Christian Writers, No. 46." New York: Newman Press, 1986.
Cyril of Jerusalem. *Mystagogical Catechesis II—On the Rites of Baptism*. In *St. Cyril of Jerusalem's Lectures on the Christian Sacraments: The Procatechesis and the Five Mystagogical Catecheses*, edited by F. L. Cross. London: SPCK, 1951.
Dales, Richard C. *The Problem of the Rational Soul in the Thirteenth Century*. New York: Brill, 1995.
Daley, Brian E. *Gregory of Nazianzus*. London: Routledge, 2006.
Dalman, Gustaf. *Jesus—Jeshua*. Translated by Paul P. Levertoff. London: SPCK, 1929.
Danby, Herbert, translator. *Mishnah*. London: Oxford University Press, 1933.
Daniel-Rops, H. *Daily Life in Palestine at the Time of Christ*. Translated by Patrick O'Brian. London: Weidenfeld, 1962.
———. *Jesus in His Time*. Translated by R. W. Millar. London: Eyre & Spottiswoode, 1956.
Daniélou, Jean. *The Bible and the Liturgy*. 1956. Reprint. London: Darton, Longman & Todd, 1960.
Darwin, Charles. *The Expression of the Emotions in Man and Animals*. 1899. Reprint. New York: BiblioBazaar, 2007.
———. *The Descent of Man and Selection in Relation to Sex*. 1871. Reprint. Princeton: Princeton University Press, 1981.
Davidson, Robert. *Genesis 1–11*. Cambridge: Cambridge University Press, 1973.
Davies, Margaret. *Matthew*. Sheffield, UK: Sheffield Academic, 1993.
Davies, J. D. *Beginning Now: A Christian Exploration of the First Three Chapters of Genesis*. Philadelphia: Fortress, 1971.
Davies, Oliver, and Denys Turner. *Silence and the Word: Negative Theology and Incarnation*. Cambridge: Cambridge University Press, 2002.
Davies, W. D., and Dale C. Allison Jr. *Matthew*. Edinburgh: T. & T. Clark, 1997.
Davis, C. et al. "Personality Correlates of a Drive for Muscularity in Young Men." *Personality and Individual Differences* 39 (2005) 349–59.
Davis, Stephen J. "Fashioning a Divine Body: Coptic Christology and Ritualized Dress." *HTR* 98.3 (2005) 355–62.
Dawe, Donald. "A Fresh Look of the Kenotic Christologies." *SJT* 15 (1962) 337–49.
Delitzsch, Franz. *Biblical Commentary on The Prophecies of Isaiah*. Vol. 1. Edinburgh: T. & T. Clark, 1890.
Demarest, Gary W. *Leviticus*. TPC. Nashville: Thomas Nelson, 1990.
Deme, Daniel. *The Christology of Anselm of Canterbury*. Aldershot, UK: Ashgate, 2003.
Dennett, Daniel C. "The Self as a Center of Narrative Gravity." In *Self and Consciousness: Multiple Perspectives*, edited by F. Kessel, P. Cole and D. Johnson, 103–12. Hillsdale, NJ: Erlbaum, 1992.
Dennett, Daniel. "Why Everyone is a Novelist." *Times Literary Supplement* 4459 (1988) 1016–29.
DeRoche, Michael. "Israel's 'Two Evils' in Jeremiah II 13." *VT* 31 (1981) 369–71.
Descartes, René. *A Discourse on Method*. 1637. Translated by John Veitch. London: Dent & Sons, 1989.
———. *The Meditations and Selections from the Principles*. 1644. Translated by John Veitch. La Salle, MI: Open Court, 1988.
"Destruction of Judean Fortress Portrayed in Dramatic Eight Century B.C. Pictures." Book Review. *BAR* 10.2 (1984) 48–65.

Dijk-Hemmes, Fokkelien Van. "The Metaphorization of Woman in Prophetic Speech: An Analysis of Ezekiel XXIII." *VT* 43 (1993) 162–70.
Dillistone, F. W. "Atonement." In *A New Dictionary of Christian Theology*, edited by Alan Richardson and John Bowden, 50–53. London: SCM, 1983.
———. *Christianity and Symbolism*. London: SCM, 1955.
———. *The Christian Faith*. London: Hodder and Stoughton, 1964.
———. *The Christian Understanding of the Atonement*. London: SCM, 1968.
———. *The Power of Symbols*. London: SCM, 1986.
Dion, Karen K. "Physical Attractiveness, Sex Roles, and Heterosexual Attraction." In *The Bases of Human Sexual Attraction*, edited by Mark Cook, 3–22. London: Academic Press, 1981.
Dionysius the Pseudo-Areopagite. *The Ecclesiastical Hierarchy*. Translated by Thomas L. Campbell. Washington, DC: The Catholic University of America Press, 1955.
Divakar, Jain Darshan Vidya Varidhi. *The Nudity of Jain Saints*. Delhi: The Jain Mittra Mandal, 1931.
Đô, Quốc. "Khởi đúc tượng Thánh Gióng đúng thời khắc trùng cửu." *Dân Trí*, Monday, October 26, 2009, No pages. Online: http://dantri.com.vn/c20/s20-358382/khoi-duc-tuong-thanh-giong-dung-thoi-khac-trung-cuu.htm.
Dockery, David S. et al. *Foundation for Biblical Interpretation*. Nashville: Broadman & Holman, 1994.
Dockery, David S. *The Challenge of Postmodernism: An Evangelical Engagement*. Wheaton, IL: Victor, 1995.
Doctrine Commission of the Church of England. *The Mystery of Salvation: The Story of God's Gift*. London: Church House, 1995.
Dodd, C. H. *History Tradition in the Fourth Gospel*. Cambridge: Cambridge University Press, 1963.
Donath, Judith S. "Identity and Deception in the Virtual Community." In *Communities in Cyberspace*, edited by Marc A. Smith and Peter Kollock, 29–59. London: Routledge, 1999.
Donovan, Peter. *Religious Language*. London: Sheldon, 1976.
Donzelot, J. *The Policing of Families*. New York: Pantheon, 1979.
Dorner, Isaac August. *A System of Christian Doctrine*. Vol. 3. Edinburgh: T. & T. Clark, 1882.
Douglas, Mary. *Purity and Danger: An Analysis of Concepts of Pollution and Taboo*. London: Routledge and Kegan Paul, 1966.
Dowling, Melissa Barden. *Clemency and Cruelty in the Roman World*. Ann Arbor, MI: The University of Michigan Press, 2006.
Doyle, Brian. "Howling Like Dogs—Metaphorical Language In Psalm LIX." *VT* 54 (2004) 70.
Drane, John. *Celebrity Culture*. Edinburgh: Rutherford House, 2005.
Duguid, Iain M. *Ezekiel*. NIVAC. Grand Rapids: Zondervan, 1999.
Dunn, James D. G. *Romans 1–8*. WBC. Dallas: Word, 1988.
Dunseath, Kirsty. *A Second Skin*. London: Women's, 1998.
Durham, John I. *Exodus*. WBC. Waco, Texas: Word, 1987.
Dwivedi, A. N. *Essentials of Hinduism, Jainism & Buddhism*. New Delhi: Books Today, 1978.
Dworetzky, John P. *Human Development*. New York: West, 1989.
Dyer, Richard. *Only Entertainment*. London: Routledge, 1992.

Eagleton, Terry. *The Illusion of Postmodernism*. Oxford: Blackwell, 1996.
Eddy, G. T. "The Proofs of Original Sin: An Eighteenth Century Critique." *ExpT* 110.9 (1999) 286.
Edelmann, Robert J. *The Psychology of Embarrassment*. Chichester, UK: Wiley, 1987.
Edersheim, Alfred. *The Life and Times of Jesus the Messiah*. Vol. 2. 11th ed. New York: Longmans, Green and Co., 1901.
Edgerton, Robert B. *The Balance of Human Kindness and Cruelty: Why We Are the Way We Are*. Lewinston, NY: Mellen, 2005.
Edwards, Dan. "Deification and the Anglican Doctrine of Human Nature: A Reassessment of the Historical Significance of William Porcher DuBose." *Anglican and Episcopal History* 58 (1989) 196–212.
Edwards, David L. *After Death?* London: Continuum, 1999.
Edwards, Douglas R. "Dress and Ornamentation." In *The Anchor Bible Dictionary*, Vol. 2, edited by David Noel Freedman, 232–38. London: Doubleday, 1992.
Edwards, James R. *The Gospel according to Mark*. Leicester, UK: Apollos, 2002.
Edwards, Mark. *John through the Centuries*. Oxford: Blackwell, 2004.
Eichrodt, Walther. *Ezekiel*. Old Testament Library. Philadelphia: Westminster, 1970.
Eilberg-Schwartz, H. *The Savage in Judaism*. Bloomington, IN: Indiana University Press, 1990.
Ellingworth, Paul. *The Epistle to the Hebrews*. NIGTC. Grand Rapids: Eerdmans, 1993.
Ellis, E. Earle. *Paul and His Recent Interpreters*. Grand Rapids: Eerdmans, 1961.
———. "II Corinthians V. 1–10 in Pauline Eschatology." *NTS* 6 (1959–1960) 219–20.
Ellis, Henry Havelock. *Psychology of Sex*. Vol. 1. London: Heinemann Medical, 1948.
Ellens, Deborah. *Women in the Sex Texts of Leviticus and Deuteronomy: A Comparative Conceptual Analysis*. London: T. & T. Clark, 2008.
Elshtain, Jean Bethke. "The Body and Projects of Self-Possession." In *Having: Property and Possession in Religious and Social Life*, edited by William Schweiker and Charles Mathewes, 141–61. Grand Rapids: Eerdmans, 2004.
Elwell, Walter A. *Evangelical Dictionary of Theology*. Grand Rapids: Baker, 1984.
End, L., and J. Danks. *Comprehension of Metaphors: Priming the Ground*. Kent, OH: Kent State University, 1982. No pages. Downloadable online: http://www.eric.ed.gov/ERICWebPortal/contentdelivery/servlet/ERICServlet?accno=ED220812.
Epstein, Louis M. *Sex Laws and Customs in Judaism*. New York: Bloch, 1948.
Ericksen, Janet S. "Penitential Nakedness and the Junius 11 Genesis." In *Naked Before God: Uncovering the Body in Anglo-Saxon England*, edited by Benjamins C. Withers and Jonathan Wilcox, 257–74. Morgantown, VA: West Virginia University Press, 2003.
Erickson, Millard J. *Christian Theology*. 3 vols. Grand Rapids: Baker, 1983.
Ertelt, Steven. "Scientist Says British Human Cloning Bill Would Allow Human-Chimp Mating." *LifeNews.com* May 2, 2008. No pages. Online: http://www.lifenews.com/bio2424.html.
Eslinger, Lyle M. "The Infinite in a Finite Organical Perception (Isaiah VI 1–5)." *VT* 45 (1995) 145–69.
Evans, C. F. *Saint Luke*. London: SCM, 1990.
Evans, C. Stephen. "Kenotic Theories." In *Pocket Dictionary of Apologetics & Philosophy of Religion*, edited by C. Stephen Evans, 65. Downers Grove, IL: InterVarsity, 2002.
Evans, Mary J. *1 & 2 Samuel*. Carlisle, UK: Paternoster, 2000.

Evans, Vyvyan. *A Glossary of Cognitive Linguistics.* Edinburgh: Edinburgh University Press, 2007.
Evans, Vyvyan. "Cognitive Linguistics." No pages. Draft article online: http://www.vyvevans.net/cognitiveLinguisticsPRAG-ENCYC.pdf. 2007.
Evans, Vyvyan, et al. "The Cognitive Linguistics Enterprise: An Overview." No pages. Online: http://www.port.ac.uk/departments/academic/psychology/staff/downloads/filetodownload,68131,en.pdf. 2006.
Evans, Vyvyan, and Melanie Green. *Cognitive Linguistics: An Introduction.* Edinburgh: Edinburgh University Press, 2006.
Ewen, Stuart, and Elizabeth Ewen. *Channels of Desire: Mass Images and the Shaping of American Consciousness.* London: McGraw-Hill, 1982.
Exum, J. Cheryl. "The Ethics of Biblical Violence against Women." In *The Bible in Ethics: The Second Sheffield Colloquium,* edited by John W. Rogerson, 248–71. Sheffield, UK: Sheffield Academic, 1995.
Fairlie, Henry. *The Seven Deadly Sins Today.* Notre Dame, IN: Nortre Dame University Press, 1978.
Farley, Edward. *Good & Evil.* Minneapolis: Fortress, 1990.
Farrer, Austin. *Finite and Infinite.* Westminster, UK: Dacre, 1943.
Farrbairn, A. M. *The Place of Christ in Modern Theology.* New York: Scribner's Sons, 1893.
Fawcett, Thomas. *The Symbolic Language of Religion.* London: SCM, 1970.
Featherstone, M. "The Body in Consumer Culture." *Theory, Culture and Society* 1 (1982) 18–33.
Fee, Gordon, and Douglas Stuart. *How To Read The Bible For All Its Worth.* Grand Rapids: Zondervan, 1982.
Fee, Gordon D. *The First Epistle to the Corinthians.* NICNT. Grand Rapids: Eerdmans, 1987.
———. *Paul's Letter to the Philippians.* Grand Rapids: Eerdmans, 1995.
Fekkes III, Jan. "'His Bride Has Prepared Herself': Revelation 19-21 and Isaian Nuptial Imagery." *JBL* 109 (1990) 269–87.
Fensham, F. Charles. "The Marriage Metaphor in Hosea for the Covenant Relationship between the Lord and His People (Hos. 1:2–9)." *Journal of Northwest Semitic Languages* 12 (1984) 71–78.
Fenton, J. C. *The Gospel according to John.* Oxford: Clarendon, 1970.
Fiddes, Paul S. *Past Event and Present Salvation: The Christian Idea of Atonement.* London: DLT, 1989.
———. *Tracks and Traces: Baptist Identity in Church and Theology.* Milton Keynes, UK: Paternoster, 2003.
Field, Benjamin. *The Student's Handbook of Christian Theology.* London: Hodder and Stoughton, 1883.
Filson, Floyd V. *A Commentary on the Gospel according to St. Matthew.* London: Black, 1960.
Fina, Barbara De (producer), and Martin Scorsese (director), *The Last Temptation of Christ.* Universal Studios, 1988.
Finlan, Stephen, and Vladimir Kharlamov. *Theosis: Deification in Christian Theology.* Eugene, OR: Pickwick, 2006.
Fisher, Fred. *Commentary on 1 & 2 Corinthians.* Waco, TX: Word, 1975.
Fisher, G. P. *History of Christian Doctrine.* Edinburgh: T. & T. Clark, 1896.

Fisher, John H. *The Complete Poetry of Geoffrey Chaucer*. New York: Holt, Rinehart and Winston, 1977.
Fiske, John. *Television Culture*. London: Methuen, 1987.
Fitzmyer, Joseph A. "Crucifixion in Ancient Palestine, Qumran Literature, and the New Testament." *CBQ* 40 (1978) 493–513.
Fitzmyer, Joseph A. *Romans*. New York: Doubleday, 1993.
Fleddermann, Harry. "The Flight of a Naked Young Man." *CBQ* 41 (1979) 412–18.
Fleming, John V. "*The Dream of the Rood* and Anglo-Saxon Monasticism." *Traditio* 22 (1966) 43–72.
Flew, Antony. *Body, Mind, and Death*. London: Collier-Macmillan, 1964.
Flugel, J. C. *The Psychology of Clothes*. London: Hogarth, 1930.
Fohr, Sherry E. "Restriction and Protection—Female Jain Renouncers." In *Studies in Jaina History and Culture*, edited by Peter Flügel, 157–80. London: Routledge, 2006.
Forsyth, P. T. *The Church and the Sacraments*. London: Independent, 1947.
———. *God the Holy Father*. 2nd ed. London: Independent, 1957.
———. *Positive Preaching and the Modern Mind*. London: Hodder & Stoughton, 1909.
———. *The Work of Christ*. 2nd ed. London: Independent, 1938.
Foss, Martin. *Symbol and Metaphor in Human Experience*. Princeton: Princeton University Press, 1949.
Fowl, Stephen E. *Philippians*. Two Horizons. Grand Rapids: Eerdmans, 2005.
Fox, Emerson (Script writer), and Wolfgang von Schiber (Executive Producer). *Shocking Asia* DVD. Hong Kong: Geiselgesteig-Film and First Film Organisation, 1981.
France, R. T. *The Gospel according to Matthew*. Leicester, UK: InterVarsity, 1985.
———. *The Gospel of Mark*. NIGTC. Carlisle, UK: Paternoster, 2002.
———. *The Gospel of Matthew*. Grand Rapids: Eerdmans, 2007.
———. *Jesus and the Old Testament*. London: Tyndale, 1971.
Francis of Assisi. *Little Flowers of St. Francis of Assisi*. Typed by Kathy Sewell, London: Bagster, 1997.
Francis of Sales. *Treatise on the Love of God*. 1884. Reprint. New York: Cosimo, 2007.
Frank, Doug. "Naked but Unashamed." In *Proclaiming the Scandal of the Cross: Contemporary Images of the Atonement*, edited by Mark D. Baker, 122–34. Grand Rapids: Baker Academic, 2006.
Franks, Robert S. *The Work of Christ: A Historical Study of Christian Doctrine*. London: Nelson, 1962.
Franklin, John. "Art, Imagination, and Theology." *Canadian Evangelical Review* 21 (2001) 5.
Frede, Michael. "Monotheism and Pagan Antiquity." In *Pagan Monotheism in Late Antiquity*, edited by Polymnia Athanassiadi and Michael Frede, 58–62. Oxford: Clarendon, 1999.
Fredrickson, Roger L. *John*. Dallas: Word, 1985.
Frei, Hans W. et al. *Theology and Narrative: Selected Essays*. Oxford: Oxford University Press, 1993.
Fretheim, Terence E. *Interpretation Exodus*. Louisville, KY: John Knox, 1991.
Freud, S. *The Interpretation of Dreams*. Translated by James Strachey. New York: Avon, 1965.

———. "Three Essays on the Theory of Sexuality." In *The Standard Edition of the Complete Psychological Works of Sigmund Freud*, vol. 7, translated and edited by J. Strachey. 1905. Reprint. London: Hogarth, 1953.

Frisby, D., and M. Featherstone. *Simmel on Culture: Selected Writings*. London: SAGE, 1997.

Frye, N. *Anatomy of Criticism: Four Essays*. Princeton: Princeton University Press, 1971.

Frymer-Kensky, T. "The Strange Case of the Suspected Sotah." *VT* 34 (1984) 18–24.

Fung, Ronald Y. K. "Some Pauline Pictures of the Church." *EQ* 53 (1981) 97–100.

Furlong, Andy, and Fred Cartmel. *Young People and Social Change: Individualization and Risk in Late Modernity*. Philadelphia: Open University Press, 1997.

Furnish, Victor Paul. *II Corinthians*. New York: Doubleday, 1984.

Futrell, Alison. *The Roman Games: A Source Book*. Oxford: Blackwell, 2006.

Gabriel, Yiannis, and Tim Lang. *The Unmanageable Consumer: Contemporary Consumption and Its Fragmentations*. London: SAGE, 1995.

Gaca, Kathy L. *The Making of Fornication*. Berkeley: University of California Press, 2003.

Gager, John G. "Body-Symbols and Social Reality: Resurrection, Incarnation and Asceticism in Early Christianity." *Religion* 12 (1982) 345–64.

Gamble, Richard C. *Calvin's Opponents*. Vol. 5: Of *Articles on Calvin and Calvinism*. New York: Garland, 1992.

Gandhi, Virchand. *Religion and Philosophy of the Jainas*. Ahmerdabad, India: Jain International, 1993.

Garner, David. "Survey Says: Body Image Poll Results." *Psychology Today*. February 1997. No pages. Online: http://www.psychologytoday.com/articles/index.php?term=pto-19970201-000023&page=2.

Garnsey, Peter. *Social Status and Legal Privilege in the Roman Empire*. Oxford: Clarendon, 1970.

Garrett, Valery. *Chinese Clothing*. Oxford: Oxford University Press, 1994.

Garrigou-Lagrange, R. *Christian Perception and Contemplation—According to St Thomas Aquinas and St John of the Cross*. Translated by Sr. Dorothea Doyle. St. Louis: Harder, 1939.

Geeraerts, D., and H. Cuyckens. *The Oxford Handbook of Cognitive Linguistics*. New York: Oxford University Press, 2007.

George, A. Raymond. "The Number of the Sacraments." *SJT* 4 (1951) 157–72.

Gerrish, B. A. "'To the Unknown God': Luther and Calvin on the Hiddenness of God." *The Journal of Religion* 53 (1973) 263–92.

Gerstenberger, Erhard S. *Leviticus: A Commentary*. Louisville, KY: Westminster John Knox, 1993.

Gess, W. F. "Nature or God?" and "Christ's Atonement for Sin." In *The Foundations of Our Faith: Ten Papers Read before a Mixed Audience of Men*, edited by Gess Auberlen et al., 27–45. London: Strahan, 1863.

Geyer, Douglas W. *Fear, Anomaly and Uncertainty in the Gospel of Mark*. London: Scarecrow, 2002.

Gibbs, Norman B., and Lee W. Gibbs. "'In Our Nature': The Kenotic Christology of Chales Chauncy." *HTR* 85 (1992) 217–33.

Gibbs, R. "Comprehending Figurative Referential Descriptions." *Journal of Experimental Psychology: Learning, Memory, and Cognition* 16 (1990) 56–66.

Gibson, Mel (producer, director and writer). *The Passion of the Christ* (film). Icon Production, Newmarkets Films, 2004.

Gibson, Michael. "The Absurdity and Sublimity of Christ: Christology in the Films of Ingmar Bergman." No pages. Online: http://gradtheo.yak.net/12/The_Absurdity_and_Sublimity_of_Christ.pdf.

Giddens, Anthony. *Modernity and Self-Identity: Self and Society in the Late Modern Age.* Cambridge: Polity, 1991.

———. *Sociology.* Cambridge: Polity, 1989.

———. *The Transformation of Intimacy: Sexuality, Love and Eroticism in Modern Societies.* Cambridge: Polity, 1992.

Gilbert, Paul. "Body Shame: A Biopsychosocial Conceptualisation and Overview with Treatment Implications." In *Body Shame*, edited by Paul Gilbert and Jeremy Miles, 6–14. New York: Brunner-Routledge, 2002.

Gilbert, Paul, and Jeremy Miles. *Body Shame.* New York: Brunner-Routledge, 2002.

Gilby, Thomas. *St. Thomas Aquinas Philosophical Texts.* Durham: Labyrinth, 1982.

Gilmore, David D. "Honor, Honesty, Shame: Male Status in Contemporary Andalusia." In *Honor and Shame and the Unity of the Mediterranean*, edited by David D. Gilmore, 90–103. Washington, DC American Anthropological Association, 1986.

Girard, René. *The Scapegoats.* London: Athlone, 1986.

Glasson, T. Francis. "2 Corinthians v. 1–10 *versus* Platonism." *SJT* 43 (1990) 146–47.

Glover, Jonathan. *The Philosophy and Psychology of Personal Identity.* London: Penguin, 1988.

Goatly, Andrew. *The Language of Metaphors.* London: Routledge, 1997.

Godden, Malcolm. "An Old English Penitential Motif." *Anglo-Saxon England* 2 (1973) 221–39.

Godet, Frederick. *Commentary on the Gospel according to St. John.* Translated by Timothy Dwight. New York: Funk and Wagnells, 1886.

Godet, F. *The Gospel of St. Luke.* Vol. 2. Translated by M. D. Cusin. Edinburgh: T. & T. Clark, 1957.

Goldingay, John. "Old Testament Sacrifice and the Death of Christ." In *Atonement Today*, edited by John Goldingay, 3–20. London: SPCK, 1995.

———. "Your Iniquities Have Made a Separation between You and God." In *Atonement Today*, edited by John Goldingay, 39–53. London: SPCK, 1995.

Goldhill, Simon. "Viewing and the Viewer: Empire and the Culture of Spectacle." In *The Body Aesthetic*, edited by Tobin Siebers, 42–45. Ann Arbor, MI: University of Michigan, 2000.

Goodacre, Mark. "Scripturalization in Mark's Crucifixion Narrative." In *The Trial and Death of Jesus: Essays on the Passion Narrative in Mark*, edited by Geert Van Oyen and Tom Shepherd, 34–47. Paris: Peeters, 2006.

Goodson, Aileen. *Therapy, Nudity, and Joy.* Los Angeles: Elysium, 1991.

Gore, Charles. *Dissertations on Subjects Connected with the Incarnation.* New York: Scribner's Sons, 1895.

———. *The Incarnation of the Son of God.* New York: Scribner's Sons, 1905.

Gorham, Karen, and Dave Leal. *Naturism and Christianity: Are They Compatible?* Grove Ethics E118. Cambridge: Grove, 2000.

Gorman, Michael J. *Apostle of the Crucified Lord: A Theological Introduction to Paul and His Letters.* Grand Rapids: Eerdmans, 2004.

———. *Cruciformity: Paul's Narrative Spirituality of the Cross*. Grand Rapids: Eerdmans, 2001.

———. *Elements of Biblical Exegesis: A Basic Guide for Students and Ministers*. Peabody, MA: Hendrickson, 1998.

———. *Inhabiting the Cruciform God: Kenosis, Justification & Theosis in Paul's Narrative Soteriology*. Grand Rapids: Eerdmans, 2009.

Gorringe, Timothy J. *The Education of Desire*. London: SCM, 2001.

Goschler, Juliana. "Embodiment and Body Metaphors." No pages. Online: http://www.metaphorik.de/09/goschler.htm.

The Gospel of Nicodemus. Or *Acts of Pilate*. In *The Apocryphal New Testament*, 60. Boston: Chase, Nichols & Hill, 1860.

Goulder, M. D. "Exegesis of Genesis 1–3 in the New Testament." *Journal of Jewish Studies* 43 (1992) 226–29.

———. *Isaiah as Liturgy*. Aldershot, UK: Ashgate, 2004.

Gowan, Donald E. *Ezekiel*. Atlanta: John Knox, 1985.

———. *From Eden to Babel: A Commentary on the Book of Genesis 1–11*. Grand Rapids: Eerdmans, 1988.

Gowen, Donald E. *Genesis 1–11*. Edinburgh: Handsel, 1988.

Graaf, John de. *Affluenza: The All-Consuming Epidemic*. 2nd ed. San Francisco: Berrett-Koehler, 2005.

Grant, Colin. "The Abandonment of Atonement." *Kings Theological Review* 9 (1986) 1–8.

Gray, Michael. "Postmodernism: The Church and Its Response as We Move toward the Twenty-First Century." M.Div. thesis, Western Evangelical Seminary/GFU 1997.

Grayston, Kenneth. *Dying, We Live*. London: 1990.

Grazer, Brian (producer), and Ron Howard (director). *Da Vinci Code* (film). Imagine Entertainment, 2006.

Green, E. M. B. *The Meaning of Salvation*. London: Hodder and Stoughton, 1965.

Green, Joel B. *Body, Soul, and Human Life: The Nature of Humanity in the Bible*. Milton Keynes, UK: Paternoster, 2008.

———. "Death of Jesus." In *Dictionary of Jesus and the Gospel*, edited by Joel B. Green et al., 146–63. Leicester, UK: InterVarsity, 1992.

———. "Kaleidoscopic View." In *The Nature of the Atonement: Four Views*, edited by James Beilby and Paul R. Eddy, 157–85. Downers Grove, IL: InterVarsity, 2006.

———. "Must We Imagine the Atonement in Penal Substitutionary Terms? Questions, Caveats and a Plea." In *The Atonement Debate: Papers from the London Symposium on the Theology of Atonement*, edited by Derek Tidball et al., 153–71. Grand Rapids: Zondervan, 2008.

Green, Joel B., and Mark D. Baker. *Recovering the Scandal of the Cross: Atonement in New Testament & Contemporary Contexts*. Downers Grove, IL: InterVarsity, 2000.

Green, Michael. *Matthew*. BST. Leicester, UK: InterVarsity, 1988.

Greengus, S. "Old Babylonian Marriage Ceremonies and Rites." *Journal of Cuneiform Studies* 20 (1966) 55–72.

———. "The Old Babylonian Marriage Contract." *Journal of the American Oriental Society* 89 (1969) 515.

Gregory I. *Dialogues*. Translated by Odo John Zimmerman. FOC 39. New York: OSB, 1959.

Grensted, L. W. *A Short History of the Doctrine of the Atonement*. Manchester, UK: Manchester University Press, 1920.
Grenz, Stanley J. *A Primer on Postmodernism*. Grand Rapids: Eerdmans, 1996.
———. *Theology for the Community of God*. Grand Rapids: Eerdmans, 1994.
———. *The Social God and the Relational Self: A Trinitarian Theology of the Imago Dei*. Louisville, KY: Westminster John Knox, 2001.
Grenz, Stanley J., and John R. Franke. *Beyond Foundationalism: Shaping Theology in a Postmodern Context*. Louisville, KY: Westminster John Knox, 2001.
Grenz, Stanley J., et al. "Kenosis, Kenoticism." In *Pocket Dictionary of Theological Terms*, 70–71. Downer Grove: InterVarsity, 1999.
Grohmann, Marianne. "Ambivalent Images of Birth in Psalm VII 15." *VT* 55 (2005) 439–49.
Guest, Deryn. "Hiding Behind the Naked Women in Lamentations: A Recriminative Response." *Biblical Interpretation* 7 (1999) 413–48.
Gumbel, Nicky. *Question of Life*. Eastbourne, UK: Kingsway, 1993.
Gundry, Robert H. *Matthew*. Grand Rapids: Eerdmans, 1982.
Gunton, Colin. *The Actuality of the Atonement: A Study of Metaphor, Rationality and the Christian Tradition*. Edinburgh: T. & T. Clark, 1988.
———. "Karl Barth's Doctrine of Election as Part of His Doctrine of God." *JTS* 25 (1974) 381–92.
———. *The One, the Three, and the Many: God, Creation, and the Culture of Modernity*. Cambridge: Cambridge University Press, 1993.
———. "Two Dogmas Revisited: Edward Irving's Christology." *SJT* 41 (1988) 359–76.
———. *Yesterday and Today: A Study of Continuities in Christology*. Grand Rapids: Eerdmans, 1983.
Guy, Laurie. "'Naked' Baptism in the Early Church: The Rhetoric and the Reality." *JRH* 27 (2003) 133–42.
Haak, Robert D. *Habakkuk*. New York: Brill, 1992.
Habets, Myk. "Reforming Theosis." In *Theosis: Deification in Christian Theology*, edited by Stephen Finlan and Vladimir Kharlamov, 146–48. Eugene, OR: Pickwick, 2006.
Hagner, Donald A. *Matthew 1–13*. WBC. Dallas: Word, 1993.
———. *Matthew 14–28*. WBC. Dallas: Word, 1995.
Hall, Carrie A. *From Hoopskirts to Nudity*. Caldwell, ID: Caxton, 1938.
Hall, Manly P. *Self Unfoldment by Disciplines of Realization*. Los Angeles: Philosophical Research Society, 1942.
Hall, Robert G. "Circumcision." In *Anchor Bible Dictionary*, edited by David Noel Freedman, 1025–31. New York: Doubleday, 1992.
Hall, Stuart. "The Work of Representation." In *Representation: Cultural Representations and Signifying Practices*, edited by Stuart Hall, 1–74. London: SAGE, 1997.
Hammond, T. C. *In Understanding Be Men*. 6th ed. Leicester, UK: InterVarsity, 1936.
Harakas, Stanley Samuel. *Health and Medicine in the Eastern Orthodox Tradition*. New York: Crossroad, 1990.
Hardy, Daniel W. "Created and Redeemed Sociality." In *On Being the Church: Essays on the Christian Community*, edited by Colin E. Gunton and Daniel W. Hardy, 21–47. Edinburgh: T. & T. Clark, 1989.
Hardy, Edward Rochie. "An Exposition of the Faith: Selections from the Work *Against Heresies* by Irenaeus, Bishop of Lyons." In *The Library of Christian Classics*, Vol. 1, translated and edited by Cyril C. Richardson et al., 343–98. London: SCM, 1953.

Haren, Michael J. "The Naked Young Man: A Historian's Hypothesis on Mark 14.51–52." *Biblica* 79 (1998) 525–31.
Hargreaves, John. *A Guide to St. Mark's Gospel*. London: SPCK, 1965.
Harman, Allan. *Isaiah*. Fearn, UK: Christian Focus, 2005.
Harnack, Adolph von. *History of Dogma*. Translated by James Millar. 7 vols. London: Williams & Norgate, 1897.
Harris, Murray J. *The Second Epistle to the Corinthians*. NIGTC. Grand Rapids: Eerdmans, 2005.
Harrison, Nonna Verna. "Theosis as Salvation: An Orthodox Perspective." *Pro Ecclesia* 6 (1997) 432–33.
Hart, Bentley David. "The Bright Morning of the Soul: John of the Cross on *Theosis*." *Pro Ecclesia* 12 (2003) 324–43.
Hart, Trevor. "Redemption and Fall." In *The Cambridge Companion to Christian Doctrine*, edited by C. E. Gunton, 189–206. Cambridge: Cambridge University Press, 1997.
Hartley, John E. *Leviticus*. WBC. Dallas: Word, 1992.
Hartman, William E., and Marilyn A. Fithian. "Nudism." No pages. Online: http://www2.hu-berlin.de/sexology/GESUND/ARCHIV/SEN/CH18.HTM.
Harvey, John. "A New Look at the Christ Hymn in Philippians 26–11." *ExpT* 76 (1965) 337–39.
Harvey, Susan Ashbrook. "Embodiment in Time and Eternity: A Syriac Perspective." *SVTQ* 43 (1999) 121–24.
Hastings, Anne Stirling. *Treating Sexual Shame*. Northvale, NJ: Aronson, 1998.
Hatt, Christine. *Clothes of the Ancient World*. London: Belitha, 2001.
Hatton, Stephen B. "Mark's Naked Disciple: The Semiotics and Comedy of Following." *Neotestamentica* 35 (2001) 35–48.
Hawkins, D. J. B. *The Essentials of Theism*. New York: Sheed and Ward, 1950.
Hayden-Roy, Priscilla. "Hermeneutica Gloriae vs. Hermeneutica Crucis: Sebastian Franck and Martin Luther on the Clarity of Scripture." *Modern Languages and Literatures*. Department of German Language and Literature Papers, University of Nebraska, Lincoln. 1990. No pages. Online: http://digitalcommons.unl.edu/modlanggerman/24.
Hayes, Stephen. "Evangelism and Liberation." *Theologia Evangelica* 25.2 (1992) 49–57.
———. *The IViyo loFakazi bakaKristu and the KwaNdebele Mission of the Anglican Diocese of Pretoria*. M.Th. thesis, Pretoria: University of South Africa, 1993.
Healey, Antonette DiPaolo. *The Old English Vision of St. Paul*. Cambridge, MA: Speculum Anniversary Monographs 2, 1978.
Hegel, Georg Wilhelm Friedrich. *The Christian Religion: Lectures on the Philosophy of Religion*. Translated and edited by Peter C. Hodgson, based on the edition by Georg Lasson. Missoula, MT: Scholars, 1979.
Heger, Paul. "Source of Law in the Biblical and Mesopotamian Law Collections." *Biblica* 86 (2005) 324–42.
Heim, S. Mark. *Saved from Sacrifice: A Theology of the Cross*. Grand Rapids: Eerdmans, 2006.
Hemer, Colin J. *The Letters to the Seven Churches of Asia*. Sheffield, UK: JSOT, 1986.
Hendriksen, William. *Luke*. Edinburgh: Banner of Truth, 1978.
———. *Matthew*. New Testament Commentary. Grand Rapids: Baker, 1973.
Hengel, Martin. *Crucifixion*, London: SCM, 1977.

Herbal Vitality. No pages, Online: http://www.herbalvitality.info/.
Herbert, A. S. *The Book of the Prophet Isaiah: Chapters 1–39*, Cambridge: Cambridge University Press, 1973.
Herbert, George. *The Temple: Sacred Poems and Private Ejaculations*. London: Bell & Daldy, 1857.
Herek, Gregory M. "Homosexuality." In *Encyclopedia of Psychology*, edited by Alan E. Kazdin, 149–150. Oxford: Oxford University Press, 2000.
Hettlinger, R. F. "2 Corinthians 5.1–10" *SJT* 10 (1957) 179–94.
Hewes, Gordon. "The History of Man's Culture." In *Man, Earth and the Challenges*. Planet Earth Conference. London: Synergetic, 1981.
Hillar, Marian. "Philo of Alexandria (c.20 BCE–40 CE)." *The Internet Encyclopedia of Philosophy*. No pages. Online: http://www.iep.utm.edu/p/philo.htm.
Hiler, Hilaire. *From Nudity to Raiment*. London: Foyle, 1929.
Hillers, Delbert R. *Covenant: The History of a Biblical Idea*. Baltimore: Johns Hopkins Press, 1969.
———. *Lamentations: Introduction, Translation, and Notes*. Anchor Bible. New York: Doubleday, 1972.
———. *Treaty Curses and the O. T. Prophets*. Biblica et Orientalia 16. Rome: Pontifical Biblical Institute, 1964.
Hippolytus. *The Apostolic Tradition of Hippolytus*. Translated by Burton Scott Easton. Cambridge: Cambridge University Press, 1934.
Hobbs, T. R. "Reflections on Honor, Shame, and Covenant Relations." *JBL* 116 (1997) 501–20.
Hodge, A. A. *The Atonement*. Grand Rapids: Baker, 1974.
Hodge, Charles. *Second Epistle to the Corinthians: An Exposition*. London: Banner of Truth, 1959.
———. *Systematic Theology*. London: Clarke, 1960.
Hoebel, E. Adamson. *Anthropology: The Study of Man*. New York: McGraw-Hill, 1972.
Holland, D., and N. Quinn. *Cultural Models in Language and Thought*. Cambridge: Cambridge University Press, 1987.
"The Holy Scriptures: Like Christ, Divine and Human." No pages. Online: http://www.angelfire.com/ny4/djw/lutherantheology.divineandhuman.html.
Hook, Sidney. *Religious Experience and Truth*. New York: New York University Press, 1961.
Hooker, Morna D. *From Adam to Christ: Essays on Paul*. Cambridge: Cambridge University Press, 1990.
———. *The Gospel according to St Mark*. London: Black, 1991.
———. *Interchange and Atonement*. Manchester, UK: John Rylands University Library of Manchester, 1978.
———. *Not Ashamed of the Gospel: New Testament Interpretations of the Death of Christ*. Carlisle, UK: Paternoster, 1994.
———. "Philippians 2:6–11." In *Jesus und Paulus*, edited by E. Earle Ellis and Erich Grässer, 151–64. Göttingen: Vandenhoeck & Ruprecht.
Hopko, Thomas. *The Lenten Spring*. Crestwood, NY: St Vladimir's Seminary Press, 1983.
Horan, B. W. "The Apostolic Kerygma in Philippians ii. 6–9." *ExpT* 62 (1950) 60–61.
Horn, Marilyn J., and Lois Gurel. *The Second Skin*. Boston: Mifflin, 1981.
Hughes, Philip E. "Adam and His Posterity." *EQ* 14 (1942) 164–65.

———. *The True Image*. Grand Rapids: Eerdmans, 1989.
Hunter, David G. "On the Sin of Adam and Eve: A Little-known Defense of Marriage and Childbearing by Ambrosiaster." *HTR* 82 (1989) 291–92.
Hurtado, Larry W. *Mark*, NIBC. Peabody, MA: Hendrickson, 1983.
Hyatt-Williams, Arthur. *Cruelty, Violence, and Murder: Understanding the Criminal Mind*. London: Aronson, 1998.
Iersel, Bas M. F. van. *Mark. A Reader-Response Commentary*. Translated by W. H. Bisscheroux, Sheffield, UK: Sheffield Academic, 1998.
Indurkhya, B. *Metaphor and Cognition*. Dordrecht: Kluwer, 1992.
International Association for Near-Death Studies. No pages. Online: http://www.iands.org/.
Irenaeus. *The Scandal of the Incarnation: Irenaeus Against the Heresies*. Edited by Hans Urs von Balthasar, translated by John Saward. San Francisco: Ignatius, 1990.
Irving, Edward. *The Collected Writings of Edward Irving in Five Volumes*. Vol. 5. Edited by G. Carlyle. 1828. Reprint. London: Strachan, 1865.
Jackson, Howard M. "Why the Youth Shed His Cloak and Fled Naked: The Meaning and Purpose of Mark 14:51–52." *JBL* 116 (1997) 273–89.
Jacobus de Voragine. *The Golden Legend: Readings on the Saints*. Vol. 1. Translated by William Caxton Volone, edited by F. S. Ellis. New York: AMS, 1973.
Jaggard, Alison M., and Susan Bordo. *Gender, Body, Knowledge: Feminist Reconstructions of Being and Knowing*. London: Rutgers University Press, 1989.
Jain Cultural Reseach Society. *Jainism the Oldest Living Religion*. Varanasi, India: Jain Cultural Research Society, 1951.
Jakes, T. D. *Naked and Not Ashamed*. Shippensburg, PA: Treasure House, 1995.
James, Oliver. *Affluenza: How to be Successful and Stay Sane*. London: Vermilion, 2007.
———. *The Selfish Capitalist: Origins of Affluenza*. London: Vermilion, 2008.
James, William. *The Principles of Psychology*. Vol. 1. London: Macmillan, 1902.
Janzen, J. Gerald. *Job*. Interpretation. Atlanta: John Knox, 1985.
Jeffery, Steve, et al. *Pierced for Our Transgressions: Rediscovering the Glory of Penal Substitution*. Nottingham, UK: InterVarsity, 2007.
Jennings, Willie James. "The Desire of the Church." In *The Community of the Word: Toward an Evangelical Ecclesiology*, edited by Mark Husbands and Daniel J. Treier, 235–50. Downers Grove, IL: InterVarsity, 2005.
Jenson, Robert W. "Theosis." *Dialog* 32.2 (1993) 108–12.
Jeremias, Joachin. "Zu Phil ii 7: ΕΑΥΤΟΝ ΕΚΕΝΩΣΕΝ." *Novum Testamentum* 6 (1963) 182–88.
Jerome. *Homilies of St Jerome*. Washington, DC: The Catholic University of America Press, 1964.
Jewett, Robert. *Romans: A Commentary*. Minneapolis: Fortress, 2007.
Jobling, D. "The Myth Semantics of Gen. 2.4b—3.24." *Semeia* 18 (1980) 41–49.
John of Ruysbroeck. *The Adornment of the Spiritual Marriage*. Ch. 5—Of Patient Endurance (1293–1381). Translated by C. A. Wynschenk Dom, edited by Evelyn Underhill. London: Watkins, 1951.
John of the Cross. *The Complete Works of Saint John of the Cross*. Translated and edited by E. Allison Peers. Wheathampstead, UK: Clarke, 1974.
Johnson, Alan F., and Robert E. Webber. *What Christians Believe: A Biblical and Historical Summary*. Grand Rapids: Zondervan, 1993.

Johnson, Ian. "Clothing and Nakedness in the Bible." No pages. Online: http://members.tripod.com/ian_j_site2/.
———. "The Law of Moses, Nakedness, Worship and Close Relatives." No pages. Online: http://members.tripod.com/ian_j_site2/NWR.htm.
———. "Nakedness as a Form of Symbolic Expression in the Old Testament." No pages. Online: http://members.tripod.com/ian_j_site2/OTSymbolic.htm.
———. "Nakedness as Judgement." No pages. Online: http://members.tripod.com/ian_j_site2/NJ.htm.
Johnson, M. *The Body in the Mind: The Bodily Basis of Meaning, Imagination, and Reason*. Cambridge: Cambridge University Press, 1987.
Johnson, Kim K. P., et al. *Fashion Foundations: Early Writings on Fashion and Dress*. Oxford: Berg, 2003.
Johnstone, William. *1 & 2 Chronicles*. Vol. 2. Sheffield, UK: Sheffield Academic, 1997.
Jones, Alexander. *The Gospel according to St Mark*. London: Chapman, 1965.
Jones, Doug. *Physical Attractiveness and the Theory of Sexual Selection*. Ann Arbor, MI: Museum of Anthropology, University of Michigan, 1996.
Jones, Tony. *Soul Shaper: Exploring Spirituality and Contemplative Practices in Youth Ministry*. Grand Rapids: Zondervan, 2003.
Jordan, James B. *The Law of the Covenant: An Exposition of Exodus 21-23*. Tyler, TX: Institute for Christian Economics, 1984.
Jordan, Mark D. "God's Body." In *Queer Theology: Rethinking the Western Body*, edited by Gerard Loughlin, 281–92. Oxford: Blackwell, 2007.
Josephus, Flavius. *The Antiquities of the Jews*. In "The Work of Flavius Josephus." No pages. Online: http://bible.christiansunite.com/jos.cgi?b=ant13&c=14.
Josephus. *Jewish Antiquities*. Translated by Louis H. Feldman, London: Heinemann, 1969.
Josephus. *The Jewish War: Newly Translated with Extensive Commentary and Archaeological Background Illustrations*. Edited by Gaalya Cornfield. Grand Rapids: Zondervan, 1982.
Josephus. *The Jewish War*, in *Josephus: In Nine Volumes*, Vol. 3—The Jewish War. Books IV–IV. Translated by H. St. J. Thackeray, London: Heinemann, 1968.
Jubilees. No pages. Online: http://wesley.nnu.edu/biblical_studies/noncanon/ot/pseudo/jubilee.htm.
Jubilees. Translated by R. H. Charles, *Apocrypha and Pseudepigrapha of the Old Testament*. Oxford: Clarendon, 1913.
Jury, Louise. "Artist Apes the Crucifixion to Save Threatened Gorillas." No pages. Online: http://www.thisislondon.co.uk/standard/article-23756203-artist-apes-the-crucifixion-to-save-threatened-gorillas.do.
Jüngel, Eberhard. *God as the Mystery of the World*. Translated by Darrell L. Guder. Grand Rapids: Eerdmans, 1983.
Kaiser, Walter C. *Micah-Malachi*. Nashville: Thomas Nelson, 1992.
Karlberg, Mark W. "The Original State of Adam: Tensions Within Reformed Theology." *EQ* 87 (1987) 291–309.
Kartsonis, Anna D. *Anastasis: The Making of an Image*. Princeton: Princeton University Press, 1986.
Kashubeck-West, S., et al. "Separating the Effects of Gender and Weight-loss Desire on Body Satisfaction and Disordered Eating Behavior." *Sex Roles: A Journal of*

Research (October 2005). No pages. Online: http://findarticles.com/p/articles/mi_m2294/is_7-8_53/ai_n16083940.

Kasliwal, R. M. "Concept of Soul in Jaina Philosophy and its Scientific Interpretation." In *Perspectives in Jaina Philosophy and Culture*, edited by Jain Shri Satish Kumar and Kamal Chand Sogani, 4–5. New Delhi: Ahimsa, 1985.

Kass, Leon R. *The Beginning of Wisdom*. Chicago: University of Chicago Press, 2003.

Katz, A. "On Choosing the Vehicles of Metaphors: Referential Concreteness, Semantic Distance, and Individual Differences." *Journal of Memory and Language* 28 (1989) 486–99.

Kawano, Satsuki. "Japanese Bodies and Western Ways of Seeing in the Late Nineteenth Century." In *Dirt, Undress, and Difference*, edited by Adeline Masquelier, 151–53. Bloomington, IN: Indiana University Press, 2005.

Kazantzakis, Nikos. *The Last Temptation of Christ* (1883–1957). Translated by P. A. Bien. Oxford: Bruno Cassirer, 1961.

Käsemann, E. *Perspectives on Paul*. Translated by Margaret Kohl. London: SCM, 1971.

Keener, Craig S. *A Commentary on the Gospel of Matthew*. Cambridge: Eerdmans, 1999.

———. *Matthew*. Leicester, UK: InterVarsity, 1997.

———. *The Gospel of John*. Vol. 2. Peabody, MA: Hendrickson, 2003.

Keil, C. F., and F. Delitzsch, *Commentary on the Old Testament*. Vol. 7 *Isaiah (1866)*. Peabody, MA: Hendrickson, 2006.

Kellett, Stephen. "Shame–Fused acne." In *Body Shame*, edited Paul Gilbert and Jeremy Miles, 135–20. New York: Brunner-Routledge, 2002.

Kellner, Douglas. "Popular Culture and the Construction of Postmodern Identities." In *Modernity & Identity*, edited by Scott Lash and Jonathan Friedman, 141–77. Oxford: Blackwell, 1992.

Kennedy, H. A. A. *St Paul's Conception of Last Things*. London: Hodder and Stoughton, 1904.

Kennedy, Maev. "Christ Portrayed as Naked, Human and Divine." No pages. Online: http://www.guardian.co.uk/print/0,,3966434-103690,00.html.

Kenny, Anthony. *The Metaphysics of Mind*. Oxford: Clarendon, 1989.

Kent, Gerry, and Andrew R. Thompson. "The Development and Maintenance of Shame in Disfigurement." In *Body Shame*, edited by Paul Gilbert and Jeremy Miles, 103–14. New York: Brunner-Routledge, 2002.

Kessler, Martin, and Karel Deurloo. *A Commentary on Genesis: The Book of Beginnings*. New York: Paulist, 2004.

Kidner, Derek. *Genesis: An Introduction and Commentary*. Tyndale Commentary. Leicester, UK: InterVarsity, 1967.

———. *Psalms 73–150: A Commentary on Books III–V of the Psalms*. London: InterVarsity, 1975.

Kierkegaard, Søren. *The Concept of Anxiety: A Simple Psychologically Orienting Deliberation on the Dogmatic Issue of Hereditary Sin*. 1844. Translated by Reidar Thomte and Albert B. Anderson. Princeton: Princeton University Press, 1980.

Kim, Jung Hoon. *The Significance of Clothing Imagery in the Pauline Corpus*. London: T. & T. Clark, 2004.

Kimmel, Sara B., and James R. Mahalik. "Body Image Concerns of Gay Men: The Roles of Minority Stress and Conformity to Masculine Norms." *Journal of Consulting and Clinical Psychology* 73 (2005) 1185–90.

King, Philip J. "Circumcision—Who Did It, Who Didn't and Why." *BAR* 32.4 (2006) 52–53.
Kitayama, S. et al. "Culture, Self, and Emotion: A Cultural Perspective on 'Self-Conscious' Emotion." In *Self-Conscious Emotions: Shame, Guilt, Embarrassment, and Pride*, edited by J. P. Tangney and K. W. Fischer, 439–64. New York: Guilford, 1995.
Kittay, Eva Feder. *Metaphor*. Oxford: Clarendon, 1987.
Kittay, E. F., and A. Lehrer. "Semantic Fields and the Structure of Metaphor." *Studies in Language* 5 (1981) 31–63.
Kitwood, T. M. *What is Human?* London: InterVarsity, 1970.
Klager, Andrew P. "Retaining and Reclaiming the Divine: Identification and the Recapitulation of Peace in St. Irenaeus of Lyons' Atonement Narrative." In *Stricken by God? Nonviolent Identification and the Victory of Christ*, edited by Brad Jersak and Michael Hardin, 422–80. Grand Rapids: Eerdmans, 2007.
Klausner, Joseph. *Jesus of Nazareth: His Life, Times and Teaching*. London: Allen & Unwin, 1929.
Klawans, J. *Impurity and Sin in Ancient Judaism*. Oxford: Oxford University Press, 2000.
Klein, Naomi. *No Logo*. London: Flamingo, 2001.
Kline, Meredith G. *By Oath Consigned*. Grand Rapids: Eerdmans, 1968.
Knights, Chris. "Nudity, Clothing, and the Kingdom of God." *ExpT* 110.6 (1999) 178.
Knight, Jonathan. *Revelation*. Sheffield, UK: Sheffield Academic, 1999.
Knight, Kevin. "St. Cyril of Jerusalem." No pages. Online: http://www.newadvent.org/cathen/04595b.htm.
———. "St. Hippolytus." No pages. Online: http://www.newadvent.org/cathen/07362a.htme.
Knutson, F. B. "Naked." In *The International Standard Bible Encyclopedia*, Vol. 3, edited by Geoffrey W. Bromiley, 480. Grand Rapids: Eerdmans, 1986.
Koester, Craig R. *Hebrews: A New Translation with Introduction and Commentary*. Anchor Bible: New York: Doubleday, 2001.
———. *Symbolism in the Fourth Gospel*. Minneapolis: Fortress, 1995.
Koester, Helmut. "The Divine Human Being." *HTR* 78 (1985) 243–52.
Kohler, Kaufmann, and Emil G. Hirsch. "Crucifixion." No pages. Online: http://jewishencyclopedia.com/view.jsp?artid=905&letter=C.
Kohut, Heinz. *The Analysis of the Self*. New York: International University Press, 1971.
Korpel, M. C. A. *A Rift in the Clouds: Ugaritic and Hebrew Description of the Divine*. Ugaritic-Biblische Literatur 8. Münster: Ugarit, 1990.
Korsmeyer, Jerry D. *Evolution & Eden*. New York: Paulist, 1998.
Kraus, Hans-Joachim. *Psalms 60–150: A Commentary*. Translated by Hilton C. Oswald. Minneapolis: Augsburg, 1989.
Kruger, Paul A. "The Hem of the Garment in Marriage: The Meaning of the Symbolic Gesture in Ruth 3:9 and Ezek 16:8." *Journal of Northwest Semitic Languages* 12 (1984) 79–86.
Kruse, Colin G. *John*. Tyndale Commentary. Leicester, UK: InterVarsity, 2003.
———. *The Second Epistle of Paul to the Corinthians: An Introduction and Commentary*. Leicester, UK: InterVarsity, 1987.
Kulkarni, V. M. *Sudies in Jain Literature*. Ahmedabad, India: Shresthi Kasturbhai Lalbhai Smarak Nidhi, 2001.

Kuriyama, Shigehisa. *The Expressiveness of the Body and the Divergence of Greek and Chinese Medicine*. New York: Zone, 1999.
Kurz, G. *Metapher, Allegorie, Symbol*. 2nd ed. Kleine Vandenhoeck-Reihe. Göttingen: Vandenhoeck & Ruprecht, 1988.
De Lacey, D. R., and M. M. B. Turner. *Discovering the Bible: Jesus and the Gospels*. Amersham, UK: Hulton, 1983.
LaFollette, Hugh. *Personal Relationships, Love, Identity, and Morality*. Oxford: Blackwell, 1996.
Lagrange, M. J. *The Gospel according to Saint Mark*. London: Burns Oates & Washbourne, 1930.
Laidlaw, James. *Riches and Renunciation*. Oxford: Clarendon, 1995.
Lakoff, G. "A Figure of Thought." *Metaphor and Symbolic Activity* 1 (1986) 215–25.
———. "The Metaphorical Logic of Rape." *Metaphor and Symbolic Activity* 2 (1987) 73–79.
———. *Women, Fire, and Dangerous Things: What Categories Reveal about the Mind*. Chicago: University of Chicago Press, 1987.
Lakoff, George, and Mark Johnson. *Metaphors We Live By*. London: University of Chicago Press, 1980.
———. *Philosophy in the Flesh*. New York: Basic Books, 1998.
Lakoff, George, and Mark Turner. *More Than Cool Reason: A Field Guide to Poetic Metaphor*, Chicago: University of Chicago Press, 1989.
Lambden, Stephen N. "From Fig Leaves to Fingernails: Some Notes on the Garments of Adam and Eve in the Hebrew Bible and Select Early Postbiblical Jewish Writings." In *A Walk in the Garden*, edited by Paul Morris and Deborah Sawyer, 82–84. Sheffield, UK: Sheffield Academic, 1992.
Lampe, G. W. H. *A Patristic Greek Lexicon*. Oxford: Clarendon, 1961.
———. *The Seal of the Spirit*. London: Longmans, Green and Co., 1951.
Landy, Francis. "The Song of Songs and the Garden of Eden." *JBL* 98 (1979) 513–28.
Lane, Anthony N. S. "Lust: The Human Person as Affected by Disordered Desires." *EQ* 78 (2006) 21–35.
———. *The Lion Concise Book of Christian Thought*. Oxford: Lion, 1984.
Lane, William L. *The Gospel according to Mark*. London: Marshall, Morgan & Scott, 1974.
Langman, L. "Neon Cages: Shopping for Subjectivity." In *Lifestyle Shopping: The Subject of Consumption*, edited by R. Shields, 40–82. London: Routledge, 1992.
Langner, Lawrence. *The Importance of Wearing Clothes*. London: Constable, 1959.
Langer, Susanne Katherina Knauth. *Feeling and Form: A Theory of Art Developed from Philosophy in a New Key*. London: Routledge & Kegan Paul, 1985.
———. *Philosophy in a New Key: A Study in the Symbolism of Reason, Rite, and Art*. Cambridge: Harvard University Press, 1942.
Lasch, Christopher. *The Culture of Narcissism: American Life in an Age of Diminishing Expectations*. London: Norton, 1991.
Lash, Scott. *Sociology of Postmodernism*. London: Routledge, 1990.
Latimer, Joanna. "All-Consuming Passions: Materials and Subjectivity in the Age of Enhancement." In *The Consumption of Mass*, edited by Nick Lee and Rolland Munro, 157–73. Oxford: Blackwell, 2001.
Lawton, John Steward. "Books on the Person of Christ: Creed's Essay in 'Mysterium Christi.'" *ExpT* 64 (1952) 46–49.

Leach, Edmund. *Culture and Communication: The Logic By Which Symbols Are Connected. An Introduction to the Use of Structuralist Analysis in Social Anthropology.* Cambridge: Cambridge University Press, 1976.
Leech, Kenneth. *Experiencing God: Theology as Spirituality.* San Francisco: Harper & Row, 1985.
Lemos, T. M. "Shame and Mutilation of Enemies in the Hebrew Bible." *JBL* 125 (2006) 225–41.
Lerner, Anne Lapidus. "Pacing Change: The Impact of Feminism on Conservative Synagogues." In *New Jewish Feminism: Probing the Past, Forging the Future,* edited by Elyse Goldstein, 175–85. Woodstock, VT: Jewish Lights, 2009.
Letham, Robert. *The Work of Christ.* Leicester, UK: InterVarsity, 1993.
Leupold, H. C. *Exposition of the Psalms.* Welwyn, UK: Evangelical, 1974.
Lewinski, Jorge. *The Naked and the Nude.* London: Weidenfeld & Nicolson, 1987.
Lewis, C. Day. *The Poetic Image: The Clark Lectures given at Cambridge in 1946.* 1947. Reprint. London: Cape, 1972.
Lewis, C. S. *Mere Christianity.* New York: Macmillan, 1952.
———. *The Weight of Glory and Other Addresses.* New York: Macmillan, 1965.
Lightfoot, J. B. *Saint Paul's Epistle the Philippians.* Grand Rapids: Zondervan, 1953.
Litman, Jane Rachel. "If the Shoe Doesn't Fit, Examine the Soul." In *New Jewish Feminism: Probing the Past, Forging the Future,* edited by Elyse Goldstein, 250–57. Woodstock, VT: Jewish Lights, 2009.
Lloyd, Genevieve. *The Man of Reason: "Male" and "Female" in Western Philosophy.* London: Methuen, 1984.
Lloyd, Peter, et al. *Introduction to Psychology: an Integrated Approach.* London: Fontana, 1984.
Lloyd-Jones, D. M. "The Wedding Garment." *The Banner of Truth* 238 (1983) 11–18.
Locke, John. *An Essay Concerning Human Understanding.* 1690. Edited by A. S. Pringle-Pattison. Oxford: Clarendon, 1924.
Lods, A. *Israel From Its Beginnings to the Middle of the Eighth Century.* Translated by S. H. Hooke. London: Kegan Paul, Trench, Trubner, 1932.
Long, A. A., and D. N. Sedley. *The Hellenistic Philosophers.* Cambridge: Cambridge University Press, 1987.
Longman III, Tremper. *The Book of Ecclesiastes.* NICOT. Grand Rapids: Eerdmans, 1998.
Lorenz, Kate. "Do Pretty People Earn More?: Research, Reality Can be at Odds Over the Ugly Truth." No pages. Online: http://www.cnn.com/2005/US/Careers/07/08/looks/.
Lossky, Vladimir. *In the Image and Likeness of God.* Crestwood, NY: St. Vladimir's Seminary Press, 1974.
———. *The Vision of God.* Bedfordshire, UK: Faith, 1963.
Louis of Blois. *Oratory of the Faithful Soul; or, Devotions to the Most Holy Sacrament, and to Our Blessed Lady.* London: Richardson and Son, 1848.
———. *Spiritual Works of Louis of Blois.* 4th ed. Edited by John Edward Bowden. London: Washbourne, 1903.
Luther, Martin. *Luther's Works.* Edited by Jaroslav Pelikan and Helmut T. Lehmann. Saint Louis: Concordia, 1955.
Lyall, Francis. "Of Metaphors and Analogies: Legal Language and Covenant Theology." *SJT* 32 (1979) 1–17.

Lycan, William G. "An Irenic Idea about Metaphor." No pages. Online: http://www.unc.edu/~ujanel/Metaphor.htm (draft document 30/08/2003).
Lyon, David. *Postmodernity*. 2nd ed. Milton Keynes, UK: Open University Press, 2000.
―――. *Surveillance Society: Monitoring Everyday Life*. Milton Keynes, UK: Open University Press, 2001.
MacCormac, E. *A Cognitive Theory of Metaphor*. Cambridge: MIT, 1985.
MacKinnon, D. M. "Subjective and Objective Conceptions of Atonement." In *Prospect for Theology*, edited by F. G. Healey, 167–82. Welwyn: Nisbet, 1966.
Macky, P. W. *The Centrality of Metaphors to Biblical Thought: A Method for Interpreting the Bible*. Studies in the Bible and Early Christianity 19. New York: Mellen, 1990.
MacLaren, Alexander. *Expositions of Holy Scripture: St John Chs. XV to XXI*. London: Hodder & Stoughton, 1952.
MacQuarrie, John. "Kenoticism Reconsidered." *Theology* 77 (1974) 115–24.
―――. "The Pre-Existence of Jesus Christ." *ExpT* 77 (1966) 199–202.
Magonet, Jonathan. "The Themes of Genesis 2–3." In *A Walk in the Garden*, edited by Paul Morris and Deborah Sawyer, 39–46. Sheffield, UK: Sheffield Academic, 1992.
Mahalik, J. R., et al. "Development of the Conformity to Masculine Norms Inventory." *Psychology of Men and Masculinity* 4 (2003) 3–25.
Malina, Bruce J., and Richard L. Rohrbaugh. *Social-Science Commentary on the Synoptic Gospels*. Minneapolis: Fortress, 1992.
Mann, Alan. *Atonement for a "Sinless" Society: Engaging with an Emerging Culture*. Milton Keynes, UK: Paternoster, 2005.
Mann, C. S. *Mark*. Garden City, NY: Doubleday, 1986.
Mann, Thomas W. *Deuteronomy*. Louisville, KY: Westminster John Knox, 1995.
Mannermaa, Tuomo. "Justification and Theosis in Lutheran-Orthodox Perspective." In *Union with Christ: The New Finnish Interpretation of Luther*, edited by Carl E. Braaten and Robert W. Jenson, 26. Grand Rapids: Eerdmans, 1998.
Mannermaa, Tuomo. "Theosis as a Subject of Finnish Luther Research." *Pro Ecclesia* 4 (1995) 37–47.
Mannix, D. P. *The History of Torture*. 1964. Reprint. New York: Dell, 1983.
Marinatos, Nannó. *The Goddess and the Warrior*. London: Routledge, 2000.
Marshall, I. Howard. *Aspects of the Atonement: Cross and Resurrection in the Reconciliation of God and Humanity*. Milton Keynes, UK: Paternoster, 2007.
―――. "The Theology of the Atonement." In *The Atonement Debate: Papers from the London Symposium on the Theology of Atonement*, edited by Derek Tidball et al., 49–68. Grand Rapids: Zondervan, 2008.
Martin, Ralph P. "Bride, Bridegroom." In *New Bible Dictionary*, 3rd ed., edited by I. H. Marshall et al., 148. Leicester, UK: InterVarsity, 1996.
―――. *Philippians*. London: Oliphants, 1976.
―――. *Philippians*. WBC. Nashville: Thomas Nelson, 2004.
―――. *Reconciliation: A Study of Paul's Theology*. Atlanta: John Knox, 1981.
―――. *Worship in the Early Church*. Grand Rapids: Eerdmans, 1964.
Marx, Dalia. "Gender in Israeli Liberal Liturgy." In *New Jewish Feminism: Probing the Past, Forging the Future*, edited by Elyse Goldstein, 206–17. Woodstock, VT: Jewish Lights, 2009.
Mascall, E. L. *Existence and Analogy*. London: Longmans, Green and Co., 1949.
Maslow, Abraham. *Motivation and Personality*. 3rd ed. New York: Harper & Row, 1987.

Masquelier, Adeline. "An Introduction." In *Dirt, Undress, and Difference*, edited by Adeline Masquelier, 2–3. Bloomington, IN: Indiana University Press, 2005.

Maxwell, John C. *TPC—Deuteronomy*. Nashville: Thomas Nelson, 1987.

Mayes, A. D. H. *Deuteronomy*. New Century Bible Commentary. Grand Rapids: Eerdmans, 1979.

Mayo Clinic. "Crucifixion." No pages. Online: http://www.the-crucifixion.org/crucifixion.htm.

Mazza, Enrico. *Mystagogy: A Theology of Liturgy in the Patristic Age*. Translated by M. J. O'Connell. New York: Liturgical, 1989.

McCallum, Dennis. *The Death of Truth*. Minneapolis: Bethany House, 1996.

McCant, Jerry W. *2 Corinthians*. Sheffield, UK: Sheffield Academic, 1999.

McCarthy, Dennis J. *Old Testament Covenant: A Survey of Current Opinions*. Oxford: Blackwell, 1972.

———. *Treaty and Covenant: A Study in Form in the Ancient Oriental Documents and in the Old Testament*. Rome: Pontifical Biblical Institute, 1963.

McCauley, L. P., and A. A. Stephenson. *The Works of Saint Cyril of Jerusalem*. Vol. 2. FOC 64. Washington, DC The Catholic University of America Press, 1970.

McCloskey, Mary A. "Metaphor." *Mind* 73 (1964) 215–33.

McCormack, Bruce L. "Karl Barth's Christology as a Resource for a Reformed Version of Kenoticism." *IJST* 8 (2006) 243–51.

McCormich, Steve K. "Theosis in Chrysostom and Wesley: An Easter Paradigm on Faith and Love." *WTJ* 26 (1991) 38–103.

McCreary, D. R., et al. "The Drive for Muscularity and Masculinity: Testing the Associations Among Gender Role Traits, Behaviors, Attitudes, and Conflict." *Psychology of Men and Masculinity* 6 (2005) 83–94.

McCurley, Foster R. *Proclamation Commentaries: Genesis, Exodus, Leviticus, Numbers*. Philadelphia: Fortress, 1979.

McDonald, H. D. *The Atonement of the Death of Christ: In Faith, Revelation, and History*. Grand Rapids: Baker, 1985.

McDowell, Colin. *The Designer Scam*. London: Hutchinson, 1994.

McFague, Sallie. *Metaphorical Theology: Models of God in Religious Language*. Philadelphia: Fortress, 1982.

———. *Models of God: Theology for an Ecological, Nuclear Age*. Philadelphia: Fortress, 1987.

McFarland, Barbara, and T. L. Baker-Baumann. *Shame and the Body Image*. Deerfield Beach, FL: Health Communications Inc., 1990.

McFarlane, Graham. "Atonement, Creation and Trinity." In *The Atonement Debate: Papers from the London Symposium on the Theology of Atonement*, edited by Derek Tidball et al., 192–207. Grand Rapids: Zondervan, 2008.

McGee, Kevin J., and Merryn Gott. "Shame and the Ageing Body." In *Body Shame*, edited by Paul Gilbert and Jeremy Miles, 75–81. New York: Brunner-Routledge, 2002.

McGrath, A. E. *Christian Theology: An Introduction*. Oxford: Blackwell, 1994.

———. *The Enigma of the Cross*. London: Hodder & Stoughton, 1987.

McGuire, M. B. "Religion and the Body: Rematerializing the Human Body in the Social Sciences of Religion." *Journal for the Scientific Study of Religion* 29 (1990) 283–97.

McIlroy, David. "Honour and Shame." *Cambridge Papers: Towards a Biblical Mind* 14.2 (2005) 1–4.

McInerny, Ralph. *The Logic of Analogy*. The Hague: Nijhoff, 1961.
McIntyre, John. "Analogy." *SJT* 12 (1959) 1–20.
———. *Faith, Theology and Imagination*. Edinburgh: Handsel, 1987.
———. *The Shape of Soteriology*. Edinburgh: T. & T. Clark, 1992.
———. *St Anselm and His Critics: A Re-Interpretation of the Cur Deus Homo*. Edinburgh: Oliver and Boyd, 1954.
McKenna, David L. *Isaiah 40–66*. Nashville: Thomas Nelson, 1994.
———. *Job*. TPC. Nashville: Thomas Nelson, 1986.
McKnight, Scot. *A Community Called Atonement*. Nashville: Abingdon, 2007.
———. *Jesus and His Death: Historiography, the Historical Jesus, and Atonement Theory*. Waco, TX: Baylor University Press, 2005.
McLaren, Brian D. "The Cross as Prophetic Action." In *Proclaiming the Scandal of the Cross: Contemporary Images of the Atonement*, edited by Mark D. Baker, 110–21. Grand Rapids: Baker Academic, 2006.
Mehta, Mohan Lal. "Jaina Yoga." In *Perspectives in Jaina Philosophy and Culture*. Edited by Shri Satish Kumar Jain and Kamal Chand Sogani, 21. New Delhi: Ahimsa, 1985.
Melito of Sardis. *Homily on the Passion*. In *Studies and Documents—XII The Homily on the Passion by Melito Bishop of Sardis and Some Fragments of the Apocryphal Ezekiel*. Edited by Kirsopp Lake and Silva Lake. London: Christophers, 1940.
Mertens, Herman-Emiel. *Not the Cross, But the Crucified: An Essay in Soteriology*. Louvain: Peeters, 1992.
Miall, D. "The Body in Literature: Mark Johnson, Metaphor, and Feeling." *Journal of Literary Semantics* 26 (1997) 191–210. No pages. Online: http://www.ualberta.ca/~dmiall/reading/BODYMIND.htm.
———. *Metaphor: Problems and Perspective*. Brighton, UK: Harvester, 1982.
Midgley, Mary. "The Soul's Successor: Philosophy and the 'Body.'" In *Religion and the Body*, edited by Sarah Coakley, 53–70. Cambridge: Cambridge University Press, 1997.
Miles, Margaret R. *Carnal Knowing*. Tunbridge Wells, UK: Burns & Oates, 1989.
Miles, Steven. *Consumerism: As a Way of Life*. London: SAGE, 1998.
Milgrom, Jacob. *Leviticus 17–22: A New Translation with Introduction and Commentary*. Anchor Bible. London: Doubleday, 2000.
———. *Leviticus 23–27*. Anchor Bible. New York: Doubleday, 2002.
Millar, J. G. "Living at the Place of Decision: Time and Place in the Framework of Deuteronomy." In *Time and Place in Deuteronomy*, JSOTSup 179, by J. Gordon McConville and J. G. Millar, 15–88. Sheffield, UK: Sheffield Academic, 1994.
Miller, Patrick D. *Deuteronomy: A Bible Commentary for Teaching and Preaching*. Interpretation. Louisville, KY: John Knox, 1990.
Miller, Rowland S. *Embarrassment: Poise and Peril in Everyday Life*. New York, Guilford, 1996.
Miller, Theo K., et al. "Therapy of Fashion." In *Dress, Adornment and Social Order*, edited by Mary Ellen Roach and Joanne Bubolz Eicher, 269–70. New York: Wiley & Sons, 1965.
Milne, Bruce. *Know the Truth*. Leicester, UK: InterVarsity, 1982.
———. *The Message of John*. Leicester, UK: InterVarsity, 1993.
Miscall, Peter D. *Isaiah*. Sheffield, UK: JSOT, 1993.
Molinos, Miguel de. *Spiritual Guide which Disentangles the Soul*. Edited and introduction by Kathleen Lyttelton, note by H. Scott Holland. London: Methuen, 1907.

Moltmann, Jürgen. *The Crucified God: The Cross of Christ as the Foundation and Criticism of Christian Theology.* Translated by R. A. Wilson and John Bowden. London: SCM, 1974.

———. *Experiences of God.* Translated by Margaret Kohl. London: SCM, 1980.

———. *The Spirit of Life.* Translated by Margaret Kohl. Minneapolis: Fortress, 1992.

———. *The Trinity and the Kingdom of God: The Doctrine of God.* London: SCM, 1986.

Moltmann-Wendel, Elisabeth. *I Am My body: New Ways of Embodiment.* London: SCM, 1994.

Monteath, Sheryl A., and Marita P. McCabe. "The Influence of Societal Factors on Female Body Image." *The Journal of Social Psychology.* 137 (1997) 708–27.

Moo, Douglas. *Romans 1–8.* The Wycliffe Exegetical Commentary. Chicago: Moody, 1991.

Moore, George Foot. *Judaism.* Vol. 1–2, Cambridge: Harvard University Press, 1927.

Moreland, J. P., and Scott B. Rae. *Body and Soul: Human Nature and the Crisis in Ethics.* Downers Grove, IL: InterVarsity, 2000.

Morris, Henry M. *The Genesis Record.* Grand Rapids: Baker, 1976.

Morris, Leon. *The Apostolic Preaching of the Cross.* Grand Rapids: Eerdmans, 1956.

———. *The Atonement: Its Meaning and Significance.* Leicester, UK: InterVarsity, 1983.

———. *The Cross in the New Testament,* Grand Rapids: Eerdmans, 1999.

———. *The Epistle to the Romans.* Grand Rapids: Eerdmans, 1988.

———. *The Gospel according to John.* NICNT. Grand Rapids: Eerdmans, 1995.

———. *The Gospel according to Matthew.* Leicester, UK: InterVarsity, 1992.

———. *The Gospel according to St. Luke.* Leicester, UK: InterVarsity, 1974.

———. "Guilt and Forgiveness." In *New Dictionary of Theology,* edited by Sinclair B. Ferguson and David F. Wright, 285. Leicester, UK: InterVarsity, 1988.

Morrison, Andrew. "The Eye Turned Inward: Shame and the Self." In *The Many Faces of Shame,* edited by Donald L. Nathanson, 271–91. London: Guildford, 1987.

Mosser, Carl. "The Greatest Possible Blessing: Calvin and Deification." *SJT* 55 (2002) 36–57.

Motyer, Alec. *Isaiah.* Leicester, UK: InterVarsity, 1999.

Moule, C. F. D. "Further Reflection on Philippians 2:5–11." In *Apostolic History and the Gospels,* edited by W. Ward Gasque and Ralph P. Martin, 264–76. Grand Rapids: Eerdmans, 1970.

———. *Worship in the New Testament.* London: Lutterworth, 1961.

Mounce, Robert H. *Matthew.* Peabody, MA: Hendrickson, 1985.

Muirhead, I. A. "The Bride of Christ." *SJT* 5 (1952) 178–84.

Muller, Richard A. *Christ and the Decree: Christology and Predestination in Reformed Theology from Calvin to Perkins.* Grand Rapids: Baker, 1988.

Murphy, Yolanda, and Robert F. Murphy. *Women of the Forest.* London: Columbia University Press, 1974.

Murray, John. *The Epistle to the Romans: The English Text with Introduction, Exposition and Notes.* Edinburgh: Marshall, Morgan & Scott, 1967.

Müller, Jac. J. *The Epistles of Paul to the Philippians and Philemon.* Grand Rapids: Eerdmans, 1955.

Nasr, Seyyed Hossein, and Oliver Leaman. *History of Islamic Philosophy.* London: Routledge, 1996.

Natura Fellowship. "Naturist Christians." No pages. Online: http://www.naturist-christians.org/, 2003–2007.

"Near-Death Experiences and the Afterlife." No pages. Online: http://www.near-death.com/.

Need, Stephen W. *Human Language and Knowledge in the Light of Chalcedon*. New York: Lang, 1996.

Negrut, Paul. "Orthodox Soteriology: *Theosis*." *Churchman* 109 (1995) 154–70.

Nellas, Panayiotis. *Deification in Christ: Orthodox Perspectives on the Nature of the Human Person*. Translated by Normal Russell. Crestwood, NY: St. Vladimir's Seminary Press, 1987.

Nelson, James B. *Body Theology*. Louisville, KY: John Knox, 1992.

Nelson, P. G. *Nudity and Sexual Activity in the Media*. Caithness, UK: Whittles, 1992.

Neusner, Jacob. *The Mishnah: A New Translation*. New Haven, CT: Yale University Press, 1988.

Newbigin, Lesslie. *Foolishness to the Greeks: The Gospel and Western Culture*. London: SPCK, 1986.

———. *The Gospel in a Pluralist Society*. London: SPCK, 1989.

Neyrey, Jerome H. "Despising the Shame of the Cross: Honor and Shame in the Johannine Passion Narrative." *Semeia* 68 (1994) 113–37.

Neyrey, Jerome H. *Honor and Shame in the Gospel of Matthew*. Louisville, KY: Westminster John Knox, 1998.

———. "Nudity." In *Biblical Social Values and Their Meanings: A Handbook*, edited by John J. Pilch and Bruce J. Malina, 122–23. Peabody, MA: Hendrickson, 1993.

Nguyễn, Hưng, "Đúc tượng Thánh Gióng 85 tấn vào ngày 'trùng cửu'." *VNexpress* Friday 23 October 2009. No pages. Online: http://www.vnexpress.net/GL/Xa-hoi/2009/10/3BA14E18/.

Nhandan. "Hanoi Starts Casting of Thanh Giong Statue." No pates. Online: http://www.nhandan.com.vn/english/life/271009/life_dl.htm.

Niesel, Wilhelm. *The Theology of Calvin*. Translated by H. Knight. London: Lutterworth, 1956.

Nilsson, Kjell Ove. "Martin Luther: Is He Still Relevant?" *Currents in Theology and Mission* (April, 2005). No page. Online: http://findarticles.com/p/articles/mi_moMDO/is_2_32/ai_n15652762/pg_6.

Nineham, D. E. *Saint Mark*. Harmondsworth, UK: Penguin, 1963.

Nixon, Sean. "Exhibiting Masculinity." In *Representation: Cultural Representations and Signifying Practices*, edited by Stuart Hall, 291–336. London: SAGE, 1997.

Nochlin, Linda. *Bathers, Bodies, Beauty*. London: Harvard University Press, 2006.

Nolland, John. *Luke 18:35—24:53*. WBC. Dallas: Word, 1993.

———. *The Gospel of Matthew*. NIGTC. Grand Rapids: Eerdmans, 2005.

Noonan, Harold W. *Personal Identity*. London: Routledge, 1989.

Noppen, J. P. van., et al. *Metaphor: A Bibliography of Post-1970 Publications*. Amsterdam Studies in the Theory and History of Linguistic Science 17. Amsterdam: Benjamins, 1985.

Noppen, J. P. van., and E. Hols. *Metaphor II: A Classified Bibliography of Publications 1985 to 1990*. Amsterdam Studies in the Theory and History of Linguistic Science 20. Amsterdam: Benjamins, 1990.

Norden, Bryan W. Van. "The Virtue of Righteousness in Mencius." In *Confucian Ethics*, edited by Kwong-loi Shun and David B. Wong, 168–70. Cambridge: Cambridge University Press, 2004.

Norris, F. W. "Deification: Consensual and Cogent." *SJT* 49 (1996) 411–28.

Noth, Martin. *Leviticus: A Commentary.* London: SCM, 1965.
O'Brien, Peter T. *The Epistle to the Philippians: A Commentary on the Greek Text.* NIGTC. Grand Rapids: Eerdmans, 1991.
O'Connor, Kathleen M. "Jeremiah." In *The Women's Bible Commentary*, edited by Carol A. Newsom and Sharon H. Ringe, 178–86. Louisville, KY: Westminster John Knox, 1998.
Oden, Thomas C. *Life in the Spirit: Systematic Theology: Volume Three.* New York: HarperCollins, 1992.
Oepke, Albrecht. "γυμνός, γυμνότης, γυμνάζω, γυμνασία." In *Theological Dictionary of the New Testament*, Vol. 1, edited by Gerhard Kittel, 773–76. Grand Rapids: Eerdmans, 1964.
Ogilvie, Lloyd J. *Hosea, Joel, Amos, Obadiah, Jonah.* Nashville: Thomas Nelson, 1990.
Olivardia, R., et al. "Biceps and Body Image: The Relationship between Muscularity and Self-Esteem, Depression, and Eating Disorder Symptoms." *Psychology of Men and Masculinity* 5 (2004) 112–20.
Olyan, Saul M. "Honor, Shame, and Covenant Relations in Ancient Israel and Its Environment." *JBL* 115 (1996) 201–18.
Onians, Richard Broxton. *The Origins of European Thought.* Cambridge: Cambridge University Press, 1951.
Osborn, Eric. *Irenaeus of Lyons.* Cambridge: Cambridge University Press, 2001.
Osborne, Grant R. *Romans.* Leicester, UK: InterVarsity, 2004.
Osei-Bonsu, Joseph. "Does 2 Cor. 5.1–10 Teach the Reception of the Resurrection Body at the Moment of Death?" *JSNT* 28 (1986) 89.
Oshana, Marina A. L. "Moral Taint." *Metaphilosophy* 37 (2006) 363–64.
Ostriker, Alicia Suskin. *The Nakedness of the Fathers.* New Brunswick, NJ: Rutgers University Press, 1994.
Oswalt, John N. *The Book of Isaiah 1–39.* NICOT. Grand Rapids: Eerdmans, 1986.
Overland Club Vietnamese Culture Class. "Vietnamese Folk Literature." No pages. Online: http://www.overlandclub.jp/en/info/folk_literature.html.
Owen, John. *The Death of Death in the Death of Christ.* In *The Works of John Owen*, Vol. 10, edited by W. H. Goold, 140–421. London: Banner of Truth, 1967.
Painter, John. *Mark's Gospel.* London: Routledge, 1997.
Paivio, A., and Begg, I. *Psychology of Language.* Englewood Cliffs, NJ: Prentice-Hall, 1981.
Palmer, Nathaniel Humphrey. *Analogy: A Study of Qualification and Argument in Theology.* London: Macmillan, 1973.
Pannenberg, Wolfhart. *Jesus—God and Man.* Philadelphia: Westminster, 1974.
———. *Systematic Theology.* Vol. 2. Translated by Geoffrey W. Bromiley. Grand Rapids: Eerdmans, 1994.
Parker, David. "Original Sin: A Fresh Approach." *ERT* 13 (1989) 228–45.
Parry, Ryan. "Statue of Christ Made from Chocolate." *Mirror News.* No pages. Online: http://www.mirror.co.uk/news/top-stories/tm_headline=statue-of-christ-made-from-chocolate&method=full&objectid=18837036&siteid=89520-name_page.html.
Partee, Charles. "Calvin's Central Dogma Again." *Sixteenth Century Journal* 18 (1987) 191–99.
———. *The Theology of John Calvin.* Louisville, KY: Westminster John Knox, 2008.
Passion8. No pages. Online: http://www.passion8.co.uk.

Paster, Gail Kern. *The Body Embarrassment: Drama and the Disciplines of Shame in Early Modern England*. London: Cornell University Press, 1993.

Pattison, E. M. "Gender Identity." In *Baker Encyclopedia of Psychological & Counseling*, edited by David G. Benner and Peter C. Hill, 487–89. Grand Rapids: Baker, 1985.

Pattison, Stephen. *Shame: Theory, Therapy, Theology*. Cambridge: Cambridge University Press, 2000.

Patzia, Arthur G., and Anthony J. Petrotta. "Kenosis." *Pocket Dictionary of Biblical Studies*, 69. Downers Grove, IL: InterVarsity, 2002.

Paul, R. S. *The Atonement and the Sacraments*. London: Hodder & Stoughton, 1961.

Paulve, Dominique, and Boye, Marie. *In Fashion*. London: Cassell, 2001.

Pauwels, Paul, and Anne-Marie Simon-Vandenbergen. "Body Parts in Linguistic Action: Underlying Schemata and Value Judgements." In *By Word of Mouth: Metaphor, Metonymy and Linguistic Action in Cognitive Perspective*, edited by Louis Goossens et al., 36–40. Amsterdam: Benjamins, 1995.

Perdue, L. G. *Wisdom in Revolt: Metaphorical Theology in the Book of Job*. JSOTSup. 112. Sheffield, UK: JSOT, 1991.

Perniola, Mario. "Between Clothing and Nudity." In *Fragments for a History of the Human Body*, edited by Michel Feher, 237–65. New York: Urzone, 1989.

Peters, Ted. "Resurrection: What Kind of Body?" *Ex Auditu* 9 (1993) 60–64.

Peterson, David. "Atonement in the New Testament." In *Where Wrath and Mercy Meet: Proclaiming the Atonement Today*, edited by David Peterson, 26–67. Carlisle, UK: Paternoster, 2001.

Pettersen, Alvyn. *Athanasius and the Human Body*. Bristol, UK: Bristol, 1990.

Phelan, Gerard B. *St. Thomas and Analogy*. Milwaukee: Marquette University Press, 1941.

Phillips, K. A. *The Broken Mirror: Understanding and Treating Body Dysmorphic Disorder*. New York: Oxford University Press, 1996.

Phillips, Katharine A. "Suicidality in Body Dysmorphic Disorder." *Primary Psychiatry* 14.12 (2007) 58–66.

Phillips, Katharine A., and William Menard. "Suicidality in Body Dysmorphic Disorder: A Prospective Study." *Am J Psychiatry* 163 (2006) 1280–82.

Philo of Alexandria. *Legum allegoria*. Translated by F. H. Colson and G. H. Whitaker. Cambridge: Loeb Classical Library, 1929.

Piers, G., and M. Singer. *Shame and Guilt*. New York: Norton, 1971.

Plass, Paul. *The Game of Death in Ancient Rome: Arena Sport and Political Suicide*. Madison, WI: The University of Wisconsin Press, 1995.

Plantinga, Alvin. "Two (or More) Kinds of Scripture Scholarship." In *Behind the Text: History and Biblical Interpretation*, edited by Craig Bartholomew et al., 19–57. Carlisle, UK: Paternoster, 2003.

Plummer, Alfred. *Second Epistle of St. Paul to the Corinthians*. Edinburgh: T. & T. Clark, 1915.

Pocknee, Cyril E. *Cross and Crucifix: In Christian Worship and Devotion*. London: Mowbray, 1962.

Polinska, Wioleta. "Dangerous Bodies: Women's Nakedness and Theology." *Journal of Feminist Studies in Religion* 16 (2000) 49–51.

Pomazansky, Michael. "The Oneness of Essence, the Equality of Divinity, and the Equality of Honor of God the Son with the God the Father." In *Orthodox Dogmatic*

Theology: A Concise Exposition Protopresbyter, 92–95. Platina, CA: Saint Herman, 1984.

Pope, H. G., et al. *The Adonis Complex: The Secret Crisis of Male Body Obsession*. Sydney: Free, 2000.

———. "Evolving Ideals of Male Body Image as Seen through Action Toys." *International Journal of Eating Disorders* 26 (1999) 65–72.

Pope, John C., editor. *Homilies of Ælfric: A Supplementary Collection*. Vol. 2, 770–81. London: Oxford University Press, 1968.

Popper, Karl R., and John C. Eccles. *The Self and Its Brain*. London: Springer, 1977.

Porter, Stanley E. *The Nature of Religious Language: A Colloquium*. Sheffield, UK: Sheffield Academic, 1996.

———. "Peace, Reconciliation." In *Dictionary of Paul and His Letters*, edited by G. F. Hawthorne et al., 695–99. Downers Grove, IL: InterVarsity, 1993.

Powell, H. T. *The Fall of Man: It's Place in Modern Thought*. London: SPCK, 1934.

Prasadji, Brahmachari Sital. *A Comparative Study of Jainism and Buddhism*. Madras: Jain Mission Society, 1932.

Prestige, G. L. *Father and Heretics*. London: SPCK, 1940.

Pritchard, James B. *Ancient Near Eastern Texts*. 3rd ed. Princeton: Princeton University Press, 1969.

Provan, Iain. *Ecclesiastes/Song of Songs*. NIVAC. Grand Rapids: Zondervan, 2001.

Punt, Jeremy. "Paul, Body Theology, and Morality: Parameters for a Discussion." *Neotestamentica* 39 (2005) 359–88.

Purchas, John. "Sermon III. Nakedness. Gen. iii. 11: 'Who told thee that thou wast naked?'" In *Miscellaneous Sermons*, edited by Frederick George Lee, 31–32. London: Masters, 1860.

Quasten, J. "The Garment of Immortality: A Study of the 'Accipe Vestem Candidam.'" In *Miscellanea Liturgica in onore di sua Eminenza il cardinale Giacomo Lercaro*, 391–401. Rome: Desclee, 1967.

Rad, Gerhard von. *Deuteronomy: A Commentary*. London: SCM, 1966.

———. *Genesis: A Commentary*. London: SCM, 1972.

Raine, Susan. "Reconceptualising the Human Body: Heaven's Gate and the Quest for Divine Transformation." *Religion* 35 (2005) 98–117.

Rakestraw, Robert V. "Becoming Like God: An Evangelical Doctrine of Theosis." *JETS* 40 (1997) 257–69.

Ramaswamy, Vijaya. *Walking Naked: Women, Society, Spirituality in South India*. Shimla, India: Indian Institute of Advanced Study, 1997.

Ramsey, Boniface O. P. *Ambrose*. London: Routledge, 1997.

Ramsey, I. T. *Models for Divine Activity*. London: SCM, 1973.

———. *Religious Language: An Empirical Placing of Theological Phrase*. London: SCM, 1957.

———. "Talking about God: Models, Ancient and Modern." In *Myth and Symbol*, edited by F. W. Dillistone, 76–97. London: SPCK, 1966.

Ransome, Paul. *Work, Consumption & Culture: Affluence and Social Change in the Twenty-First Century*. London: SAGE, 2005.

Rapske, Brian. *Paul in Roman Custody*. The Book of Acts in Its First Century Setting. Vol. 3. Grand Rapids: Eerdmans, 1994.

Rashdall, Hastings. *The Idea of the Atonement in Christian Theology*. London: Macmillan, 1919.

Ratzel, Friedrich. *The History of Mankind*. Vol. 1. London: Macmillan, 1896.
Ray, Darby Kathleen. *Deceiving the Devil: Atonement, Abuse, and Ransom*. Cleveland, OH: Pilgrim, 1998.
Reale, Giovanni. *A History of Ancient Philosophy: Plato and Aristotle*. Translated by John R. Catan. Albany, NY: State University of New York Press, 1985.
Redding, Graham. *Prayer & the Priesthood of Christ in the Reformed Tradition*. Edinburgh: T. & T. Clark, 2003.
Reichenbach, Bruce R. "Healing View." In *The Nature of the Atonement*, edited by James Beilby and Paul R. Eddy, 117–42. Downers Grove, IL: InterVarsity, 2006.
Reicke, Bo. "Body and Soul in the New Testament." *Studia Theologica* 19 (1965) 200–212.
Reid, J. K. S. "The Office of Christ in Predestination." *SJT* 1 (1948) 5–19.
Renkema, Johan. *Lamentations*. Leuven: Peeters, 1998.
Reyes, Alina, and Bernard Matussière. *Female Nudes*. Paris: Fitway, 2005.
Ribeiro, Aileen. *Dress and Morality*. London: Batsford, 1986.
Richards, I. A. *The Philosophy of Rhetoric*. London: Oxford University Press, 1936.
———. *Practical Criticism: A Study of Literary Judgement*. 1929. Introduction by Richard Hoggart. New Brunswick, NJ: Transaction, 2004.
Riches, Aaron. "After Chalcedon: The Oneness of Christ and the Dyothelite Mediation of His Theandric Unity." *Modern Theology* 24 (2008) 199–224.
Ricoeur, Paul. *The Symbolism of Evil*. 1960. Translated by Emerson Buchanan. Boston: Beacon, 1967.
Ridderbos, Herman. *The Gospel of John: A Theological Commentary*. Grand Rapids: Eerdmans, 1997.
———. *Paulus: Ontwerp van zijn Theologie*. Kampen: Kok, 1966.
Ridgeway, R. T., and T. L. Tylka. "College Men's Perceptions of Ideal Body Composition and Shape." *Psychology of Men and Masculinity* 6 (2005) 209–20.
Ridley, Matt. *The Red Queen: Sex and Evolution of Human Nature*. London: Viking, 1993.
Riezler, Kurt. "Comment on the Social Psychology of Shame." *American Journal of Sociology* 48 (1943) 457–65.
Riley, Hugh M. *Christian Initiation: A Comparative Study of the Interpretation of the Baptismal Liturgy in the Mystagogical Writings of Cyril of Jerusalem, John Chrysostom, Theodore of Mopsuestia and Ambrose of Milan*. Washington, DC: Catholic University of America Press, 1974.
Rist, John M. *Augustine: Ancient Thought Baptized*. Cambridge: Cambridge University Press, 1994.
Robbins, Anna M. "Atonement in Contemporary Culture." In *The Atonement Debate: Papers from the London Symposium on the Theology of Atonement*, edited by Derek Tidball et al., 329–44. Grand Rapids: Zondervan, 2008.
Roberts, Christopher C. *Creation and Covenant: The Significance of Sexual Differences in the Moral Theology of Marriage*. London: T. & T. Clark, 2007.
Roberts, J. J. M. *Nahum, Habakkuk, and Zephaniah: A Commentary*. Louisville, KY: Westminster John Knox, 1991.
Roberts, Michael. *Critique of Poetry*. London: Cape, 1934.
Robertson, O. Palmer. *The Books of Nahum, Habakkuk, and Zephaniah*. Grand Rapids: Eerdmans, 1990.

Robertson, O. Palmer. "Current Critical Questions Concerning the 'Curses of Ham' (Gen 9:20–27)." *JETS* 41 (1998) 177–88.
Robinson, A. B. "Nudity, As Mentioned in the Bible." No pages. Online: http://www.religioustolerance.org/nu_bibl.htm.
Robinson, Gnana. *1 & 2 Samuel*. Edinburgh: Handsel, 1993.
Robinson, John A. T. *The Body: A Study in Pauline Theology*. London: SCM, 1952.
Rockel, Jeff. "The Bible, Society and Nudity: A Study of Social Nudity from a Biblical and Secular Perspective." No pages. Online: in http://www.heritageimports.ws/.
Rodger, Symeon. "The Soteriology of Anselm of Canterbury: An Orthodox Perspective." *GOTR* 34 (1989) 19–43.
Rogerson, J. *Genesis 1–11*. Sheffield, UK: Sheffield Academic, 1991.
Rohrer, Tim C. "Embodiment and Experientialism." In *The Handbook of Cognitive Linguistics*, edited by Dirk Geeraerts and Herbert Cuyckens, 25–47. Oxford: Oxford University Press, 2005.
Rose, Nikolas. *Inventing Our Selves: Psychology, Power, and Personhood*. Cambridge: Cambridge University Press, 1996.
Rosenak, C., and H. Looy. "Homosexuality." In *Baker Encyclopedia of Psychology & Counseling*, edited by David G. Benner and Peter C. Hill, 571–78. Grand Rapids: Baker, 1985.
Rosenberg, J. *King and Kin: Political Allegory in the Hebrew Bible*. Indiana Studies in Biblical Literature. Bloomington, IN: Indiana University Press, 1986.
Ross, Allen P. *Holiness to the Lord: A Guide to the Exposition of the Book of Leviticus*. Grand Rapids: Baker Academic, 2002.
Ross, Chad. *Naked Germany: Health, Race and the Nation*. Oxford: Berg, 2005.
Rowley, H. H. "Jewish Proselyte Baptism." *Hebrew Union College Annual* 15 (1940) 313–34.
Rozemond, Marleen. *Descartes' Dualism*. Cambridge: Harvard University Press, 1998.
Rubin, Nissan, and Admiel Kosman. "The Clothing of the Primordial Adam as a Symbol of Apocalyptic Time in the Midrashic Sources." *HTR* 90 (1997) 155–74.
Rudofsky, Bernard. *The Unfashionable Human Body*. New York: Doubleday, 1971.
Ruiz, Jean-Pierre. *Ezekiel in the Apocalypse*. Frankfurt am Main: Lang, 1989.
Rull, Carmelo Pérez. "The Emotional Control Metaphors." *Journal of English Studies* 3 (2001–2) 180.
Rushdoony, Rousas John. *The Institutes of Biblical Law*. Phillipsburg, NJ: Presbyterian and Reformed, 1973.
Russsell, J. B. *The Prince of Darkness: Radical Evil and the Power of Good in History*. London: Thames & Hudson, 1989.
Russell, Norman. "The Doctrine of Deification in the Greek Patristic Tradition." *IJST* 9 (2007) 227–31.
Ryken, Leland, et al. *Dictionary of Biblical Imagery*. Downers Grove, IL: InterVarsity, 1998.
Ryle, J. C. "The Cross: A Call to the Fundamentals of Religion by J. C. Ryle." No pages. Online: http://www.crcgv.org/lit/jcryle/the%20cross.htm.
Sambusky, S. *Physics of the Stoics*. Princeton: Princeton University Press, 1959.
Sanders, E. P. *Paul and Palestinian Judaism: A Comparison of Patterns of Religion*. Philadelphia: Fortress, 1977.
Santis, A. De, and W. A. Kayson. "Defendants Characteristics of Attractiveness, Race, & Sex and Sentencing Decisions." *Psychological Reports* 81 (1999) 679–83.

Sapir, J. D., and J. C. Crocker. *The Social Use of Metaphor: Essays on the Anthropology of Rhetoric.* Philadelphia: University of Pennsylvania Press, 1977.

Satlow, Michael. *Tasting the Dish: Rabbinic Rhetoric of Sexuality.* Atlanta: Scholars, 1995.

Satlow, Micheal L. "Jewish Constructions of Nakedness in Late Antiquity." *JBL* 116 (1997) 431–40.

Schaab, Gloria L. "I Will Love Them Freely: A Metaphorical Theology of Hosea 14." *American Journal of Biblical Theology* 8.30 (2007). No pages. Online: http://www.biblicaltheology.com/Research/SchaabG01.pdf.

Schaeffer, Francis A. *Genesis in Space and Time: The Flow of Biblical History.* London: Hodder and Stoughton, 1972.

Schaff, Philip. *History of the Christian Church.* Vol. 2: Ante-Nicene Christianity. A. D. 100–325. Edinburgh: T. & T. Clark, 1884.

Scheff, Thomas J. *Microsociology: Discourse, Emotions, and Social Structure.* Chicago: University of Chicago Press, 1990.

Schiebinger, Londa. "Skeletons in the Closet: The First Illustration of the Female Skeleton in Eighteenth-Century Anatomy." In *The Making of the Modern Body*, edited by Catherine Gallagher and Thomas Laqueur, 42–82. Berkeley: University of California Press, 1987.

Schiller, Gertrud. *Iconography of Christian Art.* Vol. 2. *The Passion of Jesus Christ.* Translated by Janet Seligman. London: Humphries, 1972.

Schmid, Josef. *The Gospel according to Mark.* Translated by Kevin Condon. Cork, Ireland: Mercier, 1968.

Schmidt, Thomas E. *A Scandalous Beauty: The Artistry of God and the Way of the Cross.* Grand Rapids: Brazos, 2002.

Schmiechen, Peter. *Saving Power: Theories of Atonement and Forms of the Church.* Grand Rapids: Eerdmans, 2005.

Schöpflin, Karin. "The Composition of Metaphorical Oracles within the Book of Ezekiel." *VT* 55 (2005) 101–20.

Schreiber, Lynne. *Hide and Seek: Jewish Women and Hair Covering.* Jerusalem: Urim, 2003.

Schreiner, T. A. "Penal Substitution Response." In *The Nature of the Atonement: Four Views*, edited by James Beilby and Paul R. Eddy, 50–53. Downers Grove, IL: InterVarsity Academic, 2006.

Schroeder, Edward H. "Using Luther's Concept of *Deus absconditus* for Christian Mission to Muslims." Presented at the Luther Research Congress, Copenhagen, Denmark, 4–9 August, 2002. Seminar: Luther's Writings on the Turks. No pages. Online: http://www.crossings.org/archive/ed/LuthersWritingsTurks.pdf.

Schurr, George M. "On the Logic of Ante-Nicene Affirmations of the 'Deification' of the Christian." *Anglican Theological Review* 51 (1969) 99–105.

Schweitzer, Albert. *The Mysticism of Paul the Apostle.* London: Black, 1931.

Schweizer, Eduard. *The Good News according to Mark.* Atlanta: John Knox, 1971.

Scott, George Ryley. *The History of Corporal Punishment.* London: Torchstream, 1950.

Scragg, D. G. *The Vercelli Homilies and Related Texts.* Oxford: Oxford University Press, 1992.

Scroggs, Robin, and Kent I. Groff. "Baptism in Mark: Dying and Rising with Christ." *JBL* 92 (1973) 537–38.

Sedikides, C., and S. J. Spencer. *The Self.* New York: Psychology, 2007.

Seevers, Boyd V. "עָרָה." In *New International Dictionary of Old Testament Theology and Exegesis*, Vol. 3, edited by Willem A. VanGemeren, 527–28. Grand Rapids: Zondervan, 1977.
Segal, Alan. "The Da Vinci Code and The Passion of the Christ—What They Tell Us about American Religion Today." In *Jesus in Twentieth-Century Literature, Art, and Movies*, edited by Paul C. Burns, 212–16. London: Continuum, 2007.
Seifrid, Mark A. "Cultural Background of the New Testament." In *Foundation for Biblical Interpretation*, edited by David S. Dockery et al., 489–90. Nashville: Broadman & Holman, 1994.
Self, David. *Struggling with Forgiveness: Stories from People & Communities*. Toronto: Anglican, 2003.
Seneca's *Dialogue 6 (De consolatione ad Marciam)* 20.3 ("To Marcia on Consolation"). In *Moral Essays*, Vol. 2, translated by John W. Basore. The Loeb Classical Library 254. London: Heinemann, 1932.
Senior, Donald C. P. *The Passion of Jesus in the Gospel of Luke*. Collegeville, PA: Liturgical, 1989.
Setel, T. Drorah. "Prophets and Pornography: Female Sexual Imagery in Hosea." In *Feminist Interpretation of the Bible*, edited by Letty Russell, 86–95. Philadelphia: Westminster, 1985.
Sevenster, J. N. *Studia Paulina*. Haarlem: De Erven F. Bohn N. V., 1953.
Shelton, R. Larry. *Cross and Covenant: Interpreting the Atonement for 21st Century Mission*. Milton Keynes, UK: Paternoster, 2006.
Shemesh, Yael. "Punishment of the Offending Organ in Biblical Literature." *VT* 55 (2005) 343–65.
Sherlock, Charles. *The Doctrine of Humanity*. Leicester, UK: InterVarsity, 1996.
Sherman, Robert J. "Toward a Trinitarian Theology of the Atonement." *SJT* 52 (1999) 346–74.
Sherry, Patrick. *Religion, Truth & Language Games*. London: Macmillan, 1977.
Sherwood, Stephen K. *Studies in Hebrew Narrative & Poetry*. Collegeville, PA: Liturgical, 2002.
Shields, Mary E. "Multiple Exposures: Body Rhetoric and Gender Characterization in Ezekiel 16." *Journal of Feminist Studies in Religion* 14 (1998) 5–18.
Shuster, Marguerite. *The Fall and Sin: What We Have Become as Sinners*. Grand Rapids: Eerdmans, 2004.
Silva, Moisés. *Philippians*. 2nd ed. Grand Rapids: Baker Academic, 2005.
Singgih, E. G. "Let Me Not be Put to Shame: Towards an Indonesian Hermeneutics." *The Asia Journal of Theology* 9 (1995) 80–81.
Sinha, K. P. *The Philosophy of Jainism*. Calcutta: Punthi Pustak, 1990.
Skinner, John. *A Critical and Exegetical Commentary on Genesis*. Edinburgh: T. & T. Clark, 1910.
Smalley, Stephen S. *The Revelation of John*. London: SPCK, 2005.
Smith, Alison. *The Victorian Nude: Sexuality, Morality and Art*. Manchester, UK: Manchester University Press, 1996.
Smith, Craig Dennis, and William Sparks. *The Naked Child: Growing Up Without Shame*. Los Angeles: Elysium Growth, 1986.
Smith, C. R. "Chiliasm and Recapitulation in the Theology of Ireneus." *Verbum Caro* 48 (1994) 313–31.
Smith, Dennis. *Zygmunt Bauman: Prophet of Postmodernism*. Cambridge: Polity, 1999.

Smith, Jonathan. "The Garments of Shame." In *Map Is Not Territory: Studies in the History of Religions*, edited by Jonathan Z. Smith, 1–23. Chicago: University of Chicago Press, 1993.

Smith, Morton. "Clement of Alexandria and Secret Mark: The Score at the End of the First Decade." *HTR* 75 (1982) 449–61.

Smith, Ralph L. *Micah-Malachi*. WBC. Waco, TX: Word, 1984.

Smith, S. M. "Kenosis, Kenotic Theology." In *Evangelical Dictionary of Theology*, edited by Walter A. Elwell, 600–602. Grand Rapids: Baker, 1984.

Smith, Warren J. "The Body of Paradise and the Body of the Resurrection: Gender and the Angelic Life in Gregory of Nyssa's *De hominis opificio*." *HTR* 99 (2006) 209–11.

Snaith, N. H. *Leviticus and Numbers*. London: Thomas Nelson, 1967.

Sorabji, Richard. *Self: Ancient and Modern Insights about Individuality, Life, and Death*. Chicago: University of Chicago Press, 2006.

Sorokin, P. A. *The Crisis of Our Age*. Oxford: Oneworld, 1992.

Soskice, Janet Martin. *Metaphor and Religious Language*. Oxford: Clarendon, 1985.

Spaulding, Henry II. "Milbank's Trinitarian Ontology and a Re-Narration of Wesleyan-Holiness Theology." *Wesleyan Theological Journal* 36.1 (2001) 146–59.

Speiser, E. A. *Genesis: Introduction, Translation, and Notes*. Anchor Bible. New York: Doubleday, 1964.

Spence, Alan. *The Promise of Peace: A Unified Theory of Atonement*. London: T. & T. Clark, 2006.

———. "A Unified Theory of the Atonement." *IJST* 6 (2004) 404–20.

Spong, John Shelby. *Liberating the Gospels*. New York: HarperCollins, 1996.

Spurgeon, Charles Haddon. *Spurgeon's Sermon Volume 4: 1858*. Sermon 212—The New Heart. No pages. Online: http://www.ccel.org/ccel/spurgeon/sermons04.xlviii.html.

Stancliffe, Michael. "Symbolism and Preaching." In *Myth and Symbol*, edited by F. W. Dillistone, 98–105. London: SPCK, 1966.

Stanford, W. B. *Greek Metaphor*. Oxford: Blackwell, 1936.

Stanley, D. M. *Christ's Resurrection in Pauline Soteriology*. Rome: Pontificium Institutum Biblicum, 1961.

Stanton, Graham. *The Gospels and Jesus*. 2nd ed. Oxford: Oxford University Press, 2002.

Stebbing, Susan. *A Modern Introduction to Logic*. London: Methuen, 1953.

Steele, Valerie. "Clothing." Microsoft Encarta Online Encyclopedia. 2009. No pages. Online: http://encarta.msn.com.

Steenberg, M. C. "Children in Paradise: Adam and Eve as 'Infants' in Irenaeus of Lyons." *Journal of Early Christian Studies* 12.1 (2004) 1–22.

———. "The Role of Mary as Co-Recapitulator in St. Irenaeus of Lyons." *Vigilae Christianae* 58.2 (2004) 117–37.

Steinmetz, Devora. "Vineyard, Farm, and Garden: The Drunkenness of Noah in the Context of Primeval History." *JBL* 113 (1994) 193–207.

Steintrager, James A. *Cruel Delight: Enlightenment Culture and the Inhuman*. Bloomington, IN: Indiana University Press, 2004.

Stewart, Andrew. *Art, Desire, and the Body in Ancient Greek*. Cambridge: Cambridge University Press, 1997.

Steward, F. "The Adolescent as Consumer." In *Youth and Policy in the 1990s: The Way Forward*, edited by J. C. Coleman and C. Warren-Anderson, 203–26. London: Routledge, 1992.

Stewart, Roy A. "Judicial Procedure in New Testament Times." *EQ* 47 (1975) 94–109.
Stienstra, N. *YHWH is the Husband of His People: Analysis of a Biblical Metaphor with Special Reference to Translation*. Kampen: Kok Pharos, 1993.
Stock, Augustine. *The Method and Message of Mark*. Wilmington, KY: Glazier, 1989.
Stockwell, Peter. *Cognitive Poetics: An Introduction*. London: Routledge, 2002.
Stordalen, T. *Echoes of Eden: Genesis 2–3 and Symbolism of the Eden Garden in Biblical Hebrew Literature*. Leuven: Peeters, 2000.
Stott, John R. W. *The Cross of Christ*. Leicester, UK: InterVarsity, 1986.
———. *The Message of Romans: God's Good News for the World*. Leicester, UK: InterVarsity, 1994.
Strong, A. H. *Systematic Theology*. Valley Forge, PA: Judson, 1907.
———. *Systematic Theology*. Vol. 1. Philadelphia: Judson, 1945.
———. *Systematic Theology*. 3 vols. Philadelphia: American Baptist Publication Society, 1907–1909.
———. *Union with Christ: A Chapter of Systematic Theology*. Philadelphia: American Baptist Publication Society, 1913.
Strunks, Emily Jo. "The Metaphors of Clothing and Nudity in the 'Essais' of Montaigne." *Romance Notes* 19 (1978) 83–89.
Studer, B. "Divinization." In *Encyclopedia of the Early Church*, Vol. 1, edited by A. Di Beradina, 242–43. New York: Oxford University Press, 1992.
Stuhlmacher, Peter. *Paul's Letter to the Romans: A Commentary*. Translated by Scott J. Hafemann. Edinburgh: T. & T. Clark, 1994.
Summers, Ray. *Commentary on Luke*. Waco, TX: Word, 1972.
Swinburne, Richard. *The Evolution of the Soul*. Oxford: Clarendon, 1986.
Szeemann, Harald. "Here I Am Human Here I Am Free." In *Naked in Paradise*, edited by Michael von Graffenried, 1–5. Stockport, UK: Lewis, 1997.
Taft, R. "Baptism." In *Oxford Dictionary of Byzantium*, Vol. 1, edited by A. P. Kazhdan, 251. Oxford: Oxford University Press, 1991.
Talmud. The Minor Tractates of the Talmud. 2 vols. Many translators, edited by A. Cohen. London: Soncino, 1965.
Tangney, June Price. "Shame." In *Encyclopedia of Psychology*, edited by Alan E. Kazdin, 266–69. Oxford: Oxford University Press, 2000.
Tangney, J. P., et al. "Are Shame, Guilt and Embarrassment Distinct Emotions?" *Journal of Personality and Social Psychology* 10 (1996) 1256–69.
Tauler, John. *Meditations on the Life and Passion of Our Lord Jesus Christ*. London: Richardson and Son, 1875.
Taylor, Barry. "Fashion—Dress Up the Soul." In *A Matrix of Meanings: Finding God in Pop Culture*, edited by Craig Detweiler and Barry Taylor, 221–42. Grand Rapids: Baker Academic, 2003.
Taylor, Jeremy. *The Rules and Exercises of Holy Living*. London: Rickerby, 1838.
Taylor, Vincent. *The Gospel according to St. Mark*. London: Macmillan, 1966.
Terry, Justin. *The Justifying Judgement of God: A Reassessment of the Place of Judgement in the Saving Work of Christ*. Milton Keynes, UK: Paternoster, 2007.
TeSelle, Sallie. *Speaking in Parables: A Study in Metaphor and Theology*. London: SCM, 1975.
Tesser, Abraham, and Richard Reardon. "Perceptual and Cognitive Mechanisms in Human Sexual Attraction." In *The Bases of Human Sexual Attraction*, edited by Mark Cook, 93–144. London: Academic, 1981.

Thayer, Bill. "Dionysius of Halicarnassus: Roman Antiquities." No pages. Online: http://penelope.uchicago.edu/Thayer/E/Roman/Texts/Dionysius_of_Halicarnassus/7C*.html.

Thielicke, Helmut. *Theological Ethics I: Foundations*. London: Black, 1968.

Thielman, Frank. *Philippians*. Grand Rapids: Zondervan, 1995.

Thiselton, Anthony C. *The Hermeneutics of Doctrine*. Grand Rapids: Eerdmans, 2007.

Thomas à Kempis. *Imitation of Christ*. Milwaukee: Bruce, 1949.

Thomas, Robert L. *Revelation 1–7*. Chicago: Moody, 1992.

Thomas, Thomas A. "Kenosis Question." *EQ* 42 (1970) 142–51.

Thomas, W. H. Griffith. *The Principles of Christian Theology*. Grand Rapids: Baker, 1979.

Thompson, Leonard L. *Revelation*. Nashville: Abingdon, 1998.

Thornton, L. S. *The Common Life in the Body of Christ*. 3rd ed. London: Dacre, 1950.

Tidball, Derek. *Leviticus*. Leicester, UK: InterVarsity, 2005.

———. "Penal Substitution: A Pastoral Apologetic." In *The Atonement Debate: Papers from the London Symposium on the Theology of Atonement*, edited by Derek Tidball et al., 345–60. Grand Rapids: Zondervan, 2008.

Tietje, Louis, and Steven Cresap. "Is Lookism Unjust?: The Ethics of Aesthetics and Public Policy implications." *Journal of Libertarian Studies* 19 (2005) 31–50.

Timonen, Asko. *Cruelty and Death: Roman Historians' Scenes of Imperial Violence from Commodus to Philippus Arabs*. Turku, Finland: Turun Yliopisto, 2000.

Timpe, R. L. "Shame." In *Baker Encyclopedia of Psychology*, edited by David G. Benner, 1074–75. Grand Rapids: Baker, 1985.

Tinsley, E. J. "Coming of a Dead and Naked Christ." *Religion* 2 (1972) 32–33.

Torrance, J. B. "Cross, Crucifixion." In *New Bible Dictionary*, edited by I. H. Marshall et al., 253–54. Leicester, UK: InterVarsity, 1962.

Torrance, T. F. *Theology in Reconstruction*. London: SCM, 1965.

Towner, W. Sibley. *Genesis*. Louisville, KY: Westminster John Knox, 2001.

Trexler, Richard C. *Naked before the Father: The Renunciation of Francis of Assisi*. New York: Lang, 1989.

Trible, P. "The Gift of a Poem: A Rhetorical Study of Jeremiah 31:15–22." *Andover Newton Quarterly* 17 (1977) 271–80.

Trigg, Jonathan D. *Baptism in the Theology of Martin Luther*. Leiden: Brill, 1994.

Trilling, Wolfgang. *The Gospel according to St. Matthew*. London: Burns & Oates, 1969.

Tulloch, John. *Luther and Other Leaders of the Reformation*. Edinburgh: Blackwood and Sons, 1883.

Turner, Bryan S. "The Body in Western Society: Social Theory and Its Perspectives." In *Religion and the Body*, edited by Sarah Coakley, 15–17. Cambridge: Cambridge University Press, 1997.

Tzaferis, Vassilios. "Crucifixion: The Archaeological Evidence." *BAR* 11.1 (1985) 48–49.

Uno, Atsushi. "Some Relationships between Buddhism and Jainism." In *Buddhism & Jainism*, edited by Das Harish Chandra, 45–52. Cuttack, Orissa: Institute of Oriental and Orissan Studies, 1976.

Utriainen, Terhi. "Naked and Dressed: Metaphorical Perspective to the Imaginary and Ethical Background of the Deathbed Scene." *Mortality* 9 (2004) 132–49.

Vanhoozer, Kevin J. "The Atonement in Postmodernity: Guilt, Goats and Gifts." In *The Glory of the Atonement: Biblical, Historical and Practical Perspectives*, edited by Charles E. Hill and Frank A. James III, 370–71. Downers Grove, IL: InterVarsity, 2004.

Vawter, Bruce. *On Genesis: A New Reading*. London: Chapman, 1977.
Veale, David. "Shame in Body Dysmorphic Disorder." In *Body Shame*, edited by Paul Gilbert and Jeremy Miles, 267–82. New York: Brunner-Routledge, 2002.
Veenker, Ronald A. "Forbidden Fruit: Ancient Near Eastern Sexual Metaphors." *Hebrew Union College Annual* 70–71 (1999–2000) 57–73.
Verma, B. R., and S. R. Bakshi. *Hinduism, Buddhism and Jainism in Ancient India*. New Delhi: Commonwealth, 2005.
Vermes, Geza. "Genesis 1–3 in Post-Biblical Hebrew and Aramaic Literature before the Mishnah." *Journal of Jewish Studies* 43 (1992) 221–225.
Verspoor, Cornelia. "What are the Characteristics of Emotional Metaphors?" 1993. No pages. Online: http://public.lanl.gov/verspoor/pubs/rice/met-thesis.pdf.
Viladesau, Richard. *The Beauty of the Cross: The Passion of Christ in Theology and Arts, from the Catacombs to the Eve of the Renaissance*. Oxford: Oxford University Press, 2006.
Vine, W. E. *The Epistles to the Philippians and Colossians*. London: Oliphants, 1955.
Vo, Nhu Cau, *Vietnamese Proverbs, Folk Poems and Folk Songs*, Dong Nai, Vietnam: Nha Xuat Ban Dong Nai, 1998.
Vogelzang, M. E., and W. J. van Bekkum. "Meaning and Symbolism of Clothing in Ancient Near Eastern Texts." In *Scripta Signa Vocis*, edited by H. L. J. Vanstiphout et al., 265–84. Groningen: Egbert Forsten, 1986.
Waetjen, Herman C. *The Gospel of the Beloved Disciple*. London: T. & T. Clark, 2005.
Wagner, J. R. "Piety, Jewish." In *Dictionary of New Testament Background*, edited by Craig A. and Stanley E. Porter, 796–803. Downers Grove, IL: InterVarsity, 2000.
Walaskay, Paul W. *Acts*. Louisville, KY: Westminster John Knox, 1998.
Walker, Andrew. "Sectarian Reactions: Pluralism and the Privatization of Religion." In *20/20 Visions: The Futures of Christianity in Britain*, edited by Haddon Willmer, 46–64. London: SPCK, 1992.
Walker, Simon. "Grounding Biblical Metaphor in Reality: The Philosophical Basis of Realist Metaphorical Language." *Churchman* 112 (1998) 214–24.
Wall, Robert W. *Revelation*. Carlisle, UK: Paternoster, 1995.
Wallace, Daniel B. "When Did Jesus Know? The Translation of Aorist and Perfect Participles for Verbs of Perception In the Gospels." No pages. Online: http://www.bible.org/page.php?page_id=1223.
Wallace, Howard N. *The Eden Narrative*. Atlanta: Scholar, 1985.
Wallace, R. S. "Christology." In *Evangelical Dictionary of Theology*, edited by Walter A. Elwell, 221–27. Grand Rapids: Baker, 1984.
———. *The Gospel of John: Pastoral and Theological Studies*. Edinburgh: Rutherford House, 2004.
Walters, Margaret. *The Nude Male*. London: Paddington, 1978.
Walton, John H. "Cultural Background of the Old Testament." In *Foundation for Biblical Interpretation*, edited by David S. Dockery et al., 256–57. Nashville: Broadman & Holman, 1994.
Wan, Gok. *How to Look Good Naked: Shop for Your Shape and Look Amazing!* London: HarperCollins, 2007.
Wan, Gok, and Dawn Porter. "How to Look Good Naked?" In the Lifestyle Channel.
Ward, Graham. *The Blackwell Companion to Postmodern Theology*. Oxford: Blackwell, 2003.

Ward, William Hayes. "A Critical and Exegetical Commentary on Habakkuk." In *A Critical and Exegetical Commentary on Micah, Zephaniah, Nahum, Habakkuk, Obadiah and Joel*, edited by J. M. P. Smith et al., 3–28. Edinburgh: T. & T. Clark, 1911.

Ware, Kallistos. "The Hesychasts: Gregory of Sinai, Gregory Palamas, Nicolas Cabasilas." In *The Study of Spirituality*, edited by C. Jones et al., 251–53. New York: Oxford University Press, 1986.

Ware, Timothy. *The Orthodox Church*. London: Penguin, 1993.

Watson, Francis. *Agape, Eros, Gender*. Cambridge: Cambridge University Press, 2000.

Watson, G. R. *The Roman Soldier*. London: Thames and Hudson, 1969.

Watts, Fraser. "Shame, Sin and Guilt." In *Forgiveness and Truth: Explorations in Contemporary Theology*, edited by Alistair McFadyen and Marcel Sarot, 54–55. Edinburgh: T. & T. Clark, 2001.

Watts, Fraser N., et al. *Psychology for Christian Ministry*. London: Routledge, 2002.

Watts, John D. W. *Isaiah 34–66*. Waco, TX: Word, 1987.

Way, E. C. *Knowledge Representation and Metaphor*. Studies in Cognitive Systems 7. Dordrecht: Kluwer, 1991.

Weaver, J. Denny. *The Nonviolent Atonement*. Grand Rapids: Eerdmans, 2001.

Webb, Barry. *The Message of Isaiah*. BST. Leicester, UK: InterVarsity, 1996.

Webber, Robert E. *Ancient-Future Faith: Rethinking Evangelicalism for a Postmodern World*. Grand Rapids: Baker, 1999.

Weems, Renita R. J. *Battered Love: Marriage, Sex, and Violence in the Hebrew Prophets*. Minneapolis: Fortress, 1995.

Weinfeld, Moshe. *Deuteronomy and the Deuteronomic School*. Oxford: Clarendon, 1972.

Weis, James. "Calvin Versus Osiander on Justification." *The Springfielder* 30 (1965) 31–47.

Welby, William. *"Naked and Unashamed": Nudism from Six Points of View*. London: Thorsons, 1934.

———. *The Naked Truth about Nudism*. London: Thorsons, 1935.

Wendel, François. *Calvin: The Origins and Development of His Religious Thought*. New York: Harper & Row, 1963.

Wenham, David. "Being 'Found' on the Last Day: New Light on 2 Peter 3.10 and 2 Corinthians 5.3." *NTS* 33 (1987) 477–79.

Wenham, Gordon. *The Book of Leviticus*. NICOT. Grand Rapids: Eerdmans, 1979.

———. *Genesis 1–15*. WBC. Waco, TX: Word, 1987.

———. "Original Sin in Genesis 1–11." *Churchman* 104 (1990) 309–12.

Wesche, Kenneth Paul. "Eastern Orthodox Spirituality: Union with God in *Theosis*." *Theology Today* 56 (1999) 29–43.

Wesley, John. *Sermons on Several Occasions*. London: Kershaw, 1825.

West, Canon Edward N. *Outward Signs: The Language of Christian Symbolism*. New York: Walker, 1989.

Westcott, B. F. *The Gospel according to St John*. London: Murray, 1892.

Westermann, Claus. *Creation*. Translated by John J. Scullion. London: SPCK, 1974.

———. *Genesis*. Translated by David E. Green. Edinburgh: T. & T. Clark, 1988.

———. *Genesis 1–11: A Commentary*. Translated by John J. Scullion. London: SPCK, 1984.

Westermarck, Edward. *The History of Human Marriage*. New York: Macmillan, 1891.

Westhelle, Victor. *The Scandalous God: The Use and Abuse of the Cross*. Minneapolis: Fortress, 2006.

Weston, Paul. "Proclaiming Christ Crucified Today: Some Reflections on John's Gospel." In *Where Wrath and Mercy Meet: Proclaiming the Atonement Today*, edited by David Peterson, 136–63. Carlisle, UK: Paternoster, 2001.

White, James Emery. "Evangelism in a Postmodern World." In *Postmodernism: An Evangelical Engagement*, edited by David S. Dockery, 359–73. Grand Rapids: Baker, 1995.

White, Hugh C. *Narration and Discourse in the Book of Genesis*. Cambridge: Cambridge University Press, 1991.

Whitefield, George. *Sermons on Important Subjects*. London: Tegg, 1854.

White, James Emery. "Inspiration and Authority of Scripture." In *Foundation for Biblical Interpretation*, edited by David S. Dockery et al., 19–23. Nashville: Broadman & Holman, 1994.

Whitehouse, Mary. *Cleaning-up TV*. London: Blandford, 1967.

Whiteley, D. E. H. *The Theology of St. Paul*. Oxford: Blackwell, 1974.

Whybray, R. N. *Ecclesiastes*. London: Marshall, Morgan & Scott, 1989.

Wijngaards, John. "Naked Without Shame." No pages. Online: http://www.womenpriests.org/body/nakedwos.asp.

Wilcox, Jonathan. "Naked in Old English: The Embarrassed and the Shamed." In *Naked Before God: Uncovering the Body in Anglo-Saxon England*, edited by Benjamin C. Withers and Jonathan Wilcox, 278–309. Morgantown, VA: West Virginia University Press, 2003.

Wiles, Maurice Frank. *The Making of Christian Doctrine: A Study in the Principles of Early Doctrinal Development*. Cambridge: Cambridge University Press, 1967.

Wiley, H. Orton. *Christian Theology*. Vol. 2. Kansas City: Beacon Hill, 1952.

Wilkinson, L. P. *Classical Attitudes to Modern Issues*. London: Kimber, 1979.

Wilkinson, John. "The Body in the Old Testament." *EQ* 63 (1991) 195–210.

Willard, Dallas. *Renovation of the Heart*. Leicester, UK: InterVarsity, 2002.

Willems, Boniface A. *The Reality of Redemption*. New York: Herder & Herder, 1970.

Williams, A. N. *The Ground of Union: Deification in Aquinas and Palamas*. New York: Oxford University Press, 1999.

Williams, David John. *1 and 2 Thessalonians*. Peabody, MA: Hendrickson, 1992.

Williams, Gary. "Penal Substitution: A Response to Recent Criticisms." In *The Atonement Debate: Papers from the London Symposium on the Theology of Atonement*, edited by Derek Tidball et al., 171–91. Grand Rapids: Zondervan, 2008.

Williams, Jay G. "Genesis 3." *Interpretation* 35 (1981) 274–80.

Williams, Rowan. "Deification." In *The Westminster Dictionary of Christian Spirituality*, edited by Gordon S. Wakefield, 106–8. Philadelphia: Westminster, 1983.

Willis, Susan. *Specifying: Black Women Writing the American Experience*. London: Routledge, 1990.

Willis-Watkins, D. "The Unio Mystica and the Assurance of Faith according to Calvin." In *Calvin: Erbe und Auftrag*, edited by Willen van't Spijker, 77–84. Kempen: Kok Pharos, 1991.

Wilson, Geoffrey B. *2 Corinthians: A Digest of Reformed Comment*. Carlisle, UK: Banner of Truth, 1979.

Wilson, Michael P. "Nakedness, Bodiliness and the New Creation." *Modern Believing* 47.3 (2006) 43–49.

Wistrand, Magnus. *Entertainment and Violence in Ancient Rome: The Attitudes of Roman Writers of the First Century A.D.* Göteborg: ACTA Universitatis Gothoburgensis, 1992.

Witherington III, Ben. *1 and 2 Thessalonians: A Socio-Rhetorical Commentary.* Grand Rapids: Eerdmans, 2006.

———. *The Gospel of Mark.* Grand Rapids: Eerdmans, 2001.

———. *John's Wisdom.* Cambridge: Lutterworth, 1995.

———. *Revelation.* Cambridge: Cambridge University Press, 2003.

Wolde, E. van. *A Semiotic Analysis of Genesis 2–3. A Semiotic Theory and Method of Analysis Applied to the Story of the Garden of Eden.* Assen: Van Gorcum, 1989.

———. *Stories of the Beginning.* London: SCM, 1996.

Wolf, Naomi. *The Beauty Myth: How Images of Beauty Are Used against Women.* New York: HarperCollins, 1991.

Wolff, Hans Walter. *Hosea.* Translated by Gary Stansell, edited by Paul D. Hanson. Philadelphia: Fortress, 1974.

Worricker, Julian. "You and Yours." BBC Radio 4. Broadcast on 29 September, 2009.

Wright, Christopher J. H. *Deuteronomy.* New International Biblical Commentary. Peabody, MA: Hendrickson, 1996.

———. "Future Trends in Mission." In *The Future of Evangelicalism: Issues and Prospects*, edited by Craig Bartholomew et al., 149–63. Leicester, UK: InterVarsity, 2003.

Wright, J. Stafford. *Man In the Process of Time: A Christian Assessment of the Powers and Functions of Human Personalities.* Grand Rapids: Eerdmans, 1956.

———. *What is Man?* London: Paternoster, 1955.

Wright, Lawrence. *Clean and Decent: The Fascinating History of the Bathroom and Water Closet.* London: University of Toronto Press, 1960.

Wright, N. T. *Mark for Everyone.* London: SPCK, 2001.

———. *Matthew for Everyone.* Pt. 2. London: SPCK, 2002.

———. *The New Testament and the People of God.* Christian Origins and the Question of God 1. London: SPCK, 1992.

Yarbrough, R. W. "Forgiveness and Reconciliation." In *New Dictionary of Biblical Theology*, edited by T. D. Alexander and B. S. Rosner, 498–503. Leicester, UK: InterVarsity, 2000.

Yates, John C. "The Origin of the Soul: New Light on an Old Question." *EQ* 61 (1989) 121–40.

Yates, Roy. "From Christology to Soteriology." *ExpT* 107.9 (1996) 268–70.

Young, J. Z. *Philosophy and the Brain.* Oxford: Oxford University Press, 1988.

Zizioulas, John D. *Being as Communion.* Crestwood, NY: St. Vladimir's Seminary Press, 1985.

Zumapress. "Sculpture of Naked Christ Caused Scandal in Moscow." No pages. Online: http://www.limamug.com/photo/1812158/?k=j83s12y12h94s27k02.

Subject Index

acceptance, 9, 24, 28, 30–31, 43, 47, 75, 110, 182, 191, 240, 243
achievement, 2, 32, 194, 199, 208, 210, 233, 235
Adam,
   Adam and Christ typology, 129, 176, 194–95, 199, 201, 217, 220–22, 224, 226, 229
   Adam and Eve, 5, 18, 39, 52, 58, 79, 90–94, 97–103, 109, 114, 120–24, 126–27, 194
   First and Last Adam, 176, 181, 194–95, 222
adoption, 37, 44, 205, 206, 208
adornment, 34, 37–38, 41–42, 73, 174–75
adultery, 58, 111, 132–34
age, ageing, 28, 75
almsgiving, 82, 178–80
altar, 143
animal, 28, 34, 37, 42–43, 98, 103, 120–21, 149–50
anthropology, 22, 141, 235, 239, 242
appearance, 2–3, 22–28, 30, 32, 42, 63, 206, 240
attraction, attractiveness, 3–4, 17, 19–21, 24–25, 28, 39–43, 47, 75, 157, 213, 246–47
autonomous, 32, 71, 120, 125, 128, 241–42

baptism, 5–6, 8, 59, 80–81, 118, 142–49, 162–63, 173, 175, 177–79, 184, 193, 195–96, 208, 218, 222, 229–30, 242, 244
bather, 35, 60
battlefield, 194, 220
beast, 154, 157, 159, 166

beauty, 20, 25, 29, 35, 40, 42–45, 48–50, 53, 57, 175, 187, 240–41, 244
bed, 133
bible, biblical, 6, 8, 35, 47, 52–53, 80, 89–90, 93, 110–12, 114–16, 118–19, 124, 129, 140, 146–48, 164–65, 185, 207, 214–15, 222, 233, 235, 237, 239, 245–46
bipolar, 16, 24–25, 31, 53, 239–40
birth, 30–31, 38, 57, 90, 127, 147, 152
blaming, blame, 74, 97, 101, 115, 121, 124, 127
body,
   body and mind, 17, 64,
   neurotic body, 25–29, 31,
   regulated body, 22–23, 28
body-obsessed culture, 2–5, 7–9, 31–33, 61, 63–64, 233, 235–36, 238–42, 244–45, 247
bride, 78–79, 134, 136–37, 174
brokenness, 6, 59, 96, 98, 100–102, 118, 122–26, 128–29, 198, 222–23, 240
brutality, 112, 166
Buddhist, Buddhism, 1, 47–48
buried, 149, 158, 246
buttocks, 113, 154, 161, 164, 169

carnal, 117
Carthage, 107, 151, 175, 178
Chalcedon, 78, 191
Christ, 191–95,
clothes, clothing, 56, 60–63, 70, 72, 76–85, 89–90, 94–98, 100–3, 105–13, 117–18
cognitive, 8, 15, 18–19, 40, 43, 62–65, 76, 79, 96, 215, 240
commandment, 93, 99, 111, 137

295

communication, 7-8, 28-29, 85, 94, 206, 239, 251, 275, 277
conceal, concealment, 8, 38, 40, 44, 58, 70-74, 76, 79-80, 83-84, 96, 101, 123, 126-27, 174, 180-81, 183, 185, 190-91, 196, 217, 226, 246
concession, 3, 164-68
condemnation, 81-82, 111, 117, 135, 137, 150
consumer, consumerism, 2, 4, 9, 13-14, 17, 20-31, 61, 242, 244, 258, 262, 264, 278, 288
convention, 51, 64, 69, 73-74, 80, 83-84, 112, 228, 240
corruptible, corruption, 22, 53, 98, 126-27, 129-30, 139, 145, 194-95, 198, 207-8
couple, 91-92, 94, 98-102, 116, 119-22, 124
covenant, 81, 84, 104, 118, 130-36, 146, 148, 193, 211, 215-16
creator, 98, 121, 125, 186-88, 204, 235
criminal, 59, 151, 155, 158-59, 166-67, 169, 270
cross, vii-viii, 2-7, 24, 63, 65-66, 83-85, 98, 117, 129, 145, 153-67, 170, 173-75, 177-79, 182-83, 186-88, 191-201, 204, 206-14, 216-17, 221, 223-27, 229-32, 234-35, 238-47
crucifixion, 5-6, 8, 59, 87, 113, 145, 149, 151-63, 165-70, 174-75, 179, 186, 194, 197, 208, 217, 227, 230, 238-39, 245
cruciform, 33, 191-92, 195, 217, 266
cruelty, 149-52, 154-56, 158-59, 170
culture, 11, 28, 48, 74, 247
  popular culture, 20, 25, 30
cup, 139, 190, 199-200
curiosity, 44, 138

damage, 57, 71, 75, 134, 147, 193, 216, 228
death, 2, 50, 59, 80, 117, 138, 150, 155-56, 158, 161, 170, 197, 199
decency, 3, 38, 49, 108, 133, 155, 166
defeat, 102, 108, 110, 116, 176, 195, 215, 221,
defense, 19, 94, 103, 108, 119, 125, 140, 240, 270
degradation, 49, 112-13, 135, 158-60, 242

desire, 20, 23-27, 29, 31, 39-40, 42, 45-46, 48, 71, 78, 101, 123, 139, 146, 150, 152, 183, 231, 244
Devil, 14, 53, 60, 110, 180, 219, 220-21, 228
dictate, 19-20, 25, 28, 241
  dictatorship, 13, 20
  dictation, 20, 29
dignity, 108, 112-14, 116, 136, 158-59,
discourse, 13, 22, 64-65, 85, 76-78, 118, 126, 237
disembodiment, 50, 140-41
disgrace, 105, 136-37, 140, 164
disobedience, 38-39, 97, 102, 104, 119, 116, 124-25, 130, 133, 144, 176, 193-95, 219-20, 231
disorder, 27, 31, 52, 75, 123
dysmorphia, 31, 75
divine, 68, 81, 99, 120, 123, 130, 135, 174, 179, 181-92, 194, 196, 198, 200-206, 208-9, 221, 223, 229-31, 235, 243, 245
divinity, 47, 174, 188, 191, 193, 202, 206, 209, 230
dress, 28, 36, 38-39, 51-52, 55, 79, 83, 126, 168, 178, 183,
  undress, 55, 60
  undressing, 43, 160, 181, 186,

early centuries, 83, 118, 245
early Christian, 56-58, 118, 143, 163, 187, 196, 245,
early Christianity, 45, 57, 144, 162,
early Church, 5, 56, 58, 129, 143-44, 162, 180, 220, 227, 244
Eastern Orthodox, 193, 203
economic theory, 36-37, 39
Eden narrative, 38, 90, 92-93, 95, 97, 100-2, 109, 114, 116, 119, 123, 127, 130, 144, 217, 220, 235
ego, 16, 24, 125
Egypt, 36, 49, 104
elect, 173, 183-85, 187, 192, 194, 198, 201, 204-6, 208-10, 242
embarrassment, 70-72, 74, 81, 83, 96, 99, 101, 121-22, 125-26
emotion, 2, 23, 62, 64, 70-71, 75, 84, 106
emotive: metaphor, model, 62, 70, 77, 84, 96, 100, 131, 135,
empire, 44, 56, 150, 155-56, 159
emptying kenosis, 80, 174, 182, 187-89, 191-92, 195-96, 202, 210,

226–27, 229–30, 234–35, 243, 246–47
enemy, 105, 113, 136, 145, 185, 194, 215, 218
enhancement, 26, 28–29, 31, 33, 43
Enlightenment, 184
entertainment culture, 2–3, 29, 44, 61, 112, 167, 169, 238
environment, 19–20, 43, 218, 239, 242
equality, 55, 121, 125, 185, 191, 193, 205
error, 77, 79
essence, 15, 59, 123, 127–28, 154, 184, 189, 190, 193, 204–5, 207
estranged, 214–15, 232
eternal life, 92, 121, 179, 192, 198
ethical values, 61, 72
ethic, 28, 51, 60–61, 72, 106, 108, 122, 127, 132, 148,
euphemism, 54, 56, 110, 111, 148
evil, 42, 58, 92–93, 97, 99–102, 105, 110, 116, 120–22, 124–25, 136–37, 218, 221–22, 231, 243
evolution, 43
example, 159, 196, 201, 206, 211, 214, 216, 228–29, 231–32, 235, 241, 244
  exemplar, 33, 178–80, 182, 187, 215, 230–32
exchange, 147, 182, 191, 195–96, 206, 213, 217–19, 228
execution, 3, 149–52, 155–56, 158–60, 166, 238
exegesis, 89, 97
existence, 14–15, 18, 21–22, 34, 103, 139, 174, 188–90
experiential knowledge, 21–22, 31, 65
experimentation, 22–23, 26
exposure, 54, 71–74, 80–81, 101, 104, 115–16, 126, 131, 134, 136, 138, 143, 164, 191,
external body, 14, 16–17, 21, 27, 29–30, 240, 242
eye, 26, 50, 96, 99, 149, 154, 156, 161–62, 168

face, 37, 69, 92, 121
failure, 25, 32, 53, 58, 75, 102, 116, 120, 198, 201, 217, 220
Fall, 53, 91–100, 102, 112, 117–19, 121–28, 130, 144, 147–48, 190–91, 193, 198, 231
family, 68, 110–11, 115–16, 206, 213

fashion, 2, 24, 28–31, 35, 64, 77, 240
fear, 30, 41–42, 54–55, 73–74, 98–101, 109, 116, 119–22, 124, 140–41, 151, 155, 199, 229
feeling, 35, 38, 46, 57, 64, 70–72, 74, 76, 119, 135, 150, 240, 244, 246,
female,
  body, 27, 58
  genitalia, 56
  imagery, 131
  modesty, 55
  nakedness, 6, 53, 55–56, 60, 110
  role, 132
fig leaves, 101, 116
flesh, 21, 81, 144, 147, 150, 153, 157, 170, 181, 186, 188, 190, 198, 202, 208
flogging, 152–67
forbidden fruit, 93
forensic debt, 216
forgiveness, 8, 32, 84, 147, 215–16, 219–20, 225–26, 231–32, 235, 242
fornication, 45

games, 48, 76
gang rape, 132, 134
garment, 37, 39, 41, 45, 48–50, 58, 81, 84, 103, 107, 113, 130, 136–37, 142–43, 145, 147, 165, 173, 175–78, 180, 196, 207, 217, 229–30, 244
gaze, 45, 55, 116, 240
gender identity, 19
genital, 9, 19, 26, 35, 38, 46, 54, 56, 72–73, 93, 100, 111, 123, 133, 137, 150, 154, 158, 160
Germany, 45
glamorous bride, 136–37
glorification, 8, 127, 205–7, 209, 242
glory, 8, 54, 94, 147, 162, 176, 178, 182, 187–90, 192, 200, 202, 205–7, 209–10, 217, 232, 244, 246–47
Gnostic, 50, 58, 141
God,
  wisdom, 3, 186, 188, 191, 221
  wrath, 184, 198–200, 217, 226–27, 233
  YHWH, 131, 135–36, 143, 148
Golgotha, 166–67, 199
Gospel of Nicodemus, 165
Greco-Roman, 5, 53, 56–57, 59, 61, 144, 197

Greece, Greek, 18, 21, 35–36, 44–45, 47–58, 66, 83, 110, 138–41, 148–49, 205, 208, 218–19, 246
grief, 105–6, 108

Ham, 112, 114–16
Han Chinese, 51
hanging, 150–51, 156–59, 166, 174, 195
Harlot of Babylon, 135–36
head covering, 55, 165
health, 17, 20, 28, 46, 104–5
heaven, 1, 50, 107, 138, 142, 162, 180, 193, 205, 224
Hebrew, Hebraic, 21, 47, 53, 91, 96, 107, 110, 113, 115, 122, 141, 143, 188, 197
hedonism, hedonistic, 2, 20, 25–26, 28–29, 31–32, 61
Hellenistic, 46, 203
heretics, 58
heuristic
    experience, 63–64, 70, 84
    metaphor, 70, 72, 84
Hinduism, 16, 47–48
history, historian, 7, 34–35, 36, 51–52, 72, 79, 119, 149, 174, 193–94, 224
homily, 162
honor, 6, 8, 49, 70, 94, 111, 113, 115–16, 137, 196, 215
horror, 59, 124, 135, 159, 170, 187, 199
humiliation, vii, 105, 108, 112–13, 116, 132, 135, 152, 159, 161, 188
husband, 39, 55, 75, 93, 131–32, 134–36

image,
    bearers, 198, 201
    culture, 13, 20,
    dominance, 24–25, 30–31, 240
imitating Christ, 145, 147, 163, 196, 229
immorality, 117, 133, 135, 145
impalement, 160, 169
incarnation, vii, 180–85, 187–92, 194–95, 214, 221, 234, 243
incest, 114–16
individual, 4, 7, 20–21, 28, 42, 71, 74, 106, 127–29, 154, 214, 244
infidelity, unfaithfulness. See sex.
inheritance, 127–27, 207, 209–10, 215
interim, intermediate, 118, 140–41, 218

Israel, Israelite, 54, 82, 98, 100, 104, 108, 110, 112–13, 117, 132–33, 135–36, 143, 162, 218

Jain, Jainism, 47–48
Jerusalem, 134
Jesus,
    clothes, 107–8, 160, 164–68, 181
    nakedness, 145, 160, 163, 165, 170, 174, 176–77, 196, 199–200, 221, 226
Jewish,
    abhorrence, 53, 165, 168
    death, 158, 166
    nakedness, 52–56,
    sensitivity, 164, 168–69
    War, 153, 155, 158
Jubilees, 94, 143, 165, 167
Judaism, 57, 97
judgment, 71, 75, 81–82, 93, 102, 112, 128, 131–33, 135–38, 140, 142, 168, 218
justification, 6, 8, 137, 175, 192, 196, 206, 208–10, 226, 235, 241

kaleidoscope, kaleidoscopic, 7, 9, 211, 212–18, 232–35, 246
kenosis, 8, 182, 187–97, 199–202, 210, 217, 227, 231, 234–35, 245–46
kingdom, 244

label, 24, 29, 192
last day, 147
last temptation, 2
late antiquity, 53, 56
law, 110, 113, 131, 133, 197, 221–22, 225
legal language, 4, 198, 217, 223, 226
liberation, 7, 20, 55, 216, 218–20, 222, 227, 241
lifestyle, 23–24, 59, 107, 163, 178–79, 209–10, 231, 244
limitation, 18, 77, 101, 103, 188, 190–91, 211, 235
liturgy, 118–19, 143–44, 146, 148, 163, 174, 177, 245
logo and identity, 24, 29
logos, 187–90, 192, 196
loincloth, 163–68, 170, 217
lower class, 157, 169
lust, 45–46, 59, 110, 117, 120, 123–24, 134, 145

male,
  body, 26–27, 93
  nakedness, 53–56, 58, 143
  masculinity, 27
march, 152, 156, 159, 166–67, 230, 244
marriage contract, 131
mass crucifixion, 149, 155, 169
media culture, 13, 20, 24–25, 27, 29, 45, 238
Medieval, 59–60, 149
mercy, 107, 158, 179–80, 200
Messiah, 130, 173, 182, 217
metaphor
  theories, 62–76, 83–84, 96
  retired metaphor, 69
  root metaphor, 64, 70, 78
  metaphorical language, 62–63, 65–71, 74, 76, 78, 82, 84, 142, 196
metaphysics, 14, 189
Midrashic, 130
mimesis, 175, 177, 179–80, 195, 216
mind, 16–17, 49, 64, 120–1, 185,
Mishnah Sanhedrin, 3, 111, 166
mockery, 49, 126, 158, 160
model,
  analogy, 64, 67, 76–77, 79, 81, 206, 212
  atonement model, 211–18, 232–47
  moral influence, 178, 182, 198, 209, 211, 215–18, 228–31
  philanthropic soteriology, 82, 175, 180, 197, 231
modern, modernity, 2, 13, 18, 20, 22, 28, 30, 44–45, 51–52, 60–61, 188
modesty, 8, 34, 37–38, 41, 43–44, 53–55, 61, 70–74, 83, 94, 98, 122
modus operandus, 239, 243–45
moral value, 71–72, 98, 122, 127
morality, 29, 38, 47, 98
Mosaic theory, 8, 37, 90
Moses, 110, 113, 148
motif, 8, 91, 95–99, 102, 111, 114, 116, 118–19, 121–22, 124, 129–30, 137, 146–48, 176–77, 180–81, 193, 195–96, 215, 218, 220, 222, 235
motto, 59, 82, 149, 163, 173, 232,
multiply, 93, 121, 230
mystery, 4, 76, 100, 102, 186, 202, 207, 245–46
myth, 2, 24, 27, 36–38, 52, 90–91, 95, 97, 99, 119, 125, 183

nakedness, semi-nakedness, 110, 144
narcissism, narcissistic, 20–21, 25–26, 61, 240
national identity, 79, 143
naturism, 60
neurosis, 28
New Testament, 95, 136, 138, 146, 212–13, 224
  liturgy, 144, 146. *See* liturgy.
Noah and nakedness, 112, 114–16, 162
nudum jesum nudus, 59, 163
nuptial imagery, 136

oath, 148
obedience, 51, 98, 188, 191, 195, 219–23, 231, 244
observer, 71, 74–75, 84, 159
obsession, 3, 13, 18–19, 29, 32, 146, 240, 242
offender, 135, 216
offense, 54, 55, 115, 127, 152, 154, 169
offering, 67, 97, 182, 219, 229, 241
Old Testament, 58, 89, 107, 112, 136, 138, 140–41, 143, 146
Oneirocritica, 158–59
  organ, 22, 38, 40–41, 46, 92–93, 134–37, 141, 148, 153, 157, 160
Oriental, 50–52
origin, 8, 34–36, 38, 40–41, 43, 61, 64, 72, 90, 96, 98, 103, 138, 149, 151–52, 173, 220
  Original Sin, 58, 95, 118–19, 124, 126–30, 215
ornaments, 34, 40–44, 49

pain, 51, 103–6, 109, 134–35, 134–35, 150, 154–58, 161, 166, 186, 197
paradise, 91, 139, 195
paradox, 162, 186, 190–91, 221, 244–45
parousia, 117, 137, 142, 148
partakers, 145, 201, 205–6
participation, 59, 177, 201, 205–6, 208, 220, 222, 227, 229, 231, 232, 234–35, 243–44
passibility, 186, 190, 198
Passion, 160–63, 199–200
  patristic, 162, 187, 190, 192, 205, 209, 233–34
Paul, Pauline, 91, 105, 118, 129, 136, 140, 141–42, 186–88, 192–93, 205, 207, 217, 226

penalty, 128,155, 157, 159, 166, 182, 194, 224
penance, 107, 125, 180
penis, 19, 54–55, 93
penitential, 6, 81–82, 130
personal identity, 15–20, 24, 28, 31, 242
personality, 15, 18, 21, 27–28, 42, 242
philosophy, 13, 15, 35, 48, 57, 64, 117, 138–39, 244
physical,
   attractiveness, 17, 24, 28, 40
   pain, 104–6, 154, 156–58, 161
   qualities, 53
   state, 103, 117, 120, 127, 130, 132, 141
   vulnerability, 70, 103–6, 130, 132
   world, 17–18
plan, 183, 187
pleasure and consumption, 26, 29, 31
poetry, poetic, 35, 62, 64, 80, 83, 135, 203, 215
politics, 17, 26, 56, 60, 104, 113, 159, 213,
political tool, 155
poor, 39, 82, 103, 106–7, 137, 202
   poverty, 39, 59, 103–5, 108, 137, 180, 196, 202
post biblical, 91
postlapsarian/prelapsarian, 90, 94, 97, 116, 120, 125, 130
postmodern, postmodernism, postmodernity, 3–4, 20–21, 23, 27, 31, 61, 237–39, 244, 246
power, 21, 53–54, 58, 63, 66, 74, 80, 102, 105, 117, 129, 133, 137, 145, 152, 161–62, 181, 186, 189, 193, 198, 204–7, 218, 221, 224, 227–28
predestination, 184
primordial state, 91, 95
private parts, 73, 158
profane, 53–54, 56
prohibition, 54, 92, 99, 120, 143–44
promiscuity, 2, 45, 134–33
prophet, prophetic
   covenantal, 118, 130–31, 133–34, 148
   imageries, 117, 131, 136
   language, 83, 130–31, 137, 148
   writings, 106, 134, 141, 148
protection, 34, 37, 39, 41–43, 47, 118, 135
provincial, 155, 169, 170

provision, 81, 103, 132, 191, 220
psyche, 43, 70, 76, 141, 170
psychology,
   psychological infliction, 155
   perception, 16–18, 35, 70
public,
   bath, 5, 51, 55–59, 169
   exposure, 71, 81, 131, 134
   nakedness, 5, 48, 75, 81, 109, 131, 134–35, 144, 165, 167–69,
   view, 71, 149
punishment,
   corporal punishment, 149–54, 170
   scourging, 153, 160, 166–68, 170
purged, 179–80, 231
purity and impurity, 112, 131, 133, 135
put on/off, 36, 84, 137, 144–45, 147, 176, 178, 205, 208–9, 243–44

rabbis, 53, 55, 144
race, 17, 90, 152, 181,
rage, 170, 200
raiment, 36, 107, 179–80
ransom, 213, 216, 218–221, 223
rape. See gang rape
recapitulation, 177, 192–95, 199, 211, 213, 217–20
reconciliation, 212, 214–16, 220, 222, 224–25, 228, 231–32, 235, 240–42, 245–47
redemption, 107, 129, 179, 190–91, 193–94, 201, 210, 220, 225, 228
rejection, 80, 180, 182, 223, 227, 237–38, 240
relational,
   brokenness, 124, 126
   context, 33, 123, 245
   metaphor, 77, 84, 118, 245
religion, 13, 35, 41, 48, 47
   religious identity, 18, 35, 41, 79, 81
   religious language, 76–79, 82, 131, 142
   religious model, 78–79
   religious nakedness, 41, 47–50, 53, 60, 81, 85
   religious practice, 48, 50, 73, 81, 143, 146, 151
renunciation, 41, 47, 81–82, 108, 145, 147, 177–80, 182, 191, 218, 231, 243–44
representation, representative model, 107, 128, 193, 198, 218, 220, 223–24, 234, 245,

responsibility, 106, 121, 132, 220
restoration, 6, 129-30, 198, 205, 208, 214-17, 223, 228, 232, 235
resurrection, 6, 33, 139-40, 142, 148, 173, 177-78, 192, 201, 206-7, 212, 214, 217, 221, 226, 229-30, 235, 243-45, 247
revelation, 182-88, 190-91, 198-99, 234-35
revelatus, 183-85, 226
rhetoric, 8, 80, 82
rich, 39, 49, 103, 196, 202
righteous,
  justified as righteous, 82, 130, 148, 210
  robes of righteousness, 6, 84, 136, 147, 175-77, 182, 192, 196, 201, 207-8, 217, 221, 226-28, 230, 244
rites, ritual, 4, 35, 44, 47, 50, 106, 118, 144-46, 148, 163, 215
robe, 54, 58, 132, 138, 142, 147-48, 175, 177-78, 181, 201, 210
  disrobe, 160
Roman,
  Catholic, 138, 193
  citizen, 151, 153, 155-56, 169
  crucifix, crucifixion, 8, 113, 149, 151-55, 158-62, 166-70, 238, 245
  cruelty, 149-59, 170
  culture, 5, 53, 56-57, 144, 150, 167, 169,
  empire, 56, 150-51, 155-56, 159
  flogging, 152-61, 167
  rulers, 150, 168
  society, 56-61, 150, 154, 169, 197
  soldiers. *See* soldier
  times, 150-56, 187
  world, 2

sacred, 55, 151, 158,
sadistic, 158-60, 167-68, 238
salvation, 1-4, 31-32, 45, 82, 84, 91, 107, 137, 179-80, 187, 191, 193-94, 198, 201, 207, 214-15, 218, 224, 226, 229, 239-43, 245-46
sanctification, 127, 145, 180, 192, 204, 207-9
Sanhedrin, 3, 111, 166
Satan, 190, 218-19
satisfaction, 23-25, 198, 211, 212, 218, 222-28, 230, 232, 234-35

scandal, 2-7, 162, 187, 214, 238, 243, 246
science, 13, 23, 35, 48, 52, 62, 65, 78, 89
scourging, 153, 160, 166-68, 170
self,
  abnegation, 179-80
  awareness, 15, 35
  and body, 4, 15-33, 35, 71, 75,
  consciousness, 15-16, 26
  emptied, 80, 174, 182, 187-89, 192, 195-96, 202, 210, 226-30, 234-35, 246
  esteem, 27, 46,
  forgiveness, 32, 147, 215, 242
  identity, 15-19, 28
  image, 19, 23-24, 30
  renunciation, 108, 178-79, 191
  revealing, 183-84
  saving, 32-33
  shame, 32, 75
semantics, 110, 173
semiotics, 110, 173
Serpent, 97-98, 231
servant, 138, 189-90, 197, 223
set free, 113, 176, 217, 219-20, 222, 228,
sexuality, sex, sexual, 3, 19, 22, 35, 40, 44, 52, 54-55, 58, 71, 74, 93, 102, 116-17, 123, 135, 146, 148-49
  arousal, 40, 46, 92, 123
  attraction, 19-20, 24, 39-43
  body, 3, 19-20, 25, 31, 39-40, 55, 58, 72-74, 112, 117, 141
  connotation, 42, 46, 55-56, 110, 114, 133
  impurity, 112, 131, 133, 135
  innocence, 91, 93
  intercourse, 56, 93, 111, 114, 127, 132
  laws, 131, 133
  lust, 45-46, 110, 117, 123-24, 134
  misconduct, 56, 134, 144
  modesty, 54-55, 72-74
  organ, 38, 40-41, 46, 92-93, 132, 134, 137, 141, 148, 160
  overtones, 29, 92
  relation, 92-93, 114
  selection, 31, 40
  shame, 35, 46, 57, 72, 100, 135, 137, 149
  sin, 45, 52, 114-17, 123-24, 127, 131-35, 143, 146

unfaithfulness, 117, 131, 133–34
shame,
  guilt, 35, 70–71, 74–76, 84–85, 96, 99–101, 116, 119–24, 126–27, 176, 213, 216, 223, 236, 239, 240–42, 245
  vulnerability, 41, 70, 94, 102, 104–5, 108, 116–18, 126, 130–31, 135, 148–49
  shameless, 45–46, 60, 83, 94–95, 99, 147
shopping, 24, 30, 257, 274
Sin,
  nakedness, vii, 3, 8, 102, 117, 130–31, 176, 179, 217, 227
  shame and sin, 63, 75–76, 84, 95–96, 98, 102, 116–28, 142, 182, 239–41, 247
skin, 17, 28–29, 34–35, 37, 46, 53, 94, 103, 157
slave, 104, 113, 136, 151–55, 169–70, 176, 191, 195–97, 218, 222
society, 4, 17, 20, 23, 25–26, 28–30, 32, 34, 45–46, 52, 56–57, 59, 61, 63, 82, 150, 169, 197, 240
  social change, 74,
  social context, 6, 19, 21, 30, 60, 70, 89
  social dilemma, 27, 63
  social hierarchy, 54–55, 113
  social justice, 106–8, 150
  social norm, 19, 28, 35, 43, 131
  social propriety, 3, 19, 35, 43–44, 46, 55, 72, 115
  social status. *See* status
  social welfare, 82, 108
sociology, 13, 35
soldier, 158, 161, 164, 166, 168–70, 238
soul, 15–16, 21, 35, 47, 49–50, 58, 82–83, 127, 138–41, 148, 152, 173, 180, 197, 219, 231
speech, 64, 66–68, 102
spiritual,
  condition, 78, 82, 96, 116–17, 122, 138, 140, 178
  forces, 41–42
  knowledge, 17, 21–23, 31
  maturity, 57, 100
  poverty, 137
  relationship, 81, 102, 133
  shame, 126, 142
  spirituality, 16, 35, 47

statue, 1–2, 56, 174, 238
status, 29, 43, 55, 57, 75, 113, 142, 159
strip, stripped, stripping, 41–42, 44, 49–50, 56–57, 75, 80–81, 106, 108, 112, 122, 131, 144–45, 147, 152–54, 156–57, 159–60, 162, 164, 166, 174, 176, 178, 191, 196–97, 208, 227
substance, 15–16, 21, 42, 139, 198, 205–6, 208
suffering, vii, 3, 8, 102–6, 134–35, 154, 157, 160–62, 173–74, 182, 186, 190–91, 195, 197, 199–200, 204, 223, 225, 243–44
summa theologiae, 79
superiority, 53, 57, 73, 113, 155
symbol, 64, 77, 80, 83, 131–32, 142, 144, 177
  symbolism, 62–63, 79–80, 90, 94, 111, 124, 178, 233–34, 245
Synoptic Gospels, 6, 161
Syriac, 94

Talmud, 55–56, 111
target domain, 80, 83
telos, 8–9, 33, 206, 239, 241–43, 246–47
temple, 1, 54, 142
temptation, 2, 55, 190, 221
tenor, 67, 162
tension, 2–3, 5, 60–61, 66, 119, 183–84, 213–15, 238, 242–46
theology, 6, 8, 58–59, 76, 78, 80, 84, 91, 95, 104, 107, 118–19, 130–31, 133, 135, 138, 140, 142, 144, 146, 163, 187, 189, 191–92, 197, 202, 212, 237, 239, 241,
  eschatology, 8, 118, 136–38, 173
  kenotic Christology, 188–192, 209
  soteriology, 82, 126, 174–75, 177, 180, 191, 193, 197, 210–12, 217–18, 234–35, 239, 245
  systematic theology, 131, 191
theosis, 8, 174, 181, 187, 192–94, 200–210, 217, 227, 231, 234, 243, 245–46
therapy, therapeutic, 28, 30, 71, 216, 239–40
tomb, 49–50, 58, 139
Torah, 52, 54
torment, 2, 24, 135, 150, 156–58
tou sómatos, 35, 50

tradition, vii, 3–4, 6–7, 15, 21, 31, 35, 47, 50–53, 55, 69, 74, 82, 96, 104, 110–11, 114, 116, 129, 131, 138, 144, 163, 173–74, 185, 192, 199, 203, 211, 217, 233–34, 245–46
transcendence, 183
transformation, 177, 182, 201, 207–8, 229–30, 244
transmission, 127–28, 130
transparency, 80–81, 100–101
trial, 126, 168
trickery, 221
trinity, 191, 225–26,
trust, x, 84, 98, 104, 119–21
truth, 24, 49, 65, 76, 78–79, 186, 197–98, 237–38
union, 8, 129, 177, 196, 200–201, 203–10, 217, 219, 227, 229, 231–32, 235, 242, 246–47
universality, 103, 124, 136, 128–30

victim, 27, 74, 113, 149, 151–54, 156–60, 166, 170,
Victorian, 35, 45, 60
victory, 49, 176–77, 193–96, 212, 216–22, 232–35, 241, 243, 247
Vietnam,
 Soc mountain, Thánh Gióng, 1–2
Vietnamese, ix, 1–2, 50
vision, 49
vulnerability, 41, 70, 94, 102–6, 108, 110, 116–18, 126, 130–32, 135, 148–49, 186, 198

war, 30, 104, 112–13, 116, 153, 155, 158, 194 246
washing, 146
wedding, 83, 107, 136, 142, 173, 180
weight, 17, 27, 137, 148, 168, 223–24
west, 110, 202
western, vii–viii, 13–15, 17, 51–53, 198, 203, 234
wholeness, 98, 118, 123, 126, 240
wisdom, 2–3, 62, 90, 186, 188, 191, 221

Author Index

Ambrose, 92, 125, 129-30, 163, 176-78, 180-81, 195, 219-20, 230
Aristotle, 13, 15, 62, 66-67, 139
Augustine, Augustinian, 5, 15, 21, 38, 82, 90-95, 98, 103, 107, 117, 120-21, 123, 129-30, 139, 142, 147, 162-63, 173, 176, 180, 190, 197, 202, 206, 217, 219-21, 231
Avicenna, 15

Barth, 16, 129, 184-85, 188, 190-91, 197-200, 204-5, 223, 227, 237, 243
Bauman, 2, 4, 21, 23-24, 26, 28, 31, 71, 74-75
Bordo, 19-21, 25, 27, 30, 65

Calvin, 6, 82, 114, 137, 139-40, 170, 175, 178, 183-84, 187, 191, 196-98, 210, 203-6, 209, 212, 217
Coleridge, Samuel Taylor Coleridge, 64, 96
Cyprian, 82, 107-8, 163, 175-180, 204, 231
Cyril of Jerusalem, 145, 147, 162-63, 173, 177-78, 187, 193, 208, 217, 242
Cyril of Alexandria, 219

Descartes, René Descartes, 13, 15-16, 23

Edersheim, 3, 151, 166
Eslinger, 56, 117, 134-35

Fawcett, 76-78, 83
Fitzmyer, 5, 105, 158
Francis of Assisi, 82, 173, 178

Francis of Sales, 177, 229
Freud, Freudian, 13, 19, 71-72, 74, 263

Giddens, 18, 20, 22, 24
Glasson, 18, 50, 57-58, 140-41
Glover, 17, 35
Goodson, 6, 37-38, 45, 48-49, 51, 58-59
Gowan, Gowen, 100, 102, 114-15, 119, 132
Gregory of Nazianzus, 181, 187, 202, 208, 219
Gregory of Nyssa, 120, 202, 204, 208, 219
Grenz, 4, 29, 189, 193, 206, 237-38, 242-43, 246
Gunton, 65, 68, 75, 185, 190-91, 198, 200, 212, 216, 222-24, 226, 237, 243

Harris, 5, 105, 141-42, 217
Hatt, 34, 36
Hettlinger, 117, 139-42
Hiler, 36-42, 90
Hippolytus, 144, 163
Hoebel, 37-38, 72-73
Hooker, 128, 169, 193, 195, 212, 214-15, 217, 222-24, 226, 229-31, 233
Horn and Gurel, 36-41, 90

Irenaeus of Lyons, 18, 90-92, 127, 130, 142, 177, 181, 187, 190, 192-96, 198, 201-2, 205, 207-8, 211, 217, 219, 221
Jacobus, 163, 176, 181, 195, 220
Jerome, 59, 82, 92, 107, 163, 173, 177-78, 180, 203, 208, 230, 270
John of Ruysbroeck, 174-75

Author Index

Jordan, 4, 104, 143, 217
Josephus, 153–54, 158, 167, 169

Lakoff, 63–71, 75, 84
Lane, Anthony, 49, 117, 123, 128, 130
Langer, 62–64, 73
Lasch, 13, 26, 28, 240
Louis of Blois, 175
Luther, 98, 173, 178, 183–87, 196–97, 203, 205, 207–9, 230, 234

Martin, 136, 144, 182–85, 191, 212
Masquelier, 44, 52–53
Mazza, 80, 177, 229
McFague, 65–66, 78
McFarland, 71, 74–75
McFarlane, iv-v, viii-ix, 188
McIntyre, 7, 67, 76, 78–79, 219, 223–24, 245
McKnight, 4, 192, 194, 196, 200, 211–12, 215, 223, 226–27, 231, 238, 242, 245
Melito of Sardis, 59, 162, 175, 186, 190
Mertens, 186, 193–94, 201, 207, 212
Miall, 64–65, 69
Miles, Margaret R., 6, 35, 52, 58–59, 93, 143, 145–47, 163, 193
Miles, Steven, 20, 29–30
Miller, 30, 71, 83, 104
Milne, 94, 140, 163
Moltmann, 186, 197, 199–200, 207, 230
Moltmann-Wendel, 13–14, 16, 22
Moore, 53, 55, 94
Morris, Henry M., 39, 101, 115
Morris, Leon, 129, 153, 158, 160–61, 164, 169, 198–99, 217, 223, 239
Mosser, 201–5, 209
Motyer, 117, 133, 136
Moule, 144, 197
Mounce, 151, 156–58
Muirhead, 78–79, 136
Müller, 189, 191

Need, 62, 64, 66–68, 77–78
Negrut, 181, 202
Neyrey, 5–6, 137–38, 154, 157–61, 163, 169
Nilsson, 183, 185–86
Nochlin, 35, 60
Nolland, 159, 161–62, 167
Norris, 187, 202–4

Ogilvie, 111, 117, 134
Osborn, 192–96, 198, 201–2, 205, 207
Osei-Bonsu, 117, 137, 140–41

Parker, 126–29
Partee, 204, 212
Pattison, 112, 138, 240–41
Perniola, 35, 43, 49, 50, 53–54, 58–59, 282
Petrotta, 189, 282
Plato, 15, 49–50, 57–58, 139, 141
Plass, 160, 167, 169
Polinska, 58, 110
Prasadji, 47–48

Rakestraw, 203, 209
Ramsey, I., 76–77
Richards, 64, 66–68, 76–77, 118
Rohrer, 62, 65, 68–71, 75
Ross, 45, 47

Satlow, 43–44, 53–56, 113–14
Scott, 149–54
Shelton, 98, 211, 215–16, 219, 222, 225, 243–44
Shemesh, 132, 134
Shields, 132–33
Shuster, 91–94, 101, 120, 124
Skinner, 91, 103
Sorabji, 15–16
Soskice, 67–69, 78
Socrates, 15
Steenberg, 18, 90–91, 193
Steinmetz, 144
Stewart, 48, 52, 154–55, 157
Stordalen, 62, 64, 66–69, 95, 118, 124–25
Stott, 105, 200, 225

Tangney, 74
Tauler, 176, 178, 180, 220
Terry, 4, 200, 212–13, 216, 229, 233, 246
Theodore, 147, 193
Thielman, 182, 196
Thoby, 3, 163, 166, 167
Thomasius, 188–89, 192
Timpe, 35, 70–71, 83
Tinsley, 3, 144, 147, 158, 162–64, 166–67
Torrance, 156–57, 203
Trigg, 184
Tzaferis, 5, 151–52, 155–56

Verspoor, 62, 65, 67–70

Welby, 38, 41, 45–50, 57

Wesley, 107, 179–80, 191, 202

West, 217

Scripture Index

Genesis

1:28	92–93
2–3	38, 52, 81, 84
2:17	176
2:25	53, 91–92, 94–95, 147, 193
3	93, 141
3:7–11	90
3:17–18	102
3:4	99, 120
3:7	38, 53, 91–92, 95, 107, 148
3:10	100
3:21	94
9:20–27	165
9:20–23	114
9:21	112
17	148
19:14	184
34:13–26	134

Exodus

4	148
6:12	148
6:30	148
20:26	52, 54, 143
28:42–43	143

Leviticus

16:4	165
18	111
18:6–23	110
18:7–8	114
18:25–29	111
19	111
20:17–19	112
20:23–24	111
20:10	134

Numbers

5:11–31	134

Deuteronomy

10:16	148
28:1–4	104
28:15–58	104
28:45–48	104
32:21	164
33:13–15	102

Joshua

5	148

Ruth

3:9	132

1 Samuel

19:20–24	108
19:24	47
24:4	113

2 Samuel

10:4	113
3:31	106
6:14–20	143

2 Chronicles

28	113
28:15	112

Ezra

3:20	91

Job

1:21	103, 147
8:22	83
14:4–5	129
22:26	106
24:7–10	106
24:15	55
26:6	80
29:14	207

Psalm

34:5	83
35:26	83
44:15	83
51:2	215
51:7	215
51:9	215
51:5	129
51:7	178
69:7	83
83:16	83
103:12	215
109:29	83
132:9	208
132:16	84, 207
132:18	83
141:8	197
149:4	207

Proverbs

7:9	55

16:6	108, 179–80
30:15–16	110

Ecclesiastes

5:15	103

Songs of songs

5:3	144

Isaiah

1:18	178
1:21	103
6:8	191
11:5	84
20	104
20:2	47
20:3	104
20:4	112
28:29	203
45:15	184
47	131
47:2–3	135
52:13–53:12	223
53	223
53:12	197
53:23	197
57:17–20	191
57:8	133
58:7	106–7
59:17	207–8
61:10	84, 136, 207–8
64:6	208

Jeremiah

2–3	131
6:10	148
9:25–26	148
13	56
31	134

Lamentations

1:8	135
4:21	135

Ezekiel

16	131, 134–35
16:6–39	135
16:7–8	132
16:8	132
16:26	133
16:36	93, 133
18:7–16	106
23	131, 135
23:9–30	135
23:20	133

Daniel

10:5	94
12:7	94

Hosea

1–2	134
2	131
2:2–10	135

Amos

2:16	108–9
5	131

Micah

1:8–10	106
6:8	107

Nahum

3	131
3:5	135

Habakkuk

2:15	93, 112

Zephaniah

3	131

Matthew

3:15	223
6:25–26	105
9:14–17	136
10:28	140
17:2	178
22:1–14	81, 83, 126
22:11–14	142
24:45–46	138
24:36	190
25:36–43	106
26:31	110
27:26	160
27:28	160
27:31	160
27:35	160

Mark

2:19	136
8:34–35	232
9:12	223
10:45	223
13:34–36	138
13:32	190
14:50–52	108
14:24	223
14:32–34	200
15:15	160
15:17	160
15:20	160
15:24	160

Luke

2:52	190
5:33–35	136
11:22	223
12:36–38	138
12:42–43	138
16:19–31	140
16:23–24	139
22:37	223
23:33–34	160
23:16	167
23:22	167

John

1:29	222
2:13–22	222
3	129
3:2	147
4:16	205
6:38	186
6:65	186
8:24	129
8:58	188
14:6	186
14:9	186
15:23	160
17:21–23	205
17:11	205
18:8–9	109
18:10–11	109
18:15	109
19:31–32	156
19:31	158
19:1	160, 167
19:2	126, 160
19:12	167
20:6	59

Acts

4:12	1
16:37	153
17:23	184
19:1–6	148
19:16	108

Romans

3	129
4:25	221
5	191, 193
5:12	129
5:19	195
8:35	105
12:1	143
13:14	208

1 Corinthians

15	193
4:2	138
5:7	222
6:15	143
6:17	142
6:19	142–43
9:27	139
15	193
15:17	221
15:21	129
15:49	205
40:22	129

2 Corinthians

3:18	147
5:3–4	117
5:1–3	140
5:1	35
5:3	139–40, 142–43
5:4	142
5:8	141
5:21	199, 208
8	202
8:9	187
11:27	105

Galatians

1:12	186
2:20	205, 232
3:1	175
3:27	5, 142, 147, 208

Ephesians

1:10	194
2:3	129
3:16–19	205
3:3	186
4:13–15	205
4:22–24	147
4:24	142
5:26	142
6:17	207

Philippians

2	187–88, 202
2:6–11	182
2:9–11	231
2:5	195

3:20–21	147
3:11	138
3:21	191

Colossians

1:15–20	243
1:15–18	243
3	81
3:9–12	5
3:9–10	147
3:10	142

1 Thessalonians

5:8	207
5:23	140

2 Timothy

4:8	208

Hebrews

4:12	140

1 Peter

1:18	222

1 John

3:2	147
4:16	205

Revelation

3:17–18	137
3:5	191
3:17	164
3:18	142
6:11	138
7:13–14	208
16:5	243
16:15	35, 117, 140, 164
17–18	136
17	131
17:16	135
19–22	136
19–21	136
19	131
19:8	136
21–22	131

www.ingramcontent.com/pod-product-compliance
Lightning Source LLC
Chambersburg PA
CBHW050620300426
44112CB00012B/1583